Evaluating Mental Health Disability in the Workplace

Liza H. Gold · Daniel W. Shuman

Evaluating Mental Health Disability in the Workplace

Model, Process, and Analysis

 Springer

Liza H. Gold
Georgetown University
  Medical Center
Washington, DC
USA
lhgoldmd@gmail.com

Daniel W. Shuman
Dedman School of Law
Southern Methodist University
Dallas, TX 75275
USA
dshuman@mail.smu.edu

ISBN 978-1-4419-0151-4   e-ISBN 978-1-4419-0152-1
DOI 10.1007/978-1-4419-0152-1
Springer Dordrecht Heidelberg London New York

Library of Congress Control Number: 2009928456

© Springer Science+Business Media, LLC 2009
All rights reserved. This work may not be translated or copied in whole or in part without the written permission of the publisher (Springer Science+Business Media, LLC, 233 Spring Street, New York, NY 10013, USA), except for brief excerpts in connection with reviews or scholarly analysis. Use in connection with any form of information storage and retrieval, electronic adaptation, computer software, or by similar or dissimilar methodology now known or hereafter developed is forbidden. The use in this publication of trade names, trademarks, service marks, and similar terms, even if they are not identified as such, is not to be taken as an expression of opinion as to whether or not they are subject to proprietary rights.

Printed on acid-free paper

Springer is part of Springer Science + Business Media (www.springer.com)

We dedicate this book to our friend and mentor, Robert I. Simon, MD.

Acknowledgments

Liza H. Gold – As anyone who has undertaken writing a book knows, many people contribute to the project, although the authors take full responsibility for the quality, or lack thereof, of the final product. I would like to thank Springer and Sharon Panulla for agreeing to publish a book on this important subject. I also thank Professor Dan Shuman, without whom this book would not have been completed. As Robert I. Simon, MD, says, the most important part of writing is finishing. Without Professor Shuman's contributions, I could not have finished this book.

I would also like to thank the members of the American Academy of Psychiatry and the Law's (AAPL) Task Force on Disability Guidelines: Stuart A. Anfang, MD, Albert M. Drukteinis, MD, JD, Jeffrey L. Metzner, MD, Marilyn Price, MD, Barry W. Wall, MD, and Lauren J. Wylonis, MD. Their clinical and forensic expertise and their collaboration in the creation of the AAPL's *Guidelines for Forensic Evaluation of Psychiatric Disability* (Gold et al., 2008) are reflected throughout this book. I also offer special thanks in regard to the AAPL's *Disability Guidelines* to Douglas Mossman, MD, Debra A. Pinals, MD, and John Davidson, Esq.

Thanks go to the leadership of AAPL, in particular Howard V. Zonana, MD, Medical Director, and Jacquelyn T. Coleman, CAE, Executive Director, as well as to Ezra E.H. Griffith, MD, Editor of the *Journal of the American Academy of Psychiatry and the Law*, for giving their permission to reprint text and concepts from the *Guidelines for Forensic Evaluation of Psychiatric Disability* in this text.

I also thank my friends and colleagues upon whose support and exchange of ideas I depend. Our relationships make continued striving to improve forensic skills and practice particularly gratifying. These include Erica Schiffman, MD, Cheryl D. Wills, MD, Jeffrey L. Metzner, MD, Renée L. Binder, MD, Debra A. Pinals, MD, Marilyn Price, MD, and Patricia R. Recupero, MD, JD, among others.

I wish to particularly thank Carmel Heinsohn, MD, for her support and friendship.

My love and appreciation also goes to my family, Ian J. Nyden, PhD, Joshua Nyden, and Alix Nyden, for their unfailing love and support. They have made all things possible.

Last but certainly not least, I thank the many patients and evaluees who have taught me about the complexities of the meaning of work and disability.

Daniel W. Shuman – My heartfelt thanks to Dean John Attanasio, Southern Methodist University School of Law, the Michael and Jacqueline M. Barrett Endowed Faculty Research Fund, and the M.D. Anderson Foundation, for supporting my work. My appreciation to Matthew Thomas, who assisted me on this project during his legal education at SMU and to my assistant, Michele Oswald, who keeps it all coordinated. My wife and family are not merely how I manage, they are the reason why.

Contents

1 **Taking the High Road: Ethics and Practice in Disability and Disability-Related Evaluations** 1
   Introduction 1
   The Ethical Obligation to Practice Within Areas of Expertise 2
   Ethics and Relationships in Third-Party Evaluations 3
      The Relationship with the Third Party 3
      The Physician–Evaluee Relationship in Employment
      Evaluations 4
   Disclosure and Informed Consent 5
   Confidentiality in Third-Party Employment Evaluations 7
   Obligation for Honesty and Objectivity: Sources of Bias
   in Employment Evaluations 8
      Common Sources of Bias in Disability and Disability-Related
      Evaluations 10
      Advocacy Bias 11
      Bias Associated with Mental Health Training and Experience ... 12
   Administrative Consequences of Not Conforming to Ethical
   Guidelines 22
      Disciplinary Actions and Mental Health Employment
      Evaluations 22
      Implications for Impeachment 23
   Conclusion 24

2 **Employment Evaluations and the Law** 25
   Introduction 25
   Obligations to the Retaining Party in Employment
   Evaluations 26
      Consent 27
   Obligations to the Evaluee in Disability and Disability-Related
   Evaluations 29
      The Question of Duty in Third-Party Evaluations 30
      Breach of Duty and Harm 34

Immunity in the Provision of Disability and Disability-Related
Evaluations 35
Privacy and Confidentiality: Access to Information............. 36
Qualitative Standards for Employment Evaluations 39
  Psychiatric and Psychological Evaluations Intended
    for Judicial Consumption 39
  Psychiatric and Psychological Evaluations Intended
    for Administrative Consumption 40
Conclusion... 42

3 Why We Work: Psychological Meaning and Effects 43
Introduction 43
The Central Role of Work in Daily Life........................ 43
Work and Its Effects on Mental Health 44
The Benefits of Work 45
  Job Satisfaction.. 48
Work: The Downside 48
Assessing "Goodness of Fit"................................... 49
  Constant Effect Determinants 51
  Variable Effect Determinants 51
Occupational Stress... 53
Outcomes of Occupational Stress: Job Burnout and Withdrawal ... 60
  Job Burnout... 60
The Effects of Job Loss and Unemployment 62
Conclusion... 68

4 Psychiatric Disorders, Functional Impairment, and the Workplace ... 69
Introduction 69
Psychiatric Disorders, Impairment, and Disability............. 70
Psychiatric Diagnoses and Disability: Caveat Emptor 71
Psychiatric Disorders in the Workplace 74
Evidence-Based Assessment of Psychiatric Impairment........... 78
  Affective Disorders 78
  Anxiety Disorders 87
  Substance Use and Dependence 91
  Comorbidity 92
Conclusion... 94

5 Psychiatric Disability: A Model for Assessment................. 97
Introduction 97
Disability: A Psychological Process 98
The Relationship Between Impairment and Disability............ 99
Work Capacity: Supply, Demand, and Domains of Function 101
  Work Demand: The Job Description 102
  Work Supply: Performance and Employment History............. 104

Contents xi

    Decreased Work Supply: Diagnosis, Symptoms, Impairments,
    and Treatment... 106
    Decreased Work Supply: Personal and Social
    Circumstances 107
Work Capacity Models: The Process and Patterns of Disability
Development... 107
    Change in Work Capacity Due to Sudden Illness
    and Impairment.. 108
    Change in Work Capacity Due to Sudden Illness
    and Impairment with Relatively Rapid Recovery to Baseline ... 109
    Increasing Impairment and Decreasing Work Capacity over
    Time Due to Progression of Illness........................ 110
    Cumulative Effect of Prior Impaired Function with New
    Impairment Resulting in Decreased Work Capacity 111
    Change in Work Demands Outpacing Change in Work Supply,
    Resulting in Decreased Work Capacity 113
    Repeated Episodes of Impairment with Decreasing Baseline
    Work Capacity Between Episodes 114
Work Capacity Models and Disability Evaluations.............. 116
Motivation 118
Cultural and Ethnic Issues 120
Conclusion.. 122

**6 Practice Guidelines for Mental Health Disability Evaluations
in the Workplace** 123
Introduction 123
The Benefit of Practice Guidelines 123
Definitions and Related Issues 125
    Disability and Impairment: Related but Not Synonymous 125
    Restrictions and Limitations.............................. 127
    Impairment vs. Illegal Behavior 127
Insurance Issues for Forensic Evaluators 129
Safety Issues for Evaluators 129
General Practice Guidelines for Psychiatric Disability
Evaluations 130
    Clarify the Nature of the Referral with the Referral Source..... 130
    Review Records and Collateral Information 131
    Conduct a Standard Examination......................... 135
    Correlate the Mental Disorder with Occupational Impairment... 138
    Consider Alternatives That Might Account for Claims
    of Impairment and Disability 147
    Formulate Well-Reasoned Opinions Supported by Data....... 151
    Write a Comprehensive Report That Addresses Referral
    Questions... 152
Conclusion.. 161

7 The Maze of Disability Benefit Programs: Social Security Disability, Workers' Compensation, and Private Disability Insurance ... 163
Introduction ... 163
Public Disability Insurance: The SSDI Program ... 164
  SSDI Definitions and Process ... 165
  The Role of Mental Health Professionals in SSDI Disability Claims ... 173
  Additional Guidelines for Conducting SSA Disability Evaluations ... 178
Workers' Compensation Programs ... 178
  The Basic Components of Workers' Compensation Legislation ... 179
  Differences Between Workers' Compensation, Tort Law, and SSDI ... 180
  Causation in Workers Compensation: No Fault Does Not Mean No Conflict ... 181
  The Decision-Making Process in Workers' Compensation Claims ... 181
  Evidentiary Issues in Worker's Compensation Claims ... 182
  Definition of Disability in Worker's Compensation Cases ... 183
  Psychiatric Claims in Workers' Compensation ... 184
  Mental Health Evaluations in Workers' Compensation Claims ... 186
  Dual Roles in Worker's Compensation Claims ... 190
  Additional Guidelines for Conducting Workers' Compensation Evaluations ... 192
Private Disability Insurance Claims ... 192
  Private Disability Insurance: Benefits by Contract and Differences from Other Disability Benefits Programs ... 195
  Legal Disability vs Factual Disability ... 196
  Private Disability Insurance: Definitions and Terms ... 197
  Mental Health Professionals and Private Disability Insurance Claims ... 201
  Dual Roles and Ethical Conflicts in Private Disability Insurance Evaluations ... 206
Additional Guidelines for Conducting Workers' Compensation Evaluations ... 207
Conclusion ... 208

8 Working with Disabilities: The Americans with Disabilities Act ... 209
Introduction ... 209
The ADA in Action: How Does it Work? ... 210
  Enforcement of the ADA ... 213

Contents

Mental Disabilities: The ADA and Employment	215
Referrals for ADA Mental Health Evaluations	216
Mental Health Professionals: Understanding the ADA	219
The ADA's Statutory Definitions and Relevant Terms	219
Conclusion	234
Additional Guidelines for Conducting ADA Evaluations	235

9 Fitness-for-Duty Evaluations 237

Introduction	237
The Public's Stake in FFD Decisions	239
The Legal Basis for FFD Examinations	240
Forced FFD Evaluations	244
FFD Evaluations and the ADA	244
Referral Issues	246
Triaging the FFD Referral	246
Qualifications for Conducting FFD Evaluations	247
Constraints on FFD Evaluations	247
Confidentiality	248
Consent	250
Role Clarification and Dual-Agency Issues	250
Conducting a Mental Health FFD Evaluation	252
Documentation	252
The FFD Interview	255
Dissimulation	257
Opinions	257
Degree of Certainty of Opinions	261
Return-to-Work Evaluations	262
Conclusion	263
Additional Guidelines for Conducting FFD Evaluations	263
Key Points in Conducting RTW Evaluations	264

Conclusion 265

Appendix A: The American Academy of Psychiatry and the Law: Ethics Guidelines for the Practice of Forensic Psychiatry, 2005 ... 269

I. Preamble	269
Commentary	269
II. Confidentiality	270
Commentary	270
III. Consent	270
Commentary	271
IV. Honesty and Striving for Objectivity	271
Commentary	271

V. Qualifications. 273
  Commentary. 273
VI. Procedures for Handling Complaints of Unethical
  Conduct 273
  Commentary. 273

Appendix B: The American Psychology-Law Society, Committee on Ethical Guidelines of Division 41 of the American Psychological Association and the American Academy of Forensic Psychology: Specialty Guidelines for Forensic Psychologists (1991) 275
  I. Purpose and Scope 276
    A. Purpose 276
    B. Scope 276
    C. Related Standards 277
  II. Responsibility 277
  III. Competence 277
  IV. Relationships 278
  V. Confidentiality and Privilege. 280
  VI. Methods and Procedures 280
  VII. Public and Professional Communications 283

Appendix C: The Disability Report 287

References 291

Legal Citations 309
  Cases 309
  Statutes, Regulations, Model Acts 312
    Rules 313

Index 315

Introduction

To earn one's bread by the sweat of one's brow has always been the lot of mankind. At least, ever since Eden's slothful couple was served with an eviction notice.... No matter how demeaning the task, no matter how it dulls the sense and breaks the spirit, one *must* work. Or else (Studs Terkel: *Working: People Talk about What They do All Day and How They Feel about What They Do*, 1972, p. xii).

Workplace Conflict and Crisis

Studs Terkel, in his homage to workers and their work, teaches us that work is not a choice but an imperative. When personal, medical, or social problems threaten an individual's ability to function in the workplace, serious problems arise. These problems often result in an escalating series of crises, which can take over the individual's life, leading to disability, job loss, loss of relationships, career loss or change, conflict, litigation, and financial ruin. When the causes or consequences of these problems are psychiatric disorders, mental health professionals are asked to provide clinical treatment as well as evaluation of and guidance in managing issues relating to disability and the ability to work.

People have complicated relationships with their work, whether they are 9–5 blue-collar workers or 24/7 professionals. As one group of psychiatrists observed:

> At least one third of our lives is spent at work. It is the cause and cure of many of our ills. We feel loved through the admiration our work earns. We are empty and dejected when work fails. Goals we work toward define us; without them we lack purpose and direction. We discharge aggression when we attack our tasks, and our successes protect us from the debilitating stress of frustrated ambition. We feel masterful and strong in achievement, weak and impotent in failure. We earn our place in civilization through our work. We reduce guilt through hard labor and defy time with accomplishment. Work organizations structure our lives and, for many of us, the people we love, hate, fear, and need comes as importantly from our offices, factories, and shops as from our families and communities (Committee on Psychiatry in Industry 1994, p. xi).

Interpersonal relationships are widely recognized to encompass complicated and powerful psychological dynamics, requiring specialized training and expertise. Less attention has been paid to the dynamics of people's relationship with work. It appears axiomatic that people need to work to make money and ensure that basic material needs are met. On closer scrutiny, it quickly becomes evident that there is more to work than making money. People work to achieve psychological, emotional, and social satisfaction, and often work even if fortunate enough to be able to meet financial needs without working.

The price to be paid for underestimating the complexity of troubled relationships between people and their work can be catastrophic. The emotional fallout resulting from problems in the workplace can be as severe as those of disintegrating marriages or other important personal relationships. Psychiatric disorders that wax and wane due to their chronic or episodic nature may result in work impairments. During periods of relative stability, many individual may function without impairment or be only mildly impaired, even if they are experiencing symptoms. During acute exacerbations, individuals may develop symptoms that significantly impair their work function. Workplace problems may themselves result in the onset or exacerbation of psychiatric disorders. The overwhelming personal, social, and economic costs associated with these problems can include behavioral and interpersonal work conflicts, voluntary or involuntary withdrawal from the workplace, claims for disability, requests for accommodations, extended and expensive litigation, and sometimes, tragically, even workplace violence and death.

The Extent and Cost of Mental Health Disorders in the Workplace

Statistics relating to workplace psychiatric illness claims underline just how commonly psychiatric disorders and their associated problems burden individuals, employers, and society as a whole. Large numbers of individuals either enter the workplace with preexisting psychiatric disorders or develop psychiatric disorders during the course of their working lives. Depending on the study reviewed, between 20 and 25% of adults of working age suffer from a diagnosable psychiatric disorder in any given year. The Surgeon General's Report on Mental Health (United States Department of Health and Human Services, 1999) estimated that about one in five Americans experiences a psychiatric disorder in a given year. The National Institute of Mental Health has estimated that 26.2% of Americans aged 18 and older, about one in four adults suffer from a diagnosable psychiatric disorder in a given year (National Institute of Mental Health, 2007). When applied to the 2004 United States Census residential population estimate for ages 18 and older, this figure translates to 57.7 million people (National Institute of Mental Health, 2007).

Statistical analyses have also found that large numbers of individual with psychiatric illness are employed. One study found that of individuals with any psychiatric illness, 48–73% are employed; 32–61% of individuals with serious psychiatric illness are employed. Of all adults, 76–87% are employed (Jans, Stoddard, & Kraus, 2004). In 2005, an estimated 29% of individuals (or 2,185,000 people) between the ages of 21 and 64 who reported having a mental disability were employed (Cornell University Disability Statistics, 2005).

The monetary costs of psychiatric disorder and disability due to psychiatric disorder are staggering. Annual income in those with psychiatric illness who work is reduced due to psychiatric illness between $3500 and $6000 on an individual basis, and between $100 and $170 billion collectively every year (Marcotte & Wilcox-Gok, 2001). The first national estimate of lost earnings associated with mental disorders in the United States was $44.1 billion in 1985 (Rice, Kelman, Miller, & Dunmeyer, 1990). Costs of reduced or lost productivity in 1990 were estimated to total $78.5 billion, including both lost earnings and productivity (Jans et al., 2004). In 1992, this estimate was updated to a loss of $77 billion (Harwood et al., 2000). The most recent estimate, for the year 2002, is $193.2 billion. Of this, 75.4% was due to reduced earnings among mentally ill persons with any earnings and the remaining 24.6% was due to reduced probability of having any earnings (Kessler et al., 2008). Comparative cost of illness studies have demonstrated that the magnitude of this association is high in relation to most physical disorders.

Statistics measuring employment rates and disability are challenging to collect. Definitions and conceptualizations of disability vary in scope and severity between studies and data collection systems. In addition, there are multiple data sources, including broad epidemiological surveys, some of which are better than others. Nevertheless, the scope of problems associated with psychiatric disorders in the workplace is clear.

- In 1999, mental or emotional problems represented one of the top 10 causes of disability among adults in the United States, at a rate higher than disability caused by diabetes or stroke (Centers for Disease Control and Prevention, 2007).
- Of individuals with psychiatric disorders in any given year, 30% (or approximately 6.1 million) report some form of work disability (Jans et al., 1996).
- Psychiatric disorders are the leading cause of disability in the United States and Canada for individuals aged 15–44 (National Institutes of Mental Health, 2007).
- The World Health Organization reports that depression, a condition characterized by episodic exacerbations, is the fifth leading cause of disability worldwide and predicts that it will be the second leading cause of disability after heart disease by 2020 (Murray & Lopez, 1996).
- The National Health Survey Interview (1998–2000) found that for younger adults, aged 18–44, psychiatric illness was the second most frequently reported cause of activity limitation (10.4 per 1,000 people), exceeded only

by musculoskeletal conditions. For mid-life adults, 45–64 years, psychiatric illness ranked as the third most frequently mentioned cause of activity limitation (18.6 per 1,000) (Centers for Disease Control and Prevention, 2007).

The costs of disability benefits paid out by private and public agencies are another way to assess the prevalence and extent of mental health disability issues. In 2004, SSDI paid out $78.2 billion dollars in total claims benefits to approximately 6.2 million disabled workers (Social Security Administration, 2006). Psychiatric disorders that prevent substantial gainful employment are the leading reason that people receive SSDI, represent the largest single diagnostic category, are associated with the longest entitlement periods, and are the fastest growing segment of SSDI recipients. In 2003, 28% of SSDI recipients received payment based on a psychiatric disorder (not including mental retardation) (International Center for Disability Information, 2005; Jans et al., 2004; JHA, 2006).

Disability insurance is also available through workers' compensation programs and private insurers. National statistics regarding the number and cost of mental health-based disability claims in workers compensation programs are difficult to obtain. However, the amount of money involved in workers' compensation claims is substantial. In 1996, total benefit payments had reached $42.5 billion (Larson & Larson, 2000). Indications are that mental health-based claims also represent a significant percentage of those made to workers' compensation boards.

National statistics regarding the number and cost of mental health-based disability claims in private insurance programs are also difficult to obtain, as they are compiled by private companies and often not made public. In 2004, short-term disability (STD) benefits were available to 39% of workers, long-term disability (LTD) benefits were available to 30% of workers in private industry, and nearly all participated (United States Department of Labor, 2005a). One research and consulting firm that serves the disability industry reported that in 2004, 6% of new LTD claims and 4% of STD claims submitted were for psychiatric disorders (JHA, 2006). This firm noted that the average LTD and STD duration for psychiatric disorders represented the second longest averages of 99 days for STD and 28 months for LTD, exceeded only by average duration of disability for claims of fibromyalgia (JHA, 2006).

Costs of employment litigation associated with mental health claims, which often include claims of disability or impaired work capacity, are also impressive. Mental and emotional injuries constitute the bulk of exposure in most employment litigation (Lindemann & Kadue, 1992; McDonald & Kulick, 2001). The Equal Employment Opportunity Commission (EEOC) reported that approximately 95,000 charges of employment discrimination were filed in 2008 alone resulting in almost 300 million dollars of monetary benefits paid out through settlement, conciliations, or resolutions (United States Equal Employment Opportunity Commission, 2008). Social Security cases occupy a significant portion of the federal appellate case load (Metzner & Buck, 2003). Statistics on other types of litigation may be impossible to calculate, but are clearly high. Many law firms specialize in and employ multiple lawyers to deal with the number of state and federal cases related to various types of employment litigation. The American Bar Association Labor and Employment Law Section reports a membership in excess of 22,000 attorneys (American Bar Association, 2008).

Disability and Disability-Related Mental Health Evaluations: The Need for Expertise

Disability and disability-related mental health evaluations require specialized knowledge, training, and experience, just as do evaluations of competency to stand trial or criminal responsibility. The purpose of disability and disability-related mental health evaluations is to provide an administrative or legal system with relevant and reliable information it can translate into concrete actions, such as accommodations, award of benefits, or modification of job responsibilities (Brodsky, 1987b). Mental health professionals who undertake these evaluations should be familiar with the employment context that generated the evaluation and the legal or administrative regulations that apply to that context.

Employers, third-party private or public agencies, or workers themselves may request disability and disability-related evaluations in order to meet the administrative requirements of the social and legal contracts that structure paid employment. The need for such evaluations can arise in the context of claims for short-term or long-term psychiatric disability benefits, disability claims under the Social Security Act, or workers' compensation claims. Mental health evaluations may also be requested when employees make requests for accommodations under the Americans with Disabilities Act (ADA) or when employers have questions regarding an employee's fitness for duty or ability to return to work after disability absence or medical leave.

Litigation that arises from employment conflict covers a wide array of employment issues and can also result in mental health assessments. Claims against employers can be made under federal laws and regulations such as the ADA, the Occupational Safety and Health Act, the Equal Employment Opportunity Commission, public or private disability, workers' compensation, or torts such as premises liability, negligence, wrongful termination, negligent, or intentional infliction of emotional distress. Claims of psychiatric illness, disability, or injury in such cases often precipitate an attorney's request for a mental health evaluation to assist in proving causation, entitlement to benefits, or damages.

Providing thorough and competent evaluations based on standardized guidelines is critical to adjudication of such claims, not least because claims for benefits, damages, or entitlements based on mental or emotional problems often elicit skepticism from observers. Judicial and administrative compensation systems have historically been and often remain hostile to claims of injury and disability due to psychiatric disorder. Reviewers, administrators, and the legal system often subject evaluations of psychiatric disorders to heightened scrutiny. For example, employers typically offer more limited coverage and benefits and voice greater suspicion about malingering when employees claim disability due to psychiatric illness. The legal system initially expressed its doubts by denying compensation in the absence of physical impact and more recently by imposing damage caps on intangible losses such as emotional damage.

Concerns regarding manipulation and abuse are epitomized by claims of work-related stress disorders. In the employment arena, concerns regarding the reality of disability and disability-related claims based on stress frequently lead to referrals for mental health evaluation (Bonnie, 1997b). Patients, employers, insurers, administrators, and attorneys believe mental health professionals have the necessary knowledge and experience to answer questions regarding the credibility of employment claims of disability, causation of injury, restrictions, limitations, and return-to-work potential.

Mental health professionals become involved in disability and disability-related evaluations when a problem related to psychiatric illness is claimed or identified and some employment action needs to be taken. Most psychiatrists and psychologists can report some experience with requests for disability evaluations or for documentation for employment purposes. Many clinicians fill out paperwork for their patients to obtain medical leave, disability, accommodations, or provide opinions regarding impairment or ability to function in the workplace. Indeed, some evaluations require treating clinicians to provide assessment and are straightforward enough to present no challenge beyond that addressed by general clinical training.

However, general clinical training does not encompass the education or experience needed to perform competent disability and disability-related evaluations in more complex situations involving crisis or conflict. Evaluations relating to fitness for duty or the ADA, for example, can be well outside a general clinician's expertise. Even relatively straightforward disability claims can result in litigation, drawing unsuspecting clinicians into court to defend diagnosis, treatment, and opinions on disability.

General clinicians without experience in medico-legal evaluations will as a matter of course refer mental health evaluations of individuals for criminal issues, such as competency to stand trial or criminal responsibility to a forensic specialist, even if the evaluee is the clinician's own patient. Yet, clinicians often will not hesitate to offer an opinion that an individual is fit for duty despite workplace problems or is disabled due to psychiatric illness and needs to withdraw from the workplace, unaware that such opinions might draw them into a complex labyrinth of legal and administrative adjudication that can sometimes rival that of criminal matters.

The difficulties and ambiguities that arise at the interface of psychiatry and psychology and the legal system have been extensively discussed (Appelbaum, 1997; Mossman, 1994; Stone, 1984). These challenges take on another dimension of complexity when mental health fields interact with the world of paid employment and the different bodies of law in the administrative and judicial systems charged with administering employment benefits and resolving employment conflicts. The law governing the employment relationship in the United States has undergone rapid change in recent years, and employment conflict and litigation covers complex legal, statutory, and administrative arenas. Even experienced forensic clinicians often find the integration of these disparate worlds challenging.

The medical model of disability conceptualizes disability as a problem whose locus resides in an individual. In this model, disability is assumed to be caused by disease, trauma, or some other health condition. A competing model, the social model of disability, posits that the cause of disability does not arise from within individuals alone but results from a combination of an environment that fails to accommodate persons with disabilities and negative attitudes toward individuals with disabilities.

For more than two decades, institutions concerned with disability have struggled to integrate these two models (Iezzoni & Freedman, 2008). This has resulted in varied definitions and roles for physicians in the assessment of disability. For example, Social Security disability programs are based almost exclusively on the medical model of disability, and in Social Security evaluations, the role of physicians is central. The role of physicians in the social model of disability, best typified perhaps in ADA evaluations, is less clear. Although physicians' expertise is required in assessing aspects of disability in the social model, medical education and training generally does not confer expertise in issues such as the evaluation of work environments and whether accommodations are reasonable.

The popularity of the medical model of disability has waxed and waned but seems to have outlasted the competition, assuring that physicians, and in the case of psychiatric disorders, psychiatrists and psychologists, will continue to be asked to provide opinions regarding these complex workplace problems. Therefore, mental health professionals providing disability and disability-related assessments need to understand both the definitions associated with disability and other work ability-related evaluations, as well as their own roles in these evaluations, regardless of the model or combination of models being utilized.

Formulating competent opinions regarding issues relating to disability and employment problems may appear to be matters of common sense or logical extensions of clinical practice. Unfortunately, in many situations, such is not the case. General clinicians often believe they know what is needed for the capacity to work, if only by virtue of experience. Everyone knows people who work. In contrast, not everyone knows someone who has been accused of a crime. Most clinicians typically do not assume they understand how to assess mental states in questions of criminal responsibility or competency to stand trial. Nevertheless, common sense and personal experience are often not enough to address sometimes the complex concepts and problems relating to disability and associated employment issues.

Despite the central role of work in peoples' lives, relatively little clinical training has centered on this aspect of functioning and the problems that may occur. Few mental health professionals have had any formal training in performing disability and disability-related assessments during their clinical training. In contrast with diagnosis and treatment, most clinicians receive little or no training in how to evaluate their patients' ability to function in the workplace (Talmage & Melhorn, 2005a). As a result, the quality of disability and disability-related evaluations varies widely and often fails to meet the needs for which they have been solicited.

Forensic specialists are also often unprepared to respond to requests for many types of disability evaluations. Unless one specializes in a practice directed specifically at disability or occupational evaluations, a clinician may have little opportunity to learn how best to conduct an evaluation, obtain the necessary data, and effectively communicate results and relevant opinions. Moreover, unlike clinical practice, no consistent continuing education process in which clinicians who wish to improve their skills can engage exists. Relatively few continuing education programs offer training in conducting employment-related assessments.

"Peer review" for learning purposes, another common avenue for professional development, is almost nonexistent in regard to disability and disability-related evaluations. The exception to this is in litigation, where the opposing expert's in-depth review of one's opinions is inevitable but not necessarily constructive. In addition, unlike clinical practice where treatment outcome may provide some indication of quality of services, outcomes in disability-related evaluations rarely include an opportunity to review one's performance or skills. In the absence of litigation, once a report has been submitted, often no further contact regarding the quality of the report, the outcome of the case, or how relevant the evaluation was to that outcome occurs. (As in litigation, complaints should the opinions be contrary to the interests of the retaining party are not uncommon but are also rarely constructive.) Referral sources will simply avoid future referrals if examiners provide inadequate reports or poor quality evaluations.

Who Can Use the Information in This Book

This book will provide empirically based, legally grounded analysis as well as practical guidelines and suggestions regarding mental health evaluations associated with disability claims, ADA claims, and fitness-for-duty evaluations. It is intended for mental health practitioners varying in levels of experience, from the general clinician to the forensic expert, all of whom may be confronted with clinical, legal, or administrative situations that require specialized disability assessments. General practitioners will find much that is helpful regarding some of the common types of disability evaluations they are asked to provide in the course of their clinical practice. More experienced forensic specialists will find the information and suggestions provided will increase their expertise and level of comfort in providing more complex disability-related evaluations.

Although this text will be helpful to general mental health practitioners, clinicians uncomfortable with performing disability and disability-related evaluations should consider referring them to forensic specialists. Circumstances sometimes compel a practitioner to assume the dual role of treatment provider and forensic evaluator (Strasburger, Gutheil, & Brodsky, 1997). For example, an application for Social Security Disability benefits requires an extensive report from the clinical treatment provider. Many forms of workers' compensation insurance require evaluation of treatment, progress, and prognosis from the treating clinician.

Nevertheless, circumstances may suggest referral for various reasons to those with more specialized forensic training. Many disability-related evaluations are essentially independent medical examinations, that is, clinical assessments by a provider, not otherwise involved in the care or treatment of the patient, at the request of a third party who is not the provider's employer. Such examinations differ significantly from clinical evaluations conducted for treatment purposes (American Medical Association, 2008), particularly in regard to issues of confidentiality and the involvement of third parties. In addition, in the event of a dispute, evaluators need to be prepared to defend their opinions in trial or hearing, a situation with which forensically trained specialists are familiar.

General clinicians may encounter other circumstances that suggest a referral to a forensic specialist. Clinicians may encounter difficulty in moving from the therapeutic to the forensic role due to the conflict presented by the differences between clinical and forensic methodology, ethics, alliances, and goals (Appelbaum, 1997; Shuman & Greenberg, 1998; Strasburger et al., 1997). The terms, requirements, and legal or administrative process involved in employment evaluations may be unfamiliar. In such cases, reliance on clinical skills alone may result in erroneous conclusions or irrelevant reports. Even where the issues in clinical and employment evaluation are similar, the consequences of different types of disability evaluations differ dramatically and cannot help but frame the opinions rendered.

Clinicians who provide disability and disability-related evaluations should also be aware that should questions arise, they are likely to be held to the standards of forensic specialists (*Sugarman v. Board of Registration in Medicine*, 1996). In a related vein, by statute or judicial determination, some states consider forensic diagnosis and testimony the practice of medicine and require compliance with the same rules that govern clinicians (Federation of State Medical Boards, 2007; Simon & Shuman, 1999).

Finally, this book will also be of use to other professionals such as attorneys, human resource specialists, and insurance administrators. These groups frequently call upon the services of mental health practitioners when conflicts or disputes arise in the workplace and either the employee or the employer raises issues of disability or fitness for duty related to mental health. This book will familiarize them with what they can expect and reasonably ask of mental health practitioners whom they ask to provide evaluations that help them resolve or adjudicate difficult employment claims related to mental health.

Readers should be aware this text focuses on disability and disability-related evaluations that arise in paid employment contexts, that is, work for which one is receiving monetary compensation. There are many kinds of work and not all of them result in payment for the labor provided. For example, many women and some men provide household labor and childcare essential to their partners' successful functioning in the workplace but for which no monetary compensation is directly received.

In addition, this text addresses disability evaluations that arise due to disorders typically encountered in the workplace rather than disorders that prevent individuals from entering the workplace. Although serious psychiatric illness does not necessarily preclude competitive employment, labor force participation among people with serious psychiatric disorders is very low. Community surveys indicate that of those with schizophrenia and related illnesses, only 22-40% are employed (Jans et al., 2004). However, many of these individuals work in sheltered situations and 75-85% with these disorders do not hold any type of competitive employment (Bonnie, 1997a; Estroff, Zimmer, Lachicotte, Benoit, & Patrick, 1997; Kirsh, 2000; Yelin & Cisternas, 1997). Thus, for individuals with serious disorders such as developmental disabilities or schizophrenia, which arise during childhood, adolescence, or young adulthood, and therefore preexist opportunities for paid employment, the types of employment evaluations discussed here are not common.

This book will also not address areas the authors believe are adequately covered elsewhere or do not represent a significant number of evaluations. For example, preemployment evaluations conducted for various jobs outside any litigation or administrative process are common and may include a mental health evaluation, but will not be covered here. The overwhelming majority of evaluations, disputes, and complaints in the workplace come from those who are still employed or those who have quit or suffered a termination. Only a very small percentage of complaints come from individuals who claim they were improperly rejected for employment. In addition, certain highly regulated and specialized disability evaluations, such as those conducted within the military and Veterans Administration, are well covered in those administrative systems and so will also not be addressed here.

Further, this discussion will not address any of the professional fields associated with employment-related attempts to prevent illness or disability or return disabled individuals to the workplace. Although relevant to the ability to reenter the workplace and maintain employment, the literature and evaluations related to vocational rehabilitation, occupational illness, sheltered employment, employee assistance programs, and other employment-related fields are beyond the scope of this discussion. Finally, the issues addressed here are not intended to be a guide to occupational psychiatrists and psychologists whose primary obligation is to their employer. For example, the challenges encountered by mental health professionals employed by insurance companies for claim review purposes will not be discussed.

This book will address the types of evaluations, conflict, and crisis related to mental health disability issues that commonly arise in the workplace. Such crises may result from an employee's wish to withdraw from the workforce due to psychiatric disorder. Such individuals generally require a mental health professional's evaluation to qualify them to receive benefits to which they may be entitled by administrative law or by private insurance contract. When individuals claim the psychiatric disorder from which they suffer was caused by the workplace, they may file a workers' compensation claim or a claim of discrimination under federal or state law, or one of many tort claims related to employment law. Again, such claims will typically require an evaluation by a mental health professional in order to result in monetary compensation or damage awards.

Disability-related assessment also includes individuals who already are employed and wish to remain in the workplace but who request or require accommodations to do so. If individuals request accommodations for a disability, as they are legally entitled to do under the ADA, they may be referred for a mental health evaluation to determine their ability to continue working and the types of accommodations necessary.

Sometimes employers question an employee's ability to meet the requirements of their job or their ability to do so without presenting a risk to themselves or others. In these cases, employees may be referred for evaluations for fitness-for-duty and/or risk assessment. Such evaluations may include concerns about the potential for workplace violence or the ability to safely manage an employment-issued firearm, or public safety concerns regarding an impaired physician or other medical care provider. Generally, as in ADA evaluations, the subjects of such evaluations wish to remain at work but their employers question their ability to do so or to do so safely. This difference of opinions generally results in some type of conflict or crisis. Requests for evaluation may arise at any point in the crisis, up to and including litigation that may arise from the dispute between employer and employee.

Unique Perspectives on Workplace Mental Health Evaluations

This book offers a number of unique perspectives in the quickly evolving arena of mental health assessments arising at the interface of psychiatry, psychology, and employment. The first of these is a focus on the critical dynamic in any disability or disability-related evaluation: the relationship between the individual's internal world and external circumstances. The evaluee's internal world comprises the individual's psychiatric status, psychological issues, and the meaning and value of work to that individual. The meaning and value of work is influenced by many of the social aspects of employment. External circumstances, also a component of the model, consist of the job requirements, the social, hierarchical, and cultural aspects of any job situation, and other non-job-related factors, such as family or health circumstances.

The relationship between work and psychiatric disorders requires a model that accounts for a complex, dynamic, and changing relationship between relevant factors. Contrary to what many believe, the relationship between work and psychiatric illness cannot always be predicted on the basis of severity of illness or the stress of the work. Many individuals with severe psychiatric disorders are able to function in work settings, and even to utilize work settings to maintain or improve their functioning by increasing structure, social contact, and maintaining an income and employment benefits. Work is also an important outcome variable in its own right, correlated with although not identical to other outcome variables such as symptom severity, need for hospitalization, and social relations functioning. Work is therefore an area of functioning over time that is both semi-independent of and related to other areas of functioning in psychiatric disorders (Straus & Davidson, 1997).

Our model assumes that the dynamic relationship between the individual's internal world and external circumstances is the key issue in understanding disability problems and conflicts. Disability and disability-related evaluations differ in regard to which aspects of the dynamic relationship are of interest, such as level of impairment, causation of injury, accommodations to continue working, or fitness for duty. This model of assessment will be supported by a review of empirical evidence and scientific data regarding the relationships between specific psychiatric disorders and associated functional impairments. This data is then reviewed in the context of the process of the development of work disability, and visual models are offered to assist mental health professionals develop case formulations to help analyze the data and the process, unique to each individual, of the development of disability.

The subject matter and approach are also unique in that when such topics are reviewed, they are not typically placed simultaneously in a mental health and legal context. This text represents a collaboration between two experienced and award-winning professionals, a clinical professor of psychiatry and legal scholar. This collaboration has resulted in a text that provides a review of relevant case, statutory, and administrative law regarding each type of specific evaluation as well as the legal issues such as liability and confidentiality relating to the performance of such evaluations generally.

Finally, this text is the first to suggest both general and specific guidelines for these work-related evaluations. Such guidelines have only recently become available from the American Academy of Psychiatry and the Law (Gold et al., 2008), an effort in which one of the authors was instrumental. This text expands on these guidelines, updating evolving law and placing the discussions of general and specific types of disability and disability-related evaluations in their legal contexts.

The book provides extensive discussion of different and relevant factors in disability and disability-related evaluations before suggesting guidelines. Chapter 1 reviews relevant ethical obligations; Chapter 2 reviews relevant legal duties that arise in these employment evaluations, including those related to confidentiality and the Health Insurance Portability and Accountability Act; Chapter 3 explores the positive and negative psychological aspects of work; and Chapter 4 gives an overview of the relationship between specific psychiatric disorders and potential work-related impairments. These chapters are also unique in their reliance on evidence-based studies to support opinions and provide guidance in employment evaluations. Chapter 5 describes the process of psychiatric disability development, a process that has not been widely discussed in any context. These discussions inform the suggested guidelines for evaluation provided in Chapter 6.

The last three chapters of the book provide specific and focused discussion of disability evaluations relative to Social Security, workers' compensation programs, and private disability insurance benefits (Chapter 7); evaluations related to the ADA (Chapter 8); and fitness-for-duty issues (Chapter 9). These chapters will provide a review of the legal or administrative standards that govern how the mental health evaluation is conducted or used, the types of information to which the evaluator is entitled or must use to form an opinion, mental health issues specific to type of employment conflict, specific issues for evaluation, and guidelines specific to type of evaluation where they differ from the general guidelines reviewed in Chapter 5.

In conclusion, this text addresses the issues regarding mental health disability and disability-related evaluations requested due to the common challenges, crises, and conflicts arising in the workplace. It is inevitable that general clinicians' patients will encounter such problems, bringing them into the realm of clinical practice. It is also inevitable that these problems will result at times in the need for forensic evaluations and expert testimony. Learning to provide competent and thorough disability and disability-related evaluations will help mental health professionals at all levels of practice and experience meet their responsibilities to patients and to the administrative and legal systems that govern the world of competitive, paid labor.

Chapter 1
Taking the High Road: Ethics and Practice in Disability and Disability-Related Evaluations

Introduction

When Studs Terkel penned that people must work "or else," it is unlikely he was thinking about mental health disability and disability-related evaluations. Nevertheless, such evaluations commonly occur, often in a highly charged context of claims, conflict, and dispute. The outcome of these mental health evaluations can be life altering. Careers, financial stability, benefits, or legal decisions and awards can hinge upon the opinion of a mental health professional.

These circumstances create multiple opportunities for ethical and practical conflicts that can potentially influence opinions in mental health evaluations. Many of the assumptions, practices, and habits arising from clinical training and practice can create biases that may affect the provision of disability and disability-related evaluations. Although the law sets standards for some types of these assessments, many occur outside the legal process. In any event, professional requirements for ethical conduct and competency may exceed those set by law. This chapter will review ethical obligations; related legal obligations will be reviewed in depth in the next chapter.

Professional ethics associated with disability and disability-related evaluations, often referred to as third-party evaluations, differ in some significant respects from those associated with clinical care. Understanding the ethical obligations attendant upon third-party employment evaluations and the practical implications of these ethical obligations can provide guidance to mental health professionals when addressing some of the challenges that arise in conducting them. No systematic ethical guidelines specific to mental health disability or disability-related evaluations have to date been accepted by any professional organization. However, both psychiatric and psychological organizations have adopted ethical guidelines that are relevant and provide guidance to those conducting disability and disability-related evaluations.

The ethical guidelines and principles referenced here include

1. The American Academy of Psychiatry and the Law (AAPL): Ethics Guidelines for the Practice of Forensic Psychiatry, 2005 (http://www.aapl.org) (see Appendix A).
2. The American Medical Association (AMA): Code of Medical Ethics and Current Opinions, 2006–2007 (http://www.ama-assn.org).
3. The American Psychiatric Association (APA): Opinions of the Ethics Committee on the Principles of Medical Ethics, With Annotations Especially Applicable to Psychiatry, 2008.
4. The American Psychological Association: Ethical Principles of Psychologists and Code of Conduct, 2002.
5. Committee on Ethical Guidelines for Forensic Psychologists of Division 41 of the American Psychological Association and the American Board of Forensic Psychology: Specialty Guidelines for Forensic Psychologists (1991) (see Appendix B).
6. The American Psychology-Law Society (AP-LS), Division 41 of the American Psychological Association, and the American Board of Forensic Psychology: Specialty Guidelines for Forensic Psychologists, fourth revised draft, 2008 (not yet adopted).

The Ethical Obligation to Practice Within Areas of Expertise

One of the primary ethical obligations of any mental health professional is to practice within their area of expertise (American Medical Association, 2006; American Psychological Association, 2002; American Psychiatric Association, 2008). Specialty guidelines and ethics opinions address this obligation directly in regard to forensic evaluations (American Academy of Psychiatry and the Law, 2005; American Medical Association, 2006, Opinion E 9.07, Committee on Ethical Guidelines for Forensic Psychologists, 1991; American Psychological-Law Society, 2008). As previously discussed, mental health professionals providing disability and disability-related evaluations should consider the possibility that litigation or administrative processes may arise from claims requiring mental health assessments. Thus, the specialty guidelines for forensic clinicians may be interpreted to apply to third-party evaluations of all kinds whether litigation has occurred or not. Failure to support claims of expertise can have significant legal implications (see Chapter 2).

Evaluators should have experience with the various types of disability and disability-related evaluations and be familiar with the variety of subjects that form the basis of well-reasoned opinions in these assessments. In any given case, any or all these areas may be relevant in supporting or refuting employment claims. These include

- the relevant legal or administrative contexts of the evaluations;
- mental health issues that commonly arise in the workplace;

- the manifestations of mental disorders that can specifically affect functioning and how they relate to the specific context of each evaluation;
- the research that supports these assessments; and
- the requirements of competent disability and disability-related evaluations, including the questions that need to be addressed in each specific evaluation.

Ethics and Relationships in Third-Party Evaluations

Mental health professionals conducting disability and disability-related evaluations should understand their ethical obligations to all the involved parties. The ethical obligations of the mental health professional associated with treatment relationships typically are owed only to the patient, except in situations in which the patient presents a danger to self or others. However, disability evaluations generally involve three parties: the mental health professional, the evaluee, and the retaining or referring employer, agency, attorney, or institution. The retaining or referring party, commonly referred to as the third party, is the recipient of the information obtained in the evaluation.

This three-way relationship creates new and different ethical obligations than those associated with patient treatment and is the source of many of the ethical challenges associated with disability and disability-related evaluations. Many mental health professionals assume that in a third-party evaluation, the lack of the traditional physician/patient relationship means that traditional ethical obligations to the evaluee are abrogated. As the fields of forensic psychiatry and psychology have evolved over recent years, this analysis has come to be considered overly simplistic. In fact, the involvement of the third party creates new ethical obligations to the third party and alters rather than eliminates some of the traditional clinical ethical obligations toward the evaluee.

The Relationship with the Third Party

The clinician's primary ethical duties in disability and disability-related evaluations are owed to the third party. The purpose of the evaluation, even if initiated by the evaluee, is to provide information to a third party for consideration of some administrative, legal, or financial action. Thus, the primary ethical obligation is to strive to provide the third party with opinions regarding the issue in question. The guidelines adopted by the Committee on Ethical Guidelines for Forensic Psychologists Guidelines (1991), their proposed revision (American Psychology-Law Society, 2008), the APA ethical guidelines (American Psychiatric Association, 2008), and the AAPL ethical guidelines (2005) all recognize that this obligation affects the traditional relationship between the mental health professional and the individual undergoing evaluation.

The Physician–Evaluee Relationship in Employment Evaluations

The existence of a relationship with the third party in a disability or disability-related evaluation does not automatically preclude the existence of ethical duties owed to the evaluee. For example, basic ethical principles such as proscriptions against inappropriate sexual or physical behavior are obviously not abrogated by the primary ethical obligation to the third party. Although the view that ethical principles attendant upon a treatment relationship do not apply in employment evaluations is inaccurate, the nature of the obligations attendant upon the relationship must be different in a relationship where the primary ethical obligation is owed to a third party. For example, the obligation to maintain confidentiality cannot apply without modification in an evaluation whose express purpose is to communicate to a third party information that would normally be considered confidential.

The question of whether mental health professionals have ethical obligations to evaluees in third-party evaluations such as in independent medical evaluations (IMEs), given the primary relationship with a third party, and if so, the nature of those obligations, has been extensively discussed (Appelbaum, 1990; Candilis et al., 2007; Stone, 1984; Weinstock & Garrick, 1995; Weinstock & Gold, 2004). As the ethical guidelines clarify, mental health professionals performing employment-related evaluations do have ethical obligations toward an evaluee.

The AMA explicitly states, "When a physician is responsible for performing an isolated assessment of an individual's health or disability for an employer, business or insurer, a limited patient–physician relationship should be considered to exist..." (American Medical Association, 2006, Opinion E-10.03). The AMA ethics guidelines also state that physicians performing IMEs have the same obligations as physicians in other contexts to provide objective evaluations, maintain patient confidentiality, and disclose conflicts of interest.

The APA has not directly addressed the nature of the physician–patient relationship in any guidelines adopted to date. However, the APA Principles of Medical Ethics (2008) and the AAPL ethical guidelines (2005) imply the existence of a limited relationship in third-party evaluations. AAPL's ethical guidelines state, "Psychiatrists in a forensic role are called upon to practice in a manner that balances competing duties to the individual and to society" (American Academy of Psychiatry and the Law, 2005), acknowledging ethical obligations both to the evaluee and to the third party who often represents a public interest such as justice, disability benefits, or civil rights. The underlying rationale for some of AAPL's guidelines implies an ethical obligation toward the evaluee's welfare that follows from a physician–patient relationship.

The AP-LS also addresses the issue of whether a relationship exists between a psychologist and an evaluee in a third-party evaluation. Their proposed revised ethical guidelines (2008) specifically state, "In their work, forensic practitioners establish relationships with those who retain their services (e.g., retaining parties, employers, insurers, the court) and those with whom they interact (e.g., examinees, collateral contacts, research participants, students). Forensic practitioners recognize that associated obligations and duties vary as a function of the nature of the relationship" (p. 8). These guidelines advise psychologists that "Forensic practitioners are aware that there are some responsibilities, such as privacy, confidentiality, and privilege that may attach when the forensic practitioner agrees to consider whether a forensic practitioner–client relationship shall be established" (American Psychology-Law Society, 2008, p. 8).

Nevertheless, the AMA, the APA, the AAPL, and the AP-LS acknowledge that despite the existence of a relationship with the evaluee, an ordinary physician–patient or psychologist–client relationship does not exist in third-party evaluations, including disability and disability-related evaluations. As APPL (2005) states, the ethical duties owed to the evaluee have to be balanced against the primary ethical obligations to the third parties requesting or utilizing the evaluation. Mental health professionals providing disability and disability-related evaluations might therefore best be seen as having a primary duty to the third party and a "secondary" duty to an evaluee (Weinstock & Garrick, 1995).

Inevitably, conflicts between the secondary ethical obligation to the evaluee and the primary duty to the third party will arise. In most circumstances, the primary obligation to the third party will outweigh the duties to the evaluee. For example, the fundamental medical ethic of nonmaleficence, generally rendered as "Do no harm," is not straightforward in disability and disability-related evaluations. Information gathered in the course of a disability evaluation or IME may ultimately be used in ways that may cause the evaluee emotional distress or result in financial harm. However, mental health professionals are obligated to provide honest assessments, even if these turn out not to advance the evaluee's interests.

In other circumstances, the primary duty to the third party can and should be overridden. Situations may arise in which the welfare of the evaluee cannot be ignored, such as when an evaluee presents with high risk of suicide or harm to others. Some authors suggest that circumstances that create concern of harm to the evaluee, such as distortion of proceedings or process due to uncontrolled bias or racism, override all other ethical obligations (Candilis et al., 2007). However, other ethical issues, such as the extent of confidentiality and what constitutes informed consent, arise more commonly in disability and disability-related evaluations. The resolution of these conflicts is less straightforward and raises ethical and sometimes legal concerns that should be carefully evaluated.

Disclosure and Informed Consent

One of the clinician's primary responsibilities to evaluees in disability and disability-related assessments is to be honest regarding the nature and purpose of the examination (American Academy of Psychiatry and the Law, 2005;

American Medical Association, 2006, Opinion E10.03; American Psychiatric Association, 2008; American Psychology-Law Society, 2008). This process reflects a variety of fundamental ethical principles and obligations (American Medical Association, 2006; American Academy of Psychiatry and the Law, 2005), one of which is respect for an individual's autonomy. Disclosure and informed consent issues, even when reviewed before beginning an evaluation, may have to be revisited during the course of the evaluation. Informed consent is an ongoing process that requires dialogue between the evaluator and the evaluee.

Evaluees should be advised of the nature of the evaluation, who will have access to the information, and the limits of confidentiality before proceeding with the evaluation (see Table 1.1). If evaluees do not agree to the conditions, the evaluation should not proceed and the referring party should be consulted. Ideally, the disclosure should be provided in writing, reviewed with the evaluee, and signed at the time of the evaluation. This will help to avoid claims that the evaluee was not adequately advised of the limitations of the examination should conflicts regarding informed consent arise later.

Table 1.1 Elements of disclosure and informed consent in disability and disability-related evaluations

1. Purpose of the evaluation
2. Limits of confidentiality
3. Purpose for which information will be used
4. Absence of current or future treatment relationship
5. Caveat that once information is released to the third party, the evaluator has no control over whether the information goes further and if so, where

Clinicians should be sensitive to the fact that the circumstances that result in evaluees undergoing disability and disability-related assessments may also result in evaluees feeling they have no choice in accepting or rejecting the terms of the evaluation. In fitness-for-duty examinations, for example, employees may lose their jobs if they do not agree to undergo evaluations. In private insurance disability evaluations, individuals may not be able to access their benefits if they refuse to undergo assessment. Thus, clinicians should be certain that evaluees understand not only the purpose of the evaluation but also to whom the information will be distributed and, to the best of their knowledge, the purpose to which it will be used.

Ethical obligations require that mental health professionals also advise evaluees that the evaluation does not establish a treatment relationship (American Academy of Psychiatry and the Law, 2005; American Medical Association, 2006; American Psychology-Law Society, 2008). As mentioned above in regard to informed consent, initially advising evaluees of the lack of the traditional clinical relationship may not be sufficient. Evaluees may not be able to discriminate between the mental health professional's role as a treatment provider and a role as a clinical evaluator in a disability and disability-related evaluation. In fact, despite adequate informed consent, evaluees often assume the existence of a therapeutic alliance and ask for clinical opinions or treatment advice, thus "slipping" into the role of a patient.

Mental health providers who perform third-party evaluations may also unintentionally encourage an evaluee's belief that a therapeutic relationship is being established, even after disclosure, by themselves "slipping" into a familiar treatment or advisory role. Unintentional slippage on the part of mental health professionals is an artifact of familiar treatment roles. Examiners should monitor and address slippage in both their own interactions and the evaluee's perception of the relationship during the course of the evaluation. AAPL's ethical guidelines (American Academy of Psychiatry and the Law, 2005) remind clinicians they have "a continuing obligation to be sensitive to the fact that although a warning has been given, there may be slippage and a treatment relationship may develop in the mind of the evaluee."

Mental health professionals who intentionally foster belief in a therapeutic relationship to induce evaluees to reveal information are of more concern from an ethical standpoint (Bush et al., 2006; Shuman, 1993; Simon & Wettstein, 1997; Stone, 1984). Clinicians should avoid presenting themselves as overly friendly or empathic as a way of encouraging evaluees to provide information they might not otherwise volunteer. Active attempts to influence evaluees in this way exploit an evaluee's natural tendency to presume the existence of a traditional physician–patient or therapist–client relationship and are unethical.

Confidentiality in Third-Party Employment Evaluations

The ethical guidelines of all professional associations emphasize that confidentiality is an ethical imperative, even when limited by other obligations such as those present in third-party disability and disability-related evaluations. Mental health professionals conducting these evaluations also have an ethical obligation to maintain evaluee confidentiality whenever possible and release information only with the consent of the evaluee (American Medical Association, 2006, Opinion E-5.09; American Medical Association, 2006, Opinion E-9.07; American Psychological Association, 2002; Simon & Wettstein, 1997). However, this can create conflicts, as the purpose of third-party evaluations is to advise third parties of information that would normally be entirely confidential. Evaluators may be hard pressed to determine what information should or should not be considered and maintained as confidential under these circumstances.

Evaluators are advised that if possible, information not relevant to the decision that needs to be made should be kept confidential. Even when evaluees provide a release, the AMA ethical codes direct physicians to disclose only that information that is "reasonably relevant to the employer's decision regarding that individual's ability to perform the work required by the job" (American

Medical Association, 2006, Opinion E-5.09). Similarly, the AP-LS guidelines (Committee on Ethical Guidelines for Forensic Psychologists, 1991) state, "In situations where the right of the client or party to confidentiality is limited, the forensic psychologist makes every effort to maintain confidentiality with regard to any information that does not bear directly upon the legal purpose of the evaluation" (p. 660). The 2008 revised draft of the AP-LS guidelines takes an even stronger position, stating, "Forensic practitioners maintain the confidentiality of information relating to a client or retaining party, except insofar as disclosure is consented to by the client or retaining party, or required or permitted by law" (American Psychology-Law Society, 2008, p. 12). AAPL's ethical guidelines state that psychiatrists should maintain confidentiality to the extent possible given the context of the evaluation (American Academy of Psychiatry and the Law, 2005).

Forensic clinicians may at times find themselves in the difficult position of determining whether certain information is relevant and therefore not confidential, or not relevant and therefore should be kept confidential if possible. In IMEs conducted for litigation purposes, such considerations are less significant. All information acquired that is relevant, not privileged, and either admissible or likely to lead to the discovery of admissible information is discoverable (Federal Rules of Civil Procedure 26(b)). While the Supreme Court has recognized a psychotherapist–patient privilege that limits compelled disclosure of therapist–patient communications, as have most states, the privilege is only intended to protect confidential communications in furtherance of treatment (*Jaffee v. Redmond*, 1996). Since treatment is not the purpose of an IME, no privilege applies to limit discovery as long as the subject of the examination has received appropriate disclosure of the purpose for the examination, the lack of confidentiality, and recipient of the results.

Conflicts regarding confidentiality are more problematic when evaluations take place outside litigation and employers or insurance companies may not need to be apprised of certain information in order to make a determination regarding accommodations or benefits. In these situations, mental health professionals should bear the ethical obligation of confidentiality in mind as they provide their reports. For example, the APA states, "Ethically, the psychiatrist may disclose only that information which is relevant to a given situation.... Sensitive information such as an individual's sexual orientation or fantasy material is usually unnecessary" (American Psychiatric Association, 2006, p. 6).

Obligation for Honesty and Objectivity: Sources of Bias in Employment Evaluations

Honesty and objectivity are basic ethical tenets of all mental health professional organizations. The APA (American Psychiatric Association, 2006), the AAPL (American Academy of Psychiatry and the Law, 2005), the AMA (American

Medical Association, 2006, Opinion E-10.03), the American Psychological Association (American Psychological Association, 2002), and the AP-LS (American Psychology-Law Society, 2008) all endorse the ethical principle of honesty in all professional interactions. The value of disability and disability-related evaluations to employers, employees, administrative agencies, the social services system, and the justice system lies in the honesty and objectivity of the evaluation.

The key assessment in most disability and disability-related evaluations involves understanding the dynamics of the relationship between the evaluee's internal world, that is, the meaning the individual ascribes to work as well as to psychiatric disorders or symptoms, and the individual's external circumstances relative to employment as well as to other spheres of life. Any factor that affects evaluators' abilities to assess the evaluee's internal world, external circumstances, and the dynamic relationship between the two can create bias and limit objectivity in disability and disability-related evaluations.

As noted, disability and disability-related evaluations present many opportunities for direct and indirect pressures to influence a mental health professional's attempts to remain objective. In addition, mental health professionals often have limited or minimal formal training and clinical expertise regarding the psychological or social aspects of employment and disability issues. The influence of any type of bias potentially becomes more problematic in the absence of structured training, assessment techniques, or guidelines. In the absence of this informed guidance, personal beliefs and experiences are more likely to influence judgment.

Nevertheless, the obligation to strive for objectivity in all forensic mental health evaluations remains an ethical imperative in employment evaluations. Some professional organizations have specifically extended this ethical obligation to third-party evaluations. For example, the AMA states, "...IMEs [Independent Medical Examiners] are responsible for administering an objective medical evaluation..." (American Medical Association, 2006, Opinion E-10.03). The AP-LS-proposed ethical guidelines revisions state, "When offering expert opinions to be relied upon by a decision maker ... forensic practitioners demonstrate commitment to the goals of accuracy, objectivity, fairness, and independence. ... [T]hey strive to treat all participants and weigh all data, opinions, and rival hypotheses objectively" (American Psychology-Law Society, 2008, p. 5).

Inevitably, the endeavor to be honest and objective involves complex practical issues (Gutheil, 1998). All people, including mental health professionals, have personal and professional beliefs or biases that can potentially compromise their objectivity. Thus, mental health professionals' challenge in providing an honest and objective opinion is to recognize and address biases that might influence their opinions.

For example, the AMA advises, "In order to maintain objectivity, ... IMEs should not be influenced by the preferences of the patient-employee, employer or insurance company when making a diagnosis during a work-related or independent medical examination" (American Medical Association, 2006, Opinion E-10.03). However, in recognition of the difficulties involved in achieving absolute objectivity, AAPL's ethical guidelines (American Academy of Psychiatry and the Law, 2005) state forensic psychiatrists are obligated to strive for, not guarantee, objectivity. Similarly, the AP-LS-proposed revisions to their ethical guidelines state, "Forensic practitioners identify, make known and address real or apparent conflicts of interest in an attempt to maintain the public confidence and trust, discharge professional obligations, and maintain responsibility, objectivity, and accountability" (American Psychology-Law Society, 2008, p. 5).

Familiarity with some of the biases associated with disability and disability-related evaluations will assist practitioners in minimizing their potential influence. The influence of any type of bias on the ability to provide objective assessments depends to a great extent on how bias is defined and the degree to which it is present. Personal preferences, attitudes, professional biases, and the pressures of partisanship may not rise to a level that adversely influences expert opinions. Even the presence of significant bias regarding a particular case may not necessarily represent an insurmountable obstacle, provided the expert recognizes the bias and continues to strive for objectivity (Simon, 2002; Simon & Wettstein, 1997).

Common Sources of Bias in Disability and Disability-Related Evaluations

The adversarial nature of many disability and disability-related evaluations and the financial stakes involved increase the vulnerability of these evaluations to the same potential sources of bias as those that arise in any litigation proceeding, even if litigation has not been undertaken. Biases that may influence opinions in mental health evaluations (see, e.g., Simon & Shuman, 2002) and in employment-related evaluations (Gold, 1998) have been widely acknowledged and discussed. For example, bias can arise from individuals' tendency to under-revise initial hypotheses or to over-rely on memory in forensic evaluations (Borum et al., 1993). In addition, individuals' self-concepts, beliefs, and implicit theories influence recollection (Ross & Wilson, 2000). Research on "retrospective" or "hindsight" bias in autobiographical memory has shown that memory can be distorted toward consistency with current beliefs and expectations (LeBourgeois et al., 2007; Ross, 1989). Events that are not in fact related may become so when seen from a retrospective vantage point.

In addition, individuals may be strongly biased by their motives, and yet may be convinced that they are completely rational and objective in retrieving information from memory. Strongly held expectations may make it difficult for individuals to distinguish actual from simply expected results (Hirt et al., 1998). Finally, individuals may demonstrate errors of attribution, where they overattribute their behaviors to certain external events. Observers of the same situation may overattribute individuals' behaviors to stable personal characteristics. This dynamic makes it more likely for mental health professionals to attribute patient or examinee symptoms to character traits, whereas examinees will be more likely to attribute their symptoms to external events (Bush et al., 2006).

Advocacy Bias

Advocacy bias, that is, an inclination to present an opinion or interpret facts in a way most favorable to one side or another, is one of the most widely discussed and powerful sources of bias that can compromise mental health practitioners' opinions and testimony. Partisanship is often an implicit condition of retention by a third party. It may also result unintentionally from empathy or identification with a party or to a litigation team (Shuman & Greenberg, 2003). The influence of advocacy bias can be reinforced by the ethics of the legal profession, which requires vigorous advocacy on the part of attorneys for their clients. Concern regarding this form of bias is so significant that forensic specialty organizations' ethics guidelines explicitly warn practitioners to be wary of its influence and maintain impartiality (American Academy of Psychiatry and the Law, 2005; American Psychology-Law Society, 2008).

Despite these clear ethical directives, the fact that the legal system and mental health professional ethics have differing expectations can create a fundamental conflict. Tension in the roles that experts are expected to play is inherent in the way in which experts are used in the legal system. An adversarial legal system demands that experts serve the parties who retain them; the ethical codes and guidelines demand that experts impartially assist the court. These create competing tensions that can result in evaluators feeling they must choose between integrity and advocacy (Shuman & Greenberg, 2003).

Practical resolution of these conflicts is challenging. Mental health professionals conducting third-party evaluations should bear in mind that any issue that comes into dispute whether litigation has ensued or not always has at least two sides. The ethical obligation for objectivity requires evaluators to weigh all perspectives fairly (Bush et al., 2006). Mental health professionals should be certain that they examine information from both sides of the argument, assign a fair weight to each perspective, not engage in confirmatory or hindsight bias, and not allow the inherent pressures of the situation to influence decision making (Shuman & Greenberg, 2003).

Some have concluded that involvement in an adversarial legal system precludes the provision of objective opinions (Diamond, 1959). The eminent jurist Learned Hand reached the same opinion almost a century ago (Hand, 1915). Perhaps the only acceptable form of partisanship for evaluators is partisanship for their own opinions (Gutheil, 1998). Indeed, this type of partisanship may be an unavoidable artifact of human nature (Diamond, 1959) and is not inherently unethical. As the AP-LS-revised guidelines draft state, the principle of impartiality "does not preclude forceful representation of the data and reasoning upon which a conclusion or professional product is based" (American Psychology-Law Society, 2008, p. 5). Nevertheless, the partisanship of mental health professionals, as far as any is appropriate, should be limited to their own opinions.

Bias Associated with Mental Health Training and Experience

Intraspsychic Bias

Traditional psychodynamic theory, derived primarily from Freudian psychoanalytic theory, is the predominant theoretical training model in the Unites States. This theory focuses on the individual's intrapsychic dynamics as the source of emotional conflict and distress. Although psychodynamic theory allows that external experiences can affect an individual's psychological functioning, when life circumstances result in distress, such experiences are typically considered in light of the intrapsychic conflicts they activate or as manifestations of interpersonal dynamics.

Mental health professionals trained in psychodynamic theory and practice therefore often have a tendency to minimize external events except as they activate or reflect the internal dynamics of the individual (Simon, 1996a). They tend to place the locus of causality of emotional problems within individuals rather than in their circumstances. This results in an intrapsychic bias, that is, a bias toward assuming that an individual's psychological processes and the behavior associated with them are responsible for the individual's distress.

For example, individuals involved in legal disputes or insurance conflicts regarding claims of disability often report that they feel they are being watched or followed. Mental health professionals not infrequently interpret such statements as evidence of paranoid fantasies, traits, or personality disorders. However, many law firms and insurance companies routinely hire private investigators to photograph or videotape claimants who have asserted personal injury, including emotional injury, or disability. Given the external circumstances involving a legal or workplace claim, the perception of being watched or followed may reflect excellent reality testing rather than delusional thinking.

The tendency to pathologize what might in fact be responses to rather than causes of damaging external stresses is another risk of an intrapsychic focus in evaluation. Individuals who have experienced adverse employment events or who are involved in litigation often experience significant emotional distress, physical disturbances associated with anxiety and depression, and exacerbations or recurrences of preexisting psychiatric disorders. These individuals may appear excessively distressed, angry, or agitated. They may compulsively focus on and discuss in detail events that "prove" they have been victims of unfair treatment or that interpersonal conflicts are the fault of others. Such behavior

Obligation for Honesty and Objectivity

may lend credibility to a claim that the individual had a preexisting psychiatric disorder that resulted in the workplace problem. In fact, the stress associated with the conflict or its consequences commonly result in an agitated or obsessive presentation.

In disability and disability-related evaluations, an intrapsychic approach, without regard to legal, social, or cultural contexts, can exert a profound influence on evaluators' interpretations. Evaluators who conduct independent, psychiatric examinations without enough longitudinal history regarding evaluees and their functioning or who lack enough information about external circumstances are particularly prone to erroneous conclusions due to the influence of psychodynamic training. Intrapsychic dynamics may be a significant part of an individual's work conflicts. Nevertheless, an employment setting is one of the primary places where the external world interacts with the individual in ways that may render the contribution of internal dynamics less significant than external circumstances, even when the individual has unresolved intrapsychic conflicts or even an acute psychiatric disorder.

Bias Associated with an Extrapsychic or External Focus

Conversely, an external focus can result in a bias toward minimization of an individual's dynamics and potential contributions to a problematic employment situation. Individuals who develop employment-related problems or work impairment often put the blame for their difficulties on their employers, supervisors, or co-workers, even when the difficulties originate with their own perceptions, personality traits, or interpersonal styles. Uncritical acceptance of reports of external events in which evaluees portray themselves as passive victims of illness or of unscrupulous or incompetent supervisors or co-workers can result in incomplete and inaccurate assessments.

Mental health clinicians are familiar with the process of externalizing distress and assigning blame to others as a means of avoiding self-examination and responsibility for managing problems, but may not have enough information to recognize the extent to which this process is occurring in any given evaluation. For example, employees with escalating substance abuse problems will frequently blame deteriorating work performance and interpersonal relationships on unreasonable supervisors, unsupportive co-workers, or unfairly increased work demands. They may acknowledge depression or anxiety as problems, without mentioning substance abuse. Evaluators who focus on and accept these explanations without considering the possibility of substance abuse, a factor related only to the employee, may miss the key issue in the deteriorating relationship between the employee and the job.

Treatment providers may be particularly susceptible to this bias. In a treatment relationship, clinicians are naturally and appropriately inclined to accept patients' reports of symptoms and circumstances. In addition, they may appropriately empathize with patients' fears of consequences if employment is threatened or disrupted. For example, in sexual harassment cases, experienced clinicians recommend adopting the therapeutic stance of assuming that sexual harassment did in fact occur if a patient complains of this problem. They base this recommendation on the need to avoid causing further harm or "second injury" by expressing disbelief (Charney & Russell, 1994; Sherer, 1996; Shrier & Hamilton, 1996). This recommended therapeutic stance exaggerates the natural tendency to accept, at least initially, patients' reports of unfair treatment as accurate, but is incompatible with the provision of an objective evaluation (Gold, 2004).

Independent evaluators, especially those without forensic training, are also not immune to the bias of external focus. They may not understand the complex relationship between individuals and their work. As clinicians, evaluators generally and appropriately assume that the individuals seeking treatment are being candid about their circumstances and symptoms. In addition, mental health professionals are aware that unfair or stressful events occur in the workplace. Reports of unfair treatment or problematic supervisors or co-workers are not usually overtly unbelievable or bizarre, as may be reports of psychotic delusions. Thus, assumptions of veracity and ingrained clinical habits of trust can carry over to disability and disability-related assessments, rendering the independent evaluator susceptible to a less critical acceptance of external causation of distress.

Competent assessment requires that mental health professionals consider both internal and external aspects of workplace evaluations equally and avoid overemphasizing internal or external factors when reliable evidence supporting such conclusions is not available. As noted, the bias associated with a focus on intrapsychic factors can be most effectively addressed by obtaining as much information as possible regarding external circumstances. Similarly, minimizing the bias associated with an external focus requires obtaining enough psychiatric history to demonstrate that an evaluee has not had long-standing behavioral, psychiatric, or personality problems that might indicate patterns of distorted perception or tendencies to consistently blame external events for personal problems.

The Bias Toward Diagnosis: Stress vs. Disorder

Another source of bias in disability and disability-related evaluations lies in mental health professionals' tendencies to view signs and symptoms of emotional distress as diagnosable pathology in terms of the *Diagnostic and Statistical Manual of Mental Disorders* (DSM-IV-TR) (American Psychiatric Association, 2000). As the saying goes, to a hammer everything looks like a nail. Mental health professionals are predisposed by training and clinical experience to interpret signs of emotional distress and stress-related symptoms as evidence of a diagnosable disorder.

External pressures operative in disability and disability-related evaluations can reinforce this tendency. The pressure toward assigning diagnoses relatively quickly can be significant. In some types of evaluations, such as those associated with the Americans with Disabilities Act or Social Security benefits, the law makes diagnosis an essential element of a claim (Greenberg et al., 2004). This renders assigning a diagnosis an essential component of the evaluation.

In addition, one of the reasons for such regulations in statutory and administrative law is that a diagnosis generally is considered a threshold indicator of severity of illness. Individuals are generally not entitled to disability benefits or legal compensation for normal and expectable reactions to common but adverse events. Insurance benefits or workplace accommodations may not be available unless a diagnosis can be made.

The legal context for employment evaluations can result in increased pressures to assign diagnosis, and sometimes very specific diagnoses. The ability to diagnose a plaintiff's distress as a DSM-IV mental disorder lends credibility to claims of emotional distress, workplace injury, or disability. In civil litigation, for example, plaintiffs not given formal DSM diagnoses are often perceived as less damaged, although their emotional distress and suffering may have been profound (Greenberg et al., 2004).

In addition, third parties may exert pressure to ascribe or not ascribe certain diagnoses to support their arguments. A diagnosis of PTSD, for example, is highly favorable to plaintiff's arguments about causation and plaintiffs' attorneys may actively seek such a diagnosis (Greenberg et al., 2004; Simon, 2002). A diagnosis of a personality disorder is equally appealing to defense attorneys because by definition the development of this disorder predates employment issues and can even be ascribed a role in causation (Gold, 2002, 2004).

As a result of these pressures and biases, withholding diagnostic judgment is often more difficult than making definitive diagnostic statements. Psychiatric illnesses should be distinguished from expectable, nonpathological emotional reactions to adverse events. Mental health professionals do not accept as axiomatic the proposition that adverse events inevitably lead to psychiatric disorders. Similarly all emotional distress does not rise to the level of diagnosable illness. Feelings commonly associated with adverse work experiences, such as conflict with supervisors or sudden job loss, may include anxiety, anger, grief, and embarrassment. These feelings may be intensified if the individual feels unfairly treated or victimized. Nevertheless, intense and distressing feelings, in and of themselves, do not amount to diagnosable disorders.

Even in the absence of an identifiable adverse event, stress in the workplace is inevitable and can create various problems. These too may be erroneously ascribed to a psychiatric disorder, which can become the basis of a legal or disability claim. Occupational stress has become a common problem in the United States (see Chapter 3). Work-related stress can result in diagnosable physical and psychiatric symptoms. Stress at work can impair work performance, which in turn can increase the stress. If a stress state continues for a prolonged period of time, these symptoms may result in consulting a physician or mental health professional (Brodsky, 1984).

Most physicians and mental health professionals are aware that high levels of stress can have negative effects on physical and mental health and lead to or exacerbate health-damaging behaviors such as smoking or substance abuse. Treating clinicians will often diagnose these symptoms as mental disorders, and based on their patient's report, ascribe causation of the disorder to work-related stress. However, a person struggling with a difficult job is likely to experience symptoms indistinguishable from those that may result, for example, from wrongful termination. When claimants believe symptoms and associated impairments are due to unfair treatment rather than to their capacity to cope with workplace stress, misattribution becomes compounded (Greenberg et al., 2004).

Nevertheless, not every stressful situation will inevitably result in a physical or mental disorder, even if some stress-related symptoms are present. Employment-related problems may result in stress-related symptoms such as sleep disturbance, anxiety, or depressed mood, but at such a mild or infrequent level as to be below a diagnostic threshold. Transient symptoms, even if severe, are not typically signs of a mental illness and would not generally meet the criteria for a formal DSM psychiatric diagnosis. The standard for determining whether a collection of symptoms qualifies as a diagnosable mental disorder is provided by DSM-IV-TR (American Psychiatric Association, 2000). If symptoms are severe, are persistent, and begin to impair an individual's ability to function, they may indeed represent symptoms of a mental disorder that meets DSM diagnostic criteria.

For example, many individuals experience significant distress upon being required to relocate to another area in order to continue working for their current employer. This distress is magnified if the job transfer occurs under difficult circumstances, for example, workplace conflict with a supervisor. Evaluation might reveal this individual's primary symptoms are anxiety or difficulty sleeping, for which a primary care physician may have prescribed medication. Unless the individual meets the criteria for an anxiety or mood disorder, the application of these diagnoses on the basis of anxiety or insomnia alone would be inappropriate.

The value of DSM diagnoses when used for purposes other than treatment and research, such as legal or administrative claims, has been the subject of extensive discussion (Gold, 2002; Greenberg et al., 2004; Simon & Gold 2004). Diagnosis will not provide information regarding the specific functional impairment associated with any mental disorder in any given individual (Greenberg et al., 2004; Simon, 2002). Moreover, individuals described as having the same mental disorder are not alike in all ways, including degrees of functional impairment. The DSM contains a number of caveats that are intended to address these problematic issues. The DSM points out that

1. although potentially relevant, diagnosis is only one factor, and often not the most significant factor, that must be considered in assessing the severity and possible duration of psychological symptoms and associated impairment;
2. assignment of a particular diagnosis does not imply a specific level of impairment or disability since impairments, abilities, and disabilities vary widely within each diagnostic category;

3. it does not encompass all conditions;
4. its nomenclature was not developed for purposes other than clinical treatment and research; and
5. its use for forensic purposes carries a significant risk that diagnosis information will be misunderstood (American Psychiatric Association, 2000).

Despite these caveats and the concerns raised by legal scholars, the DSM has become something of a Bible in legal and administrative contexts. Rarely, if ever, is a psychological claim made that is not accompanied by a DSM diagnosis offered by a treatment provider or independent expert. Some have therefore argued that diagnostic categories should not be used in forensic contexts if not legally required because their circumstantial use is potentially more misleading than it is helpful (Greenberg et al., 2004).

Mental health professionals providing third-party evaluations for disability and disability-related issues should be aware of the pressures that might lead them to make diagnoses in the absence of symptoms meeting DSM criteria. They should also be aware that supplying a diagnosis, if required, is not a substitute for an analysis of the relevant behaviors, capacities, and functioning (Greenberg et al., 2004; Simon & Gold, 2004), particularly impairment in work functioning. Opinions involving diagnoses in disability and disability-related evaluations should be offered judiciously and should be well supported by the available data, not least because they may need to be defended should litigation arise. Evaluators required to provide a diagnosis who feel that they do not have enough information to make one should state as much and, if appropriate, suggest additional information that could be obtained or reviewed for purposes of diagnostic clarification.

Bias Associated with Role Conflict

The most common type of role conflict in disability and disability-related evaluations occurs when a mental health professional assumes the dual role of treating clinician and independent evaluator. Occupying these dual roles inevitably affects evaluators' perceptions of the dynamics of the relationship between the patient/evaluee's psychological issues and external work-related circumstances. The processes associated with a treatment role and evaluation role typically create irreconcilable conflicts due to differences in methodology, ethics, alliances, and goals. These difficulties have been extensively discussed (Appelbaum, 1997; Bush et al., 2006; Shuman & Greenberg, 1998; Strasburger et al., 1997).

Attempting to fill both roles simultaneously often compromises the effective execution of the tasks of both forensic evaluator and treating clinician. The required clinical stances of empathy, nonjudgmental listening, and the clinical imperative of forming a treatment alliance with a patient are typically not congruent with the characteristics of objectivity, balance, and healthy skepticism required in the forensic evaluator. For example, one of the first casualties of attempting to fill both roles is generally confidentiality. Although an essential component of a therapeutic relationship, confidentiality cannot be assured in disability and disability-related evaluations, as discussed above. Clinicians' desires to preserve confidential information may undermine their ability to provide complete disability and disability-related assessments. On the other hand, even with the patient's permission, the disclosure of information revealed initially in a confidential setting, especially to an employer, or in a public setting, may cause emotional distress and harm to the patient (Strasburger, 1987, 1999).

Empathy with patients, a misguided sense of obligation, or concern regarding disruption of treatment alliance can lead clinicians to agree to requests to occupy a dual role (Appelbaum, 1997). Treating clinicians, including primary care physicians, generally respond in one of several predictable ways when their patients ask them to provide documentation regarding short- or long-term disability, workplace accommodations, or fitness for duty. They may

a. fail to question or challenge the patient's assertions;
b. fail to identify malingering;
c. become overprotective out of concern for the patient's wellbeing;
d. exhibit misplaced advocacy;
e. overdiagnose pathology in the presence of minimal findings to support a disability claim or minimize pathology to facilitate return to work;
f. fail to consider personal or social factors contributing to the work issue; and
g. equate pathology and diagnosis with functional limitations and ability.

These responses often have a counterproductive effect on the patient, the physician–patient relationship, physicians themselves, and on the larger disability and health-care systems, even though they are generally motivated by the clinician's genuine desire to help the patient.

Mental health treatment providers are ethically obligated to be their patients' allies in the pursuit of health. Both patients and their providers may interpret this ethical obligation to mean that the providers should ally themselves with their patients' goals regardless of circumstances. Patients do not infrequently seek disability certification as a means of addressing problematic workplace situations that may not be related to impairment from mental disorders. Conversely, they may seek certification that they are able to return to work or are fit for duty after being placed on medical or administrative leave. Most patients reasonably or unreasonably expect that their treatment providers' obligations to advocate for their health will result in unquestioning advocacy of their desires.

Treatment providers may feel obligated to comply with their patients' expectations out of misguided beliefs regarding their appropriate advocacy role, particularly when providers are aware of financial or employment consequences of work-related problems. Treatment providers may also be hesitant to challenge a patient's interpretation of a work problem or request for medical documentation if they believe it may harm the treatment alliance. However, many physicians rarely or only briefly discuss their patient's work life. More often, their conclusions are strongly influenced by their patients' motivations and desires or by their patients' feelings about the job environment.

Clinicians will therefore often provide the requested documentation without ever taking into account specific job information (Rigaud, 2001). This is not to suggest that clinicians are attempting to deceive anyone or are in collusion with their patients to falsify declarations of disability, fitness, or unfitness. Rather, such interventions underscore the fact that the personal relationship between doctors and patients will cause the health professionals to present their patients' interest in the perspective most favorable to their patients (Brodsky, 1996a).

Vigorous advocacy is the appropriate ethical standard for attorneys but is not the appropriate ethical stance for forensic psychiatrists and psychologists (Gutheil & Simon, 1999; Simon & Wettstein, 1997). Such advocacy is not always the appropriate clinical stance even in some treatment circumstances. For example, certifying disability that leads to long-term work absence may not be in the best interest of patients' mental health, even in the presence of a chronic psychiatric disorder. In many such cases, advocacy for the patient's interest in optimal mental health may be best served by supporting recovery to maximum functioning and return to work.

Workers' compensation cases provide a salient example of the ethical dilemmas and potential bias caused by adopting a dual role. In workers' compensation claims, the same mental health professional generally provides initial evaluation, treatment, and reevaluation of a claimant. Ordinarily, evaluating clinicians do not consider the provision of treatment to claimants to be a conflict of interest, if treatment is indicated. However, the combination of sympathy toward the patient/claimant and a tendency to justify one's own treatment renders the clinician who provides both treatment and workers' compensation evaluations for the same patient/claimant especially vulnerable to bias (Brodsky, 1990). Those treating patient/claimants are far more likely to be sympathetic to them and to become their advocates in a legal conflict.

Treating clinicians may play a legitimate and necessary role in certain types of employment-related evaluations. Medical eligibility for social security disability benefits, for example, is based largely on documentation provided by the treating mental health professional. Often, no other medical information is obtained. However, the ethical conflicts inherent even in the relatively common circumstance of documenting impairments for their own patients for Social Security Disability Insurance have been noted and discussed (Candilis et al., 2007).

Circumstances sometimes compel or may not preclude assumption of dual roles (American Academy of Psychiatry and the Law, 2005; American Psychology-Law Society, 2008; Bush et al., 2006; Strasburger et al., 1997). Nevertheless, both AAPL's ethical guidelines (American Academy of Psychiatry and the Law, 2005) and the ethical guidelines for forensic psychologists (Committee on Ethical Guidelines for Forensic Psychologists, 1991; American Psychology-Law Society, 2008) recognize the ethical conflicts inherent in assuming the dual role of forensic evaluator and treating clinician. Both recommend avoiding adopting the dual role in forensic evaluations. Such considerations apply equally to many types of disability and disability-related evaluations, even in the absence a litigation context. Clinicians should consider whether the ethical and practical problems that arise from the assumption of both treatment and forensic roles in employment evaluations argue for its avoidance if possible (Bush et al., 2006; Candilis et al., 2007).

Bias Associated with the Work Ethic: Can't Work or Won't Work?

Mental health professionals' own beliefs regarding the role and value of work can also result in bias in employment evaluations. Some beliefs amount to nothing more than personal prejudices, which obviously should not be allowed to influence opinions. For example, some clinicians may believe that a certain ethnic group is more likely to malinger or otherwise manipulate systems to avoid work, and so be less likely to consider such complaints from individuals with these backgrounds credible. Some may believe that women are more likely to complain of real or imagined somatic symptoms and hence may be more likely to interpret women's complaints in employment evaluations as evidence of somaticization or hypochondriasis (Brodsky, 1990).

Many of the commonly held beliefs regarding work are more subtle and therefore more difficult to neutralize. These stem primarily from the social work ethic, often referred to as the "Protestant work ethic," that developed alongside and facilitated the Industrial Revolution. These beliefs about the value and necessity of work arose during the Protestant reformation, which embraced the concept that work could be a means toward the desirable end of saving one's soul (Statt, 1994). Adoption of this ethic during the industrial development of western society resulted in the attachment of moral value to work-related behaviors and circumstances.

The Protestant work ethic promoted the belief, and the experience of many people, that the harder they worked, the likelier they were to be successful. People were considered to have an obligation to fill their lives with work, with little or no time for recreation and leisure. Workers were to adhere to structure and authority and have dependable attendance records with low absenteeism and tardiness. A greater good was ascribed to doing one's job well, being highly productive, and taking pride in one's work. Workers were therefore encouraged to be achievement oriented and strive for promotions and advancement (Furnham, 1990; O'Brien, 1986).

The influence of this work ethic in disability and disability-related evaluations that consider questions of disability, impairment, or accommodations can be profound, especially as the work ethic is connected with political and personal beliefs regarding social policy. When presented with individuals who claim they can't work, beliefs and moral values about that individual's "work ethic" are inevitably activated. Our society, through multiple private and public regulations and statutes, has determined that individuals who are or who become unable to work due to illness are entitled to financial support or awards through public or private insurance or legal claims. Nevertheless, political and social controversy surrounds debates regarding social programs and disability, including issues of who should have to work and under what conditions.

Mental health professionals may hold strong opinions on this social issue. Just as most people agree that some people are clearly entitled to social support due to disability, most people would also agree that volition plays a part in decisions regarding work among persons with mental disorders. This is obvious from the fact that the problems of many, if not most, persons with mental disorders do not necessarily preclude the ability to work or result in permanent withdrawal from the workplace. This is not to say that all employed individuals who develop severe disorders will be able to continue working or be able to return to work. However, the symptoms of many people with a variety of psychiatric disorders do not absolutely preclude work or dictate permanent withdrawal from the workplace (Simon, 2002; Yelin & Cisternas, 1997).

In addition, most mental health professionals have internalized the work ethic, although not for the religious values it originally embodied. Completing the education and training necessary to become a mental health professional without a strong belief in working hard in pursuit of a desired goal would be difficult. Thus, when faced with making a judgment regarding an evaluee's functional impairment and the degree to which it creates a disability or was caused by an adverse event, mental health professionals' own attitudes toward work is inevitably at least one of the yardsticks against which the evaluee is measured.

Discussions of employment evaluations require recognition of the influence of this subtle but powerful bias. For example, many clinicians do not consider the possibility that an evaluee does not share our society's work ethic. Individuals who experience some of the more negative aspects of work (see Chapter 3) may not ascribe the same inherent value to work or hold the same work ethic as the professionals who evaluate them. Some minority or nondominant groups have historically not able to achieve success even with strict adherence to this same ethic. Personal circumstances related to social roles unfamiliar to many evaluators can also result in misinterpretation of work choices. For example, individuals with responsibilities of caring for aging parents or young children, roles for which women typically bear primary responsibility, may find that having to work outside home produces more problems and stress than psychological and financial benefits.

In addition, cultural attitudes toward the social welfare system will significantly influence the use of the public support system and the seeking of private or legal compensation. Evaluators unfamiliar with these attitudes and who do not assess them may also misinterpret work-related behaviors. People from some groups have cultural beliefs and attitudes that tend to prize self-reliance for dealing with problems. Unless absolutely necessary, they avoid depending on others or on the public. In contrast, other cultural groups may feel that they are entitled to receive help from the public and depend on society at large to provide support even in situations where others might not (Tseng et al., 2004).

Thus, mental health professionals' judgments regarding working ability and disability, between can't work and won't work, are especially subject to evaluators' own biases. Absolute criteria for mental disability, which might decrease the influence of personal bias regarding impairment vs. volitional withdrawal from work, do not and cannot exist. As noted by the DSM (American Psychiatric Association, 2000), occupational problems are not created solely by mental disorders and can arise from experiences such as job dissatisfaction and uncertainty about career choices. Even in the presence of a documented mental disorder, diagnosis alone is not of assistance in creating an absolute standard for the determination of disability (see Chapter 4).

Assessment of the question of can't work, that is, disability, as opposed to won't work, that is, choice or motivation to work, has much in common with forensic evaluations involving other specific aspects of functioning, such as competence or dangerousness. These are also issues that diagnosis alone cannot resolve (Greenberg et al., 2004). Each of these areas of assessment involves conclusions also rooted in subtle moral intuitions about peoples' choices, responsibility, degree of control over their functional ability, and whether the claimed impairments constitute "symptoms" over which the person has no control rather than weakness of character or bad habits (Bonnie, 1997c).

Clinicians are better able to meet their ethical obligation to strive for objectivity when they recognize their own potential biases. Mental health professionals performing disability and disability-related assessments face the challenge of minimizing the projection of their own social and moral values regarding work onto evaluees. When mental health professionals evaluate cases in which mental impairment and disability are claimed, they should be certain to examine their own beliefs and practices. The minimization of the influence of all types of bias requires that mental health professionals collect as much data as possible and structure their assessments to consider all relevant aspects of the dynamic relationship between an evaluee's internal state, external circumstances, and work-related problems.

Administrative Consequences of Not Conforming to Ethical Guidelines

Disciplinary Actions and Mental Health Employment Evaluations

Ethical violations in disability and disability-related evaluations can result in professional and legal consequences. Legal issues specific to third-party evaluations are addressed in Chapter 2. However, significant consequences short of legal action can result from violations of ethical principles. Evaluees can file complaints seeking disciplinary action, separate from or in conjunction with civil complaints for monetary compensation in court, with mental health clinicians' professional organizations and with state licensing boards.

All medical, psychiatric, and psychological professional organizations have provisions for peer review and support sanction and/or disciplinary processes for complaints regarding forensic activities (American Academy of Psychiatry and the Law, 2005; American Medical Association, 2006, Opinion E-9.07; American Medical Association, 2006, Opinion H-265.992; American Psychiatric Association, 2008; American Psychological Association, 2002). Professional organizations can impose disciplinary actions resulting from peer review processes held in response to complaints regarding expert witness testimony. Expert testimony by psychiatrists and psychologists typically fits the local definition of the practice of medicine or psychology (Simon & Shuman, 1999) and therefore the experts' behavior as an expert is governed by professional ethical norms.

The authority of a professional organization to impose disciplinary actions for forensic services has been consistently recognized in the courts (Kesselheim & Studdert, 2007). For example, in *Austin v. American Association of Neurological Surgeons* (2001), the Court of Appeals for the Seventh Circuit upheld disciplinary action taken based on a finding that Dr. Austin gave "irresponsible testimony under oath in a suit for medical malpractice." In *Budwin v. American Psychological Assn.* (1994), a California Court of Appeals affirmed the American Psychological Association's censure of a member for giving false testimony as a court-appointed expert in a custody dispute about interviews he did not in fact conduct and concluded that quasi-judicial immunity does not preclude a professional organization from disciplining its members for their actions in a judicial proceeding.

In addition, mental health professionals may also be reported to their state medical boards and disciplined (Binder, 2002; Willick et al., 2003). States have taken an increasingly active role in attempting to regulate expert testimony, including entertaining complaints against physician experts for improper testimony. The medical boards have folded this activity into a firmly established area of their jurisdiction by construing inappropriate expert witness testimony as a form of unprofessional conduct (Kesselheim & Studdert, 2007).

State licensing boards generally investigate all complaints received to ascertain their merit. Filing a complaint with a state licensing board offers several advantages to evaluees over pursuing a legal claim. First, the costs of filing this type of complaint, if any, are negligible, unlike the potential costs associated with hiring an attorney and filing a lawsuit. Second, licensing board complaints do not require proof of damages, as do civil suits. Finally, no statute of limitations on board complaints exists.

Implications for Impeachment

The degree to which examiners adhere to ethical obligations will have some bearing on both the admissibility and the credibility of their testimony, should disability and disability-related evaluations result in courtroom proceedings. Some legal scholars have suggested that serious ethical violations are "red flags" that should alert the court to closely examine the expert's reliability (Jansonius & Gould, 1998; Shuman & Greenberg, 1998). Many have suggested that unexcused violations of a relevant professional ethical rule, such as the obligation to strive for objectivity, should result in a presumption in favor of exclusion of that testimony (Shuman & Greenberg, 1998). In those cases where the court does not agree that it should result in exclusion, the opposing party is free to argue that violation of these professional ethical guidelines goes to the weight or credibility of the testimony.

Assessments that ignore or distort factual data as a result of biasing influences are much easier to discredit in court and thus may ultimately harm the retaining attorney's case. In addition, mental health professionals who provide biased testimony may undermine their personal reputations and credibility as well as the credibility of their profession. Finally, in failing to meet the ethical obligations of striving for objectivity, they undermine the legal system by casting doubt on the usefulness and value of any expert testimony.

Conclusion

The challenges that arise in the provision of disability and disability-related evaluations can be most effectively addressed by understanding the relevant ethical guidelines and obligations and how they apply in third-party evaluations. Ethical codes and legal obligations change and evolve over time. Mental health professionals providing disability and disability-related evaluations should endeavor to remain abreast of these changes. They should be familiar with their professional organizations' ethical guidelines and try to recognize their own personal and professional biases. Mental health professionals are also well advised to stay abreast of evolving legal standards, reviewed in the next chapter.

Chapter 2
Employment Evaluations and the Law

Introduction

In the previous chapter, we addressed psychiatrists' and psychologists' professional ethical obligations to third parties who contract for disability and disability-related evaluations, to the subjects of these evaluations, and to the courts and administrative tribunals asked to resolve relevant disputes. In this chapter we address the legal obligations attendant upon these evaluations. Psychiatrists and psychologists should be familiar with both. Ethical codes describe what the majority of a profession expects of its members and may be based on the same moral principles as the law (Bersoff, 1995). However, ethical and legal obligations may be congruent or incongruent. Ethical codes do not bind the law (i.e., legislatures, courts, agencies), which may have different expectations on any given issue based on a different moral perspective.

For example, the professional ethical duty of confidentiality, which prioritizes effective psychotherapy, conflicts with legal norms that prioritize accurate dispute resolution. Moreover, the ethical duty of confidentiality does not limit the authority of a judge to order disclosure and punish noncompliance. That is the realm of the law of privilege.

Claims of forensic professional liability or malpractice, although relatively rare, are brought against psychologists and psychiatrists (Binder, 2002; Gold & Davidson, 2007; Greenberg et al., 2007; Heilbrun et al., 2008; Melton et al., 2007). To prevail in a malpractice case, the complainant would have to demonstrate that the outcome of the claim would have been different if the mental health professional had not performed in a substandard manner. In addition, other types of legal obligations relating to the provision of disability and disability-related evaluations do exist and require that those providing such evaluations be familiar with the legal obligations and framework within which they are conducted.

Operating at the interface of the mental health professions and the law can create challenges in understanding conflicts and priorities in clinical evaluations conducted for legal or administrative reasons. Even psychiatrists and psychologists with a good understanding of the legal issues related to clinical evaluations conducted for treatment purposes may find themselves caught in a no-man's land of competing legal obligations when conducting disability and disability-related evaluations. Although disability and disability-related evaluations have much in common with clinical evaluations conducted for therapeutic purposes, the legal rules that govern the two differ.

Understanding the rules governing disability and disability-related evaluations begins with the recognition that they are most often applied outside the courthouse and are not subjected to public scrutiny. No codified list of what must be included in these evaluations or how they should be conducted has been established. Often, cases or statutes specific to disability and disability-related evaluations do not exist and we rely on general principles of contract or tort law. In other instances, precedent setting cases involving physicians are available, but not involving psychiatrists or psychologists. When no argument that might persuade courts to reach a different result in the case of psychiatrists or psychologists is evident, we present relevant cases involving other clinical specialties to explain the law. Because many disability and disability-related evaluations are conducted at the request of a third party, we begin with how the retaining third party and the examiner's expectations for the evaluations are expressed.

Obligations to the Retaining Party in Employment Evaluations

Most mental health professionals begin their assessments of both ethical and legal obligations from the perspective of the physician–patient relationship. It may therefore seem odd that a discussion of legal obligations in disability and disability-related evaluations begins with the obligations to the third party who enters into the contract with the evaluating clinician. However, a discussion of legal obligations in disability and disability-related evaluations needs to begin with an understanding that the contract in such evaluations is between the evaluating clinician and a third party, not between the evaluating clinician and the evaluee. Beginning the legal discussion of disability and disability-related evaluations with this subject also reflects legal history in which tort law, as we know it today, was a relatively late arrival. Liability arising out of the breach of an agreement has a longer legal pedigree.

The contract between the evaluating mental health professional and the third party requesting the evaluation is the primary relationship in third-party evaluations as far as the law is concerned. The vast majority of disability and disability-related evaluations performed by psychiatrists and psychologists are not conducted for the benefit of the courts and are never judged by them. Risk assessment and fitness-for-duty evaluations, for example, are typically intended only for the private use of a third-party employer. Examinees who think they were wronged by the evaluation face a fundamental problem posed by the absence of a doctor–patient relationship, discussed in the section "A Question of Duty" found below. But the relationship between examiners and the employers or insurance companies who retain them and who feel the examiner has wronged or harmed them does not pose the same problem.

First and foremost, evaluators owe a duty to the retaining party to provide competent evaluations. Substandard evaluations violate a contractual duty owed to the party who employed the evaluator (*Ryans v. Lowell*, 1984). When these evaluations subsequently arise in a lawsuit asserting that the failure to identify serious health problems that cost the employer money for which it seeks recompense, the question they present is whether the evaluation met the expectations of the parties (*Marine Transp. Corp. v. Methodist Hosp.*, 2006). The courts evaluate and determine whether the evaluation was conducted with the agreed-upon level of competence and skill.

Explicit agreements between the parties to a contract regarding performance standards are controlling. When an explicit agreement articulating a different standard does not exist, the courts default to the tort standard of reasonable professional conduct as a performance measure (*Lambley v. Kameny*, 1997). Inability to meet that threshold because it is beyond the examiner's expertise risks nonpayment for contracted services as well as tort liability for any resulting harm.

Consider, for example, *Marine Transp. Corp. v. Methodist Hosp.* (2006). On behalf of Marine Transportation, Methodist Hospital and Rashid Khan, M.D., conducted a fitness-for-duty examination of seaman Richard Guillory and failed to identify the presence of syphilis, from which Guillory died on a ship in the plaintiff's employ. The employer then sued Methodist Hospital and Dr. Khan for the costs of Guillory's medical care on the ship. After receiving a chilly reception in the trial court, the Texas Court of Appeals upheld the claim. Under Texas law, the physician is a party to a contract for the patient's benefit and in the absence of evidence that the parties chose a different standard of care, Methodist and Khan were required to exercise a duty of reasonable care.

Consent

Although many disability and disability-related evaluations are arranged by the contracting third party, consent of the evaluee, as in the provision of all health care, is generally required by the law as well as professional ethics. Psychiatrists and psychologists enjoy no roving authority to intervene in the lives of others. Captured in Cardozo's colorful and much-quoted refrain highlighting the importance of autonomy, the fundamental legal principle underlying the necessity for consent is now beyond debate. "[E]very human being of adult years and sound mind has a right to determine what shall be done with his own body...." (*Schloendorff v. Society of New York Hospital*, 1914, p. 93). The law's recognition of autonomy extends to the mental as well as the physical realm (*Zinermon v. Burch*, 1970).

Whether in a private employment context or a court-ordered examination, consent should precede the evaluation and no evaluation should proceed without consent (*Smith v. Welch*, 1998). In the case of court-ordered examinations (although unlikely in disability and disability-related evaluations), consent, or, as some prefer, assent, is constitutionally required if statements made during the examination may be used against the evaluee in a criminal proceeding (*Estelle v. Smith*, 1981). Proceeding with an evaluation without assent is also unwise. Obtaining consent, even if not absolutely necessary or mandatory, costs nothing and treats the examinee with respect. Failing to obtain a consent later determined to be required cannot be remedied.

Despite the contract with the third party, evaluees must therefore make a stark but meaningful choice that the examiner should respect (Foote & Shuman, 2006). Refusing to participate in an employment evaluation has its consequences: evaluees may lose financial benefits or employment. The law has upheld the rights of employers to obtain such evaluations in certain circumstances. For example, employers are permitted to require employees to submit to fitness-for-duty examination as a condition of employment if it is job related and enjoys a business necessity (*Cal. Gov. Code*, 2004). "Simply put, applicants for jobs ... have a choice; they may consent to the limited invasion of their privacy resulting from the testing, or may decline both the test and the conditional offer of employment" (*Wilkinson v. Times Mirror Corp.*, 1989, p. 194). Even though these consequences may seem harsh, the examinee is entitled to make his or her own choice.

Other rules may also play a role in encouraging an informed decision about participation in disability and disability-related evaluations. In some states, the results of a court-ordered examination may be admitted if it can be shown that the evaluee was previously informed the examination would not be privileged (Tex. R. Evid. 510 (d)(4)). Providing information to the examinee about the absence of privilege makes it more likely that the true nature and purpose of the relationship and the risks and benefits that may flow from the examination are addressed.

In the context of treatment, the elements of adequate or "informed consent" generally consist of information provided regarding "(1) the condition being treated, (2) the nature and character of the proposed treatment, (3) anticipated results, (4) possible alternative treatments, and (5) possible and probable risks and side effects" (*Barcai v. Betwee*, 2002, p. 959). Different interests are at stake in nontherapeutic employment or forensic evaluations (Foote & Shuman, 2006). The information exchange that must precede a valid consent/assent is generally thought to include informing the evaluee of the *purpose* of the examination; who will have access to the results of the examination or at least to whom the report will be forwarded; and of what the examination will consist (e.g., pencil and paper tests, interviews). Examinees should also be advised that no treatment will be provided at the time of the evaluation or in the future. Before the examination begins, an examinee should know whether the sole purpose of the examination is to discover information relevant to a claim or defense and not to provide treatment.

If there is any doubt about whether the evaluee understands these conditions at any time during the assessment, mental health professionals should explain them as many times as necessary during the course of the interview. If the evaluation is occurring in the context of litigation and the examiner has concerns about the evaluee's understanding of these conditions, examiners should refer the evaluee to his or her attorney before proceeding. Examiners should obtain a signed consent before beginning the interview documenting that all these conditions have been explained. In the absence of a valid consent/assent, or relevant exception thereto, evidence resulting from the evaluation may not be admissible and the examiner may face a tort claim for battery, intentional infliction of emotional distress, invasion of privacy, or negligence.

Obligations to the Evaluee in Disability and Disability-Related Evaluations

A psychiatrist or psychologist conducting an employment evaluation wields immense power over the person being evaluated. When individuals perceive they have been harmed by an inappropriate evaluation, given the important role of work in peoples' lives, it should not be surprising that they may pursue professional disciplinary actions or civil tort remedies measures. The professional disciplinary process associated with inappropriate or substandard evaluations was discussed in Chapter 1. This discussion will address the tort remedy.

Most tort claims arising out of a disability and disability-related evaluation assert negligent rather than intentional wrongs. Intentional tort claims such as battery, intentional infliction of emotional distress, or false imprisonment are possible in the employment context and apply even if no doctor–patient relationship exists (*Smith v. Welch*, 1998). However, the assertion that a health-care professional intentionally harmed an evaluee they had not met until the evaluation presents an assertion that is intuitively unlikely and difficult to prove. Thus, negligence is the mainstay of these claims.

Negligence is the breach of a duty proximately causing harm. The conjunctive elements necessary in a claim of negligence are proof of duty, breach, cause, and harm. Duty refers to the legal recognition of an obligation to another; breach refers to conduct that does not meet that obligation; cause refers to a close connection between the breach and the harm claimed; and harm refers to injury that the law recognizes. Each must be found to be more likely than not for the plaintiff to prevail.

In many instances, courts have treated these relatively new tort claims arising out of third-party evaluations as ordinary negligence rather than as medical malpractice. Medical malpractice or professional negligence, that is, intentional and negligent tort claims against health-care professionals, applies the same basic principles as ordinary negligence with a few added wrinkles. Although most medical malpractice claims are grounded in negligence, important procedural consequences flow from their categorization as "ordinary" negligence (Gold & Davidson, 2007). For example, some tort reform efforts are limited to cases designated as medical malpractice. In addition, medical malpractice claims generally have shorter statutes of limitation than ordinary negligence claims; medical malpractice claims are more likely to require expert testimony on the standard of care; and medical malpractice claims are more likely to be covered under a professional liability insurance policy.

The Question of Duty in Third-Party Evaluations

Duty, the first element of negligence, is an issue that is likely to be contested in malpractice claims arising out of disability and disability-related evaluations because of the nature of the doctor–patient relationship in a third-party evaluation. When contested, the question of whether a duty exists is ordinarily determined by the judge. If the judge determines as a matter of law that the defendant owes no legal duty to the plaintiff, the lawsuit will be dismissed without regard to the harm the plaintiff suffered.

The common law took the position that in the absence of voluntarily assuming an obligation (e.g., when taking on a new patient), no one, not even health-care professionals, has a legal duty to come to the aid of another. In the event of a request for emergency or nonemergency services, with limited exception (see Emergency Medical Treatment and Active Labor Act; also *Greenberg v. Perkins*, 1993), mental health professionals legally have the choice of accepting or not accepting a patient for treatment. Accepting the patient for treatment gives rise to a doctor–patient relationship and resultant legal duties.

In contrast, courts have held that an evaluation conducted for the benefit of a third party does not give rise to a doctor–patient relationship and, consequently, a duty of care. Therefore, the majority rule in such cases is that a traditional medical malpractice claim by the examinee against the evaluator will not survive (*Joseph v. McCann*, 2006; *Martinez v. Lewis*, 1998; *Rogers v. Horvat*, 1975; *Tomko v. Marks*, 1992). "The general rule is that the physician who is retained by a third party to conduct an examination of another person and report the results to the third party does not enter into a physician-patient relationship with the examinee and is not liable to the examinee for any losses he suffers as a result of the conclusions the physician reaches or reports" (*Ervin v. American Guardian Life Assur., Co.*, 1988, p. 357).

For example, in *Joseph v. McCann* (2006), Joseph, a Salt Lake City police officer who shot a motorist, was required to submit to an independent medical examination (IME) regarding fitness for duty as a condition of reinstatement.

McCann, a psychiatrist, performed the IME and concluded that Joseph was not psychologically fit to perform his duties as a police officer. After unsuccessfully appealing his termination with the city, Joseph brought a malpractice claim against McCann. The trial court dismissed the claim on summary judgment. The Appeals court ruled that a fitness-for-duty examination does not result in a physician–patient relationship cognizable in an action for medical malpractice by the examinee, and affirmed reasoning that a physician–patient relationship was a prerequisite to a legal duty enforceable in a medical malpractice action. Because McCann was not treating or evaluating Joseph for treatment, no physician–patient relationship arose and no medical-malpractice claim would be recognized. Thus, a false-positive finding that results in failing a fitness-for-duty evaluation done at the behest of a third party is not grounds for a medical malpractice claim in most states. Similarly, in another case, *Harris v. Kreutzer* (2006), the Virginia Supreme Court refused to recognize a medical malpractice claim brought against a psychologist for an incorrect diagnosis in an employment evaluation.

However, mental health professionals conducting disability and disability-related evaluations should be aware that although a doctor–patient relationship is the foundation for a malpractice claim, no particular formalities are necessarily required to establish that relationship. A relationship may be established without a written document reflecting the terms or conditions of the relationship or even without direct contact. Neither doctor nor patient may realize the implications of their actions. The test courts apply to determine whether a doctor–patient relationship existed asks what a reasonable person observing their behavior would believe, not what the doctor or the patient believed (Baum, 2005).

> It is the general rule that recovery for malpractice against a physician is allowed only where there is a relationship between the doctor and patient .... This relationship may be established by contract, express or implied, although creation of the relationship does not require the formalities of a contract, and the fact that a physician does not deal directly with a patient does not necessarily preclude the existence of a physician-patient relationship. What is important, however, is that the relationship is a consensual one, and when no prior relationship exists, the physician must take some action to treat the person before the physician-patient relationship can be established *(Dehn v. Edgecombe*, 2005, p. 620).

For psychiatrists and psychologists conducting disability and disability-related evaluations, slipping into a clinical role in a forensic evaluation, or agreeing to provide future services for a forensic evaluee may establish a doctor–patient relationship. Doing so exposes the examiner to liability for medical malpractice, in addition to creating the ethical and practical problems discussed in Chapter 1.

The "no-duty-to-rescue" rule has been unpopular for many years because it is morally abhorrent. Highly publicized cases of bystanders failing to take any action to stop a sexual assault or a stabbing provoke public outrage, despite the fact that the failure to rescue in such circumstances is not illegal. While courts are reluctant to do away with the rule fearing the creation of an unworkable general duty of beneficence, they have been increasingly willing to recognize exceptions that chip away at the rule. Following in that mode are a group of decisions that reject the notion that treatment is required to establish doctor–patient relationships. These decisions recognize a limited doctor–patient relationship arising out of employment as well as other types of nontherapeutic evaluations performed for the benefit of a third party.

These decisions are carefully confined to their facts. They do not recognize a claim for any harm that would be compensable in a medical malpractice claim, such as an incorrect diagnosis. Rather, these decisions recognize a limited duty to avoid only the following specific harms.

The Duty to Not Cause Harm in the Conduct of an Examination

Many jurisdictions that reject medical malpractice claims by employee/examinees arising out of examinations for the benefit of third parties have recognized a negligence claim when the examiner engages in conduct that causes physical harm to the person being examined (*Greenberg v. Perkins*, 1993). In most of the reported cases this involves subjecting the examinee to a physical test of an injury or impairment that results in harm or dysfunction not present prior to the examination. Examinations that cause harm are disquieting and the claims of those injured have not fallen on deaf ears. "The limited relationship between the examiner and the plaintiff encompasses a duty by the examiner to exercise care consistent with his professional training and expertise so as not to cause physical harm by negligently conducting the examination" (*Harris v. Kreutzer*, 2006, p. 29; see also *Dyer v. Trachtman*, 2004).

Although most of the reported cases involve physical harm, the principle underlying the rule is not restricted by any logic to physical harm. Indeed, in one recent case, a psychologist's allegedly verbally abusive behavior during an IME of a claimant asserting traumatic brain injury resulting in psychological trauma was recognized as viable. "Because the [IME] functions only to ascertain information relative to the underlying litigation, the physician's duty in [an IME] is solely to examine the patient without harming her in the conduct of the examination" (*Harris v. Kreutzer*, 2006, p. 31; see also *Martinez v. Lewis*, 1998). Thus, the obligation of the examiner to discover relevant information regarding the subject's injuries and impairments must be balanced against the obligation not to worsen those injuries or impairments in the process of learning about them.

The Duty to Communicate Critical Information

In addition to a duty to avoid causing harm in the evaluation, a number of states have recognized a duty to report serious new abnormal test results obtained in an evaluation conducted for the benefit of a third party. These cases, like those imposing a duty to examine without causing harm, do not involve a review of the reliability of the evaluation or the failure to discover a condition. Rather they address the failure to communicate what was discovered. Thus far, no psychiatric or psychological discoveries have been at issue in the reported decisions, but there is nothing in the reasoning of those opinions that would limit their application. Case law has not yet encompassed circumstances in which a disability or disability-related psychiatric or psychological evaluation yielded evidence of suicidal ideation or intent to harm others that was not communicated to appropriate parties and resulted in harm, but such a case is not hard to imagine.

The Duty to Maintain Confidentiality

In writing reports and testifying about the results of an evaluation, psychiatrists and psychologists face a dilemma. Professional ethics require the protection of confidentiality as far as possible in third-party employment evaluations (see Chapter 1). However, the duty to maintain confidentiality is constrained by the need to make disclosures that fulfill the purpose of the evaluation. Therefore, sensitive personal data that are irrelevant to the purpose of an evaluation should be withheld in the interests of privacy and disclosure should be limited in scope and directed only for the purpose for which consent was provided.

For example, in *McGreal v. Ostrow* (2004), Mr. McGreal, a police officer, underwent a fitness-for-duty evaluation. Subsequently, the report was disseminated. Mr. McGreal's psychological evaluation included sensitive personal information not relevant to his fitness for duty and had been disseminated far beyond the superiors responsible for the determination of his fitness and the purposes for which the report was created. Mr. McGreal brought a claim under the state confidentiality act. The trial court dismissed the claim on a motion for summary judgment but the appeals court reversed and remanded. The Illinois Supreme Court held that a police chief had the authority to order fitness-for-duty evaluations of officers in the interest of public safety and that logically the police chief was entitled to the results of the examination. However, the act allowed disclosure only under narrow circumstances and a reasonable doubt existed whether those circumstances were present in this case, implying that the state confidentiality act had to be followed in disseminating the fitness-for-duty report.

Protecting confidentiality by withholding seemingly irrelevant information disclosed by the examinee risks a painful cross-examination that may undermine credibility should litigation arise. Advancing the credibility of the examination by providing all information disclosed to an employer risks unnecessary breaches of confidentiality and psychological harm to the examinee. In some instances specific state privacy laws govern the procedures for disclosure of health information even in the judicial context and may serve as a third category of liability arising out of employment evaluations (*Pettus v. Cole*, 1996). For a discussion of claims that may arise under federal law, see the discussion below regarding privacy and confidentiality.

Breach of Duty and Harm

To prevail in a negligence claim, in addition to proving the existence of a duty, the claimant must also prove that the duty was breached and proximately caused compensable harm. Breach is typically assessed by measuring the defendant's behavior against what the behavior of other members of the profession would be in similar circumstances. This assessment leaves room for debate between experts about other physicians' common practices and the nature of the ordinary skill of practitioners.

> In order to establish medical malpractice, it must be shown by a preponderance of evidence that the injury complained of was caused by the doing of some particular thing or things that a physician or surgeon of ordinary skill, care and diligence would not have done under like or similar conditions or circumstances, or by the failure or omission to do some particular thing or things that such a physician or surgeon would have done under like or similar conditions and circumstances, and that the injury complained of was the direct and proximate result of such doing or failing to do some one or more of such particular things (*Bruni v. Tatsumi*, 1976, p. 675).

The claimant must also convince the jury that the doctor's breach of duty is causally linked to the harm claimed, that is, that the outcome would have been different and better if the defendant had acted appropriately. If no harm was suffered or if the same harm would have occurred regardless of the breach of duty, for example, where the condition that the defendant negligently failed to diagnose was not curable nor could its course be altered by timely treatment, the causation requirement is not met and the claim fails.

The requirement that compensable harm must be closely linked or proximate to the negligence results from the law's effort to make the financial consequences of negligence proportional to the negligent act. This link is typically expressed in terms of foreseeability of harm within the risk that made the defendant's actions negligent in the first place. For example, where the defendant's care of the patient was negligent giving rise to an increased risk of suicide, but the suicide did not occur until 2 months later when the plaintiff had stopped seeing the defendant and, in the interim, had seen a new psychiatrist, the harm would not be proximate to the defendant psychiatrist's negligence. An act of suicide 2 months after cessation of treatment with the defendant psychiatrist would not be considered a foreseeable risk despite negligent care.

Finally, the law must recognize the harm caused by the breach of duty. Thus, minor hurt feelings or the loss of one night's sleep would not suffice to support a prima facie case of negligence, but major depression or a suicide attempt would. Although the law has long been wary of mental or emotional loss as in claims of damages (e.g., capping intangible loss), at least when unaccompanied by some physical impact or injury, it remains a cognizable albeit problematic damage claim.

Immunity in the Provision of Disability and Disability-Related Evaluations

Most disability and disability-related evaluations are conducted outside the legal arena. Therefore, any type of immunity associated with providing testimony or evaluations to the legal system will not be applicable. Possible causes of action related to third-party evaluations for which no immunity is available include defamation, invasion of privacy, breach of contract, perjury, and other intentional torts. For example, negligent interference with a contractual relationship is a relatively new but developing doctrine that may create liability for third-party evaluations, including mental health professionals (Postol, 2003).

Of possible causes of action other than negligence or malpractice, defamation appears to be the most common. Although mere opinions are not actionable, other types of statements may be. Generally, physicians cannot be sued for defamation for their opinions concerning a worker's ability to work unless the statement made was false and made with recklessness (Postol, 2003).

Notwithstanding the negligence of the defendant, if evaluations or testimony are provided in certain legal circumstances, the law insulates the defendant from liability in order to advance a different agenda. This insulation may apply if the disability or disability-related evaluation is conducted within a litigation context. One way in which the law seeks to encourage witnesses' participation in the judicial system is to provide certain immunities for the benefit of citizens engaged in this community service. "[T]he claims of the individual must yield to the dictates of public policy, which requires that the paths which lead to the ascertainment of truth should be left as free and unobstructed as possible" (*Calkins v. Sumner*, 1860, p. 197).

Thus, the common law has long recognized that witnesses should not be subject to lawsuits for defamation for statements given under oath on the witness stand. "A witness is absolutely privileged to publish defamatory matter concerning another in communications preliminary to a proposed judicial proceeding or as a part of a judicial proceeding in which he is testifying, if it has some relation to the proceeding" (American Law Institute, 1981, p. 588). The rule that witnesses are immune from suits for defamation for their testimony applies to lay and expert witnesses alike.

However, witness immunity is not absolute under all circumstances. Because witness immunity is intended to assist in the administration of justice, it has no application to statements made prior to the commencement of litigation or after commencement but outside the judicial process (*Twelker v. Shannon & Wilson*, 1977). Nor does witness immunity extend beyond the courtroom. For example, the reach of professional disciplinary proceedings to address behavior on the stand (i.e., *Austin v. American Association of Neurological Surgeons*, 2001), as well as criminal proceedings, for example, to face perjury charges (*Riffe v. Armstrong*, 1996) is unaffected by immunity in conjunction with expert testimony.

The discussion of immunity often brings up the terms "witness immunity" and "quasi-judicial immunity." These labels are used differently by different courts and are a better starting point than ending point in predicting whether immunity will protect an expert providing testimony in disability and disability-related evaluation cases. In general, witness immunity tends to be more qualified or conditional than quasi-judicial immunity. Qualified immunity shields some behaviors, such as good faith mistakes. Quasi-judicial immunity tends to be less qualified and provides a broader shield, even for bad faith actions. The more unqualified the immunity, the more likely a court will dismiss the claim on its face. The more qualified the immunity, the more likely it may require completion of discovery or even taking evidence at trial to determine its application.

At one extreme are cases such as *Bruce v. Byrne-Stevens* (1989) that refuse to limit witness immunity to defamation for court-appointed experts and recognized unqualified immunity for all experts. "[E]nsuring objective, reliable testimony – dictates in favor of immunity for experts." Many jurisdictions only grant court-appointed experts this sort of immunity under the label quasi-judicial immunity, a reason many psychiatrists and psychologists will only testify if they are court-appointed. But not all jurisdictions recognize quasi-judicial immunity for all court-appointed experts (*Levine v. Wiss*, 1984). For example,

> ... [Q]uasi-judicial immunity is generally not extended to an examination conducted at the request of one of the parties to the litigation.... Rather, the cases that recognize quasi-judicial immunity for court-appointed psychiatric examiners do so only when the examiner is appointed by and reports directly to the court.... In effect, such an appointee acts as an officer of the court (*Dalton v. Miller*, 1999, p. 668).

In any event, since most disability and disability-related evaluations are conducted outside a litigation context, the question of immunity will never arise.

Similarly, a number of states have concluded that experts providing litigation support services are not cloaked with any immunity and are subject to ordinary negligence claims for harm caused by substandard services (*Murphy v. A.A. Matthews*, 1992). These cases have involved conduct such as incorrectly advising that a malpractice claim would not be recognized and incorrectly calculating damages that resulted in agreeing to a reduced settlement. Thus far, psychiatrists and psychologists are not well represented in reported decisions regarding immunity from suit for expert testimony, but the relevant cases do not appear to draw distinctions that would change the result for them.

Privacy and Confidentiality: Access to Information

In a traditional doctor–patient relationship, the subject of an evaluation is the intended recipient of information gained. In contrast, disability and disability-related evaluations are generally conducted for the express purpose of providing information to the third party who contracts for the evaluation.

Outside of litigation, mental health professionals have commonly assumed that they owe a duty to provide the information gained in a third-party evaluation to the party who retained their services and no one else. Evaluees who request voluntary disclosure of that information from the evaluator are generally referred to the third party who contracted for the evaluation and who could choose to disclose or not.

However, the Health Insurance Portability and Accountability Act's (HIPAA) Privacy Rule gives patients the right to inspect and copy their records. Clinicians who meet HIPAA's definition of a health-care provider must comply with the Privacy Rule's requirements for disclosure of protected health information (PHI). HIPAA's Privacy Rule defines PHI as all "individually identifiable health information held or transmitted by a covered entity or its business associates, in any form or media, whether electronic, paper or oral" (45 CFR §160.103). This definition does not distinguish information generated by employment-related mental health evaluations from records of treatment. Nor does the Privacy Rule explicitly make the purpose for which the information was created of any consequence (Gold & Metzner, 2006).

The Office of Civil Rights is responsible for enforcing HIPAA regulations. This office reports the case of a private medical practice that denied an individual access to medical records of the individual's IME at the direction of the retaining insurance company. The Office of Civil Rights states that it required the practice to revise its policies and procedures regarding access to "reflect the individual's right of access regardless of payment source" (United States Department of Health and Human Resources, Office of Civil Rights-HIPAA, 2007).

The Social Security Administration (SSA) takes the position that a purely diagnostic consultative examination (CE) (see Chapter 7) performed by a health-care professional for SSA disability purposes is a covered health-care function (45 CFR §164.501) requiring compliance with the Privacy Rule (Health and Human Services Summary of the HIPAA Privacy Rule, 2006). However, in contrast to the ruling of the Office of Compliance and Enforcement, SSA advises consultative examiners that requests for the report of a CE should be directed to the state disability determination service (Social Security Administration, 2006). To date, no opinions have addressed whether this is an apparent or actual conflict.

HIPAA's regulations permit a patient to authorize disclosure but require that the authorization be in writing, signed by the patient or the patient's legal representative, describe what is to be disclosed, to whom, the purpose of disclosure, include an expiration date and an explicit acknowledgment of a broad array of rights (45 CFR §154.508). They also require that the healthcare provider keep a record of all disclosures (45 CFR §164.512(e)). The Privacy Rule does authorize disclosure without patient authorization in specified cases. For example, the Privacy Rule specifically states that it is "not intended to disrupt existing workers' compensation systems as established by State law.... To this end, the Privacy Rule explicitly permits a covered entity to disclose protected health information as authorized by, and to the extent necessary to comply with workers' compensation or other similar programs established by law that provide benefits for work-related injuries or illness...." (45 CFR §164.512(j)).

Similarly, in a judicial or administrative proceeding, PHI may be disclosed without authorization pursuant to an order from the court or administrative tribunal or pursuant to a discovery request or subpoena, provided it is accompanied by an assurance that the subject of the records has been notified or reasonable efforts will be made to give notice of the request, or that reasonable efforts have been made to secure a qualified protective order limiting access to these records (*Bayne v. Provost*, 2005; 45 CFR §164.512(e)). Without these assurances or the signature of a judge, a subpoena or discovery request does not authorize disclosure. HIPAA requires a formal authorization to conduct an ex parte interview (i.e., without the presence of the opposing party) of health-care and medical personnel employed by an opposing party (see *Keshecki v. St. Vincent's Medical Center*, 2004).

In the case of conflicting requirements, one method HIPAA adopts for resolving potential conflicts between state and federal law is by requiring compliance with the law that imposes the most stringent privacy protection. Thus, HIPAA creates a minimum standard for privacy and confidentiality, which may be superseded by more stringent state laws. Another method of avoiding conflicts is by excluding certain areas of state law, such as workers' compensation (as discussed above), from HIPAA preemption.

Although disclosure of PHI to the patient/evaluee is designated as mandatory, exceptions to the right of access to personal records exist, and HIPAA specifically delineates grounds for denying access. Some of these denials may be appealed for review, others may not, again as per HIPAA regulations. For example, patients may be denied access to psychotherapy notes and are not entitled to review of this denial. Patients may also be denied access to their records if it is thought likely to endanger the patient or others, but this denial may be appealed and reviewed.

However, none of the grounds for denial of access, whether subject to appeal or not, are based on the fact that the documents were created for purposes of a third-party evaluation or were paid for by a party other than the evaluee, nor are they related to the nature of the physician–patient relationship. A psychiatrist or psychologist who is a covered entity under HIPAA conducting IMEs, disability, or disability-related evaluations, or third-party evaluations should therefore include in their initial disclosures to evaluees the relevant aspects of the Privacy Rule as well as their practices regarding obtaining reports. Finally, mental health professionals should be aware that the Privacy Rule requires covered psychiatrists and psychologists to maintain a log of all PHI disclosures.

One major exception made by HIPAA to the patient's right of access to their records which may be relevant to disability and disability-related evaluations is the limitation of disclosure of information "compiled in reasonable anticipation of, or for use in, a civil, criminal or administrative action or proceeding" (45 CFR §164.529). An examination by an expert retained after litigation has begun is cloaked by work product and does not lose that protection under HIPAA. Mental health professionals should bear in mind, however, that since most of the employment examinations occur outside litigation, work product protection would not apply.

Nevertheless, if litigation ensues, evaluees will typically obtain copies of disability and disability-related evaluations through the discovery process. When litigation is threatened or pending, it should be assumed that the author of any relevant document may be confronted with it on cross-examination. As should be standard practice, psychiatrists and psychologists should be certain that reports and disclosures adhere to professional, ethical, and legal standards.

Qualitative Standards for Employment Evaluations

Psychiatric and Psychological Evaluations Intended for Judicial Consumption

Although most evaluations are conducted outside the courts and never find their way there, some do. Some disability and disability-related evaluations conducted without any thought of judicial oversight arrive in court when the subject of the evaluation challenges a decision based on the mental health professional's opinions or report. Some examinations may be conducted explicitly to support a decision that has proceeded through administrative or company procedures and is now being challenged in a civil lawsuit.

However factually and/or technically complex the dispute the parties bring to court may be, jurors are not chosen because of their expertise or familiarity with the case. Indeed, specialized knowledge about a case acquired outside of the parties' evidentiary presentation in that case may result in juror disqualification. It follows that because of the purposeful limitations on the knowledge and skills of the jury, some minimum threshold will be necessary to prevent jurors (and judges as well) from relying upon superficially attractive but patently false claims of expertise.

Until the early twentieth century, courts relied solely on the qualifications of a proffered expert, the opportunity for cross-examination, and presentation of opposing experts to assure that jurors sensibly scrutinized claims of expertise. The D.C. Court of Appeals decision in *Frye v. United States* (1923) played a seminal role in changing exclusive reliance on qualifications for admission of expert evidence. After recognizing a distinction between the qualifications of an expert and the reliability of the science upon which the expert relies, *Frye* articulated a standard for determining the reliability of the science. According to *Frye*, courts should apply a "general acceptance" in the relevant professional communities as the standard for scientific reliability.

In using "general acceptance" as a proxy for scientific accuracy, *Frye* raised a host of new problems about who must accept, what must be accepted, as well as what constitutes general acceptance. In the midst of *Frye's* increased application and criticism, the Federal Rules of Evidence (FRE) were codified in 1975 with no references to *Frye*. It was not until 1993 that the Supreme Court resolved *Frye's* survival under the FRE in *Daubert v. Merrell Dow Pharmaceuticals, Inc.* The Court found no reference to *Frye* in the FRE and concluded that *Frye* was not intended to be the benchmark for scientific testimony under the FRE.

The Court focused on Karl Popper's work on falsifiability in science as a guide to what constitutes scientific knowledge. It articulated four factors bearing on reliability for federal trial courts to consider in the admission of scientific experts under the FRE: whether the experts' methods and procedures were testable and had been tested; whether it had been subjected to peer review and publication; if so what was the error rate and could it be controlled; and finally a rebirth of *Frye's* general acceptance test. Two subsequent decisions, *General Electric v. Joiner* (1997) and *Kumho Tire Co. v. Carmichael* (1999), clarified that these considerations applied to the admissibility of all experts. The *Daubert* analysis is at the discretion of the trial court who might apply some of these criteria but not others, or other criteria not articulated by the Court, depending on the nature of the case.

Although the vocabulary may have changed, for the most part, *Daubert* has not resulted in a sea change for most psychiatric and psychological experts. Clinical opinion testimony remains the most common psychiatric and psychological forensic contribution, as well as the most vulnerable to scientific critique (Shuman & Sales, 1998). Nevertheless, the most compelling argument for an expert to embrace *Daubert*'s preference for the use of techniques which have been validated in studies published in peer-reviewed journals is that if a laissez-fare trial court is suddenly moved to apply *Daubert* strictly, it will be too late for the unsuspecting expert to do much about it (Shuman & Sales, 2001).

Like "Pascal's Wager," designed to demonstrate why the smart money was on a belief in God, "Daubert's Wager" is intended to demonstrate why smart experts will assume that their testimony will have to meet a *Daubert* threshold (Shuman & Sales, 2001). Even though no lawsuit may be in sight when a disability or disability-related evaluation takes place, litigation is always a possibility and evaluations, which may become testimony, should therefore be conducted accordingly. Adhering to *Daubert* standards is also prudent because even if *Daubert* issues are not pursued as a matter of admissibility or legal competence, they may appear on cross-examination, where they will speak to the weight or credibility of the expert's testimony.

Psychiatric and Psychological Evaluations Intended for Administrative Consumption

Most disability and disability-related disputes decided by a third party are not heard in court but rather by administrative tribunals, such as the Equal

Employment Opportunity Commission, the SSA, and state workers' compensation boards. *Daubert*, interpreting the FRE, has no relevance for the vast majority of administrative law determinations (*Pasha v. Gonzales*, 2005). By their own terms, the FRE apply only in trials in the federal district courts (Fed. R. Evid. 1101), not in administrative hearings (*Dubose v. USDA*, 1983).

Evidentiary decision making by federal agencies is governed by 280 different regulations. Most agencies have a single evidentiary regulation applicable to all adjudications, but some distinguish among proceedings of different types or conducted under different statutes. Agency evidentiary regulations differ considerably in their precise language but they can be divided initially into two general categories. The majority, 243 of 280, makes no reference to the FRE and appear not to impose any constraints on the discretion of administrative law judges (ALJs) in regard to the admission of evidence. Often these provisions either parrot the Administrative Procedure Act (2006), which governs procedures for agency determinations, or paraphrase it. The other 37 evidentiary regulations make some reference to the FRE (Pierce, 1987).

Administrative proceedings before the SSA and Equal Employment Opportunity Commission (EEOC), for example, are heard by ALJs who are experienced attorneys and are governed by the Administrative Procedure Act. The Act provides that "any oral or documentary evidence may be received, but every agency shall as a matter of policy provide for the exclusion of irrelevant, immaterial, or unduly repetitious evidence." Whatever rules are applied under federal as well as state law, admissibility at an administrative hearing is committed to the discretion of the ALJ, which means that the judge's decision is unlikely to be reversed (*Bar-Av v. Psychology Examining Bd.*, 2007).

The threshold for admissibility in proceedings under the Administrative Procedure Act is reliability. "[B]ecause an ALJ's findings must be supported by substantial evidence, an ALJ may depend upon expert testimony only if the testimony is reliable" (*McKinnie v. Barnhart*, 2004, p. 910). Reliable expert testimony in this context is characterized by four considerations. It should:

1. rest on an adequate basis (i.e., dates and details of interviews and examinations; results of appropriate laboratory and psychological testing; school, military, and work records);
2. clearly articulate what opinion(s) or conclusion the expert draws from the raw data;
3. clearly explain how the expert reasoned from the raw data to the opinion offered, including the relevant science and its limits; and
4. fairly address these issues from the opponent's perspective (*Gilbert v. DaimlerChrysler Corp.*, 2004; Shuman, 2005).

Conclusion

Psychiatric and psychological disability and disability-related evaluations performed for the benefit of a third party may be common, but relying solely on common sense or clinical intuition to ascertain the difference in legal obligations between workplace evaluations and traditional psychiatrist/psychologist–patient relationships is not advisable. Although many of the legal obligations overlap ethical obligations, these two sets of obligations are not entirely congruent. Mental health professionals conducting disability and disability-related evaluations should be familiar with the necessary clinical skills, ethical obligations, and legal duties required to provide competent, reliable evaluations.

Chapter 3
Why We Work: Psychological Meaning and Effects

Introduction

Disability and disability-related assessments require an understanding of the relationship between the evaluee's internal world and external circumstances. The meaning of work and the psychological effects of both work and unemployment on an evaluee's mental health are major elements that influence an evaluee's internal world. The dynamic between the evaluee's internal world and external circumstances can turn upon the meaning an evaluee ascribes to work, the psychological effects of work, disability, or unemployment upon the evaluee, and/or changes in these psychologically powerful forces. The other major internal factor in the dynamic relationship individuals have with their work, mental disorders and their effect on work functioning, will be reviewed in the next chapter.

The Central Role of Work in Daily Life

Work influences people throughout their lives as few activities do. Studs Terkel recognized that work is a search "for daily meaning as well daily bread, for recognition as well as cash, for astonishment rather than torpor" (Terkel, 1972, p. xi). Social roles and social behaviors are developed and grow out of work roles and work organizations. Work is an activity central to survival, personal change, and human development. Through work, individuals are able to achieve a sense of identity, social contribution, and find meaning in their lives.

For most people, work is probably second only to love as a compelling human activity (O'Toole, 1982). No other choice people make, with the possible exception of a spouse, influences an individual's family, children, values, or status as much as a job or an occupation (Brodsky, 1987a; Chestang, 1982; Hulin, 2002; Tetrick & Quick, 2003). A major portion of peoples' waking time and energy is invested in or absorbed by their work. Thus, the psychological relationship that individuals have with their work can be as complex as any marital relationship, as beneficial as a good marriage, or as toxic as a destructive one.

Work is a principal source of identity for most adults (Brodsky, 1987a; Brown et al., 2001; Chestang, 1982; Perlman, 1982; Tausig, 1999). As individuals and as a society, we define people by their work. Questions regarding employment early in a new acquaintance are commonplace and are based on the assumption that every adult "works at" something (Perlman, 1982). The identification of an occupation provides information that we use in our initial assessment of an individual's value, status, and place in the world.

The powerful association of people's identities with their work is evident in the social historical practice of adopting occupations as last names: cooper, baker, carpenter, smith, weaver, etc. (Hulin, 2002). Work defines people even at death. Newspaper obituaries typically list deceased individuals' occupations immediately after their names. As one researcher stated, "Work is work no matter who does it or what they do. It is as important to who we are whether one is an archaeologist cataloging old garbage or a garbage collector picking up new garbage" (Hulin, 2002, p. 11).

Typically, only employment that generates income is considered legitimate "work" in our society. Individuals who feel they do not have a legitimate or socially acceptable form of employment dread the question, "What do you do?" For example, unpaid labor, such as caring for children, has traditionally not been considered "real" work. The use of the tongue-in-cheek job description "domestic engineer" rather than the term "housewife" reflects society's increasing sensitivity to the need to recognize and distinguish women (and men) who work inside the home from those who work outside the home in terms that do not devalue the unpaid work of childcare.

Similarly, people with disabilities that preclude the ability to work also dread questions regarding employment. To declare oneself as disabled is often embarrassing and considered by many to be an admission of weak moral character. Individuals attempting to return to the work force after prolonged disability struggle with how to explain "gaps" in their resumés. These individuals acutely feel the stigma associated with having a "disabled" status in a society that values productivity and paid labor.

Work and Its Effects on Mental Health

The overwhelming impact of work on an individual's mental health cannot be disputed. The definition of psychological health as the capacity to love and to work, attributed to Freud,[1] is axiomatic among mental health professionals. Nevertheless, traditional Freudian and Freudian-derived theory and practice has to a great extent neglected the psychological dimensions of work satisfaction or dissatisfaction (Axelrod, 1999; O'Brien, 1986). Thus, psychodynamically trained

---

[1] This statement was attributed to Freud by Erikson; it cannot be found in Freud's writings (Axelrod, 1999; Rudy Lamé, personal communication, 1999, Freud Archives).

mental health professionals often lack an understanding of the complicated relationships that exist between people and their work.

The meaning and psychological effects of work are complex. Many people have an ambivalent relationship with their work due to the positive and negative aspects and psychological effects associated with any work situation. As a general principle, mental health professionals agree that people derive many benefits from engaging in productive work and that unemployment negatively affects mental health. However, work can also be a source of stress, frustration, and even psychological injury and disability. Conversely, unemployment typically is detrimental to mental health, but the effects of unemployment are not necessarily uniformly negative.

The evaluation of the meaning and psychological effects of work on an individual should take into account both positive and negative effects of work. For example, a recently promoted individual is likely to experience happiness and satisfaction associated with the recognition of achievement and excitement about the opportunity to pursue new goals and challenges at work. At the same time, the individual may also experience anxiety at being faced with new responsibilities or at facing the prospect of relocation in order to obtain the promotion. An individual who has recently lost a job as a result of downsizing can be expected to feel anger and sadness due to the loss and anxiety due to the need to find a new job. Yet at the same time, the person may feel a sense of relief in leaving a stressful or unpleasant job or may experience the layoff as an opportunity to pursue a new career or to retire early (Nelson & Simmons, 2003).

The frequent blurring of boundaries between an individual's work and personal life also complicates the psychological effects and meaning of work. Very few people are able to treat work solely as an impersonal activity. People often consider relationships in the workplace as something like a second family and often behave as they might in their own family or personal relationships. In the best of circumstances, this can result in constructive and supportive social relationships. However, as in families, boundaries can become blurred or confused. When this happens, workplaces and relationships associated with them can become dysfunctional and can cause or exacerbate preexisting problems with consequences that reach beyond the workplace.

When problems in the workplace or in the individual arise, the balance between the negative and positive psychological aspects of work may shift. To understand this balance, its effects, and the ways it can change, evaluators should understand the ways in which work can be both psychologically beneficial and potentially stressful and destabilizing.

The Benefits of Work

Studies have consistently demonstrated that individuals experiencing satisfying employment demonstrate higher self-esteem, less depressive affect, and less negative mood than the dissatisfied employed and the unemployed (Boardman

Table 3.1 Potential psychological benefits of work

1. Income and sense of security
2. Source of identity
3. Source of sense of purpose in life
4. Source of self-worth and self-esteem
5. Opportunity to develop skills and creativity
6. Autonomy and independence
7. Relationships outside the family
8. Structure
9. Defines leisure time and activities

et al., 2003; Chestang, 1982; Kates et al., 1990, 2003; Perlman, 1982; Winefield et al., 1991). When beneficial, employment provides monetary recompense as well as nonfinancial benefits, all of which contribute to psychological health (see Table 3.1). Nonfinancial benefits include social identity and status, social contacts and support, a means of structuring and occupying time, activity and involvement, a sense of personal identity and achievement, and a means of gaining recognition and developing competence. For these and other reasons, as noted above, work is a significant priority for the general adult population (Corrigan et al., 2007).

1. *Income and sense of security*: Work provides the security associated with having a reliable source of income. The remuneration work provides pays for the essentials of life such as food and shelter, as well as additional "luxury" items that make life more comfortable. Income also allows participation in leisure or social activities. Frequently, work also provides longer term financial security through a pension, supplementary income after retirement, or opportunities to save money (Kates et al., 1990, 2003; Ozawa, 1982; Perlman, 1982).
2. *Source of identity*: As noted above, work is a major source of identity from which people derive a sense of recognition, belonging, and understanding (Chestang, 1982; Clemens, 2001; Furnham, 1990; Hulin, 2002; Kates et al., 2003; Ozawa, 1982; Perlman, 1982; Tausig, 1999). Work helps to form and preserve an individual's internal identity, self-worth, and sense of personal continuity, especially if the role is seen to have purpose and value. Behaviors and interactions that are part of the work role are internalized and become an integral part of a self-image. Positive work experiences, recognition by peers or superiors, and the mastering of new challenges help to enhance this self-image. Conversely, negative experiences, insufficient stimulation, or a lack of respect from peers may diminish an individual's self-esteem (Chestang, 1982; Kates et al., 1990, 2003).
3. *Sense of purpose in life*: The importance of family notwithstanding, work provides most people with a sense of purpose. The sense of social contribution growing out of the usefulness of one's products or services to others gives the sense of being purposeful and needed, both vital to a person's self-esteem (Chestang, 1982; Furnham, 1990; Hulin, 2002).

The Benefits of Work 47

4. *Source of self-worth and self-esteem*: Just as work provides a sense of purpose in life, work and all of its associated accomplishments and benefits related to this purpose are a source of feelings of self-worth and self-esteem (Chestang, 1972; Furnham, 1990; Hulin, 2002).
5. *Opportunity to develop skills and creativity*: Many of the important skills people have are either developed or honed in the performance of a succession of jobs. Work allows for the development of mastery, the exercise of control, and/or the ability to alter the environment. People acquire considerable satisfaction and confidence from the integrity and coordinating of intellectual and motor functions that lead, over time, to the development of skills (Chestang, 1982; Furnham, 1990; Hulin, 2002; Ozawa, 1982).
6. *Autonomy and independence*: Work is a source of autonomy, one of the most strongly held values in our society. Independence rests on the foundation of a job, the money it provides, and the intangible values associated with "standing on one's own feet" (Chestang, 1982; Furnham, 1990; Hulin, 2002; Ozawa, 1982).
7. *Relationships outside the family*: Opportunities to make friends and to obtain social support from coworkers and supervisors on the job can have a positive effect on well-being. The opportunity to interact with one's coworkers fills a general human need for social contact. Even when on the job companionship is maintained at a fairly superficial level, it meets in part the need to be connected with others. This connection may be expressed in sharing jokes or venting and sharing gripes, and often serves to counteract loneliness or to provide a sense of support inside the workplace in coping with workplace stresses (Kates et al., 1990, 2003; Ozawa, 1982; Perlman, 1982).

   In addition, people often develop important friendships among coworkers that are carried on after working hours and even after one or both leave the job. Through these relationships, individuals find a source of emotional outlet and support for workplace, personal, or family strain or distress, which in turn has benefits on family relationships. Work relationships may also be an escape from a dissatisfying family or personal life (Kates et al., 1990, 2003; Ozawa, 1982; Perlman, 1982; Tausig, 1999).
8. *Structure*: Work structures time into predictable, regular periods. Although generally externally imposed and often resented, considerable difficulty and hardship often ensue when work structure is lost or taken away. Individuals accustomed to going to work each day become restless, uncentered, frustrated, irritable, and often anxious if work structure is removed for an extended period of time. They find it difficult to get even small tasks accomplished and blame themselves for being lazy or lacking motivation. Even people who have no financial need to work have this response to lack of structured employment (Chestang, 1982; Kates et al., 2003; Furnham, 1990; Hulin, 2002; Perlman, 1982).
9. *Defines leisure time and activities*: Work provides a temporal framework within which other activities such as leisure gain meaning. Employed workers often feel pleasure in nonwork or "free" time. The common sentiment, "Thank

God it's Friday," only has universal meaning in our society because a standard work week ends on Friday and is followed typically by 2 days of leisure time. Individuals who do not work find themselves uneasy with the amount of time they have to find ways to fill (Chestang, 1982; Furnham, 1990; Hulin, 2002; Kates et al., 2003; Perlman, 1982).

Job Satisfaction

Positive psychological benefits derived from work are closely associated with job satisfaction. Job satisfaction is often determined by how well outcomes meet or exceed expectations. Job satisfaction is also derived from a number of related job characteristics, such as the nature of the work, pay, promotion opportunities, supervision and coworkers, working conditions, and status conferred by the work.

Individuals in a workplace with a good fit, that is, a good match between the individual's temperament and skills and the work requirements and environment, report high levels of job satisfaction (Bennett et al., 2003; Nelson & Simmons, 2003; Spielberger et al., 2003; Statt, 1994). Most individuals experience mental health benefits when work is characterized by certain features common to "good fit" jobs, including

1. challenges, but not those overly demanding in terms of time, speed, or environmental and ergonomic conditions;
2. variability, but also control;
3. role expectations which are reasonably clear and not overly conflicting;
4. supportive social relationships as well as demanding but supportive leadership; and
5. reasonable rewards and security (Greenglass, 2002; Lubit & Gordon, 2003; Perrewé & Carlson, 2002; Probst, 2002; Semmer, 2003).

The more frequently a worker achieves highly valued outcomes, the higher the level of satisfaction and the greater the psychological benefits. One meta-analysis study indicates a strong relationship between job satisfaction and employee health (Farager et al., 2005). A workplace that promotes the beneficial effects of work often exhibits high productivity, high employee satisfaction, good safety records, few disability claims and union grievances, low absenteeism, low turnover, and the absence of violence (Bennett et al., 2003; Tetrick & Quick, 2003).

Work: The Downside

Despite the advantages work can bestow, certain kinds of work or work situations can have negative psychological effects (Kates et al., 1990; Straus & Davidson, 1997). Some employment situations result in considerable stress and can cause psychological distress and even harm. The quality of the employment experience is the critical factor in determining whether or not the individual derives psychological benefits from the job (Barling & Griffiths, 2003). If the work is stifling and frustrating or if it deprives an individual of dignity, creativity, and self-esteem, the person may feel inadequate, incompetent, and a failure. In these circumstances, work can erode a sense of personal worth (Chestang, 1982) and the negative psychological consequences may outweigh the benefits of the job.

Job dissatisfaction and its respective psychological consequences, just like job satisfaction and its psychological benefits, are affected by a variety of factors (Bono & Judge, 2001; Ilies & Judge, 2003; Judge et al., 2002; Statt, 1994). Negative mental health effects, including stress-related medical and mental health problems, are closely related to job dissatisfaction. The poorer the fit between the individual and the job, the greater the likelihood that the individual will experience job stress and dissatisfaction. The less satisfied individuals are with their job and the more negative their affective reactions to workplace events are, the more psychological distress and the greater number of health conditions they will report (Brown et al., 2001; Elovainio et al., 2000; Nelson & Simmons, 2003; Probst, 2002; Spielberger et al., 2003; Statt, 1994).

Psychological stress occurs when individuals perceive that environmental demands tax or exceed their adaptive capacity (Cohen et al., 2007). People generally do not become distressed by the presence of challenge in their work but by the inability to meet the challenge (Tausig, 1999). When job demands and pressures in the work environment exceed the skills and abilities of an employee or when these demands conflict with the employee's goals and values, work overload, role ambiguity, conflicting role demands, and job dissatisfaction can result. The psychological stress and distress associated with job dissatisfaction can result in adverse behavioral consequences, such as lower productivity, absenteeism, turnover, and employee burnout, as well as physical and mental health-related problems (Nelson & Simmons, 2003; Spielberger et al., 2003; Statt, 1994).

Assessing "Goodness of Fit"

Evaluators therefore need to assess the "goodness of fit" between the individual and the job in order to assess the psychological effects of the job, a critical aspect of most disability and disability-related evaluations. A good fit between an individual and a workplace obviously depends on both the characteristics of the individual and the workplace. Each set of specific circumstances and their interactions between job and individual needs to be evaluated on a case-by-case basis.

Although the elements of what creates job satisfaction or a positive work experience are discussed above, no one set of job characteristics is either good or bad for everyone. What one individual experiences as a good work environment may not be experienced the same way by another. Moreover, even if a job seemed ideal at first, the individual or the job requirements may change over time to the point where a job that was initially a good match with an individual's temperament, personality, and skills becomes problematic or detrimental (O'Toole, 1982).

Some factors relevant to "goodness of fit" are unique to the individual. For example, aside from the effects of mental disorders (see Chapter 4), studies have consistently demonstrated a moderate relationship between an individual's propensity toward experiencing negativity and job satisfaction. Individuals who cope less well with stress often have a negative affect and tend to appraise and perceive situations more negatively. Personality factors that have been suggested and tested as determinants of health and job satisfaction include hostility and anxiety. Individuals with these traits experienced a higher number of stresses, a lowered sense of well-being, heightened physiological reactivity in stressful social situations, and less benefit from support available to them (Bono & Judge, 2001; Elovainio et al., 2000; Ilies & Judge, 2003; Judge et al., 2002).

Studies have also found correlations between job satisfaction and more specific personality traits, such as extraversion, openness to experience, agreeableness, and conscientiousness (Ilies & Judge, 2003; Rothman & Cooper, 2008). Individuals who cope better with stress tend to be individuals who display optimism, feel that they have some control over the outcomes of situations by their own actions, and display commitment and engagement in their activities. Some of the indicators of engagement in work are positive affect, being able to find meaning in work, and believing that the work demands are manageable with available resources (Lennon, 1999; Nelson & Simmons, 2003; Tausig, 1999). Factors such as social support and family interaction can also contribute to how an individual identifies meaning and satisfaction in the workplace (Brown et al., 2001).

Finally, how the individual interacts with the work environment will have an effect on "goodness of fit" and on the positive or negative psychological outcomes of a job. Some people can cope with a great deal of stress without suffering detrimental effects. Others are barely able to tolerate any stress without developing some emotional or physical problems (Hodson, 2001). Some individuals can be enthusiastically involved in and pleasurably occupied by the demands of work even when confronted with extremely demanding stressors. Others utilize stress to meet challenges, improve performance, and increase their engagement with their work (Lennon, 1999; Nelson & Simmons, 2003; Tausig, 1999).

Nevertheless, job demands and work environments can exert beneficial or detrimental effects on any individual, separate from the individual's personality and disposition and separate from the type of employment under consideration (Ilies & Judge, 2003). One model of assessing the effects of work on psychological well-being emphasizes that psychological outcomes depend on the balance between certain workplace characteristics (Warr, 1987). This model identifies nine related factors associated with any workplace (see Table 3.2).

Assessing "Goodness of Fit" 51

Table 3.2 Factors in the workplace that exert positive or negative effects

Constant effect determinants: Presence always positive, absence exerts negative effect
1. Availability of money
2. Physical security
3. Valued social position

Variables effect determinants: Can exert positive or negative effects depending on balance
4. Opportunity for control
5. Opportunity for skill use
6. Opportunity for social contact
7. Externally generated goals and structure
8. Variety
9. Environmental clarity
   a. Availability of feedback
   b. Predictability

Constant Effect Determinants

Factors whose effect on mental health is directly proportional to their presence, which results in positive effects, or their absence, which results in negative effects, may be considered "constant effect determinants" of job satisfaction or dissatisfaction (factors 1–3 in Table 3.2). These include availability of money, physical security (i.e., a safe and secure working environment), and valued social position (Hodson 2001).

Variable Effect Determinants

Variable effect determinants (factors 4–9 in Table 3.2) are variables essential for mental health, but potentially damaging if too much or too little are present. They are key elements in the dynamic relationship between internal and external factors in a work situation. When these variables are present and balanced, they promote good psychological effects. When out of balance, they can result in negative effects. These include opportunity for control, skill use, and social contact; and externally generated goals, variety, and environmental clarity (Hodson, 2001).

Problems can occur when individuals lack opportunity for control over their environment or are pressed into constant decision-making without time to consider consequences. In addition, in some positions, individuals must make decisions without being able to predict their outcomes. For example, this is an integral feature of the job of dealing with futures on the stock market or working with people with behavior difficulties. Such jobs are notorious for their detrimental effects on mental health and functional ability (Hodson, 2001).

Individuals also need to have opportunities to use and develop skills. Being able to perform a skilled job successfully can lead to high levels of personal satisfaction and high self-esteem. Individuals who work in environments where their skills are underused or undervalued frequently become demoralized. Conversely, being asked to use extremely complex skills for prolonged periods can be detrimental to mental health and can compromise functioning (Hodson, 2001).

Jobs that lack social balance can also become problematic. Social isolation can be psychologically damaging. Similarly, overcrowding can have negative psychological effects. People also require change and stimulation in their environment. However, an environment that constantly changes, particularly in ways that cannot be predicted, can be harmful to both physical and mental health (Hodson, 2001).

Individuals also require a reasonable number of externally generated goals. Work goals provide structure to the workday and, when achieved, provide opportunities for increasing feelings of self-worth and control. However, goals that are impossible to accomplish, either because they are too many or because they make unreasonable demands or adequate resources are lacking, may become damaging. Setting unrealistic targets for workers, for example, can lead to significant distress (Hodson, 2001).

Finally, environmental clarity can profoundly affect the positive or negative effects of work. Environmental clarity consists of two aspects. The first is the availability of feedback about the consequences of actions. Individuals who do not know whether their actions were acceptable or unacceptable or whether their decisions result in correct or incorrect outcomes will find the environment increasingly unpredictable and potentially stressful or even frightening. The second is predictability. People become anxious if they are uncertain of how individuals will respond to them, if they are unsure how they are to respond to other people or situations, or if they have to deal with constantly changing procedures or systems. Alternatively, a totally predictable environment where things rarely or never change can pose its own problems (Hodson, 2001).

Detrimental changes over which employees have no control can create negative effects on mental health that are often reflected in functioning (Nelson et al., 2002). Decreased job security, for example, as a result of outsourcing, downsizing, or increased reliance on technology, can result in increased anxiety and stress (Maslach & Leiter, 1997). Job elimination has been found to be related to depression and increased disability claims, with the largest increase in claims being stress related (e.g., mental or psychiatric problems, substance abuse, hypertension, and cardiovascular disease) (Tetrick & Quick, 2003). Managers who implement the layoffs and workers whose jobs survive the layoff also suffer negative mental health effects because of the effect of the layoffs on their own sense of job security as well as because of some of the other factors discussed above.

As noted, the role of organizational structure is a major factor in employee morale and productivity. Much of the positive as well as negative effects of employment are related to an organization's culture (Book, 2003). Workplace culture refers to management style and structure, values, and norms of behavior and beliefs; it also defines interactions at all levels as well as the emotional environment that will exist in the organization. Culture proscribes and prescribes certain behaviors. A strong and healthy workplace culture can help an organization guide and coordinate employees' behaviors and choices, and helps people discriminate between acceptable and unacceptable behavior.

Certain cultures are particularly toxic (Kahn, 2003; Lubit & Gordon, 2003) and can be so regardless of the psychological strengths and vulnerabilities of the individual employee. Toxic cultures are characterized by

1. lack of cooperation, when people refuse to help each other;
2. lack of support, when the human needs of individuals are ignored and people feel alienated and dehumanized;
3. intolerance, when mistakes or suggestions for alternative ways of doing things are met with derision;
4. exclusivity, when cliques replace a sense of community and newcomers are hazed; and
5. rigidity, when the boss insists on and is viewed as right even when he or she is not (Lubit & Gordon, 2003).

Toxic workplaces can be created from dysfunctional leadership or management, whose decisions, vision, and behaviors set the tone for organizational structure (Kahn & Unterberg, 2003). Such behavior can include bullying, discrimination, and unclear or poorly defined boundaries regarding appropriate and inappropriate workplace behaviors.

Occupational Stress

For many individuals, job dissatisfaction and working conditions that overwhelm the adaptive capabilities and resources of workers can result in occupational stress that can be expressed through acute psychological, behavioral, or physical reactions (Swanson, 2000). Workplace stress responses can occur as a result of any of the factors discussed above, including lack of a good fit between the job and the employee. Other circumstances that can result in significant occupational stress include job demands (work overload, lack of task control), organizational factors (poor interpersonal relations, unfair management practices, poorly defined work roles), physical conditions (noise), and financial and economic factors (Nelson & Simmons, 2003; Rothman & Cooper, 2008; Spielberger et al., 2003; Statt, 1994).

Occupational stress has become a common problem in the United States. According the National Council on Compensation Insurance, stress-related claims account for nearly one-fifth of all occupational diseases (Quillian-Wolever & Wolever, 2003). Work stress and its associated problems cost organizations an estimated $200 billion dollars or more a year, when measured in the costs of decreased productivity, absenteeism, worker conflict, higher health-care costs, and more worker's compensation claims of all kinds (Nelson & Simmons, 2003;

Quillian-Wolever & Wolever, 2003). Of the 550 million days of productivity lost yearly through sickness absence, approximately 54% are stress related in some way (Fielden & Cooper, 2002). Large-scale long-term studies have found that 60–90% of all visits to health-care providers and 60% of work absenteeism are caused by stress-related disorders. In the executive ranks alone, it is estimated that $10–$20 billion are lost annually to absenteeism, hospitalization, and early death, much of it as a result of stress.

Mental health professionals should therefore consider the role of job dissatisfaction and occupational stress in employment evaluations. Stress can be expressed as feelings of anger, anxiety, and fear, to the point where individuals find they have difficulty sleeping at night or concentrating during the day. They may become irritable because almost any request is experienced as a demand on their already strained capacities. Almost all individuals experiencing severe stress describe reduced pleasure from personal and social interactions. Some complain of fatigue or exhaustion, become depressed or anxious, or both. Physical symptoms associated with stress can include changes in blood pressure, headaches, dermatitis, and gastrointestinal symptoms such as abdominal pain and diarrhea (Brodsky, 1984).

The "goodness-of-fit" model discussed above is used to conceptualize and understand the development of occupational stress. Another model for understanding occupational stress is the demand-control model, which focuses on interactions between the objective demands of the work environment and the decision latitude of employees in meeting those demands (Lerner et al., 2004; Nelson & Simmons, 2003; Spielberger et al., 2003). The combination of high job demands with relatively little control contributes to lowered productivity and a greater risk of health-related problems. These types of jobs compounded by lack of social support from supervisors and coworkers present a high risk of negative health outcomes.

Another model, the cognitive appraisal approach, emphasizes the individual's role in classifying situations as threatening or nonthreatening (Nelson & Simmons, 2003). Any event or situation in the work environment can be a potential stressor. Whether the event leads to stress will depend on the meaning individuals attribute to it, whether of threat, harm, or challenge, and on their appraisal of effectiveness in coping with it. The more negative a person's reading of the significance of events at work, the greater the experienced stress (Brodsky, 1984). Part of the value of this model is its incorporation of the assessment of positive and negative aspects of stressors differs from individual to individual (Nelson & Simmons, 2003).

Regardless of the model used to understand occupational stress, it is clear that occupational stress can have a significant detrimental impact on individuals' workplace function and mental and physical health (Quillian-Wolever & Wolever, 2003; Semmer, 2003). The National Institute of Occupational Safety and Health identified job-related psychological disorders as among the top 10 occupational heath concerns. About a third of workers across multiple occupations experience chronic work stress. For individuals with chronic physical conditions, the additional presence of chronic work stress increased the probability of workers experiencing days in which they were unable to work. For individuals with mental illness, chronic work stress was associated with an increased probability of total and partial disability days (Dewa et al., 2007).

Although individual coping factors and social resources can modify the reaction to occupational stressors to some degree (Axelrod, 1999; Brodsky, 1984; Swanson, 2000), prolonged exposure to stressful working conditions may lead to illness or disease. Stressful life events have been linked to depressive symptoms, major depressive disorder, and cardiovascular disease. Increased stress also predicts the clinical course of major depression, including features such as longer duration, symptoms exacerbation, and relapse (Cohen et al., 2007). Chronic stress associated with the workplace has been found to be associated with hypersomnia, fatigue, and appetite gain (Keller, Neale, & Kendler, 2007). Occupational stress has been linked to hypertension, cardiovascular disease, sleep disturbances, headaches, and a variety of psychosomatic complaints (Axelrod, 1999; Cheng et al., 2000; Quillian-Wolever & Wolever, 2003; Swanson, 2000).

Adverse psychosocial work conditions and associated occupational stress are important predictors of poor functional status and decline over time, including physical functioning, social functioning, and emotional and mental health problems. These effects are independent of socioeconomic status, baseline functioning, and other variables such as age, weight, and comorbid conditions. Individuals may experience other types of acute or chronic stressors, such as financial, marital, and family conflicts, or major life events, such as family illness or death and other losses. Nevertheless, how people feel at work and about work is more strongly predicted by stressors at work than outside work (Axelrod, 1999; Cheng et al., 2000; Klitzman et al., 1990; Quillian-Wolever & Wolever, 2003; Swanson, 2000).

As discussed above, in some cases individual vulnerabilities can be as or more important than occupational stressors in the development of reactions to work stress. Personality characteristics, genetic vulnerability to illness, other life stressors, and substance abuse may be more significant than job circumstances. Stress levels are also related to multiple behaviors that affect health, including sleep, levels of exercise, and alcohol and tobacco consumption (Quillian-Wolever & Wolever, 2003).

Regardless of physical or psychological individual vulnerabilities, the great majority of the labor force would experience many types of occupational exposures as noxious, resulting in stress responses (Levi, 2003). Many tasks are intrinsically stressful but still need to be performed for the public good, for example, emergency service and public safety jobs (Levi, 2003). Certain jobs, such as emergency room physician, firefighter, airline pilot, and production manager, are well recognized to be more stressful than others (Rothman & Cooper, 2008). Jobs that score high in stress tend to be in the public sector where workloads have increased over the years, while at the same time workers feel that their professional control over their workloads has diminished. These jobs involve contact with members of the public in circumstances that may lead to confrontation, particularly if there is heightened risk of potential for violence. In addition, these jobs carry high expectations of standards of performance, but at the same time may have low public esteem (Hodson, 2001).

Shift work is also associated with significant occupational stress. Individuals who regularly work atypical hours are at greater risk for physical and psychological impairment or disease than typical day workers regardless of the type of job. This is the result of the physical and psychological stress due to schedule-related disruptions of circadian rhythms, sleep, family, and social life. Although most people seem able to cope reasonably well psychologically, particularly with a night shift, a minority of shift workers seems to have long-term problems, especially if shifts rotate frequently. The risk is further exacerbated if individuals have to work more than a standard 40 hour week (Smith et al., 2003; Statt, 1994).

Technology has introduced new areas of job stress, although it does not influence all jobs equally. Employees are constantly subjected to changes in systems involved in information and technology. Skills essential to a job one day may be obsolete the next, and require individuals to start back at zero on a learning curve while still being held responsible for work product (Rothman & Cooper, 2008). Modern-day office technology failures are often a source of stress and frustration for human operators who are unable to control technological breakdowns, malfunctions, and deficiencies. A worker's lack of control is a key component in the stress and anxiety produced by technological issues. In fact, for the first few years following the introduction of new technology, the main predictor of job dissatisfaction and stress is lack of control (Coovert & Thompson, 2003).

Although both the perceived severity and frequency of a particular stressor influence the amount of strain experienced by a worker, frequency of occurrence seems to have more adverse behavioral and health-related consequences (Spielberger et al., 2003). Measures of occupational stress have been designed, which provide information about these and a number of other factors that influence stress in the workplace (Brodsky, 1984; Coovert & Thompson, 2003; Elovainio et al., 2000; Lehman & Bennett, 2002; Maslach & Leiter, 1997; Ozawa, 1982; Probst, 2002; Rothman & Cooper, 2008; Semmer, 2003; Spielberger et al., 2003; Statt, 1994). Identified categories of occupational stress not surprisingly overlap many of the factors identified in job satisfaction and "goodness-of-fit" assessments, and include

1. pressures intrinsic to the job itself, such as time pressures and work overload;
2. organizational structure, degree of intraorganization stability, and job stability;
3. role requirements and clarity, that is, role ambiguity or confusion;
4. social conditions, such as conflicts, social support, appreciation, and perceptions of fairness, as evidenced by evaluation, promotion, distribution of workload or pay, and procedures for conflict, dispute, or grievance resolution;

5. limitations in career development, resulting in concerns about job security and opportunity for advancement;
6. degree of control over job circumstances, such as participation in decision-making;
7. predictability and frequency of changes in requirements, roles, or rewards;
8. features of tasks, such as complexity, variety, and level of stimulation involved;
9. the conditions under which tasks have to be performed, such as working time, ergonomic conditions, and speed; and
10. fear of physical harm (particularly in public safety occupations, such as police officers or firefighters, but also in anyone who works in less obviously vulnerable occupations, such as bus drivers, service station attendants, and cashiers in convenience stores).

Certain circumstances in the workplace are particularly stressful and detrimental to mental health. For example, one of the most stressful of work circumstances is the presence of chronic and unresolved interpersonal workplace conflict (Rothman & Cooper, 2008). Conflict infuses the workplace with frustration, anger, fear, anxiety, disrespect, and suspicion. Perceived or actual unfairness or favoritism is a source of severe occupational stress that can erode self-respect and self-esteem and can result in a variety of stress-related psychological and physical symptoms (Maslach & Leiter, 1997).

Certain populations of workers experience additional issues and problems that can create or exacerbate occupational stress. Society's model of an ideal worker is based on the white, male, middle-class experience of work. This model, although subject to a great deal of variation in experience, is still the social norm against which both employers and employees measure workplace behavior and performance. The experiences and circumstances of women, the poor, minorities, or those with disabilities often differ significantly from that of the "ideal" worker. Nevertheless, over the past few decades, the workforce has become increasingly diverse with respect to the age of workers, the continued entry of women into the workforce, the composition of the workface by race and ethnicity, and the increased participation of individuals with disabilities. The fact that these individuals do not easily fit into the stereotypes and patterns of the ideal worker creates unique sources of occupational stress (Crawford & Unger, 2004; Statt, 1994).

Perceived and actual prejudice and discrimination are a source of stress for minority workers, above and beyond normal sources of work stress (Fielden & Cooper, 2002; Rothman & Cooper, 2008). Similarly, membership in non-mainstream racial, religious, and ethnic categories has substantial effects on the likelihood that an individual will be employed in a job with stressful characteristics. African-Americans earn less than whites on average and within identical occupations (United States Bureau of Labor Statistics, 2008). The racial differences observed are mostly attributable to discrimination and occupational segregation (Tausig, 1999; United States Bureau of Labor Statistics, 2008).

Disabled workers may also experience unique workplace stressors. Since the implementation of the Americans with Disabilities Act, there has been a significant increase in the number of individuals with disabilities in the workforce (Tetrick & Quick, 2003). This population may experience problems such as physical access to the workplace and social stigma as profound sources of stress.

Occupational stress may be a particular problem for women (Frone, 2003; Spielberger et al., 2003; Swanson, 2000). Gender has been identified as one of the most important variables in the experience of occupational stress. Between 1970 and 2004, women increased their labor force participation rate from 43 to 59%. Women held half of all management, professional, and related occupations in 2004 (United States Department of Labor, 2007). Overall, employment has many benefits for women, including improved social networks, financial independence, and greater self-esteem (Barnett et al., 1992; Barnett & Shen, 1997; Gilbert & Rader, 2001; Swanson, 2000).

However, compared to men, the employment held by women (and minority groups) is typified by job characteristics that have been found to be stressful. Women's work is concentrated in low-paying occupations and peripheral, nonunionized industries. Women tend to predominate in occupations permitting less autonomy than those occupied by men. Even when men work in the same occupations, women tend to earn less than men and occupy jobs with less power than men; in 2007, women who were full-time wage and salary workers had median weekly earnings that were 80% of their male counterparts (United States Bureau of Labor Statistics, 2008). These are all characteristics associated with higher levels of occupational stress and job dissatisfaction (Tausig, 1999).

Occupational stressors for women, particularly women managers, include many of the same problems as those associated with belonging to a minority group, such as discrimination and prejudice. This can include experiences such as career blocks ("glass ceilings"), sexual harassment, isolation due to tokenism, stereotyping, social exclusion from male-dominated professional and work-related social groups, and a lack of role models. Women from minority ethnic backgrounds are doubly disadvantaged: the stressors associated with belonging to a minority group, when combined with the effects of sexism and racism, result in higher levels of stress reported by black female managers (Fielden & Cooper, 2002; United States Department of Labor, 2008).

Men may be psychologically vulnerable to certain gender-specific stressors related to this shift in gender distribution in the workforce (Axelrod, 1999). However, well-documented stressors that appear more specific to women, such as conflict between work and family roles, gender discrimination, and sexual harassment, pose additional risks to their health and well-being (Axelrod, 1999; Fitzgerald et al., 1997; Swanson, 2000). Despite their roles in the work force, women are still expected to take primary caretaking roles in family life. Although both men and women experience work–family conflict, women report more conflict than men do (Noor, 2002).

Conflicts between women's work and family responsibilities may exacerbate occupational stress (Rosenstock & Lee, 2000; Stellman, 2000). In 2004, of the 59% of women in the labor force, 60% were married, 71% had children under 18 years, 62% had children under 6 years, and 57% had children under 3 years (United States Department of Labor, 2007). Both men and women are measured against the ideal worker norm, that is, the (white, male) employee who works full time and even overtime and does not take time off for childbearing or child rearing. Caregiving responsibilities often directly conflict with the model and expectations of the ideal employee, resulting in conflict between the demands of work and family (Gilbert & Rader, 2001; Williams, 1999).

Studies focused on job satisfaction and job fit have demonstrated that multiple roles can be health enhancing when there is a good fit between work and job and all the roles are desired and voluntary. Some research has indicated that women who occupy multiple roles of mother, worker, and spouse experience better mental and physical health than those who occupy few roles (Barnett et al., 1992; Barnett & Shen, 1997; Gilbert & Rader, 2001; Swanson, 2000). However, if there is a poor fit, or roles are unwanted, women often experience negative effects (Stellman, 2000). In one large-scale survey, 60% of women respondents reported that job stress was their number one problem (Swanson, 2000).

The ability to successfully juggle various roles has its limits. Employed married women, for example, consistently report higher levels of distress than employed married men (Barnett & Shen, 1997). When women lack sufficient childcare and household help from spouses and work in psychologically demanding jobs, their health and well-being may suffer. It may even suffer when women work in rewarding jobs if their overall work–family workload is high (Barnett & Shen, 1997; Murray et al., 2003; Swanson, 2000). The decision to pursue work outside the home itself can be a source of chronic stress due to the perception or reality of sacrifice, feelings of guilt, and psychological conflict (Axelrod, 1999; Stellman, 2000; Williams, 2000). The guilt felt by some parents, especially mothers, for working rather than tending to children, "is enormous" (Axelrod, 1999, p. 131).

Traditional gender roles and adverse psychosocial working conditions often cause stress reactions in women in an interactive and cumulative manner (Fielden & Cooper, 2002; Krantz & Ostergren, 2001; Tausig, 1999; Tetrick & Quick, 2003). These conflicts have been found to be positively related to clinically significant mood, anxiety, and substance abuse disorders (Frone, 2003). In one study, a greater amount of domestic responsibility and job strain was independently associated with a high level of common stress symptoms in vocationally active women between the ages of 40 and 50. These women were also found to be at greater risk for symptoms of chronic pain, anxiety, nervousness, and sleeping disorders (Krantz & Ostergren, 2001). Other negative health outcomes associated with work–family conflict include job and life dissatisfaction, decreased family and occupational well-being, and increased psychological distress, self-reported poor physical health, and heavy alcohol use (Frone, 2003; Noor, 2002).

Outcomes of Occupational Stress: Job Burnout and Withdrawal

Individuals choose a variety of options for managing occupational stress, some of which result in positive change and a decrease in stress. Often those who remain at their positions resolve their conflicts through taking constructive action. They may engage in negotiation or inform superiors of the problems, resulting in improvement in the circumstances creating stress. Although changes in assignments, new managers, moves to other buildings, and resignations of peers or subordinates can be causes of stress, they may also relieve stress (Brodsky, 1984).

Some individuals take more dramatic steps to change their work or life circumstances, such as leaving their jobs or adopting a less stressful lifestyle. People often feel relief when they make the decision to leave a highly stressful job. They may be willing to permanently give up working in the stressful environment, or another similar environment, and in the process renounce the status or high pay associated with their former jobs. Some make major life changes, such as moving to less expensive communities to reduce living costs and stresses of daily living or pursuing alternate careers (Brodsky, 1984).

Frequently, however, people are reluctant to change jobs, even when experiencing severe occupational stress. It takes a good deal of self-confidence for most people to change jobs, particularly in people who have reached middle age (O'Toole, 1982). Most people are afraid to leave the security of a job, especially if they have held the job for a long time. For these individuals, work becomes an obligation rather than a resource. They choose to remain on the job because they need the money or are not prepared to search for new employment, to be unemployed, or to be categorized as disabled. Because they find the job stressful and at the same time believe that they cannot leave, they feel trapped or "locked in." This in itself becomes a source of distress and conflict (Brodsky, 1984) and may result in job burnout.

Job Burnout

Burnout is the ultimate negative consequence of a job with a poor fit, of job dissatisfaction, or of prolonged occupational stress and can lead to work withdrawal, claims of disability, or emotional harm. Prolonged strain or emotional exhaustion occurs when individuals feel they no longer have sufficient emotional resources to handle the stressors confronting them. The chronic exposure stresses leading to burnout include qualitative and quantitative overload, role conflict and ambiguity, and lack of social support (Shirom, 2003), as well as any of the other factors discussed above in relation to occupational stress.

Job burnout is a pathological affective reaction in which emotional depletion and maladaptive detachment develop in response to prolonged occupational stress. The affective state of burnout is likely to exist when individuals perceive or experience a continuous net loss of physical, emotional, or cognitive energy or resources over a period of time at work as a result of repeated and chronic stress. Burnout is distinct from depression and has been shown to be more job-related and situation-specific compared to other sources of emotional distress, such as depression (Shirom, 2003). An individual with burnout is less likely to show the global symptoms of depression. Rather, their symptoms tend to be focused on the workplace.

Burnout has three related dimensions that can coexist in different degrees:

1. emotional exhaustion, in which overwhelming work demands deplete the individual's energy resources;
2. depersonalization and cynicism, in which the individual detaches from the job; and
3. feelings of inefficacy, in which the individual perceives a lack of personal effectiveness, competency, and achievement (Maslach, 1982; Maslach & Leiter, 1997; Shirom, 2003; Thomas, 2004).

Although all three components of burnout are potentially important, emotional exhaustion characterized by physical and psychological depletion is the key dimension (Wright & Cropanzano, 1998).

In early stages of burnout, individuals may experience high anxiety as they attempt to directly and actively cope with work-related stresses. When and if these coping behaviors prove ineffective, individuals feel increasingly frustrated and helpless. They may stop attempting to actively address the problems, become emotionally detached, and engage in defensive behaviors that can lead to depressive symptoms. In advanced stages of burnout, symptoms similar to those of depression may become predominant, although as noted, distinct differences from depression have been observed. Other manifestations of advanced burnout include frustration, anger, psychological withdrawal, increasing cynicism, and dehumanizing customers or clients. Burnout may also exacerbate problematic personality traits (Maslach & Leiter, 1997; Shirom, 2003; Wright & Cropanzano, 1998).

Ultimately, burnout can result in increased job turnover, absenteeism, lower organizational commitment, lower performance and reduced personal accomplishment, and reduced levels of motivation to perform (Maslach & Leiter, 1997; Shirom, 2003; Wright & Cropanzano, 1998). Burnout has also been associated with a variety of somatic problems such as headaches, gastrointestinal illness, high blood pressure, muscle tension, chronic fatigue, and insomnia (Shirom, 2003; Wright & Cropanzano, 1998). To cope with stress, some people increase use of alcohol and drugs. If individuals bring burnout home, exhaustion and negative feelings begin to affect relationships with family and friends. Eventually some people reach the point where they feel they can no longer expose themselves to the occupational stress or tolerate burnout and withdraw from the workplace (Maslach & Leiter, 1997; Wright & Cropanzano, 1998).

Mental health professionals should be sensitive to the signs of job burnout when conducting disability and disability-related evaluations. It is not uncommon for individuals who withdraw from the workplace due to burnout to claim work-related disability or injury. Individuals genuinely may not be able to distinguish between burnout and depression or anxiety, and may believe that they are disabled by these psychiatric disorders. In addition, individuals who feel they can no longer tolerate the stress of the workplace or who feel they have been unfairly treated often feel, rightly or wrongly, they are owed compensation or medical leave by their employer, the same way spouses may rightly or wrongly feel they are owed alimony for their sacrifices and participation in a relationship that has ended badly.

Regardless of the circumstances and the validity of the claim, individuals who withdraw from the workplace claiming disability rarely find this an ideal solution to their workplace conflicts. Aside from the stigma and discomfort associated with adopting a disabled status, individuals who withdraw from the workplace and pursue compensation often experience guilt, anger, helplessness, and depression (see Chapter 5). These states may continue for years, as the individuals continue to dwell on the events that forced them to stop working and are subject to the stress of bureaucratic administrative procedures or litigation (Brodsky, 1984).

The Effects of Job Loss and Unemployment

Mental health professionals conducting disability and disability-related evaluations also often have to separate the effects of unemployment, particularly long-term unemployment, from mental disability or primary emotional injury due to work-related events. Job loss has consistently been found to be associated with negative psychological effects and increased symptoms of mental disorder. These negative effects and symptom exacerbations can be easily mistaken for symptoms ascribed to the precipitating disability. Nevertheless, in some disability and disability-related evaluations, separating the underlying disorders from the effects of unemployment may be a critical part of the assessment.

Unemployment can be a predisposing, precipitating, or perpetuating factor in the onset of mental and physical health problems. Preexisting deficits, whether physical, psychological, or interpersonal, can be exposed or uncovered by the loss of a job. The increased stress and losses may be sufficient to precipitate a further episode of a preexisting psychiatric disorder. The challenges of adjusting to job loss may also expose interpersonal weaknesses and exaggerate maladaptive personality traits.

The effects of losing a job can touch every aspect of a person's life (Kates et al., 1990). Empirical tests of the link between unemployment and mental health have linked job loss to higher rates of depression and anxiety, more physical illness, increased levels of somatic complaints, higher mental hospitalization rates, alcohol abuse, suicide rates, and violence (Dooley, 2003; Kessler et al., 1987; Murray et al., 2003; Price et al., 2002). Other common mental health issues related to job loss and unemployment include loss of self-confidence, isolation, and strain on the family (Dew et al., 1992; Murray et al., 2003; Pernice, 1997).

Research has consistently demonstrated that unemployed people report diminished levels of psychological well-being in comparison to their employed counterparts (Price et al., 2002). For example, individuals with depression who work and who do not work differ significantly in measurable ways. Working depressed persons were significantly more likely to perceive themselves as healthier, reported fewer attributable health conditions, and were less impaired by social, cognitive, and physical limitations. The perceived ability to work and self-reported disability were also significantly different between depressed persons who worked and those who did not (Elinson et al., 2004).

Anger, anxiety, sadness, and fear are normal reactions that accompany job loss, even in the absence of a diagnosable mental disorder. However, among the adverse outcomes associated with job loss and unemployment, depression emerges as a prominent mental health outcome. In addition to elevated symptoms of depression, the increased likelihood of major depressive episodes has been demonstrated for the unemployed in large-scale psychiatric epidemiological studies. Financial strain, as well as the loss of related benefits such as insurance, is the critical mediator in the relationship between unemployment, depression, and other adverse psychological and physical effects (Comino et al., 2003; Dew et al., 1992; Dooley, 2003; Kates et al., 1990, 2003; Kessler et al., 1987; Lennon, 1999; Murphy & Athanasou, 1999; Murray et al., 2003; Panzarella, 1991; Pernice, 1997; Statt, 1994; Talmage & Melhorn, 2005b).

Unemployment is, in itself, a risk factor for poor health (Talmage & Melhorn, 2005b). Unemployment has a strong positive association with many adverse physical health outcomes, including increased overall mortality and mortality from cardiovascular disease (Kates et al., 2003; Kessler et al., 1987; Talmage & Melhorn, 2005b). Stress-related psychosomatic problems found in those who are unemployed include headaches, stomach ulcers, and dermatitis, as well as more severe conditions such as heart disease and strokes and exacerbations of previously stable conditions (Statt, 1994; Kates et al., 2003). Depression-induced changes tend to be responsible for symptoms of poor health and impaired psychosocial functioning. Physical problems may deteriorate and make it harder for individuals to return to work (Price et al., 2002). Depression and anxiety may lead to increased focus on somatic symptoms as a reason for decreased functioning and inability to seek reemployment.

Decreased self-esteem is also a consistent and central finding. However resilient or self-assured an individual may be, losing a job or remaining unemployed can seriously undermine self-esteem. Loss of career identity is a narcissistic injury, especially when it occurs in an atmosphere of failure or perceived incompetence. The greater the individual's investment in the job, the greater the effects of the losses associated with unemployment. For those whose jobs define their identity, the loss of the job may lead to crisis of identity and changes in self-image (Kates et al., 2003). Narcissistic injuries and the consequent collapse of self-esteem can play a major role in precipitating emotional injury (Clemens, 2001).

Individuals who lose their jobs also often blame themselves for the loss, even when they had no control over the events that transpired. An individual's perception of events, even if inaccurate, may be just as distressing as the actual impact of job loss. Self-recrimination, self-blame, and guilt about essentially uncontrollable events and perceived loss of control promote further personal devaluation (Kates et al., 1990, 2003).

Feelings of humiliation and embarrassment associated with job loss and unemployment are also common. Individuals may avoid social contact because of misperceptions of the attitudes of friends or former colleagues or because of a sense of shame or embarrassment at being unemployed (Kates et al., 1990). Individuals may wish to avoid questions they find embarrassing or painful, sometimes to the point where they hide job loss from family and friends by getting up every day and pretending to go to work. These individuals become extremely isolated since, rather than utilizing support systems, they hide the job loss from those who might offer support.

Job loss in the context of burnout, conflict, adverse circumstances such as being fired, or as a consequence of retaliation for complaints of unfair or inappropriate treatment or behavior worsens the negative effects of job loss. In these circumstances, individuals experience more pronounced feelings of sadness, anger, and guilt. Forced or voluntary job withdrawal can be very painful if it means walking away from a career that was a source of pride, prestige, and personal identity. Complicating negative circumstances can lead to a sense of isolation and alienation and eventually to a state of helplessness and despair (Kates et al., 1990, 2003; Maslach & Leiter, 1997).

Other losses associated with job loss and unemployment have varying degrees of negative effects on individuals. The loss of a job may eliminate the social contacts, friendships, psychological support, and daily structure that had been available within and through the workplace. Opportunities for gaining recognition and developing competence through work are also lost (Kates et al., 1990, 2003; Statt, 1994).

The challenges of adjusting to job loss can aggravate preexisting marital and family problems. Negative effects on the family may also result from changes in the behavior of the unemployed individual. Someone who is depressed may be more short-tempered or may withdraw from other family members. Anxiety or stress may lead to reduced interest or involvement in family activities. Deteriorating family relationships and support can reinforce a sense of failure and diminished sense of self-worth (Clemens, 2001).

Job loss may also trigger a cascade of secondary stressors and changes in coping resources with their own significant impacts on mental health and functioning, further straining relationships with and eroding support for the unemployed individual (Kates et al., 1990, 2003). For example, the loss of an income may lead to secondary losses that affect the family if, for example, social or leisure activities have to be curtailed or possessions sold (Kates et al., 1990,

2003; Statt, 1994). As might be expected, the more basic deprivations have more substantial impacts on mental health, such as inadequate resources to meet essential needs such as food, shelter, and heat, as opposed to loss of less essential material resources (Dooley, 2003; Price et al., 2002).

Individuals with a preexisting vulnerability, such as a prior history of depression, anxiety, or other psychiatric disorders, difficulties in dealing with stress and change, problems in interpersonal relationships, or difficulties adjusting to previous job loss, are at increased risk of developing more severe emotional reactions to job loss. Concurrent personal stress can dramatically exaggerate the effects of job loss. In addition, risk for more severe responses to job loss is increased in individuals who are socially isolated, have limited coping skills, family dysfunction, physical health problems, or an excessive investment in the job or other risk factors that suggest they may have trouble coping with additional or unexpected change (Kates et al., 2003).

Workers with certain disadvantages or combinations of disadvantages are also at higher risk of developing emotional problems when they become unemployed. Older workers, for example, have a harder time finding new employment. Job loss may therefore mean the end of their working life, particularly if they opt for retirement. Lower levels of education, which frequently reflect other related impediments to reemployment such as lower socioeconomic class, poverty, or limited work skills, increase the difficulty in finding work after a job is lost. Individuals who are physically or emotionally disabled face additional hardships in entering or reentering the work force. Workers who had adapted to disabilities may again be reminded of their impairments when looking for a new position. Impairments may also restrict the kinds of work that can be considered (Kates et al., 1990, 2003).

One of the most immediate pressures individuals feel after becoming unemployed is the need to find a new job. Most unemployed individuals, despite the pain involved, adjust to or accept the job loss, make the changes necessary to adapt to an unemployed status, and ultimately find new work. However, each of the steps involved in finding work, that is, searching out work opportunities, applying for jobs, interviewing and reinterviewing, can be stressful (Kates et al., 1990, 2003). The pressure and stress may increase as time passes, personal hardships increase, and the need to find work becomes more desperate. Unfortunately, an increase in depression can have a direct effect on the likelihood of regaining employment, suggesting that while job loss and financial strain may influence depression, depression in turn may reduce access to opportunities to reduce financial strain through reemployment (Price et al., 2002).

Continuing joblessness can also erode self-confidence and create practical difficulties that can be overwhelming and reduce optimism for future change for the better. Many unemployed people develop negative work attitudes and little commitment to employment over time (Kokko & Pulkinnen, 1998; Pernice, 1997). The level of psychological distress is especially high among the long-term unemployed. These individuals can reach an emotional state where they become resigned to their position and adopt a view that they will never work again, resulting in apathy, withdrawal, and depression (Hodson, 2001; Kates et al., 1990, 2003; Kokko & Pulkinnen, 1998).

In addition, the longer individuals are out of work, the more "deconditioned" to work they become. Individuals who work develop and rely on habits, routines, and structure to maintain their productivity. Examples of these are getting up at the same time every day, setting and meeting routine daily goals, and following imposed time schedules to meet deadlines. As time passes, unemployed individuals lose the habits, routines, and structure that support productivity. Many people experience this deconditioning on a smaller scale after time off work for an extended illness or vacation. If unemployed individuals are successful in obtaining a new job, reconditioning to the habits of work poses an additional challenge, particularly if an individual has a psychiatric disorder such as anxiety or depression.

Fortunately, most individuals demonstrate a significant decrease in levels of distress following reemployment (Comino et al., 2003; Kates et al., 1990; Kessler et al., 1987; Lennon, 1999; Murphy & Athanasou, 1999; Statt, 1994; Talmage & Melhorn, 2005b). However, there is likely to be considerable variability in the extent to which reemployment can reverse the damaging psychological and physical effects of unemployment. In one study, many respondents succeeded in obtaining new jobs only by settling for lower salaries and worse job conditions. Underemployment or downscaling of job rewards may also have health implications (Kessler et al., 1987; Tausig, 1999).

Mental health evaluators should expect that nearly everyone who loses a job will experience at least some of the negative effects of job loss and unemployment. Nevertheless, despite the well-documented adverse psychological effects of unemployment, evaluators should bear in mind that the experience of job loss and unemployment is unique to each individual (Kates et al., 2003) and is not necessarily uniformly negative. This is not to suggest that becoming unemployed will necessarily confer positive benefits. However, the removal of profound workplace stress can reduce the psychological stress specifically associated with those adverse circumstances.

For example, as jobs increasingly take on undesirable qualities or characteristics, the negative effects of stressful or dissatisfying employment may be resolved by leaving adverse employment circumstances (Dooley & Catalano, 2003). In one study, a sizable percentage of male workers who had illnesses that were aggravated by their working conditions reported a perception of improved health after becoming unemployed (Hodson, 2001). Individuals suffering harassment or discrimination may accrue more negative effects than benefits from their employment. In these cases, losing a job may result in decreased immediate and short-term stress, particularly if other factors that minimize the effects of unemployment are present.

Individuals also often experience a sense of relief when withdrawal from the workforce resolves the stress associated with conflict between work and family obligations. One study found a significant increase in mental and physical problems among the unemployed. However, these researchers also found that single mothers of young children or women married to men who were the chief breadwinners in the families, a substantial subgroup of respondents, had been unemployed for a considerable period of time yet appeared to experience no adverse health effects (Kessler et al., 1987).

Mental health professionals should also consider whether individuals have access to or have been able to draw upon a variety of resources that can mitigate the negative effects of job loss and unemployment. Evaluators should assess the individual's personal deficits or preexisting problems that may have contributed to either job loss or the outcome of job loss. Problems or deficits that might hinder progress include limited coping skills, limited work skills, physical health problems, and more severe psychiatric problems (Kates et al., 1990). Access to financial resources is one of the most significant mitigating influences. Individuals who are not financially overwhelmed are better able to overcome the loss of the job and move on. In addition, they tend feel better about themselves and to suffer less emotional injury (Kates et al., 1990, 2003; Murray et al., 2003; Pernice, 1997; Statt, 1994).

For some individuals, the effects of job loss will be minimal if they possess marketable skills, live in areas where work opportunities are plentiful, are able to find work relatively quickly with little disruption to their lives, or have planned to withdraw from the workforce, for example, as in retirement. For others, the job loss provides an opportunity to pursue desired alternate career plans. Factors such as locus of control, family and social support, and positive coping skills and work attitudes also moderate the effects of unemployment (Kates et al., 1990, 2003; Murray et al., 2003; Pernice, 1997; Statt, 1994).

Evaluators should therefore not make assumptions regarding the effects of job loss. Although as discussed, the preponderance of effects of job loss is negative, some situations may result in positive changes or, at the least, the removal of some sources of acute stress due to conflicting responsibilities or noxious work environments. Evaluators assessing the effects of unemployment should consider the following:

1. What did the job mean to the individual?
2. How long did the individual work there?
3. Was the job important or useful in meeting personal or career goals?
4. Did the job further or hinder relationships?
5. What was the individual's overall level of job satisfaction?

Evaluators also need to understand how the job was lost. As noted, emotional responses to job loss differ significantly depending on the circumstances surrounding the loss. Being laid off, fired, or forced to leave due to adverse circumstances is a much different emotional and psychological experience than choosing to leave a job or starting a planned retirement (Kates et al., 1990).

Conclusion

Mental health professionals should have an understanding of the positive and negative psychological effects of employment and unemployment in order to provide disability and disability-related evaluations. At times, claims of injury or disability are strongly influenced by both the positive and negative influences of work. Even the most rewarding and satisfying job has associated stress. Stressors at work take the form of role demands, interpersonal demands, physical demands, workplace policies, and job conditions. Many of these will elicit a degree of both positive and negative responses. The balance between the positive and negative psychological factors dictates the overall psychological effect, including the effects of unemployment. When that balance changes, a net psychological gain may become a net psychological loss.

The psychological effects and meaning of employment and job loss are a major part of the internal factors in the dynamic of the relationship individuals have with their work. As noted, people bring their physical and mental health problems, the other major internal factor in the dynamic, with them to the workplace. The effect of psychiatric disorders on functional impairment will be examined in the next chapter.

Chapter 4
Psychiatric Disorders, Functional Impairment, and the Workplace

Introduction

When psychiatric disorders occur, they can impair the ability to perform job-related tasks. Some individuals may become completely precluded from competitive employment because of mental illness; some, however, are able to work despite severe illness and, at times, episodes of severe impairment. Well-known examples of individuals with severe psychiatric illnesses who have continued to work include John Nash, who suffers from schizophrenia (Nasar, 1998), William Styron, who wrote movingly of his own battles with depression (Styron, 1990), and Kay Redfield Jamison, a preeminent researcher in her own illness, bipolar disorder (Jamison, 1995). Nevertheless, despite such inspiring examples, the effects of many mental conditions are as severe in terms of disability as those of many chronic physical conditions (Merikangas et al., 2007a).

A dynamic relationship exists between an evaluee's internal world and external environment and circumstances. The understanding of this relationship is central in disability and disability-related evaluations. The last chapter discussed the meaning and role of work, one of the significant factors in the individual's internal state. The second major component of the internal state that affects the dynamic balance between internal state and external work circumstances is the individual's mental status. What symptoms is the individual experiencing? Are these symptoms creating impairments that are resulting in functional disability?

Mental health professionals providing disability and disability-related evaluations therefore need to be familiar with the evidence-based relationships between psychiatric disorders, symptoms, and potential work-related impairments. A discussion of every potential impairment associated with every psychiatric disorder is beyond the scope of this review. However, mental health professionals should be familiar with the evidence associating the most common diagnoses found in the workplace, their symptoms, and their associated work impairments encountered in disability and disability-related evaluations.

Psychiatric Disorders, Impairment, and Disability

Over the past two decades, psychiatric epidemiology studies have established that psychiatric disorders are highly prevalent in the general population. About half of all Americans will meet the criteria for a Diagnostic and Statistical Manual of Mental Disorders 4th edition (DSM-IV) disorder sometime during their lives, 27.7% will meet criteria for two or more lifetime disorders, and 17.3% for three or more (Kessler et al., 2005). Most follow a protracted or chronic course. Depending on severity and context, a mental impairment may qualify an individual for disability benefits, accommodations, or result in removal from the workplace and job loss.

Research demonstrates that psychiatric symptoms, even at a mild or moderate level, can create impairment and, at times, disability. Not every psychiatric symptom will cause a work-related impairment in every individual, and not every individual who has a psychiatric symptom, or even a psychiatric disorder, will necessarily experience work impairment or disability. Someone suffering from insomnia may have impaired judgment. If his or her job involves flying planes or carrying a weapon, he or she may be functionally disabled, even if other prominent symptoms of depression are not present. Conversely, a sales representative or administrative assistant experiencing insomnia may be able to function, even if not at the highest level of productivity, without creating undue risk to himself or herself or to the public.

Studies exploring the association between psychiatric disorders, symptoms, and impairments provide the bases for reasoned mental health opinions regarding employment-related work issues such as disability, causation, fitness for duty, or need for accommodations. Opinions based solely on an evaluee's reports or on the evaluator's personal experience are not an adequate basis for conclusions. Familiarity with research literature helps evaluators avoid relying only on evaluee's reports, stereotypic beliefs, or their own limited clinical experience. However, evaluators should bear in mind that such data are only one source of information upon which they should rely in any evaluation. Although research points out commonalities among large groups, it cannot provide a description of the evaluee in any individual case.

As a starting point, mental health evaluators should understand that the terms impairment and disability, although often used interchangeably, describe two different concepts. Psychiatric symptoms may cause mental impairment and mental impairment may reduce work functioning. Impairment is "a significant deviation, loss, or loss of use of any body structure or body function in an individual with a health condition, disorder or disease" (American Medical Association, 2008, p. 5). Disability is "activity limitations and/or participation restrictions in an individual with a health condition, disorder or disease" (American Medical Association, 2008, p. 5). Impairments may or may not result in a disability. The assessment of impairment due to illness is a medical assessment; the determination of the presence of work-related disability is a more complex matter that relies on nonmedical factors.

"Disability" is a legal term of art defined differently in different legal or administrative contexts. The definition of disability in a private disability insurance policy is defined by the insurer and presented on a take it or leave it basis. In contrast, Congress has statutorily defined disability for purposes of determining eligibility both for Social Security disability benefits and for protection under the Americans with Disabilities Act (ADA). Yet the definition of disability for purposes of the Social Security Act and the ADA is different and, of course, both differ from the definitions of any private insurance policy. An individual with a diagnosis of depression or attention deficit hyperactivity disorder (ADHD) may be eligible for accommodations under the definition of disability in the ADA, but may not qualify as disabled according to the definition applied by the Social Security Administration or by a private insurer.

Nevertheless, the synonymous use of the terms impairment and disability is so common in research and clinical practice, including many of the studies reviewed here, that it is inevitable that the terms will be used interchangeably in a discussion of research studies. Where possible, clarification of which concept is under consideration will be noted.

Psychiatric Diagnoses and Disability: Caveat Emptor

Diagnostic categories, based on the DSM-IV TR (American Psychiatric Association, 2000), are the organizing principles upon which research on impairments and functional disability associated with psychiatric disorders is conducted. However, as in clinical evaluation for treatment purposes, providing a diagnosis is not the only relevant opinion in a disability and disability-related evaluation. Mental health professionals and retaining third parties should bear in mind that a diagnosis does not provide specific information about a given individual's symptoms, impairments, history, prognosis, or functional status.

The relevance and importance of the use of diagnoses depend on the type of evaluation and what information is requested. Examiners should not assume the presence or absence of work-related dysfunction on the basis of psychological symptoms or a psychiatric diagnosis. Functional impairment and disability are not an inevitable part of the clinical presentation of any disorder (Sanderson & Andrews, 2002). In addition, a psychiatric diagnosis will not explain the specific effect on work functioning (Axelrod, 1999). Diagnosis is only one factor, and often not the most significant factor, in assessing the severity and possible duration of impairment associated with psychological symptoms (American Medical Association, 2008; Simon, 2002).

Diagnostic categories are crucial tools in clinical practice and research because they allow comparison of large numbers of cases and access to standardized and scientifically gathered information. In contrast, most disability and legal structures are not organized around diagnoses but rather around functional impairment. The imperfect fit between diagnostic emphasis in research and treatment and the emphasis on functionality in administrative or legal systems raises the question of how useful psychiatric diagnoses are to the assessment of impairment and disability (Gold, 2002; Greenberg et al., 2004; Simon & Gold, 2004).

With the exception of Social Security Disability programs, legal rules governing compensation or accommodation for mental impairment, disability, or injury do not typically rely on formal psychiatric diagnosis to come to decisions for eligibility for benefits or other types of action. Nevertheless, administrative and legal systems frequently rely informally on diagnosis as an indication of severity of emotional injury or distress. In the absence of a psychiatric diagnosis, employers and insurance companies rarely consider claims of impairment due to mental illness seriously. Without a formal diagnosis, they are often hesitant to believe that symptoms are severe enough to cause impairment or warrant compensation or accommodation.

However, as the DSM's authors point out, DSM diagnoses were not defined for nonmedical purposes such as the assessment of employment-related functional impairments (American Psychiatric Association, 2000). Diagnostic assessment typically incorporates functional status as a criterion of severity of illness but diagnostic categories were not designed to provide specific information about functional status. They do not provide the type of information that administrative or legal systems considering disability seek or require to determine eligibility for benefits, accommodations, or damages.

Research can provide a broad understanding of symptoms and the natural course of illness typical to a diagnostic category because studies are based on large numbers of individuals. It also provides useful statistical analysis and correlation of variables associated with diagnostic categories, such as comorbidity, functional impairment, and response to treatment. However, no statistical analysis or research data can identify the symptoms and associated impairments in any given individual. Any one person's presentation may or may not fit into larger statistical patterns or probabilities.

In addition, a potentially wide range of functional difficulties is associated with any diagnostic category. Not everyone with a specific disorder will have all the possible impairments associated with that disorder, and may not even have any impairments, despite the presence of severe symptoms. In studies examining disability and its association with various disorders, for all types of disorders there were some participants without disability (Sanderson & Andrews, 2002).

Even the severity of psychiatric symptoms and illness does not necessarily equate with functional impairment. The loss of function may be greater or less than the impairment might imply, and the individual's performance may fall short of or exceed that usually associated with the impairment (Bonnie, 1997a; Simon, 2002). Moreover, when individuals do experience functional impairments, many are able to prioritize work functioning and, despite symptoms, function adequately in the workplace. Many are even able to utilize work settings to maintain or improve their functioning (Straus & Davidson, 1997).

For example, although depression is widely acknowledged to be a major source of disability (Jans et al., 2004; Murray, & Lopez, 1996), not all individuals with depression experience symptoms that cause functional impairment. Depression can be disabling or it can be experienced as an uncomfortable or distressing mood state without creating actual disability. It is not the disorder "depression" itself that is disabling. Rather, symptoms of depression such as psychomotor retardation, insomnia, and impaired concentration can result in functional impairment when functional impairment exists (Enelow, 1988). The relationship between a diagnosis such as depression and a work-related impairment depends on the employment environment and the demands of particular jobs, as well as on the abilities and functional limitations of the individual (Bonnie, 1997a).

In disability and disability-related evaluations, the most significant factor in the assessment of the effect of any psychiatric disorder on work function is the interaction of the specific impairment with the specific job requirement. The ability to assess and explain how symptoms associated with a diagnosis affect a specific set of work skills is often more important than a diagnostic label and more relevant to the parties involved. For example, an individual with a back injury who cannot lift more than 50 pounds may not be impaired if employed as a computer data entry worker but might be totally disabled if employed to work in a heavy machinery loading bay. Similarly, an individual with attention deficit hyperactivity disorder may function without any significant impairment in a job that involves completion of a task at his or her own pace by no particular deadline, or may be totally disabled in a job that requires long periods of sustained attention to detail or the ability to multitask under time pressures.

Unfortunately, evaluators, employers, insurance companies, and litigators often focus on diagnosis rather than on the relationship between symptoms, impairments, and specific work skills. Legal arguments may become centered on the accuracy or appropriateness of the diagnosis rather than on the relevant functional capacity and its relationship to the employment or legal issue in question. Diagnosis may actually become an impediment to understanding the nature of an impairment (Greenberg et al., 2004).

Nevertheless, diagnoses are relevant and appropriate for use in disability and disability-related evaluations. First, statutes or regulation may require that a diagnosis be present for eligibility. For example, as noted, in order to qualify for Social Security Disability Insurance, an individual has to meet the criteria for a recognized DSM diagnosis. Second, diagnostic categorization may be relevant because diagnoses share symptom profiles that can direct an examiner to explore relevant psychiatric issues in the related research, such as patterns of symptom presentation and potential impairment (Gold, 2002; Halleck et al., 1992). This allows access to the large data bases upon which such research draws. It also helps direct exploration of relevant psychiatric issues within a context that includes patterns of symptom presentation, expected or probable response to treatment, and natural history of disorders. In addition, diagnostic categories create a common language that can facilitate communication, and therefore legal or administrative decision-making, when used appropriately.

Diagnostic categories also provide certain information regarding appropriate treatment, reasonableness of claims of impairment and disability, prognosis, and, to some degree, the likelihood of future impairment and disability. For example, broadly speaking, an individual with episodic depression who responds well to treatment should retain the ability to function in between episodes. In contrast, an individual with a paranoid delusional disorder is unlikely to be able to function well for any extended period of time in most workplaces in the absence of treatment and, even in many cases, with treatment.

Regardless of diagnosis, the assessment of symptoms, impairment, and compromised work functions depends on the interaction between the individual's symptoms and job requirements. Individuals with episodic depression may also experience chronic symptoms even between episodes that impair their workplace functioning. Individuals with paranoid delusional disorder may be able to maintain certain types of employment if those jobs do not escalate or interact with their delusional thinking. Mental health professionals are therefore advised to consider diagnostic categories as a means of organizing thinking and using evidence-based data to understand the possible types of impairments associated with that diagnosis and the types of disability that may be related to those impairments.

Psychiatric Disorders in the Workplace

Studies have consistently demonstrated substantial impairments and disability associated with all categories of psychiatric disorders, including those frequently encountered in the workplace (Kessler & Frank, 1997; Ormel et al., 1994). Psychiatric illness accounted for more than half as many disability days as all physical conditions in the United States population (Merikangas et al., 2007a). The most prevalent lifetime disorders are anxiety disorders, mood disorders, ADHD, and substance use disorders. Since most of these disorders do not preclude employment, these are among those most frequently encountered disorders in the workplace and in employment evaluations (see Table 4.1).

The psychiatric disorders most commonly associated with impairment and disability in the workplace are not necessarily those most often thought of as the most disabling. Conditions such as schizophrenia, typically considered highly disabling, are uncommon in working populations because they often preclude competitive employment (Bonnie, 1997a; Sanderson & Andrews, 2002). In contrast, and as noted above, mood disorders, anxiety disorders, and substance use disorders, the most common psychiatric disorders in the population, rarely preclude entering the competitive labor force and thus are also the most common psychiatric disorders associated with workplace disability (Corrigan et al., 2007; Druss et al., 2000; Ormel et al., 1994).

Table 4.1 Prevalence of commonly encountered workplace psychiatric disorders by class and specific diagnosis

Class of disorder	Specific diagnosis	Lifetime prevalence (%)	12-month prevalence (%)
Anxiety disorders		28.8	18.1
	Panic disorder	4.7	2.7
	Specific phobia	12.5	8.7
	Social phobia	12.1	6.8
	Generalized anxiety disorder	5.7	3.1
	Posttraumatic stress disorder	6.8	3.5
	Obsessive compulsive disorder	1.6	1.0
Mood disorders		20.8	9.5
	Major depressive disorder	16.6	6.7
	Dysthymia	2.5	1.5
	Bipolar I and II	3.9	2.6
Impulse control disorders		24.8	8.9
	Attention deficit/hyperactivity disorder	8.1	4.1
Substance use disorders		14.6	3.8
	Alcohol use	13.2	3.1
	Alcohol dependence	5.4	1.3
	Drug use	7.9	1.4
	Drug dependence	3.0	0.4

Kessler, Berglund, et al. (2005) and Kessler, Chiu, et al. (2005).

Although chronic psychotic disorders are thought of as the most disabling, any type of psychiatric disorder can result in some degree of impairment (Sanderson & Andrews, 2002). Employees with nonpsychotic psychiatric illnesses such as mood and anxiety disorders may exhibit a variety of psychiatric symptoms, including irritability, anger, inattention, apathy, loss of motivation, disinterest, and fatigue (Pflanz & Heidel, 2003). These more common illnesses have been shown to cause work impairments such as absenteeism, accidents, interpersonal conflict, and poor job performance, and all can result in disability.

The predominant effect of chronic physical conditions in the workplace is absenteeism. In contrast, the predominant effect of psychiatric disorders in the workplace is often "presenteeism," a form of disability in which an individual is present at work but does not work at full capacity and is significantly less productive (Dewa et al., 2007). Depression-related presenteeism has been found to generate up to 30 times more lost productivity than absenteeism (Marlowe, 2002). Presenteeism would be expected to be particularly likely when an employee is reluctant to report an illness such as depression or anxiety, does not believe the illness is a legitimate reason for missing work, or believes it would not be regarded as such (Druss et al., 2001).

Despite the lack of consistent research definitions of psychiatric disability, studies have attempted to quantify the degree of severity of psychiatric disorders, where one of the factors related to severity was work impairment. Investigators in one study (Kessler et al., 2005) found that although more than one-third of cases of all disorders reported in the previous 12-month period were mild, the prevalence of moderate and serious cases, using work impairment as one determinant as severity of illness, was 14% (see Table 4.2). In addition, certain common disorders had a much higher incidence of serious cases. Panic disorder was classified as serious in 44.8% of cases, generalized anxiety disorder (GAD) in 32.3% of cases, posttraumatic stress disorder (PTSD) in 36.6% of cases, and obsessive compulsive disorder (OCD) was classified as serious in 50.6% of cases. Mood disorders demonstrated high proportions of severe cases as well, with combined severe and moderate cases of major depressive disorder at 80.5% and combined severe and moderate cases of bipolar disorder, types I and II, at 100%.

A growing body of research has documented the variety of impairments caused by symptoms of these and other psychiatric disorders. As noted, psychosis compromises occupational functioning (Beiser et al., 1994; Cather et al., 2003), and psychotic symptoms can accompany a variety of psychiatric problems,

Table 4.2 Severity of commonly reported workplace psychiatric disorders in a 12-month prevalence study, utilizing work impairment as one measure of severity

Class of disorder	Specific diagnosis	Serious severity	Moderate severity	Mild severity
Anxiety disorders		22.8	33.7	43.5
	Panic disorder	44.8	29.5	25.7
	Specific phobia	21.9	30.0	28.7
	Social phobia	29.9	38.8	31.3
	Generalized anxiety disorder	32.3	44.6	23.1
	Posttraumatic stress disorder	36.6	33.1	30.2
	Obsessive compulsive disorder	50.6	34.8	14.6
Mood disorders		45.0	40.0	15.0
	Major depressive disorder	30.4	50.1	19.5
	Dysthymia	49.7	32.1	18.2
	Bipolar I and II	82.9	17.1	0
Impulse control disorders		32.9	52.4	14.7
	Attention deficit/hyperactivity disorder	41.3	35.2	23.5
Substance use disorders		29.6	37.1	33.4
	Alcohol use	28.9	39.7	31.5
	Alcohol dependence	34.3	65.7	0
	Drug use	36.6	30.4	33.0
	Drug dependence	56.5	43.5	0

Kessler, Chiu, et al. (2005).

including mood disorders. Psychotic symptoms may also be induced by substances use, or may result from medical problems such as lupus, thyroid disorders, and electrolyte imbalance (Cather et al., 2003).

ADHD can also be associated with work impairments. Although considerable variation in neuropsychological deficits is found among individuals with ADHD, the symptoms of this disorder are associated with cognitive deficits predominantly in executive functioning. Executive function describes a broad range of interrelated higher level cognitive processes involved in the selection, initiation, execution, and monitoring of complex motor and cognitive responses. These processes contribute to decision-making and higher-level thinking, such as initiation, planning, execution, and flexibility in response to changing contingencies. Judgment may be impaired, resulting in poor decisions or ineffective management, which can significantly impair work performance (Biederman et al., 2005; Brod et al., 2005; Roth & Saykin, 2004).

Other disorders may present as either primary or comorbid psychiatric disorders, or even physical disorders, and have their own associated impairments. Dementia, chronic pain syndromes, somatoform disorders, and personality disorders are all encountered in the workplace. Each of these disorders can result in severe impairments and disability. Even if not disabling, each of these disorders can predispose individuals to other disorders such as depression, anxiety, or substance use, with their associated impairments and potential disability.

As noted above, an in-depth review of all psychiatric disorders and possible associated work impairments is beyond the scope of this discussion. However, mood disorders, anxiety disorders, and substance use, the most common disorders encountered in the workplace, warrant some review. These disorders are consistently found to be the most disabling of workplace psychiatric disorders, generally with a dose–response relationship between severity of mental illness and degree of disability (Kessler & Frank, 1997; Ormel et al., 1994).

The relationship between anxiety, mood, and substance disorders and associated disability is independent of comorbid physical conditions (Sanderson & Andrews, 2002). In one large-scale study, the reported work impairments due to these psychiatric disorders were higher than those for most physical disorders (Kessler et al., 2001). A World Health Organization study that examined common psychiatric disorders in primary care settings in 14 different countries found that after controlling for physical disease severity, psychopathology was consistently associated with increased disability and was more strongly associated with disability than was severity of physical illness (Ormel et al., 1994). Considering the variety of the populations studied, "the consistency of the findings on the relationship of psychopathology and disability ... was striking" (Ormel et al., 1994, p. 1746).

Other studies have demonstrated similar findings. For example, major depression is more consistently related to poor work performance than eight major chronic medical conditions, including hypertension, diabetes, and arthritis (Lerner, Allaire, & Reisine et al., 2004; Wang et al., 2004; Wells et al., 1989).

One study found that workers with depression cost employers in the United States more than three times the amount associated with lost productivity from all other illnesses (Stewart, Ricci, Chee, Hahn, & Morganstein et al., 2003). In another study of the health and employee files of over 15,000 employees of a major United States corporation, researchers found that the cost to employers in workdays lost to depression was greater than the cost of many other common medical illnesses (Druss et al., 2001).

Psychiatric disorders typically result in more impairment and disability than physical disorders in areas of functioning critical for success in most workplaces. Whereas general medical conditions appear to affect primarily one area of function, that of physical functioning, mental conditions often result in combined deficits in more than one higher order social and cognitive skill (Druss et al., 2000; Kessler & Frank, 1997; Ormel et al., 1994). In addition, mental conditions that lead to deficits in skills and functions such as adapting to social situations, coping with stress, trouble concentrating, and confusion may be particularly important for successful functioning in the workplace. At the same time, deficits in these domains may be subtle and therefore more challenging to overcome than the more concrete barriers raised by general medical conditions (Druss et al., 2000).

In a study comparing disability associated with both medical and psychiatric conditions (Druss et al., 2000), individuals reporting disability due to a mental condition were more than five times more likely than those with disability due to a general medical condition to report difficulties in social and cognitive function. Of those with mental disabilities only, 58.8% reported having some type of difficulty in social functioning and 40.7% reported trouble coping with stress. In regard to cognitive functioning, 24.5% reported trouble concentrating and 25.4% reported frequent confusion. In addition, mental disability was more commonly associated with combined deficits in functioning than were physical impairments (Druss et al., 2000). Of those reporting mental disability, 23.3% reported deficits in two of three domains of function (social, physical, and cognitive) and 14% reported difficulties in all three domains.

Evidence-Based Assessment of Psychiatric Impairment

Affective Disorders

Affective disorders, primarily major depressive disorder and bipolar disorder, are among the most extensively studied psychiatric disorders in terms of work impairment. Multiple studies have found that depression and bipolar disorder are major causes of lost work productivity and disability (Druss et al., 2000; Greenberg et al., 2003; Kessler et al., 2006; Stewart et al., 2003; Wang et al., 2004). Although affective disorders, anxiety disorders, and substance use disorders are common in the workplace, pure affective disorders are associated with somewhat larger average numbers of both work loss and work cutback days than either pure anxiety disorders or pure substance use (Kessler & Frank, 1997).

The degree of disability associated with affective disorders is reflected in their cost both to individuals and to employers. One large-scale study of affective disorders and disability (Kessler et al., 2006) found that individuals with bipolar disorder had 65.5 lost workdays per worker per year and those with major depression 27.2 lost workdays. Projections of individual-level associations to the total civilian labor force yielded estimates of 96.2 million lost workdays and $14.1 billion worth of lost productivity associated with bipolar disorder and 225 million workdays and $36.6 billion worth of lost productivity per year associated with major depression.

Major Depression

Depression alone is believed to have the largest impact on work disability (Elinson et al., 2004; Stewart et al., 2003). In fact, depression is one of the leading worldwide causes of disability, representing the fourth most important cause of disability in the world (Murray & Lopez, 1996). By the year 2020, depression is projected to be the leading cause of disability worldwide (Smith et al., 2003). Major depressive disorder is episodic, with circumscribed, acute major depressive episodes reoccurring throughout the lifetime. However, chronic forms of depression account for 12–35% of depressive disorders. If an individual has had a major depressive episode, there is a 50% chance of having a second; after having two major depressive episodes, there is a 75% chance of having a third; after three depressive episodes, there is a 90% chance of future depression (American Psychiatric Association, 2000; Dubovsky, Davies, & Dubovsky et al., 2003).

Individuals with major depression are significantly more likely to report high levels of both social role and work impairment (Kessler, Dupont, Berglund, & Wittchen et al., 1999). The level of disability among patients with depression appears similar to or higher than the disability found among those with chronic medical illnesses (Druss et al., 2000; Hays, Wells, Sherbourne, Rogers, & Spritzer et al., 1995; Ormel et al., 1994; Pro, 2005). Functional outcome in depression is comparable to or worse than functioning in chronic medical disorders such as diabetes mellitus and cardiovascular disease (Dubovsky et al., 2003; Wells et al., 1989). Depression in addition to chronic medical conditions has unique and additive effects on patient functioning (Wells et al., 1989).

The association between depression and lost productivity has been consistently demonstrated through epidemiologic and research studies across a wide range of cultures and economies (Simon et al., 2000). In a study of primary care patients, compared to other psychiatric disorders, depression-related short-term disability generally affected more employees, lasted longer, and had a higher rate of recurrence than other disorders (Dewa et al., 2002). The relationship between depression and work dysfunction has been found to be independent of other important social influences of interpersonal stress attributed to coworkers, spouses, and others, and job stress related to work dissatisfaction (Martin, Blum, Beach, & Roman et al., 1996).

The number of previous episodes of depression is associated with degree of disability (Rytsala et al., 2005). Generally, however, the most significant predictor of functional disability is severity of symptoms (Berndt et al., 1998; Dewa et al., 2002; Lerner, Adler, Chang, et al., 2004; Lerner, Allaire, et al., 2004; Ormel, Oldehinkel, Nolen, & Vollebergh, 2004; Rytsala et al., 2005). Studies report substantial positive correlations between symptom severity and impairment in work functioning (Adler et al., 2006; Burton, Pransky, Conti, Chen, & Edington, 2004). Lower functional levels are also associated with older age and any comorbid personality disorder (Rytsala et al., 2005). Most individuals with mild impairment from depression can work without difficulty. When major depression produces moderate or severe impairments in these domains, individuals may well lack the capacity to be productive at work (Pro, 2005).

Notwithstanding the association between symptom severity and impairment in functioning, substantial decrements in social and work functioning have also been found to be associated with subclinical and less severe levels of depressive symptomatology (Martin et al., 1996). Dysthymia, also referred to as minor depression, describes a chronic, non-episodic, low-grade depressive mood disorder that never completely disappears. Symptoms associated with dysthymia can result in decreased activity, effectiveness, or productivity.

Some researchers have found only mild degrees of impairment associated with dysthymia (Liu & Van Liew, 2003). Others have asserted that when the severity of dysthymia is examined from the standpoint of functioning rather than number of symptoms, "Dysthymic disorder produces as much impairment as MDD [Major Depressive Disorder] in work ... and ability to perform social roles" (Dubovsky et al., 2003, p. 450). Perhaps most significant to assessment of impairment for individuals with chronic dysthymic conditions is the fact that dysthymia predisposes individuals to major depressive episodes. Eighty percent of patients with dysthymia also have a lifetime diagnosis of major depression (Dubovsky et al., 2003).

A number of studies have demonstrated the association between depression and absenteeism (Adler et al., 2006; Dewa et al., 2002; Druss et al., 2001; Kessler et al., 1999; Kessler et al., 2006; Lerner, Adler, Chang, et al., 2004; Lerner, Allaire, et al., 2004; Liu & Van Liew, 2003; Pflanz & Heidel, 2003; Wang et al., 2004; Yelin & Cisternas, 1997). In a study of primary care patients, depression was associated with an increase of two to four disability days per month (Dewa et al., 2002). In two major community surveys, people with depression had a fivefold or greater increase in lost time from work compared to those without symptoms of depression (Broadhead, Blazer, George, & Tse, 1990; Kessler & Frank, 1997).

As discussed above, depression-related "presenteeism" due to symptom impairment presented a bigger problem than absenteeism (Adler et al., 2006;

Dewa et al., 2002; Lerner, Adler, Chang, et al., 2004; Lerner, Allaire, et al., 2004; Liu & Van Liew, 2003; Stewart et al., 2003; Wang et al., 2004; Yelin & Cisternas, 1997). A recent study documented that although absenteeism was elevated for individuals with depression (8.7 days lost per year), presenteeism accounted for significantly more lost productivity in terms of work loss days (18.2 days lost per year) (Kessler et al., 2006). Workers with depression report significantly more total health-related lost productive time than those without depression (Stewart et al., 2003). One study found that depression was among the leading chronic conditions that resulted in limitations in time-related components in work as well as problems with physical tasks, mental tasks, and overall output, all elements of presenteeism (Burton et al., 2004). Depressed patients are less engaged in work and more likely to report "doing nothing" during work hours than healthy controls (Lerner, Allaire, et al., 2004).

The common symptoms of depression can cause cognitive, behavioral, and social impairments that may affect work capacities. Social impairments, for example, can result from irritability, angry outbursts, and isolation from coworkers, and cause impaired cooperation and communication (Liu & Van Liew, 2003). Cognitive and behavioral symptoms of depression that may affect work performance include inability to concentrate, low energy, easy fatigability, poor judgment, indecisiveness, and sleep deprivation (Berndt et al., 1998). Judgment may be impaired, resulting in poor decisions or ineffective management (Biederman et al., 2005; Brod et al., 2005; Roth & Saykin, 2004) as well as cause significant rates of absenteeism and presenteeism (Kessler, Chiu, et al., 2005).

One study (Lerner, Allaire, et al., 2004) identified two clusters of specific depression symptoms that increase employee productivity loss. First, employees having difficulty concentrating and with increased distractibility demonstrate more on the job productivity loss. Second, employees reporting fatigue and sleep disturbance had more difficulty performing mental and interpersonal tasks and reported more missed days of work. Employees in the depression groups in this study also had notable impairment in time management, difficulty managing mental and interpersonal job demands, and difficulty managing output demands 20% of the time or more, an amount equivalent to two 8-h workdays in 2 weeks.

Cognitive deficits found in depression include measurably impaired performance in tests of attention, executive function, and recall memory. An impairment in attention or immediate memory can interfere with almost every facet of daily life. Subjective complaints of memory loss are often reported by patients with mood disorders and have been confirmed by neuropsychological assessment (Marvel & Paradiso, 2004).

These cognitive impairments can also result in difficulties in handling demands, making correct decision, avoiding errors, meeting time requirements and deadlines, working without unnecessary supervision, being responsible, and handling overall job requirements (Liu & Van Liew, 2003; Martin et al.,

1996). The cognitive effects of depression are often more pronounced late in the day. It is possible that depression exacerbates the fatigue and reduction in cognitive abilities that have been found to increase naturally over the workday (Wang et al., 2004).

Increased cognitive dysfunction and productivity is most influenced by symptom severity (Lerner, Adler, Chang, et al., 2004; Lerner, Allaire, et al., 2004; Marvel & Paradiso, 2004). In severe depression, cognitive impairment can be severe and global, at times approaching and meeting criteria for dementia (Marvel & Paradiso, 2004). However, certain occupations also significantly increased employee vulnerability to productivity loss. When depressed employees had occupations that required proficiency in exercising judgment and communication, more work limitations and absences were reported. The differential effect of impairments due to depression leading to work cutback has also been noted to be greater among professional workers than in other occupations (Kessler & Frank, 1997). Occupations requiring a high degree of contact with the public also resulted in greater impairments in the ability to handle mental and interpersonal demands and physical job demands in depressed employees (Lerner, Adler, Chang, et al., 2004; Lerner, Allaire, et al., 2004).

Motor impairments can also result in work dysfunction and may arise due to psychomotor retardation or agitation. Psychomotor retardation, or slowed response time, is a prominent feature of depression, although it is not present in every individual with this disorder. Individuals with psychomotor agitation frequently present with symptoms of restlessness and anxiety. Increased time to initiate movement, accompanied by increased time to complete movement, may represent impairment in both cognitive and motor processes. Such impairments may manifest themselves as abnormal involuntary disturbances that interrupt daily activities (Marvel & Paradiso, 2004).

Fortunately, with proper diagnosis and treatment, 80% of depressed individuals can return to normal activities, including work (Liu & Van Liew, 2003; Marlowe, 2002). Successful treatment often occurs within 1–3 months (Liu & Van Liew, 2003). Improvement in work performance is rapid, with about two-thirds of the change occurring by the fourth week of treatment (Berndt et al., 1998).

Improvement in psychiatric symptoms is associated with corresponding changes in impairments and disability (Ormel et al., 1994). Treatment for depression has been shown to keep depressed persons employed and to improve the productivity of depressed persons who are already working (Elinson et al., 2004). Individuals treated for depression are significantly more likely to be working after 12 months than untreated individuals (Claxton, Chawla, & Kennedy, 1999; Marlowe, 2002). In one study, more than three quarters of those on depression-related short-term disability returned to work (Dewa et al., 2002).

Antidepressant medication has also been shown to reduce the number of disability days (Claxton et al., 1999; Marlowe, 2002). Although initiation of antidepressant medication may be associated with additional impairments, a brief time out of work, generally no longer than 1 week, if at all, is typically appropriate to permit adaptation to initial side effects (Pro, 2005). In addition, employment itself is often therapeutic: symptoms of those with affective disorders have been found to improve in the presence of employment, especially if they have established a work history prior to the onset of the condition (Yelin & Cisternas, 1997).

However, patients whose symptoms run a chronic course often experience chronic impairments and disability (Ormel et al., 1994). Some individuals will prove resistant even to skillful psychopharmacologic and psychotherapeutic management. Refractory major depression is associated with a 50% chance of work impairment (Dubovsky et al., 2003). In one study, individuals whose symptoms remained present over 2 years showed substantially higher difficulties in workplace function than did those whose symptoms had resolved (Druss et al., 2001). In addition, residual symptoms and impairment of work roles can persist after improvement of depression. In some individuals, some cognitive deficits can persist even during states of remission (Marvel & Paradiso, 2004).

Bipolar Disorder

Major depression, as noted, ranks among the world's top 5 disabling conditions; bipolar disorder is one of the world's 10 most disabling conditions (Murray & Lopez, 1996). Although less common than depression (see Table 4.1), bipolar disorder is also associated with substantial work impairments. Aggregate impairment is greater for major depressive disorder than for bipolar disorder because of the high prevalence of major depressive disorder relative to bipolar disorder. However, bipolar disorder has been found to be associated with substantially more lost work performance than major depressive disorder at the individual level (Kessler et al., 2006).

Bipolar disorder has a number of variable presentations. In bipolar I disorder, an individual alternates between three general mood states: mania, euthymia, and depression. Euthymia refers to a period of baseline, normal mood, characterized by neither manic nor depressive feelings or behavior. States may vary in duration and may be relatively pure, or mixed. In mixed states, mood includes features of both mania and depression at the same time.

A manic episode, the hallmark of bipolar disorder, consists of a persistently euphoric, expansive, or irritable mood that often includes a decreased need for sleep, grandiosity, pressured speech, racing thoughts, flight of ideas, distractibility, and an increase in goal-directed activities. Disinhibition in combination with increased energy and poor judgment can result in excessive involvement in nonproductive or destructive activities, such as substance use, sexual activity, or spending money. Disinhibition in combination with irritability can result in rage, demanding attitudes, and even assaultiveness.

Individuals with bipolar II disorder have elevated hypomanic mood states, often as a baseline state, rather than the more severe episodic manic states, but cycles of depressive episodes in bipolar I and II disorders are similar, and symptoms of depression in bipolar disorders are similar to those in major depression. Psychosis may evolve at either manic or depressive extreme but does not occur in hypomanic states.

All bipolar disorders, including bipolar II disorder, are chronic cyclic conditions. Ninety percent of those diagnosed as having a manic episode have future episodes of either mania or depression. Without treatment, individuals generally experience about four episodes of either mania or depression in a 10-year period on average. The interval between episodes tends to shorten with aging. However, some individuals experience a variant of bipolar disorder characterized by rapid cycling, in which they experience at least four separate episodes of mania or depression in 1 year (Liu & Van Liew, 2003).

Psychosocial outcomes, including employment, vary widely for persons with bipolar disorder, but are generally not favorable. Bipolar disorder has been found to be associated with increased work absenteeism owing to illness, decreased work productivity, and poorer overall functioning (Judd et al., 2005; Kessler et al., 2006). It is estimated that 30–60% of individuals with bipolar disorder do not regain full social or occupational functioning after the onset of illness (Dickerson et al., 2004). In one follow-up of patients hospitalized for a manic episode, only 43% were employed 6 months after hospitalization even though 80% were symptom-free or only mildly symptomatic (Dickerson et al., 2004).

Several studies have demonstrated persistent cognitive impairments in bipolar patients in euthymic states (Dixon, Kravariti, Frith, Murray, & McGuire, 2004; Marvel & Paradiso, 2004). One recent study suggests that persisting functional disability even with mood stabilization may result, at least in part, from persisting neurocognitive impairment (Altshuler et al., 2007). In this study, of the 80% of subjects who were symptom-free 6 months after hospitalization, only 43% were employed and only 21% were working at their expected level of employment. Neurocognitive functioning among patients with bipolar disorder in the euthymic state found continued impairment in executive function or verbal memory, two deficits which are strong predictors of poor functional outcome in other disorders (Altshuler et al., 2007).

Similarly, another group of researchers has noted a significant relationship between employment status and a variety of variables in bipolar disorder, including cognitive impairments and symptom severity (Dickerson et al., 2004). Greater cognitive functioning and lower severity of symptoms were associated with a better employment status, regardless of education, age, gender, race, and time since last hospitalization, among other variables examined. Cognitive performance, particularly immediate verbal memory, was significantly associated with employment status apart from the effects of severity of symptoms and other variables.

Cognitive function is least impaired and significantly less impaired during periods of euthymia but, as noted above, studies have found that it still differs from that in healthy controls. When individuals with bipolar disorder are asymptomatic, their psychosocial functioning is good but not as good as that of well controls (Judd et al., 2005). Psychomotor speed deficits seem to persist even with full remission and to be unrelated to medication and symptom severity. Deficits in response initiation, strategic thinking, and inhibitory control appeared to be independent of affective state, whether depressed, manic, or euthymic and may simply represent trait markers of bipolar illness (Dixon et al., 2004). These findings are consistent with other studies that have found impairments in measures of response latency, rapid visual information processing, and fine motor skills in clinically stable bipolar patients (Dixon et al., 2004).

Impairments associated with subsyndromal symptoms may also account for ongoing impairment of work-related functioning in the absence of acute symptoms. For example, one study found that minor and subsyndromal depressive symptoms, which may dominate the course of bipolar illnesses, are associated with significant psychosocial disability as compared with months when the same patients have no symptoms of a mood disorder (Judd et al., 2005).

The degree of workplace impairment associated with bipolar II disorder is the subject of some debate. Some associated workplace dysfunction due to disorganization and racing thinking may occur. However, generally speaking, many individuals with bipolar II disorder can be outstanding performers in their fields (Liu & Van Liew, 2003). In fact, individuals with bipolar II disorder have been found to experience improvement in psychosocial functioning as they go from asymptomatic status to subsyndromal hypomanic symptoms, indicating that hypomania may increase productivity and efficiency (Judd et al., 2005; Liu & Van Liew, 2003). Nevertheless, when their mood becomes unstable, individuals with bipolar II disorder can become demanding, less effective, impulsive, and may display increasingly poor judgment, which can have profound effects on work functioning (Liu & Van Liew, 2003).

At the opposite end of the mood spectrum, bipolar II disorder is comparable to bipolar I disorder in terms of psychosocial disability at corresponding levels of severity of depression. For patients with either form of bipolar disorder, minor depression or dysthymia is associated with significantly more psychosocial disability than hypomania. Depressive symptoms are at least as disabling as, and sometimes significantly more disabling than, manic symptoms at comparable levels of severity in bipolar II disorder (Merikangas et al., 2007b). Similarly, subsyndromal depressive symptoms are more disabling than subsyndromal hypomanic symptoms in bipolar II disorder (Judd et al., 2005). Episodes of depression do not vary significantly between bipolar I and bipolar II disorders, implying that in cycles of depressive episodes, impairment in either type of bipolar disorder would be equivalent given equivalent symptom severity.

A recent study yielded similar findings particularly in regard to work impairment. These researchers (Kessler et al., 2006) found that mania/hypomania in the absence of major depressive episodes was associated with significantly less work impairment than bipolar disorder with major depressive episodes. However, the higher individual level of overall work impairment of bipolar disorder compared to major depressive disorder found in this study was due largely to major depressive episodes being more impairing in the context of bipolar disorder than in major depressive disorder, rather than to mania or hypomania being more impairing than major depressive episodes. This is in part the result of measurably greater persistence and severity of major depressive episodes in bipolar disorder than in major depressive disorder (Kessler et al., 2006).

Nevertheless, impairments related to manic and hypomanic symptoms can be significant. Executive dysfunction is particularly associated with the manic state and is largely explicable in terms of the formal thought disorder that is a feature of mania (Dixon et al., 2004). Bipolar patients have shown impaired performance in tests of attention, executive function, and memory. Cognitive functioning has been postulated as a determinant of psychosocial and employment outcomes in bipolar disorder. As in depression, increased cognitive dysfunction often is associated with greater symptom severity (Marvel & Paradiso, 2004).

Also as in major depressive disorder, total symptom severity has been found to be significantly associated with employment status (Dickerson et al., 2004). One study (Judd et al., 2005) found that patients with bipolar I disorder had a significant, stepwise progression in disability associated with each increment in manic or hypomanic symptom severity. Similarly, every increase or decrease in depressive symptom severity in both bipolar I and II disorders was associated with a corresponding significant and stepwise increase or decrease in psychosocial disability. When patients with these disorders had no mood disorder symptoms, their psychosocial functioning normalized and was rated as good. When patients had symptoms at the threshold for major depression, functioning was poor.

Another study demonstrated similar findings. The wide variability with which individuals with bipolar disorder are able to successfully engage in paid work included the individual's stage of recovery from the disorder and/or effective management of the disorder. Specifically, reasonable control of the clinical symptomatology associated with bipolar disorder determined whether or not individuals could function effectively, although it did not mean that individuals with the disorder had to wait until they were symptom-free to resume workplace functioning (Tse & Yeats, 2002).

Treatment often helps ameliorate and resolve many symptoms that create work impairment. However, treatment for bipolar disorder is often more complex and may be less effective than that for major depressive disorder. Combinations of mood stabilizers, antidepressants, and even antipsychotic agents may be required, and even in appropriate doses, may not result in full remission and control of the disorder. Some of these agents may themselves have side effects, such as fatigue, memory problems, or tremors that cause or exacerbate impairments that result in work disability.

One study also found that another important theme relating to vocational outcome of people with bipolar disorder was "goodness of fit" with their job, as discussed in Chapter 3. For instance, a participant who recovered from bipolar disorder might still have a variety of functional impairments such as a short attention span or inadequate organizational skills. These difficulties did not result in disability provided the employer was willing to accommodate the employee's increased requirements (Tse & Yeats, 2002). If an individual was able to hold down meaningful work for a significant length of time it could have a beneficial effect upon that person's recovery from bipolar disorder. In turn, the better the recovery from mental health problems, the greater the opportunities to successfully maintaining employment (Tse & Yeats, 2002).

In short, symptom severity and psychosocial disability fluctuate together during the course of bipolar disorder (Judd et al., 2005). Depressive symptoms in both bipolar subtypes are at least as disabling as, and sometimes more disabling than, manic or hypomanic symptoms (Judd et al., 2005; Kessler et al., 2006). Subsyndromal depressive symptoms are associated with significant impairment in both forms of bipolar disorder as compared with asymptomatic states. In contrast, subsyndromal hypomanic symptoms are not associated with significant increases in impairment for either disorder and may even enhance some functioning in bipolar II disorder (Judd et al., 2005). Nevertheless, some impairment may remain even in euthymic states, due to either persistent cognitive deficits or subsyndromal symptom states.

Anxiety Disorders

Anxiety disorders are the most common of all psychiatric illnesses, are frequently encountered in the workplace, and can result in considerable functional impairment and distress (see Tables 4.1 and 4.2) (Hollander & Simeon, 2003; Kessler et al., 2001; Yelin & Cisternas, 1997). Anxiety disorders include panic and anxiety disorders (panic disorder, GAD, and adjustment disorder with anxious mood), phobic disorders (social anxiety disorder and specific phobias, such as agoraphobia), OCD, and PTSD. Anxiety disorders may be relatively short-lived, lasting from less than 28 days (acute stress disorder) to less than 6 months (adjustment disorder with anxiety), or may become chronic, as may occur in GAD, OCD, and some individuals with PTSD.

Anxiety disorders are frequently viewed by the public as less disabling than schizophrenic disorders and mood disorders. However, individuals with anxiety disorders may struggle with significant life disabilities for prolonged periods of time. In addition, anxiety disorders frequently co-occur with mood disorders, which is likely to increase impairments and resulting disabilities (Corrigan et al., 2007). Public lack of awareness of the impairments created by anxiety may in part be the result of the fact that anxiety is a universal emotion and can be experienced in response to many stimuli. Work itself can be a source of stress and anxiety due to the need to meet goals, deadlines, and standards and the need to interact with employers, employees, coworkers, clients, or the public (Stein & Hollander, 2003). Many individuals turn performance anxiety in the workplace into a constructive source of motivation.

In contrast, anxiety disorders are characterized by the impairment of the ability to modulate arousal. Levels of anxiety that become excessive or are experienced at inappropriate times lead to unbearable subjective distress and substantial work impairment (Kessler, Chiu, et al., 2005; Stein & Hollander, 2003). In another large study, of those who met the criteria for panic disorder,

52% reported some work impairment; of those with GAD, 53.5% reported impairment (Kessler et al., 2001).

The relationship between anxiety disorders, work impairment, and disability is complex and differs depending on the type of anxiety disorder, symptoms, and severity of the disorder. For example, panic disorder can have a significant impact in all spheres of functioning (Kessler, Chiu, et al., 2005; Kessler et al., 2006; Stein & Hollander, 2003). Panic attacks are characterized by the sudden onset of an overwhelming sense of intense anxiety and impending doom and often are accompanied by physical symptoms such as shortness of breath, dizziness, palpitations, chest pain, and nausea.

Panic attacks can be debilitating. An occasional panic attack may create minimal or no impairment. However, if the panic attacks continue, the person begins to dread the experience of having attacks and often develops anticipatory anxiety. This can result not only in increased incidence of panic attacks but also to phobic avoidance or fears of leaving home, being alone, or being trapped in public, such as when shopping in a supermarket or attending a theatre, with no escape. The more anxious individuals become, the likelier they are to have repeated panic attacks.

When events at the workplace trigger panic attacks, anticipatory anxiety may cause significant work impairment. Examples of debilitating anticipatory anxiety and panic attacks triggered by common workplace situations include interpersonal confrontations, public speaking, airline travel, and attending meetings where the individual feels physically trapped (Stein & Hollander, 2003). The symptoms of panic attacks, even without agoraphobia, may lead to severe disability and demoralization. Individuals may begin to use substances such as alcohol to obtain relief. Although suicide is often associated with mood disorders, people with severe panic disorders also have a high incidence of suicide due to despair over the quality of their lives and their unremitting anxiety (Stein & Hollander, 2003).

Panic disorder symptoms can result in work avoidance, withdrawal, and may result in complete work disability in severe cases. In one study, individuals with panic disorder were 10 times more likely to be unable to work owing to emotional problems than a control group with no current psychiatric diagnosis (Roy-Byrne et al., 1999). Approximately 60% of the panic patients in this study had at least 1 day in which they could not carry out their normal activities in comparison with less than 30% of the control group without any current psychiatric diagnosis.

OCD, a disorder characterized by recurrent obsessions or compulsions, can be one of the most disabling of all psychiatric disorders. People with OCD may experience significant impairment in functioning in every sphere of life, including the workplace. Some individuals with severe OCD function well in their daily lives but generally they must exert significant effort to compensate for their unusual behaviors or irrational thinking. Compulsions involving ritualized behavior can impair workplace performance; repetitive obsessive thoughts can impair attention and concentration. OCD symptoms often fluctuate and may be exacerbated by both personal and workplace stresses (Stein & Hollander, 2003).

One of the most disabling symptoms of OCD is inflexibility in thinking or behavior. Research has identified deficits in executive function especially with respect to flexibility on tasks requiring set shifting. Individuals with OCD do not change strategies when demands or rules of a task change and often have difficulty in set-shifting between tasks, that is, responding to changes in rules (Anderson & Savage, 2004). Neuropsychological testing has demonstrated subtle but potentially severe cognitive difficulties that support the frequently observed impairment associated with inflexibility (Anderson & Savage, 2004). Some studies of patients with OCD have found deficits associated with the ability to use high-level oversight functions to modulate memory, sensory information, cognition, and affect as a situation evolves, and the ability to shift strategies to maintain performance. Workers with OCD may have rigid ideas or approaches that persist inappropriately (Stein & Hollander, 2003). In some instances, an individual is unable to redirect focus or change strategies to accomplish a goal.

In some cases, OCD affects work indirectly. For example, going through checking routines before leaving home may result in chronically arriving late to work. In other cases, symptoms will affect job performance more directly, as discussed above. Even in the absence of problems with adapting to maintain performance, a person with OCD may check work over and over again and be unable to move on to the next task. Slowness, secondary to indecisiveness, the need to achieve a "perfect" result, or to achieve a result in a specific manner also impair work functioning. This slowness may include intrusive and perseverative features (Anderson & Savage, 2004).

GAD is a chronic and severe form of anxiety. Individuals with GAD worry excessively and are emotionally aroused most of the time. This worry exceeds a pathological threshold in its pervasiveness, intensity, and invasion into other domains including cognitive efficiency, a physical sense of well-being, ability to sleep, or interact socially. The symptoms of this type of anxiety disorder fall broadly into two categories: apprehensive anxiety and worry and physical symptoms. Individuals with GAD are constantly worried over trivial matters, fearful, and anticipating the worst. Difficulty in concentrating, irritability, insomnia, and fatigue are typical signs of generalized anxiety (Stein & Hollander, 2003).

GAD is a highly impairing condition that results in reduction in work productivity. Impairments associated with GAD are equivalent in magnitude to impairments associated with major depressive disorder, even after adjusting for other comorbid disorders (Kessler et al., 1999). Individuals with GAD are significantly more likely to report high levels of social role and work impairment and to perceive their mental health as fair to poor when compared to respondents without the disorder. Individuals with this disorder experience a significant number of days they are limited and even completely unable to perform everyday activities. Chronic and daily symptoms such as restlessness, fatigability, and difficulty in concentrating may interfere with productivity (Stein & Hollander, 2003). They also experience associated reductions in quality of life and well-being (Wittchen, Carter, Pfister, Montgomery, & Kessler, 2000).

PTSD can also lead to substantial functional impairment. This disorder is comprise of a characteristic set of symptoms that occur after a psychologically traumatic event. The traumatic stressor involves actual or threatened bodily harm and the immediate response involves feelings of fear, terror, or helplessness. The characteristic symptoms include reexperiencing the event, avoidance of the stimuli associated with the event or psychic numbing, and symptoms of increased arousal.

Some PTSD patients develop lifelong severe symptoms with exacerbations and remissions that make employment and interpersonal relationships difficult to maintain (Pro, 2005). Individuals with PTSD have higher unemployment rates and struggle with frequent family and interpersonal difficulties. More chronic forms of the disorder have impairments equivalent to those of individuals with diagnoses of other serious mental illnesses, sometimes including chronic psychotic disorders (Kimble & Kaufman, 2004).

Any of the symptoms of PTSD may be severe enough to interfere with work capacity. For example, poor concentration as a result of intrusive recollection may preclude the ability to follow instructions or to keep up a work pace (Pro, 2005). Difficulties in concentration and performance as well as strained interpersonal relations can develop from excessive arousal and psychic numbing (Stein & Hollander, 2003). Situations reminiscent of the original trauma may be systematically avoided. If PTSD arises from a workplace injury, avoidance of work may be a significant problem that can be particularly disabling (Pro, 2005; Stein & Hollander, 2003). Other symptoms of PTSD that may interfere with functioning include irritability and explosive anger, difficulty in concentrating, hypervigilance, anxiety, panic attacks, shame, and rage (Hollander & Simeon, 2003).

Even a disorder as circumscribed and focussed as simple or social phobia can be a highly disabling. Social phobia is a chronic and potentially highly impairing condition. More than half of patients with this disorder report significant impairment in some area(s) of their lives, independent of their degree of social support (Hollander & Simeon, 2003). Persons with social phobias have been found to be impaired on a broad spectrum of measures, ranging from dropping out of school to significant workplace disability (Hollander & Simeon, 2003).

Individuals who have only limited social fears or phobias may function well overall and be relatively asymptomatic unless confronted with the necessity of entering their phobic situation. In the workplace, social anxiety disorder may lead to minimal impairment if the feared situation is avoidable. However, avoidance of the feared situation may limit career advancement. If unable to avoid the feared situation, they are often subject to intense anticipatory anxiety, which can escalate to a panic attack. Typical circumstances that may result in anxiety, panic attacks, and attendant impairment are performance situations (speaking, eating, or writing in public) and social interactions (attending meetings, group discussions, or giving interviews). If the worker has multiple phobias, anxiety and avoidance can lead to chronic demoralization, social isolation, and disabling vocational and interpersonal impairment (Hollander & Simeon, 2003; Stein & Hollander, 2003).

As with affective disorders, treatment for anxiety encompasses both medication and various psychotherapeutic interventions, including cognitive and behavioral therapy. Some anxiety disorders, such as panic attacks and phobias, respond well to treatment. Antianxiety medications allow some patients to function without any impairment at all. Some disorders, such as OCD and severe cases of GAD and PTSD, are more refractory to treatment, whether with medication or therapy, and despite treatment, individuals may have chronic and even disabling impairments. In these disorders as well as other disorders, medication effects may play a role in the types of deficits seen in some studies of impairment associated with various psychiatric disorders (Anderson & Savage, 2004).

Substance Use and Dependence

Substance use can lead to psychiatric disability and psychiatric disability can contribute to chronic substance use (Cohen & Hanbury, 1987). A complete discussion of the effects of all the various types of substance use and dependence disorders alone or on underlying psychiatric illness and work functioning is beyond the scope of this review. In short, the effect of substance use on social and/or occupational function may include disturbed social relations, failure to meet important obligations, erratic or impulsive behavior, inappropriate expression of hostility, legal problems, or decreased productivity (Cohen & Hanbury, 1987).

Numerous epidemiologic surveys and clinical studies consistently indicate that mood and anxiety disorders are strongly associated with substance use disorders, a finding replicated across international studies (Compton, Thomas, Stinson, & Grant, 2007; el-Guebaly et al., 2007). One study (Kessler & Frank, 1997) found that mood and anxiety disorders and substance dependence were associated with work-specific disability and impaired functioning. The presence of more than one disorder including substance use was associated with the highest prevalence of functional impairment (el-Guebaly et al., 2007), consistent with findings in other studies of similar issues.

Any or all of the substance use or dependence disorders can create work impairment. For example, alcohol use is associated with a clear and consistent pattern of general cognitive deficits, the highest risks of which are imposed by frequent consumption of large quantities of alcohol rather than lifetime consumption (Vik, Cellucci, Jarchow, & Hedt, 2004). Heavy alcohol consumption is associated with global neurophysiological changes. Acute effects of moderate drinking include impaired immediate learning and subsequent retrieval of information learned while intoxicated. Deficits in perceptual-motor abilities, abstract reasoning, and nonverbal learning and memory can persist for months or years, even after cessation of alcohol use. Deficits in other skills such as processing speed, novel problem solving, and new learning are slowest to resolve, and functioning may not fully return to previous levels despite abstinence.

Polydrug-abusing individuals exhibit a pattern of neuropsychological deficits similar to alcohol use. In one study, the number of substances for which the individuals met dependence criteria, in addition to alcohol use variables, was related to measures of executive functioning and psychomotor speed (Vik et al., 2004). Polydrug use may have more substantive impact because of multiple assaults to the brain. These researchers found that by the time polydrug users entered treatment, between one-third and one-half had impairments in attention, encoding new information, cognitive flexibility, and problem solving (Vik et al., 2004).

Comorbidity

Psychiatric disorders rarely occur in isolation. Many people suffer from more than one psychiatric disorder at a given time. Nearly half (45%) of those with any psychiatric disorder meet criteria for two or more disorders, with severity of illness strongly related to comorbidity (National Institutes of Mental Health, 2007). Depression and anxiety, two of the most common disorders found in the workplace, are common coexisting disorders. Substance use in particular frequently occurs with serious mental illness and worsens the disease course (Corrigan et al., 2007).

In one large epidemiological study of psychiatric illness (Kessler, Chiu, et al., 2005), more than 40% of the cases reported demonstrated comorbidity of psychiatric conditions. Another study (Merikangas et al., 2007b) found that 92.3% of individuals with any type of bipolar disorder had lifetime comorbidity with other Axis I disorders. The most common comorbid disorder with bipolar disorder was anxiety disorders (74.9%). Substance use disorders were also significantly comorbid, at a rate of 42.3% for any type of substance use and 39.1% for alcohol use alone.

Psychiatric disorders also commonly exist comorbidly with medical conditions. For example, depression is commonly found in individuals who have a number of general medical conditions, including dementia and other neurodegenerative diseases, coronary artery disease, cancer, diabetes, fibromyalgia, chronic fatigue syndrome, rheumatoid arthritis, and migraine headaches (Pro, 2005).

Comorbidity increases the likelihood of experiencing impairments that result in work disability. Even when any one condition alone might not create disabling impairments, the presence of two such conditions has a synergistic effect, increasing impairment and decreasing the ability to cope effectively with those impairments. In one large study, comorbidity involving at least one disorder in at least two of the three categories of affective, anxiety, and substance use disorders was associated with larger average numbers of work loss days (49 per month per 100 workers) and work cutback days (346 per month per 100 workers) than any single disorder (Kessler & Frank, 1997). In another large epidemiological study, severity of illness, where one of the measures of severity was work impairment, was strongly related to comorbidity (See Table 4.3).

Table 4.3 Prevalence and effect of comorbidity on severity of psychiatric disorders*

	Lifetime prevalence (%)	12-month prevalence (%)	Serious severity	Moderate severity	Mild severity
Any disorder	46.4	26.2	22.3	37.3	40.4
One disorder		14.4	9.6	31.2	59.2
Two disorders	27.7	5.8	25.5	46.4	28.2
Three or more disorders	17.3	6.0	49.9	43.1	7.0

*Severity based on 12-month prevalence.
Kessler, Chiu, et al. (2005) and Kessler, Berglund, et al. (2005).

In one study (Dewa et al., 2007) examining the interaction of work stress, physical illness, and psychiatric illness on disability, the proportion of individuals with a disability day grew as the combinations of conditions increased from no condition to the co-occurrence of a psychiatric disorder, a chronic physical condition, and chronic work stress. Comorbid psychiatric disorders and chronic physical conditions were more disabling than either condition alone. Workers in this study reporting both conditions were between a third to nearly twice as likely to report disability days than workers with either condition alone (Dewa et al., 2007).

Other studies have borne out these findings in relation to specific comorbidities. For example, one group of researchers (Druss et al., 2000) found that comorbid anxiety and depression were associated with the largest number of work loss days, and comorbid anxiety–depression, anxiety–substance use, and anxiety–depression–substance use were associated with the largest average numbers of work cutback days. In another study (Wittchen et al., 2000), more than 50% of respondents with GAD and no major depression, and more than 30% of those with major depression and no GAD, reported some reduction in activity. When the major depression and GAD occurred together, 23% of the respondents with comorbid GAD and major depression experienced reductions of at least 50% in their past month's activities.

As noted, the degree of impairment and disability associated with a variety of psychiatric disorders is more severe than that associated with some common chronic medical conditions. However, comorbidity of psychiatric and medical disorders can result in even more pronounced disability. Numerous studies have found that the effects of depressive symptoms and medical conditions on functioning are additive (Wells et al., 1989). One group of researchers found that for those with both mental and general medical disabilities, combined deficits associated with work impairment are the rule rather than the exception (Druss et al., 2000). In this study, 72.5% of individuals in this category reported having social difficulty and 53.5% reported difficulty with various types of cognitive function.

Mental disorders are also more strongly associated with some work disability outcomes when they are accompanied by chronic pain. When a mood disorder was present with a physical condition such as chronic back pain, the number of work days lost was greater than the sum of days lost associated with each condition alone (Braden, Zhang, Zimmerman, & Sullivan, 2008). Comorbidity of psychiatric disorders, substance use disorders, and chronic pain is also common and contributes to overall disability. In one study, rates of chronic back or neck pain were 29.3% among individuals who met criteria for any psychiatric disorder in the past 12 months, 34.5% among those with a mood disorder, 31.4%, among those with an anxiety disorder, and 23.4% among those with a substance use disorder (Von Korff et al., 2005).

Conclusion

Whether an exacerbation of a preexisting disorder or a new onset disorder, psychiatric disorders can result in symptoms that impair workplace functioning in specific, definable ways. Disability and disability-related evaluations require assessments of impairments associated with psychiatric disorders and symptoms and should focus on available data indicating the types of social, behavioral, and cognitive deficits that may impair work performance. Research data describe large numbers of individuals. Although employment evaluations are focused on only one individual, the research data can guide mental health professional in exploring both the types of possible impairments associated with diagnoses and symptoms.

Diagnostic labels, although often used to organize research data and clinical treatment, should be used carefully and cautiously in disability and disability-related evaluations. Not all disorders result in impairments and disability and not all problems with work performance are associated with an underlying psychiatric diagnosis. The symptoms and associated impairments in an individual with a psychiatric diagnosis are significantly more important than the diagnostic label alone. In any evaluation, clinicians should ask whether a diagnosis is relevant, and if so, how.

In addition, evaluators should bear in mind that the evaluee's internal state, that is, the meaning of work to that individual and the individual's mental status, is only one half of the equation in an employment evaluation. The other half is external circumstances, such as job requirements, social or family problems unrelated to the workplace, or changes in employment conditions, such as new job responsibilities, transfers, promotions, or change in supervisors.

Conclusion

These external factors interact with the internal factors in a powerful and dynamic relationship that generally is the focus of the employee's disability and disability-related issues. The next chapter will provide guidelines for assessment of both internal and external factors in any given individual to assist evaluators in understanding this complex and dynamic relationship.

Chapter 5
Psychiatric Disability: A Model for Assessment

Introduction

The inability to work as a result of psychiatric illness, whether temporary or permanent, is a serious crisis. Occupational disability can become a chronic and treatment-resistant psychosocial condition. People who become disabled lose self-esteem, become discouraged, hopeless, and deconditioned, making the prospect of returning to work increasingly challenging. The longer an individual is unable to work, the less likely it is that he or she will be able to return to work.

The journey from unimpaired or impaired but able to work, to impaired and disabled is complicated, difficult, painful, and unique to every individual who has the misfortune to travel that road. Individuals who have been able to work rarely become disabled overnight due to psychiatric illness. The dynamic relationship between the internal and external factors that result in work impairment involves a process that is far from straightforward and takes time to develop.

Understanding the progression and process that ultimately results in a claimant seeking benefits for disability status, a label with a negative stigma (see Chapter 1), is critical to any type of disability evaluation.

This understanding allows mental health professionals to develop a case formulation explaining current circumstances, symptoms, symptom presentation, and implications for current and future functioning. Mental health professionals are not typically trained to understand the process of disability development or to think of disability evaluations in terms of case formulation. Guidelines for providing assessments of impairment and the requirements for eligibility for specific types of disability benefits programs are reviewed in subsequent chapters. However, before individuals are referred for mental disability evaluations, they must perceive themselves as disabled and apply for benefits or accommodations.

Therefore, although psychiatrists and psychologists are not the final arbiters of disability determinations, they should understand and develop a case formulation to explain the complex relationship between impairment and disability and the processes by which individuals come to see themselves as disabled.

98   5 Psychiatric Disability: A Model for Assessment

This understanding facilitates answering many of the questions involved in a disability or disability-related evaluation. This chapter provides a discussion of one model or conceptualizing the process of disability development. This model utilizes the concepts of work capacity and takes into consideration all the factors discussed in previous chapters in the dynamic balance between a functional and nonfunctional work status.

Disability: A Psychological Process

A broad spectrum of people apply for disability benefits on the basis of psychiatric illness, ranging from those with profound work impairments to individuals who are malingering,[1] from blue-collar workers to CEOs, and from hourly wage workers to salaried professionals. Most individuals with psychiatric disorders who become disabled or who perceive themselves to be disabled have reached that point after a process involving many factors in addition to psychiatric symptoms. Retrospective assessment of individuals who have reached a point where they apply for disability benefits demonstrates different patterns of development of disability. The balance and progression toward disability depend on the nature of the disorder, the job requirements, and the many other factors discussed in previous chapters.

Most people who claim disability benefits believe they are entitled to them. Many claimants report that their doctors or therapists told them they could not work anymore. In the majority of cases involving psychiatric disorders, the opposite is true: individuals typically inform their doctors they can no longer work. Self-declared disability is more common than is recognized (Brodsky, 1996b).

Few treatment providers will challenge their patients' self-assessment of disability unless there is overwhelming evidence to the contrary. A mental health treatment provider's opinion that an individual is disabled or, conversely, is ready to return to work, is often informed more by the worker's opinion than by the mental health professional's considered assessment. As discussed in Chapter 1, clinicians often do not have the time to explore the complexities of their patients' work conflicts and generally lack the necessary information to make an objective determination of impaired work capacity based on psychiatric symptoms.

In addition, challenging the patient's perception may result in disrupting the treatment alliance, a risk that many clinicians are not willing to take. Thus, when asked, most clinicians will write notes or sign forms documenting a patient' claims. Unfortunately, doing so reinforces the patient's beliefs regarding the severity of his or her impairments and allows the

---

[1] Malingering in disability claims is discussed in Chapter 6.

patient to adopt a passive position regarding the decision to stop working by saying it was the doctor's decision.

Although often self-imposed, accepting the label "disabled" has multiple psychological and practical consequences involving issues of self-esteem, status, stigma, and social relationships. As a result, the process of regarding oneself as impaired enough to be disabled and to apply for disability benefits is almost always accompanied by emotional turmoil and psychological distress. These complicated psychological reactions may include anger, entitlement, regression, and denial.

The Relationship Between Impairment and Disability

As discussed in Chapter 4, the terms "disability" and "impairment" are often used interchangeably. Nevertheless, they are not synonyms and represent two different, albeit related, concepts. Impairment, as discussed, is "a significant deviation, loss, or loss of use of any body structure or body function in an individual with a health condition, disorder or disease" (American Medical Association, 2008, p. 5). Impairment constitutes an observational description that should be measurable in some way and related to a health condition. In contrast, disability is "activity limitations and/or participation restrictions in an individual with a health condition, disorder, or disease" (American Medical Association, 2008, p. 5).

The relationship between impairment and disability is difficult, if not impossible, to predict. Some individuals may become disabled even when experiencing only mild impairments; others may experience severe impairments and not become disabled at all. "In some conditions there is a strong association between level of injury and degree of functional loss.... The same level of injury is in no way predictive of an affected individual's ability to participate in major life functions (including work) when appropriate motivation, technology, and sufficient accommodations are available" (American Medical Association, 2008, pp. 5–6).

Even the most profoundly impaired individuals may maintain remarkable productivity in their own occupations. For example, Stephen Hawking, Franklin Roosevelt, Christopher Reeve, and Ludwig von Beethoven overcame catastrophic impairments as the result of injury or disease. We can only assume that the psychological and emotional implications of accepting a disabled status were so unacceptable to these individuals that they made the extraordinarily difficult commitment to find a way to continue functioning in their chosen professions. Individuals who are able to do this often have considerable psychological resources, social support, resiliency, and adaptational capacities.

The same is true of individuals with sometimes severe psychiatric disorders. The presence of a psychiatric diagnosis does not automatically imply any significant or specific functional impairment, and functional impairment, when present, does not necessarily result in disability. As noted in Chapter 4, many individuals with severe or chronic psychiatric disorders continue to function productively at high levels in their chosen professions.

Current research validates the observations that many people with psychiatric impairments are often capable of continuing to work productively. For example, some individuals diagnosed with depression may never experience significant functional impairment because the symptoms do not interfere with occupational skills or because medication successfully manages their symptoms. What research on this subject is available has found little relationship between psychiatric signs and symptoms identified in a mental status examination and the ability to perform competitive work (American Medical Association, 2008).

The lack of a clear or direct relationship between signs and symptoms of psychiatric illness and the ability to work is not surprising. Psychiatric disorders demonstrate differential patterns of impairment and disability. The complexity of the relationships between psychiatric impairment, activity limitations, participation, and productivity are further complicated by the fact that none of these factors are linear or unidirectional. Activity limitations and participation restrictions are not static, and may vary over time as a result of numerous physical and psychological factors (American Medical Association, 2008).

In addition, the presence of some areas of psychiatric impairment does not necessarily indicate or imply an impaired capacity to perform other occupational tasks and functions. An individual with bipolar disorder might be restricted from working excessive irregular night hours. This might be disabling for a solo practitioner obstetrician but may not represent any significant problem for an office-based dermatologist. An individual with a phobia about elevators may be able to perform adequately as long as he or she works on the ground floor. Tasks that require the use of elevators might result in a disability (Enelow, 1988).

As discussed throughout this book, patterns of development of disability involve the dynamic balance between internal factors unique to the individual and external factors that affect the individual's ability to work. The balance may fluctuate in breadth and severity at different points in a person's lifetime depending on internal and external changes or circumstances. For example, an individual with depression may have a history of functioning well even when experiencing symptoms which cause impairments. When a social problem, such as the loss of a significant relationship, occurs, this individual may lose the ability to function in the workplace as a result of the combination of the impairments and distress over the loss.

Thus, a worker's decision to withdraw from the workplace, opt for a disability status, and apply for benefits may be the solution to social, employment, or psychological conflicts that have little do with impairment due to psychiatric illness, even if an illness is present. For example, an individual nearing retirement experiencing conflict with a new supervisor may find the emotional conflict associated with making the decision to apply for a disability retirement less difficult than that of continuing to work with the new supervisor. The employee may have a history of psychiatric disorder, such as depression, and may be experiencing more emotional distress due to the work conflict.

However, the actual level of impairment associated with depression may not have changed; rather, the individual may misattribute current emotional distress to the preexisting diagnosis and claim that the depression has worsened to the point where he or she is now disabled.

Alternatively, decisions to withdraw from the workplace through a claim of disability may be influenced by social or personal circumstances. A working individual with overwhelming family and social obligations, such as child care, single parenthood, or caring for ill or aging relatives, may also experience mounting emotional stress and distress. If such individuals have preexisting psychiatric disorders, such as depression or anxiety, their social or personal circumstances may exacerbate psychiatric symptoms such as anxiety, depressed mood, or irritability, but may not necessarily cause additional or new impairment. Nevertheless, withdrawal from the workplace by claiming disability and collecting benefits may resolve the practical conflicts and emotional distress caused by their difficult personal circumstances.

Some individuals, for whom a disabled status is extremely distressful, may attempt to avoid disengaging from work even if continuing to work aggravates or irreparably harms the underlying condition. Sadly however, many people find it psychologically less difficult to adopt the position that they cannot work due to illness rather than acknowledge they are withdrawing from the workplace because of internal or external conflict. Paid employment is such a highly valued and socially significant activity that in the absence of a retirement status (which implies a history of a productive work), many people cannot bring themselves to admit that it is too painful to work or they do not want to work. This reluctance may be present even if individuals have valuable and productive social and family commitments that take up most of their time or if they are financially secure enough not to need paid employment.

Similarly, some claimants may find it less distressing to claim inability to work based on psychiatric illness rather than acknowledge that they no longer like or can tolerate the stress of their job. If they acknowledge that they dislike their job circumstances, then they must acknowledge they bear the burden of seeking new employment, a difficult, stressful, and anxiety-provoking task. Many of these individuals are experiencing job stress or burnout as discussed in Chapter 1. They often genuinely mistake their emotional state for disorders such as depression. In addition, such individuals may be able to meet dependency or entitlement needs by receiving disability payments or adopting a "sick" role.

Work Capacity: Supply, Demand, and Domains of Function

Understanding the process by which individuals come to consider themselves disabled is central to the evaluation of disability and is a prerequisite to addressing the questions posed in disability evaluations. One model for understanding the development of disability, regardless of underlying psychiatric causes, work issues, or personal or social circumstances, utilizes the concept of work capacity as an assessment of the balance between work supply and work demand (Battista, 1988). Supply is defined as the individual's functional capacity and demand as job requirements. Individuals have adequate work capacity if their supply of functional capacity exceeds the minimum capacity required to meet job demands, that is, when functional capacity exceeds the demand. Disability occurs when supply does not exceed demand.

The relationship between job demands and work supply is essential in understanding the functional impact that impairment has on a person's ability to perform the tasks associated with a specific job. Work supply and demand assessments are not traditional mental health concepts. Fortunately, they translate into a series of assessments that are more familiar to mental health professionals. These involve understanding and appreciation of

1. work demand, that is, job description;
2. work supply, that is, previous and current performance and employment history;
3. possible decreased work supply due to mental health issues, that is, current diagnosis, symptoms, impairments, and treatment; and
4. possible decreased work supply due to nonmental health issues, such as personal, social, or work circumstances.

The analysis of changes in an individual's work capacity based on work supply and demand requires the type of longitudinal assessment also familiar to mental health professionals. Although ordinarily an essential aspect of an evaluation, the results of a single interview cannot provide enough information to understand a dynamic process that unfolds over time and involves many variables, especially since an individual's level of functioning may vary considerably over time and in different circumstances. The information needed for the analysis of the above issues can come from a variety of sources (as discussed in detail in Chapter 6). The significance of the information in the assessment of impairment and disability and the development of a case formulation are discussed below.

Work Demand: The Job Description

Mental health professionals should understand the relevant work skills and demands of a particular job in order to provide a meaningful opinion on the issue of work capacity relative to a specific job. They must therefore have an understanding of the essential functional requirements of the job, the evaluee's understanding of those demands, and how the employee performs those tasks. Without a detailed job description, determining whether work capacity exceeds or falls below work demand is not possible.

A typical job description may not be sufficient. Often a more detailed function-oriented job analysis is essential.

The essential functions of a job encompass more than can be communicated in a written job description. For example, evaluation of work demands should also consider the physical and mental demands that arise not only from the job tasks but also from physical working conditions such as noise, office space, or frequency of travel (Battista, 1988). Work demands can be conceptualized as involving four intersecting domains: physical, cognitive, affective, and social (see Table 5.1) (Leclair & Leclair, 2001).

Table 5.1 Work demand domains

Physical
Type of physical exertion
Degree of physical exertion
Physical endurance requirements
Work environment factors: noise, light, space, etc.

Cognitive
Intellectual, aptitude, and ability requirements
Memory requirements
Insight and judgment
Problem-solving skills
Ability to attend and follow directions
Ability to work independently
Attention and concentration requirements

Affective
General mood and consistency with expectations in the work environment
Affective response to general job or work-site requirements
Affective response to stressful events and changes in job or work-site requirements
Affective response to interaction with customers, coworkers, and supervisors

Social
Ability to work with a group or team
Ability to supervise others and to be supervised
Ability to maintain working relationships in the workplace
Ability to respond appropriately to public or customers

Adapted from Leclair and Leclair (2001).

In addition, evaluators should understand whether the demands of the job have changed. For example, promotions may result in increased job responsibilities. Layoffs or reductions in force can result in increased workloads as well as in increased job stress and decreased morale. Finally, the interaction between a psychiatric disorder and functional abilities can be influenced by physical changes in the environment, such as relocation from an enclosed office space with a window and a door, even if shared with a few others, to an open, cubicle environment with no privacy, no direct light, increased noise, and visual distractions.

Work Supply: Performance and Employment History

The assessment of an individual's baseline work supply requires a review of performance and employment history. These may provide historical evidence of high or low work functioning. Documented performance problems, frequent job transfer or turnover, or the implementation of performance improvement plans in more than one job might support a pattern of long-term functional impairments and a historically low work supply regardless of job demands. Long-term stable employment, consistent promotions and raises, and consistently good performance evaluations would support a pattern of relatively high work supply. Because the workplace itself may be a significant source of stress, if individuals have attempted to withdraw from the workplace but then tried to return, examiners should look for evidence of repeated deterioration upon the claimant's return to work.

Assessment of work supply also requires assessment of the ability of a number of work-related functions. In addition to specific tasks unique to any job, certain basic work skills must be available. These parallel the physical, cognitive, affective, and social domains listed above in Table 5.1. Many work tasks involve more than one domain of functioning. Therefore, the assessment of these domains can be combined and reviewed as certain general work abilities (see Table 5.2). These fall into two broad categories: individual functions that typically do not have a social or interpersonal component and functions that by their nature require social capacities.

Table 5.2 General work abilities

Individual functions
The ability to complete a normal workday or work week
The ability to perform simple and repetitive tasks
The ability to perform complex or varied tasks.
The ability to maintain a work pace appropriate to a given work load
The ability to accept and carry out responsibility for direction, control, and planning
The ability to handle routine or customary work stressors or pressures
The ability to handle more than routine or customary work stressors or pressures
The ability to work without supervision

Functions with significant social component
The ability to respond appropriately to supervision
The ability to get along with coworkers
The ability to supervise others
The ability to interact appropriately with the public, customers, client or others who enter the workplace.

Adapted from Enelow (1988) and Lasky (1993).

Evaluators should consider, for example, whether individuals have the ability to complete a normal workday or week, or to report to work on time and stay at work, with no unnecessary absences. The ability to perform complex tasks includes the ability to make generalizations, evaluations, or decisions without immediate supervision. Individuals must be able to follow precise details and use higher powers of attention and concentration and organizational ability. Evaluators should also assess whether individuals can handle routine work pressures, such as meeting normal deadlines, and whether they can handle more than routine or customary work stressors or pressures, such as working overtime or covering the responsibilities of others as well as doing their own job in the event of a work shortage. Evaluators should also be aware that the ability to work without supervision, to think independently, make decisions, and initiate and carry through self-directed activities are higher order work functions present in numerous jobs and always present in managerial positions.

Work functions that involve social and interpersonal skills require communication skills as well as basic empathy in dealing with others. Evaluators should consider whether an individual can accept and respond appropriately to routine supervisory comments, performance evaluations, and constructive criticism. Many jobs require a joint effort for completion of a task. In such jobs, individuals have to be able to communicate with and respond appropriately to fellow workers. The ability to supervise others requires the ability to delegate responsibility in an appropriate manner and direct other individuals who operate in support roles (Lasky, 1993). Many jobs also require the ability to interact appropriately with the general public, customers, or clients. This ability is critical in public service jobs, health care jobs, retail jobs, and many others.

Another method of assessing work functioning is used by the Social Security Administration (SSA). The SSA suggests that assessment considers four main categories of functioning (42 USC §405):

1. the ability to perform activities of daily living;
2. social functioning;
3. concentration, persistence, and pace; and
4. deterioration or decompensation in work or a work-like setting.

These categories are based on functional areas thought to be relevant to work, and the SSA provides multiple examples for each category (see Chapter 7). Although some of these are not directly related to work functioning, it is unlikely that individuals would be able to function effectively in a workplace if their psychiatric impairments are so severe that, for example, they are unable to maintain grooming and hygiene.

The ability to perform activities of daily living and social functioning are routinely assessed in any mental health evaluation. The two areas that may be less familiar to mental health professionals are the ability to maintain concentration, persistence, and pace, and repeated episodes of deterioration or decompensation in work or work-like settings. The information needed for these assessments typically goes beyond what can be gleaned from a personal interview with the evaluee and requires the type of collateral information discussed above and in Chapter 6.

One limitation to the SSA's model arises from the SSA's goal of determining whether an individual is capable of performing any gainful work (see Chapter 7).

The SSA categories and their applications are geared toward an assessment of permanent impairment, utilizing an all or none model. They are therefore limited in their applicability and usefulness in cases in which the impairment is temporary or partial. Because of this, the SSA categories do not lend themselves to devising the kind of balanced assessment possible utilizing a supply and demand model. The supply/demand equation allows evaluators to consider the pattern of development of a disability, consider temporary or partial disability, and potentially, how to minimize work demand or maximize work capacity to help regain function.

Assessment of work supply alone does not address other significant issues. For example, as reviewed above, long-term impairment of work capacity and supply may be due to factors other than an Axis I psychiatric diagnosis. Changes in an individual's motivation to work can occur at any time regardless of history of work supply and previous levels of work capacity (see discussion below). A high baseline work supply does not necessarily indicate the absence of any impairments or psychiatric disorders; it may just as easily reflect extraordinary adaptational skills or profound work commitment. At times, individuals with impairments will sacrifice other areas of functioning, such as social or family functioning, to maintain work supply due to prioritizing work functioning. Nevertheless, evaluators cannot assess changes in functional capacity without a good understanding of the evaluee's baseline work supply.

Decreased Work Supply: Diagnosis, Symptoms, Impairments, and Treatment

As noted, impairments may or may not affect work supply. Evaluators should understand the evaluee's claimed psychiatric diagnosis, associated impairments (see Chapter 4), and what kind of treatment, if any, the claimant is receiving. Evaluators should consider the effects of medication, past and present, on the individual's functioning. Some individuals may be able to sustain a satisfactory degree of functioning on medication, but be unable to function if not on medication. Some individuals may demonstrate impaired functioning due to psychiatric disorders even on medication or due to the effects of medication.

A history of stable work demands but exacerbation of psychiatric disorder, aggressively treated with medication and therapy without significant response would indicate a possible decline in work supply due to psychiatric illness alone. A history of stable symptoms, minimal or no impairment, and good response to treatment but onset of impaired functioning in the event of new social stressors raises issues that may focus more on the role of nonwork-related factors affecting work capacity. In addition, as discussed above, the presence of some areas of psychiatric impairment does not necessarily indicate or imply an impaired ability to perform other occupational tasks and functions.

Decreased Work Supply: Personal and Social Circumstances

Any of a myriad of nonvocational social, personal, or family circumstances can result in stresses or changes in symptoms which result in increased stress or decreased motivation to work and thus decreased work supply. An individual with a psychiatric disorder and adequate although impaired functioning may be especially vulnerable to a decrease in work supply if faced, for example, with divorce or with physical illness. Conversely, nonwork-related factors such as social support or care provided by a family member may support and increase work supply despite impairments caused by psychiatric disorder and nonwork-related stressors. Either way, these nonwork and nonpsychiatric factors figure prominently in any work supply/demand assessment. Personal and social factors are particularly significant in the discussion of disability-related questions such as motivation for treatment and rehabilitation, prognosis, and future ability to function.

Work Capacity Models: The Process and Patterns of Disability Development

The concept of work capacity can be utilized to conceptualize models of disability development. Work capacity represents the balance between work supply (or abilities) and work demand. Adequate work capacity indicates that an individual has enough work supply (ability) to meet current work demand. Adequate work capacity results whenever work supply exceeds work demand. This can occur in situations with high supply/high demand, high supply/low demand situations, or low supply/lower work demand. Inadequate work capacity results whenever work demand exceeds work supply.

The development of disability generally occurs over time, rather than suddenly. This means that over time, an individual's work capacity changes. Since work capacity depends on both work supply and work demand, changes in work capacity can be due to changes in either supply or demand. Symptoms of physical or mental illness can decrease work supply or ability. Job demand can be changed by increased work load, work conflict, or even relocation to a different work environment. Moreover, change in work capacity is not necessarily static: it demonstrates patterns of fluctuation over time, and may be temporary, rather than permanent. However, work capacity must fall below some minimal functional level for people to become so impaired that they consider themselves disabled.

Application of this work capacity assessment results in the projection of six prototypic models of disability development and patterns:

- change in work capacity due to sudden illness and impairment (Fig. 5.1);
- change in work capacity due to sudden illness and impairment with relatively rapid recovery to baseline (Fig. 5.2);

- increasing impairment and decreasing work capacity over time due to progression of illness (Fig. 5.3);
- cumulative effect of prior impaired function with new impairment resulting in decreased work capacity (Fig. 5.4);
- change in work demands outpacing change in work supply, resulting in decreased work capacity (Fig. 5.5); and
- repeated episodes of impairment with decreasing baseline work capacity between episodes (Fig. 5.6).

These models are stereotypical to some degree. Individuals may meet some of the features of one model at certain times, and others at another time, depending on circumstances. However, evaluators who utilize these models as a framework for understanding the development and pattern of disability in any given case will find that they facilitate developing a case formulation to describe the evaluee's present claim and circumstances. This in turn facilitates answering referral questions commonly posed in disability evaluations. It also can provide guidance in responding to questions regarding future work capacity, including prognosis, length of disability, return to work issues, restrictions, limitations, and accommodations.

Change in Work Capacity Due to Sudden Illness and Impairment

People often conceptualize the development of disability as the result of an injury or illness that occurs suddenly. In this model, these circumstances are described as decreased work capacity in a previously unimpaired individual, whose work supply falls below work demand even though threshold job requirements are stable. This pattern of disability development would occur, for example, when an otherwise adequately functioning person has a severe cardiac event, a stroke, or a serious accident, resulting in profound physical or neurological impairments.

Disability can also develop suddenly as a result of an acute psychiatric crisis. However, this pattern of psychiatric disability development is the least common. Consider, for example, the case of an individual with no previous psychiatric history who develops a first episode of mania as part of the onset of bipolar disorder. If this individual's symptoms include severely impaired attention, concentration, insomnia, and thought disorder, his or her work capacity might drop over a relatively short time from "enough" to "not enough" relative to the minimal functional capacity needed to satisfy work demand (Battista, 1988). Regardless of functional history, an individual with a relatively rapid onset of a first manic episode is unlikely to have developed adaptational skills to continue working effectively with the impairments commonly associated with a manic state. Even if the absence of adequate work capacity is temporary rather than permanent, this individual is likely to have the pattern of development of disability represented by Fig. 5.1.

```
Prior level of
unimpaired function
                    ↘
                      sudden injury or illness

------------------------+-------------------------------------
                        ↑ Minimum Required Functional Capacity


                        ↑ Available Functional Capacity
Time ──▶
                                    Adapted from Battista 1988
```

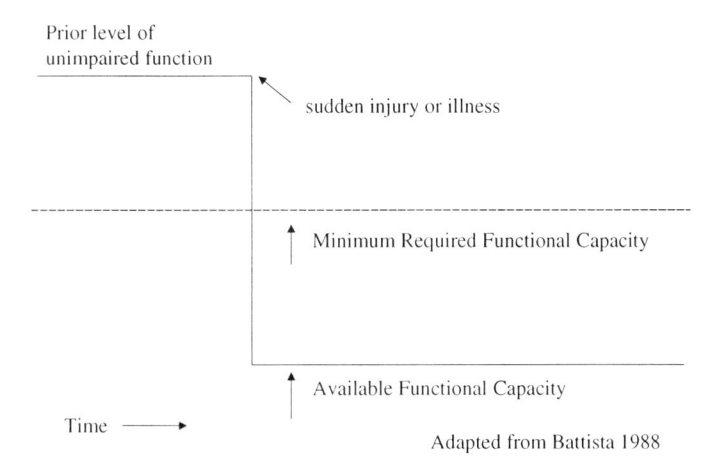

Fig. 5.1 Sudden Onset of Impairment Resulting in Disability

Change in Work Capacity Due to Sudden Illness and Impairment with Relatively Rapid Recovery to Baseline

If sudden psychiatric disability does occur, any number of outcomes may be seen. Hopefully, the outcome of such a sudden change in work capacity will be a relatively robust recovery with treatment to previous levels of functioning (see Fig. 5.2). In this case, the individual would have had a temporary disability and be able to return to previous job responsibilities.

The processes represented by Figs. 5.1 and 5.2 may recur throughout an individual's lifetime and represent periods of temporary disability followed by full recovery, with no change in baseline functioning when asymptomatic. Such outcomes are often seen, for example, with depressive episodes, recurrent episodes of anxiety, and even in bipolar disorder, particularly with successful treatment. In these cases, work demand is not a significant factor. Rather, work supply, primarily affected by symptoms of illness or possibly changes in personal, social, or medical circumstances, dictates work capacity.

Figures 5.1 and 5.2, however, are not representative of the development of more persistent, severe, or permanent psychiatric disorders and associated impairments that result in disability. Several other more common scenarios

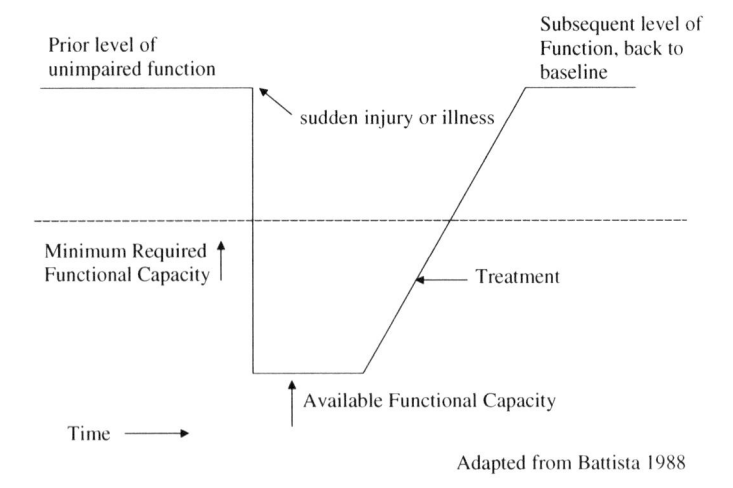

Fig. 5.2 Sudden Onset of Impairment with Full Recovery

that generally involve a combination of psychiatric and nonpsychiatric factors are more typical of these unfortunate patterns. For example, many psychiatric disorders have a gradual onset over months or years. Disability associated with these disorders often involves a slow or episodic rather than sudden loss of work capacity

Increasing Impairment and Decreasing Work Capacity over Time Due to Progression of Illness

When illness develops at a later age, after the acquisition of successful work skills, individuals with slow onset of illness often are able to successfully adapt their functioning to minimize the effects of impairments. For example, an individual who has struggled for much of her adult life with moderate depression may have had years of successful adaptation to associated impairments in work skills involving concentration, attention, or social withdrawal. Such an individual may never have lacked adequate work capacity despite chronic impairment. In the event of an acute episode of severe depression, this individual has years of adaptational coping skills upon which she can draw to try to avoid work demands outstripping work supply, resulting in a slower decline in work capacity.

However, impairments associated with new or exacerbated symptoms, such as the development of the lack of energy resulting in difficulty getting out of bed or severe insomnia, or external circumstances, such as a physical injury or loss of an important relationship, may result in an exacerbation with impairments severe enough so that work demands exceed work supply, resulting in decreased work capacity (see Fig. 5.3). Another example of the pattern in Fig. 5.3 is often

Figure

```
Prior level of
unimpaired function
              ← Onset of psychiatric illness

- - - - - - - - - - - - - - - - - - - - - - - - - - - - -
Minimum Required
Functional Capacity

                    Available Functional Capacity

Time ⟶                              Adapted from Battista 1988
```

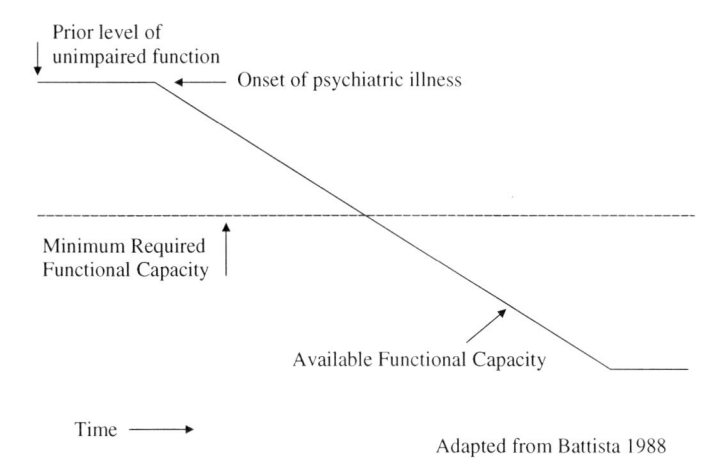

Fig. 5.3 Gradual Onset of Disability

seen with the onset of Alzheimer's dementia in later life in a high-level manager. Alzheimer's dementia develops slowly over time, resulting in incremental but progressive loss of work as well as in other capacities.

A line with a steady downward slope that eventually crosses below minimal required functional capacity depicts available functional capacity in the presence of gradual onset of increasing impairment. In reality, the slope of this line is far less consistent and predictable. Individuals whose symptoms worsen over time, or whose circumstances create additional obstacles to functioning, typically demonstrate a more stepwise pattern of decline. Nevertheless, the general slope of the line is negative, and at some point, crosses from adequate work capacity to inadequate work capacity and may not cross back again.

This pattern of disability development can be particularly heartbreaking. Individuals who function adequately or well for many years despite increasing impairment usually acquire complex work skills and years of successful and productive functioning. When their work capacity falls below the minimum level required to remain functional, they often suffer severe emotional difficulty in adapting to their decreased work capacities. For these individuals, gradual and incipient psychiatric illnesses may result in losses that are overtly threatening to their identity and psychological stability. Denial, anger, and projection of blame onto others are frequent psychological responses.

Cumulative Effect of Prior Impaired Function with New Impairment Resulting in Decreased Work Capacity

Another pattern of disability development occurs when an individual with a preexisting disorder and some impairments who is nevertheless functional develops a new psychiatric or psychosocial problem that overwhelms his or her ability to function (see Fig. 5.4). The preexisting condition and its associated impairments, combined with new comorbid psychiatric disorders or social problems, or increased work demands, might produce a greater impact on functional capacity than the sum of the impact expected from each disorder or stressor separately (see Chapter 4).

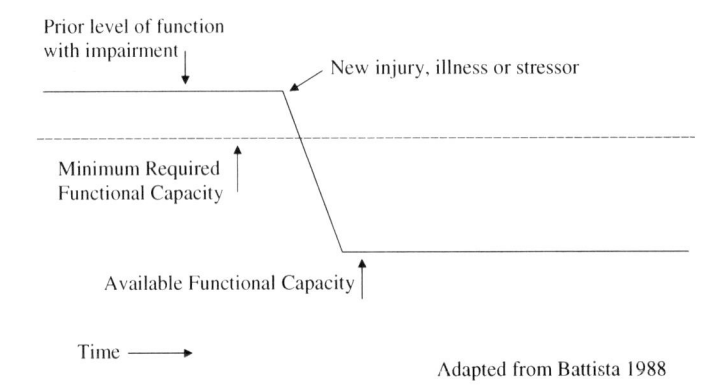

Fig. 5.4 Cumulative Effects of Prior Impairment with Additional Impairment

For example, an individual with impairments associated with anxiety and panic attacks may function despite impairments and have adequate work capacity. However, if this person develops another disorder, such as depression or alcohol abuse, common comorbid disorders, functioning may deteriorate below the minimum level required for employment. Alternatively, a severe psychosocial stressor, such as the loss of a significant relationship or serious illness in a family member, may destabilize the individual enough so that he or she is no longer be able to meet minimum functional work demands and therefore develops decreased work capacity.

This pattern of development of disability is more likely if the recent injury or illness directly affects the functional capacity the individual relied on to adapt to the prior impairment (Battista, 1988). For example, an individual with a severe anxiety disorder may have adequate work capacity as long as he gets enough sleep. If he or she develops insomnia, due perhaps to depression or to pain from a physical injury that disrupts or prevents sleep, his or her work supply or ability to function in the workplace may drop below minimal functional requirements. Alternatively, some individuals functioning despite their psychiatric impairments may not be able to adapt if changes in their environment or supervision remove a critical source of support or add a new degree of physical or interpersonal stress, even if these do not represent increased work demands. This may occur with a change as routine as the retirement of a familiar and friendly supervisor.

Change in Work Demands Outpacing Change in Work Supply, Resulting in Decreased Work Capacity

This pattern of disability development occurs when an individual with a stable impairment who has had good, adequate, or even marginal functional capacity relative to specific job requirements is confronted with increased job demands. A change in job demands, with or without an increase in work responsibility or work load, can overcome an individual's ability to adapt to the preexisting impairments (Fig. 5.5).

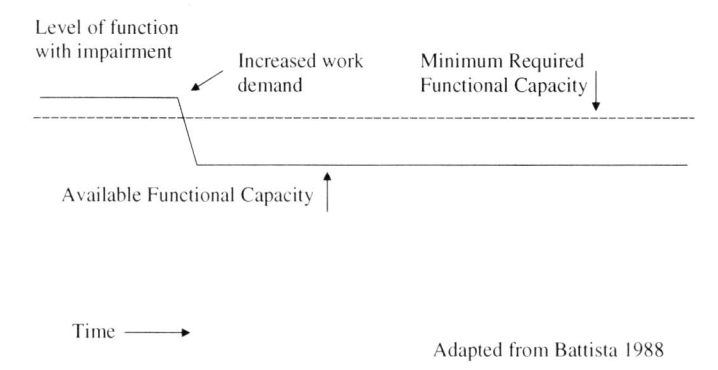

Fig. 5.5 Disability Due to Increased Demand in Context of Prior Functional Impairment

In these types of cases, the individual's impairments and work supply have not changed. Rather, changed job circumstances result in increased job demands, despite stability of workload, causing an overall decreased work capacity. This may change the balance between work supply and work demand to the point where work capacity decreases far enough past minimal functional requirements that the person becomes disabled. This pattern may be encountered in individuals who have received a promotion after excellent work performance but are incapable of meeting new and increased job responsibilities. For example, an employment history may indicate that an individual with depression who functioned well as a teacher for many years began to develop increased symptoms and problems with functioning only after being promoted to an administrative position as vice-principal. The increased workload and new job responsibilities for this individual resulted in stress severe enough to precipitate or exacerbate a psychiatric disorder, resulting in decreased work capacity and a claim of disability.

Changes in scheduling, physical conditions, work location, or even routine changes in personnel can also cause increased work demands even though they do not entail new responsibilities. An individual subject to suffering panic attacks when driving over bridges and through tunnels may never experience any impairment unless he or she is transferred to a new job location where the commute now involves experiencing these stressors on a daily basis. An individual with irritability due to depression whose work capacity is adequate despite this impairment might experience increased stress if assigned a new supervisor with whom he or she has a conflict. Work demand for this individual now includes coping with increased stress in the workplace, even though the job requirements have not changed.

Another example of these circumstances would be an individual with a schizoid personality disorder who is unable to tolerate social relationships. This individual might be able to function adequately as a technical writer as long as he or she is allowed to work from home and is assessed only on the ability to meet deadlines. If new job policies require that this individual work in an office, necessitating interaction with coworkers and supervisors, his or her functional capacity is likely to decline even though the actual work required remains the same. In this case, the increased social interaction and structure represent increased work demands even in the absence of increased workload and cause decreased work capacity.

Individuals who display this pattern of disability development frequently become distressed by their inability to meet the new work demand. However, they also often lack insight into the reasons the new work demands have created problems in their work capacity. Their previously good work functioning validates their belief that the problem in work capacity lies either internally with worsening of their disorder or externally with the new situation or conflict. These individuals may attempt to remain in the workplace by requesting accommodations or may withdraw claiming disability if their level of discomfort is unbearably high. Nevertheless, the precipitating factor in the perception of disability is the change in job demand, not change in the underlying disorder or work supply (although the stress associated with failing to successfully meet new job demands may ultimately result in exacerbation of the disorder and decrease work supply).

Repeated Episodes of Impairment with Decreasing Baseline Work Capacity Between Episodes

The last common pattern of disability development is one in which an individual experiences an episodic changes in the balance between work supply and demand, as a result, for example, of episodic psychiatric disorder, such as depression, bipolar disorder, or anxiety disorder with panic attacks (Fig. 5.6).

With each episode, the individual experiences decreased work capacity, perhaps even to the point of disability, that is, work capacity below minimal functional requirements, but then is able to regain functioning as the symptoms resolve. However, with each episode, the individual's baseline work capacity is somewhat decreased. Such individuals often reach the point where they are no

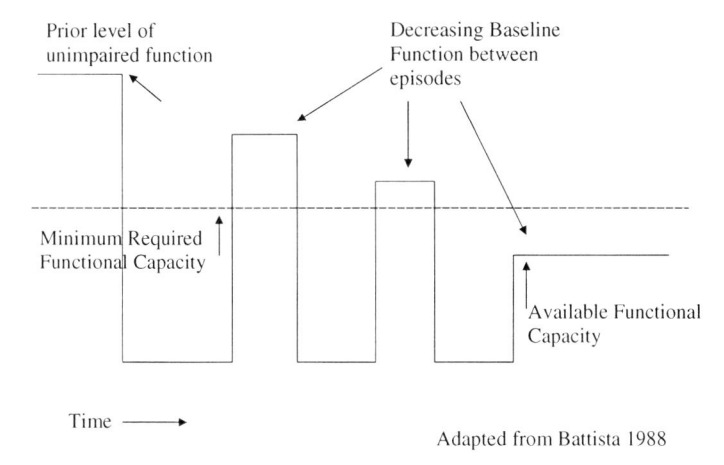

Fig. 5.6 Episodic Impairment with Decreasing Levels of Functional Recovery

longer able to "bounce back" due to residual impairments, external problems that accrue as a result of the psychiatric disorder, such as job loss and financial problems, or social losses, such as divorce, or even an unexpected external circumstance, such as family or personal illness.

For example, an individual with bipolar disorder and a high functioning baseline may experience manic episodes during which he or she also abuses alcohol. The eventual consequences of repeated episodes of psychiatric and functional impairment and alcohol abuse, despite extended periods of mood stability and no symptoms, may include job loss, financial distress, loss of important social relationships, and legal charges related to alcohol use. As these stressors accumulate, the individual's baseline work capacity after each episode may decrease and impairments may become more chronic. Ultimately, this individual may no longer be able to meet the minimal functional requirements needed to maintain employment and may seek disability benefits.

These patterns of disability development are inevitably simplified. Both internal work capacity factors and external job demand factors in various combinations can affect work function. For example, an individual could experience decreased work capacity as a result of exacerbation of a mood disorder and, at the same time, be faced with an increase in work demands. Such an individual's pattern of disability development might fit into more than one of the models described above.

These models are also limited by their lack of consideration of future risk of impairment. An individual might have adequate capacity to perform at a given point in time but the required minimum work capacity might have to include a low probability of certain future risks (Battista, 1988). For example, an airline pilot who has no impairment in regard to flying but who fails the required physical examination because of evidence of heart disease would likely be considered disabled. The disastrous consequences of suffering a heart attack while piloting a plane might result in a disability status even though the pilot's current work capacity, that is, the ability to fly a plane, and work demand, is unaffected. Similarly, a law enforcement officer with a history of bipolar disorder and impaired judgment during manic episodes, even if currently stable and without any impairment in work capacity at the time of evaluation, might be considered disabled because continued employment presents too much of a risk of future impairment with potentially disastrous consequences.

Finally, these models do not necessarily predict when work capacity that falls below a job's minimum functional requirements may be temporary or permanent. Figures 5.1 and 5.2 are likelier to describe cases where disability might be temporary; Figs. 5.3 through 5.6 are likelier to describe cases where disability is permanent. But even individuals who initially present with the patterns illustrated in Figs. 5.1 and 5.2 may go on to develop permanent disability. In any given case, whether disability is permanent or temporary may be evident from the nature of the impairments, the functional disability, the history of the disorder and its treatment, and an assessment of the individual's social and personal circumstances. These models cannot necessarily incorporate enough of these factors to provide an adequate predictive tool for this critical issue.

Work Capacity Models and Disability Evaluations

Despite these limitations, the work capacity model based on the balance of work supply and work demand provides a method for organizing a structured case formulation, which lends itself to consideration of questions relevant to disability claims (see Table 5.3).

Table 5.3 Disability evaluations: common questions referred for evaluation in psychiatric illness[1]

1. Multiaxial diagnosis, including GAF score
2. Impairments in work function and the relationship to psychiatric symptoms
3. Causation
4. Disability from one type or own type of work
5. Disability from any type of work
6. Current and past treatment, its adequacy, and claimants response to treatment
7. Treatment recommendations, including recommendations for medical consultations or psychological testing
8. Motivation
9. Prognosis
10. Maximum medical improvement
11. Restrictions and limitations
12. Malingering, primary and secondary gain

GAF, Global Assessment of Functioning Scale
[1]Guidelines for evaluating and offering opinion regarding the issues listed in Table 5.3 are suggested in Chapter 6.

Not every evaluation will ask for opinions on and responses to all these questions. For example, Social Security Disability Insurance (SSDI) programs and private disability programs are not concerned with causation of illness or disability, whereas causation is a central issue in a worker's compensation evaluation (see Chapter 7). Nevertheless, causation is always psychologically relevant. Identifying the event that triggers the process of changing psychological impairments into work-related disabilities is essential in understanding the dynamics of the process in which the individual's current claim of disability evolved.

The work capacity model also assists mental health professionals understand and describe how the evaluee came to perceive him or herself as disabled and what precipitated the filing of a related disability claim. For example, understanding causation also helps identify which of the work capacity models best describes the evaluee's development of disability. The identification of causation or a precipitating event will guide evaluation of other issues that may be relevant, even if causation is not. Identifying a pattern does not necessarily identify all the relevant factors that have resulted in a disability claim. However, once evaluators have identified a pattern that broadly fits the claimant's history, questions regarding treatment, motivation, nonwork-related issues that might affect functioning, changes in job demand or structure, and other relevant issues are often brought into clearer focus.

For example, an individual who fits in the pattern illustrated in Fig. 5.1 is someone whose functional capacity has suffered a dramatic decline over a relatively brief period of time due to acute onset of illness. Although the work capacity model does not indicate whether this is permanent or temporary, the model does imply that the primary issues in attempting to answer this and other disability-related questions are adequacy of current treatment and the evaluee's response to treatment. This model also implies that in the absence of treatment, the question of how much function this individual will regain cannot be answered at the time of evaluation.

Over time, it may become evident that this individual is displaying a pattern consistent with that illustrated in Fig. 5.2, an individual who, with treatment, recovers to previous baseline level of functioning. Such a pattern indicates that the individual is a treatment responder and may have a relatively good prognosis. Disability opinions in such a case should center on need for treatment, prognosis, and restrictions and limitations upon return to work.

However, it may become evident over time that the pattern of disability development is closer to that represented in Fig. 5.6; an individual who experiences acute episodes and dysfunction regains functional capacity between episodes, but whose baseline deteriorates between episodes. This may not be evident until several episodes have occurred. This specific pattern directs inquiry and opinions toward why this individual is unable to return to at least a minimal work capacity relative to minimal functional capacity at the time of the evaluation when he or she has done so in the past. This raises issues related to treatment, prognosis, motivation, maximum improvement, changes in external circumstances or work demand, restrictions and limitations, and possibly accommodations.

In addition, when individuals do not fit into one of these work capacity models, or when their claims seems to fit one of the models but is not supported by corroborating information, evaluators may be able to identify alternate lines of inquiry into issues relevant to disability. For example, an individual who claims previously unimpaired work capacity whose history reveals only marginal work functioning does not fit any of the illustrated patterns. Disability claims may not focus on the history of marginal work capacity, but evaluators may find that this is the single most significant issue in the particular case. Similarly, an individual whose claims seem to fit the patterns illustrated in Fig. 5.1 or 5.4, but whose reported history is not consistent with documented work capacity, raises issues involving alternative agendas or malingering.

Motivation

Of the disability questions listed in Table 5.3, motivation stands out as the only significant question commonly referred for evaluation that does not fit readily into the work capacity model. Motivation to work, although perhaps one of the most difficult characteristics to assess, is nevertheless one of the most significant links between impairment and disability. Poor motivation can be a major cause of poor work functioning as well as lack of engagement in other activities of life. Many times, an individual's motivation is not well understood even after careful consideration and assessment (American Medical Association, 2008).

Numerous theories regarding work motivation have been discussed (Rothman & Cooper, 2008). Some emphasize the primacy of the fulfillment of basic needs, such as financial, safety, and social needs, in the creation of motivation to work. Theories also include discussion of motivation to work as a means of filling the need of self-esteem and the need of receiving esteem from others. Self-actualization, achievement, recognition, responsibility, advancement, and growth are also recognized motivational needs. Other theories have emphasized the need for power and the need for affiliation.

Nevertheless, motivation to attempt to overcome or adapt to impairments so as to avoid or minimize disability and motivation to seek and comply with treatment are essential aspects of disability evaluations. Outside of work demand, motivation is the factor that can make the most difference in work capacity between two individuals with equivalent impairments or work supply. Thus, its assessment deserves special attention and consideration in the understanding of patterns of disability development.

Motivation is frequently affected by psychiatric symptoms. For example, individuals with mood disorders typically show motivational problems. People with overwhelming euphoria may experience an expansive approach to life, perceiving themselves as able to accomplish anything, with no limits.

Conversely, those who are depressed may be fatigued, lethargic, and have difficulty completing everyday activities, including those required for work duties. People with anxiety disorders may be unable to accomplish daily activities because they avoid situations that make them anxious or because they are overwhelmed with worry. Individuals with severe mood, anxiety, substance use, certain types of traumatic brain injury, and psychotic disorders often demonstrate avolition, that is, an inability to initiate and persist in goal-directed activities. People manifesting this symptom rarely show interest in work or social activities (Corrigan et al., 2007).

Many factors, medical and nonmedical, influence an individual's motivation to work (see Table 5.4).[2]

Table 5.4 Factors that may affect motivation to work

Medical
Psychiatric illness
Physical illness
Traumatic brain injury
Real or perceived effect of workplace on disorder
Side effects of medication
Substance use

Nonmedical
Demoralization due external factors, such as chronic illness or family problems
Availability and strength of support network
Attitude toward job, workplace, or company
Personality style: dependent, regressive vs. resilient, adaptive
Fear of losing entitlement
Secondary gain

Side effects of medications for both mental and physical disorders can result in both fatigue and lack of motivation. An individual's fear, real or anticipatory, that return to the workplace may exacerbate symptoms or destabilize a disorder can result in poor motivation to attempt to resume prior work functioning. Deconditioning due to long periods of unemployment, as discussed in Chapter 1, can also result in lack of motivation to attempt to return to work.

Poor motivation can also be associated with personality organization. Illness of any kind tends to foster regression since individuals often have to rely on others for care or assistance (American Medical Association, 2008). However,

---

[2] This discussion does not address some of the issues reviewed in depth in studies of motivational theory, such as job expectations or sense of equity (see Rothman & Cooper, 2008). Some of those specific issues are subsumed in this discussion within categories such as attitudes and real and perceived effects of workplace on disorder

an individual with dependent personality traits may become so regressed in the event of increasing impairments and gratification of dependent needs that return to work function becomes precluded.

Nonmedical factors can also play a major role in affecting an individual's motivation. Living with chronic diseases, whether mental or physical, can result in profound demoralization and lack of motivation to attempt to make changes, adapt to impairment, or return to work. Demoralization can also result in struggling with family and social problems, which can make continued efforts to work or efforts to return to work seem an overwhelming task. A strong support network and encouragement from significant others can help increase an individual's motivation to return to work. Conversely, fear of losing entitlements or the secondary gain of being cared for or being relieved of various responsibilities due to a formally recognized "sick" role can reduce motivation.

Certain circumstances may indicate the presence of motivation to work or lack thereof. For example, an individual who decides to file a disability claim, especially a long-term disability claim, before treatment has been obtained or has had sufficient time to be effective, might be seeking an exit from the workplace. Noncompliance with efforts at rehabilitation, medication, and other treatment, along with an evaluee's decision prematurely early in the disability process that he or she would never work again, should also raise suspicion that the impairment alone is not deterring employment and motivation to work may be a key factor.

Even though it does not fit neatly into the work capacity model, motivation may be the most significant factor in an individual's pattern of disability development. It should therefore always be considered in the evaluation of disability. Nevertheless, mental health professionals should understand that like the assessment of disability, the assessment of motivation is not a purely psychiatric or medical assessment. Opinions regarding an evaluee's motivation represent personal and social judgments based on a combination of medical and nonmedical evidence and are influenced by a multitude of factors. As a result, evaluators are subject to the biases discussed in Chapter 1 regarding whether an individual can't work or won't work. Thus, in providing opinions regarding motivation, evaluators should be certain their assessments consider all relevant factors while attempting to minimize their own biases.

Cultural and Ethnic Issues

Finally, when evaluators assess individuals whose cultural or ethnic backgrounds differ from their own, they should consider the possibility that cultural factors may be a significant issue in the evaluee's relationship to the workplace and attitudes toward identifying psychiatric illness, impairment, and disability. These factors can create issues in language, cognition, culture-related beliefs, values, and attitudes held both by the evaluator and by the evaluee. Not all individuals will automatically require cultural or ethnic considerations. Sometimes, cultural and ethnic factors, although present, may have no relevance to the issue under evaluation. However, each evaluee should have potentially relevant cultural factors taken into account. Sometimes these may be critical to an accurate evaluation.

For example, evaluators should be aware that the presentation of psychiatric disorders might vary because of the influences of culture (Tseng et al., 2004). Generally speaking, psychopathology that is predominantly determined by biological factors, such as psychotic disorders, is not profoundly influenced by cultural factors. In contrast, culture often plays a considerable role, both from etiological perspective and in the expression of symptoms, in many of the disorders commonly encountered in the workplace, such as anxiety or depression. This is also particularly true of personality disorders. For example, individuals from certain ethnic groups tend to express depression or anxiety through somatic complaints rather than through direct complaints of depressed mood or nervousness. Others will be hesitant to present any type of complaint, no matter how great the discomfort or pain (Tseng et al., 2004).

In addition, cultural attitudes toward social welfare systems will significantly influence the seeking of compensation and may be relevant in disability and disability-related evaluations. People from some groups have cultural beliefs and attitudes that tend to prize self-reliance, and unless absolutely necessary, they avoid depending on others or on the public. Some cultural groups that hold values emphasizing self-support, working hard, and avoiding being dependent on others' resources as much as possible may be reluctant to request assistance and depend on the resources of the public welfare system. In contrast, people from other cultural groups may feel they are entitled to receive help from the public and depend on society at large to maintain income. For example, certain ethnic groups have a cultural tendency to seek workers' compensation benefits and demonstrate disproportionately high numbers of applications. These groups will not hesitate to apply for this benefit if injured during work (Tseng et al., 2004).

Cultural factors may be particularly significant in the assessment of malingering. Certain behaviors thought to indicate malingering, such as an overplayed and dramatic presentation or a deliberate, slow, and careful method of presentation (see Chapter 6), may be related to cultural or ethnic norms of behavior rather than deception. Characteristic behaviors regarding authority figures, level of education, and unidentified problems with communication may also result in the appearance of deception or dissimulation. Clinical skill and an understanding of cultural patterns of problem presentation are necessary for the evaluator to assess the nature and severity of the complaints, particularly in cases involving potential compensation (Tseng et al., 2004).

Mental health professionals conducting disability and disability-related evaluations are not expected to know all about the evaluee's cultural system. Cultural, ethnic, racial, or gender matching between the evaluating mental health professional and the evaluee is not necessary. However, evaluators should actively maintain a cultural sensitivity when assessing immigrants, people of ethnic or racial minorities, hearing- or speech-impaired individuals, or people who are different from the majority in terms of age or gender (i.e., women), or whose backgrounds differ from that of the evaluator. Evaluators should be perceptive enough to sense cultural differences among people and to know how to appreciate them without bias, prejudice, or stereotypes (Tseng et al., 2004). If cultural issues with which the evaluator is unfamiliar seem prominent, evaluators may need to state this directly and seek consultation to clarify their concerns.

Conclusion

Mental health professionals conducting disability or disability-related evaluations should attempt to understand how individuals came to be or to perceive themselves as disabled. The work capacity model offers one method of conceptualizing the process of disability development. A case formulation based on this model details the development of the individual's impairments and how the individual came to make a claim of disability. By determining which pattern in this model is most relevant in any disability evaluation, evaluators can provide a narrative that will guide their exploration of the relevant issues. These relevant issues, including diagnosis, treatment, maximum improvement, are the opinions most often requested of mental health professionals in conducting disability evaluations.

These case formulations are designed to understand the development of disability from the claimant's perspective. They are not designed to help evaluators determine whether claimants are entitled to payments, benefits, accommodations, or any other type of employment action. Any definition of disability is program- or policy specific, and administrators or courts make the decision regarding whether an individual qualifies for a particular program's or policy's benefits. Nevertheless, the persistence of the medical model of disability (see Introduction) increases the likelihood that disability programs will continue to call upon mental health professionals to provide opinions regarding disability when mental disorders interfere with work. General guidelines for providing assessments of impairment and disability required by disability programs are presented in Chapter 6, and the requirements of specific types of programs or related evaluations will be reviewed in the subsequent chapters.

Chapter 6
Practice Guidelines for Mental Health Disability Evaluations in the Workplace

Introduction

This chapter will suggest practice guidelines for psychiatric disability and related work capacity assessments. As reviewed in Chapter 5 and earlier chapters, a complicated relationship exists between psychiatric symptoms, work impairment, and disability. In the previous chapter, a model for analysis of the process of development of disability was discussed. This analysis allows mental health professionals to develop case formulations based on a work capacity model that balances work demand with work supply or functional capacity. Mental health professionals can then utilize the case formulation to translate the analysis of work impairment and disability into responses to questions used by administrative and judicial systems to adjudicate disability and related workplace issues. These practice guidelines will provide a framework for this "translation."

The Benefit of Practice Guidelines

In past decades, the production of clinical practice guidelines in all fields of medicine has grown considerably, spurred by a variety of social and medical concerns including quality improvement (Recupero, 2008). Practice guidelines are "best practices" established internally by specialty fields and organizations. The development of clinical practice guidelines has been actively promoted by the American Psychiatric Association (APA, 2006) to incorporate relevant scientific and clinical findings in describing best treatments for a range of mental illnesses. The American Psychological Association (2005) cites three broad justifications for the development of practice guidelines, one of which is provision of professional guidance. Clinical practice guidelines prepared by general and specialty medical and psychological associations tend to be highly regarded, since they reflect physicians' reviews of the current literature, emphasize the provision of quality care, and define a range of acceptable practices (Zonana, 2008).

Forensic evaluation best practices have been discussed and debated over the past decades as the fields of the forensic mental health have evolved.

Nevertheless, relatively few practice guidelines for conducting forensic evaluations are available. The American Academy of Psychiatry and the Law (AAPL), the specialty organization for forensic psychiatrists, is one of the first to begin developing practice guidelines for forensic evaluations (Giorgi-Guarnieri et al., 2002; Mossman et al., 2007) to provide professional guidance and to standardize and improve the quality of forensic evaluations.

Until recently, practice guidelines for workplace evaluations provided by professional organizations have been largely unavailable.[1] The existing American Psychiatric Association clinical practice guidelines (APA, 2006) address standard practices such as clinical evaluation and treatment for various disorders but do not address workplace evaluations. General practice guidelines for conducting forensic psychiatric and psychological evaluations have been suggested (Committee on Ethical Practice Guidelines for Forensic Psychologists, 1991; Simon & Wettstein, 1997) but are also not specific to workplace or disability evaluations.

The American Medical Association's *Guides to the Evaluation of Permanent Impairment, 6th Edition* (American Medical Association, 2008) are substantively relevant to disability evaluations generally but are not practice guidelines for conducting a mental disability evaluation. The *Guides* do not provide a structured framework for mental health professionals to formulate opinions regarding disability. Rather, the *Guides* suggest "principles of assessment" for "mental and behavioral disorders" (p. 348) and offer a series of "suggestions" for conducting a "Mental and Behavioral Disorders Independent Medical Examination" (p. 352). In addition, the *Guides*' rating system is intended for use in the assessment of permanent impairment. The concept of permanency poses certain problems in regard to psychiatric disorders, as the *Guides* acknowledge. Many mental disorders are dynamic rather than static in nature and are, to some extent, never at a level that can be considered permanent (American Medical Association, 2008).

AAPL is the first professional organization to suggest practice guidelines specifically for workplace evaluations (Gold et al., 2008). The practice guidelines suggested here are congruent with the AAPL practice guidelines but expand upon them with more extensive exploration of legal and practical considerations.[2] Adherence to these suggested principles and standards can help evaluators minimize common errors that can compromise an evaluation and raise concerns regarding credibility of opinions should litigation, a common consequence of workplace problems, arise.

The use of practice guidelines can assist mental health professionals in addressing many of the challenges encountered in providing forensic evaluations. Forensic evaluations are widely recognized to vary in quality and content.

---

[1] For example, The California Division of Industrial Accidents Medical and Chiropractic Advisory Committee's Subcommittee on Permanent Psychiatric Disability developed guidelines for psychiatric disability evaluation (Enelow, 1987). These however address only the evaluation of permanent disability and are outdated.

[2] Any direct use or adaptation of text or concepts from theAAPL's *Guidelines for Forensic Evaluation of Psychiatric Disability* (2008) occurs with the permission of AAPL.

Practice guidelines assist in decreasing variation in procedures across employers, employees, and the courts and agencies that have oversight jurisdiction. In addition, practice guidelines can standardize education and research, which further decreases variation and improves consistency among examiners. Finally, if questions regarding credibility of the evaluation process arise, the use of practice guidelines can help establish whether an evaluation was conducted using best practice standards. The use of practice guidelines relevant to the type of evaluation in question can also support assertions that an evaluator adhered to accepted procedure in reaching conclusions, thus enhancing credibility.

Nevertheless, practice guidelines do not provide a solution to all the problems associated with improving the quality of forensic evaluations or the practical issues involved in evaluations (Recupero, 2008; Wettstein, 2005b). Guidelines are often not empirically based. Rather, they represent a consensus of opinions regarding best practices held by members of the organizations developing them. Therefore, not all members of the profession may agree with the guidelines' recommendations. In addition, guidelines are often not widely disseminated, and many practitioners may not be aware of their existence. Finally, clinicians may find the process of applying guidelines cumbersome and adherence to all suggested guidelines results in exceeding the resources they have available for conducting evaluations.

Practice guidelines are aspirational, not mandatory, and are not intended to supersede the judgment of mental health professionals (Heilbrun et al., 2008). The practice guidelines suggested here are not intended to establish a rigid protocol that will be relevant in their entirety for every evaluation. Mental health professionals must exercise professional judgment to determine how to proceed in any individual evaluation. Nevertheless, familiarity with accepted best practices will assist mental health professionals in improving the quality of their work, maintaining their objectivity, addressing the challenges that arise in disability and disability-related evaluations, and meeting the needs of both evaluees and referral sources in facilitating a fair and relevant decision-making process.

Some last caveats: these practice guidelines are not intended to describe exclusive methods of evaluation nor is it expected that they can be applied to reach a reliable result in the absence of professional training. Clinicians should also bear in mind that following the practice guidelines reviewed here will not lead to a guaranteed outcome (American Psychiatric Association, 2006; Gold et al., 2008; Simon & Wettstein, 1997).

Definitions and Related Issues

Disability and Impairment: Related but Not Synonymous

As discussed in Chapters 4 and 5, the definitions of "impairment" and "disability," although related, are not synonymous. The concept of disability has shifted in recent years from a focus on the presence of diseases, conditions, and impairments to more of a focus on functional limitations caused by these factors (Wunderlich et al., 2002). Thus, impairment is defined as "a significant deviation, loss, or loss of use of any body structure or body function in an individual with a health condition, disorder or disease" (AMA, 2008, p. 5). In contrast, disability is considered "activity limitations and/or participation restrictions in an individual with a health condition, disorder or disease" (AMA, 2008, p. 5). Impairments, therefore, may or may not result in a disability, and the presence of impairment does not of itself establish the presence of disability or eligibility for any type of disability program benefits.

The evaluation of impairment, that is, the loss or reduction in a body part or system, is a medical assessment. Impairment and change in functional capacities due to psychiatric illness are questions that are within mental health professionals' expertise. In contrast, the assessment of the presence of a disability requires more than medical assessment of the presence of impairment. It involves evaluation of the degree of impairment and how that impairment interacts with the requirements of the environment (Wunderlich et al., 2002). Determination of disability not only is based on an understanding of impairment but also requires information about an individual's skills, education, job history, adaptability, and age, as well as environment requirements and modification availability.

Moreover, disability is a status with many definitions, only one of which might be relevant in a particular case. The vast majority of disability definitions are work referenced and attempt to tie the disability concept to a threshold work capacity (Battista, 1988). However, any definition of disability is program or policy specific. For example, Social Security disability programs and private insurance plans define disability very differently (see Chapter 7). Mental health professionals asked for opinions on disability also need to be familiar with technical legal definition relevant to the evaluation at hand and translate it into a clinically meaningful concept.

Although administrative or legal systems make the ultimate decision regarding eligibility for benefits or accommodations, the medical model of disability (see Introduction) has assured that disability programs will continue to call upon mental health professionals to provide opinions regarding disability. Mental health professionals should nevertheless be keenly aware that the opinions regarding disability, even when requested, venture into legal and administrative areas. Evaluations of disability involve more than purely medical assessment and require specialized expertise (American Medical Association, 2008; World Health Organization, 2001). In fact, some disability evaluation referrals, in recognition of the limitations of mental health professionals' opinions in this nonmedical area, are accompanied by specific instructions to refrain from providing an opinion on whether the evaluee is disabled. These referral sources typically direct evaluators to limit their opinions to medical or psychiatric findings of how and why the capacity to meet an occupational demand is altered by illness or injury.

Despite the fact that opinions regarding disability go beyond purely medical assessments, mental health professionals may have the additional skills, qualifications, and knowledge base to provide reasonable opinions on disability

(American Medical Association, 2008). Nevertheless, psychiatrists and psychologists who provide opinions about disability rather than impairment should be aware that they will need more than information regarding the evaluee's illness and symptoms. In many cases, they will need to obtain additional expertise and information from multiple sources to provide reasonable disability assessments.

Restrictions and Limitations

Disability evaluators are often asked to consider whether evaluees' psychiatric signs and symptoms are severe enough to limit or to restrict their ability to perform general or specific occupational functions. Restrictions and limitations, like the terms disability and impairment, are not equivalent. Nevertheless, these terms are often confused with each other and therefore used inaccurately.

Restrictions address what a claimant "should not do" because of the risk of exacerbating or precipitating psychiatric symptoms. Mental health professionals offering opinions regarding restriction are offering opinions that performing the restricted activities would aggravate the individual's condition or delay healing or recovery (Battista, 1988). In contrast, limitations address what a claimant "cannot do" because of psychiatric symptoms. A limitation is a reflection of documented loss of function. For example, an evaluee with bipolar disorder, even if stable and asymptomatic, might be restricted from, that is, should not work, excessive irregular night hours due to the possibility of precipitating a manic episode. In contrast, the evaluee might be limited in the ability, that is, unable, to sustain concentration beyond one hour due to persistent racing thoughts and diminished attention even when treated.

Impairment vs. Illegal Behavior

Mental health professionals are sometimes called upon to evaluate disability and disability-related claims that involve assertions of illegal or unethical behavior and psychiatric illness. Such claims raise the difficult evaluation issue of whether a claimant is attempting to evade responsibility for or seeking to benefit from wrongful behavior by claiming illness, or whether in fact the wrongful behavior arose from symptoms of illness. For example, claimants confined for an illegal act and unable to practice their profession may attribute their wrongful behavior to a mental disorder and may seek disability benefits on the basis of the claimed disorder. Alternatively, conduct that would otherwise disqualify a physician from practice, such as inappropriate prescribing practices, if demonstrably related to a psychiatric illness, might result in a rehabilitation plan and ultimately resumption of practice rather than permanent loss of license.

As several professional organizations have attempted to clarify, such evaluations turn on the issue of causation. An American Psychiatric Association resource document on this issue states, "Under certain circumstances, a physician's problematic behavior leads to questions about fitness for duty. Boundary violations (such as sexual misconduct), unethical or illegal behavior, or maladaptive personality traits may precipitate an evaluation, but do not necessarily result from disability or impairment due to a psychiatric illness" (Anfang et al., 2005, p. 85). Similarly, the Federation of State Medical Boards (FSMB) adopted a policy that states, "In addressing the issue of whether sexual misconduct is a form of impairment, the committee does not view it as such, but instead, as a violation of the public's trust. It should be noted that although a mental disorder may be a basis for sexual misconduct, the committee finds that sexual misconduct usually is not caused by physical/mental impairment" (Federation of State Medical Boards, 1996).

These policies provide guidance for the assessment of unethical or illegal behavior that arises in the context of a claim of psychiatric impairment. The analysis of such claims needs to be case-specific and should include a detailed examination of the relationship between any psychiatric illness and the individual's problematic behavior. If, for example, an individual has a long history of bipolar disorder, steals funds, and goes on a flagrant spending spree during a well-documented manic episode while off mood-stabilizing medication, a claim of causal relationship between the behavior and the psychiatric impairment is more credible. In contrast, if an employee has been embezzling money routinely from a financial institution over 20 years but has no documented psychiatric history until after he or she is caught, a claim of a causal relationship between the behavior and a psychiatric impairment is less credible.

The inability to perform occupational tasks due to a legal barrier such as incarceration or the loss of professional license is termed "legal disability." Whether an individual with a legal disability also qualifies for purposes of disability benefits based on psychiatric illness and impairments is a perplexing question and raises issues that may be referred to mental health professionals. Causation is again the primary focus of such evaluations. The specific facts and context of the issue in the case, including the sequence of events, the claimant's clinical status, and the timeframe for seeking treatment and filing a disability claim, are critical to the analysis of a disability claim resting on legal impediment.

A Maryland federal district court captured the causal analysis in a review of a denial of Social Security disability benefits on behalf of a claimant convicted of breaking and entering, adjudicated a defective delinquent, and then committed to an institution for the treatment of repeat disordered offenders.

> There is an important difference between an impairment that results in an inability to perform the physical or mental functions necessary to engage in substantial gainful activity on the one hand and antisocial behavior that results in confinement on the other. In the latter case, it is the confinement rather than the impairment that precludes the individual from engaging in substantial gainful activity. The [Social Security] Act does not intend for simple incarceration to result in a finding of disability (*Waldron v. Secretary of Health, Education, and Welfare*, 1972, p. 1180).

Many state and private disability insurance policies turn on the same issue. In *Massachusetts Mutual v. Ouellette* (1992), for example, the Vermont Supreme Court found that an optometrist convicted and imprisoned for lewd and lascivious conduct with a minor was not entitled to disability benefits for pedophilia because he had not shown that his "mental disorder" was what precluded him from engaging in substantial gainful activity. In fact, to the contrary, the record appeared to indicate that the plaintiff's mental condition or disorder had not affected his ability to engage in his occupation.

Insurance Issues for Forensic Evaluators

Mental health professionals who routinely perform third-party evaluations and provide testimony should be certain their malpractice insurance policy contains provisions for forensic activities. Physicians should be familiar with the details of their policies and arrange for the appropriate coverage (Gold & Davidson, 2007). Although malpractice claims for forensic evaluations are rare (see Chapter 2), they may occur and not all malpractice claims are covered by all policies. In addition, in third-party evaluations or in the case of expert testimony, claims such as ordinary negligence rather than professional negligence are more common and these claims may not trigger coverage unless specifically covered by rider in a medical malpractice policy. In this situation, a plaintiff may well seek to recover the physician's personal assets. Finally, should a lawsuit rely on legal theories other than professional malpractice, professional liability insurance may not provide protection from damage awards and the caps on damages juries can award in malpractice cases enacted by some states.

Safety Issues for Evaluators

Angry evaluees may express their feelings and become threatening toward evaluating mental health professionals. Mental health professionals conducting disability and disability-related evaluations should therefore give some thought to their personal safety. The opinions rendered in a disability, Americans with Disabilities Act (ADA), or fitness-for-duty evaluation can result in lawsuits and the loss of monetary benefits, employment, or careers. Emotions associated with employment conflict and these potential consequences can be as extreme as those stirred up in interpersonal conflicts such as divorce and custody battles.

Evaluees referred because of anger management problems, substance use problems, or paranoid delusions may become overtly threatening. Some evaluees are angry about being required to undergo a psychiatric or psychological examination, considering it part of a pattern of unfair treatment. Evaluees may become further angered by an evaluator's report if it results in loss of income or tangible or intangible employment benefits to which the evaluee feels entitled.

Mental health professionals should always be aware of the setting and context in which they conduct evaluations. An interview should not be undertaken when the clinician feels threatened in any way. Evaluators should also be clear about setting limits around evaluation interviews. For example, psychiatrists and psychologists evaluating law enforcement personnel should consider routinely enquiring whether the officer's firearm has been returned to the employer pending evaluation. If not, evaluators may wish to routinely request that the evaluee refrain from carrying firearms into the office. If an evaluee becomes threatening, the evaluator should consider terminating the interview. Threats made after the evaluation should be reported to the referral source and, if appropriate, to local law enforcement agencies.

General Practice Guidelines for Psychiatric Disability Evaluations

Clarify the Nature of the Referral with the Referral Source

Mental health professionals should clarify the context and legal status of the evaluation with the referral source at the time of initial contact. Many disability and disability-related evaluations are already in the process of litigation. Mental health professionals should ask whether an attorney is involved in the case and, if so, should request that the referral be made through the attorney. This maximizes the chance that the communication will be protected by the attorney/client privilege, which applies when the expert is assisting the attorney. In many cases, especially if they are at the initial stages of evaluation or dispute, no attorneys are directly involved in the referral or disability process. In these cases, mental health professionals should be aware that the expert's communications with the client or collaterals will not be privileged.

Whether through the attorney or another party, evaluators should also clarify the nature of the referral and the role they are expected to play. Although this can be done by phone, a written referral documenting expectations and the questions that need to be addressed in the evaluation is preferable. The referral contact is a good opportunity to make certain that the conditions associated with conducting the evaluation, such as the evaluator's availability, fees, and how the conclusions of the evaluation will be communicated, are understood.

Some referral sources request only a review of records rather than an evaluation that includes an interview with the evaluee. Opinions that can be provided based on a review of documents are usually limited to very specific questions, such as whether there is enough evidence to support a psychiatric diagnosis or a specific type of impaired function. If broader questions are asked, a review of records may not provide enough information to render a reasonable opinion. If this is the case, evaluators should advise the referral source that more information or an independent medical examination (IME) is required to answer the question. Often insurance companies will arrange for an IME on the basis of the suggestion of a mental health professional conducting a record review.

Evaluators should also clarify at the initial contact that no treatment will be provided. Often, attorneys and employers are seeking both evaluation and treatment and may not understand why these two roles are usually incompatible. For example, an attorney may refer a client for treatment, not only because it seems necessary but also because he or she plans to use the clinician to provide testimony regarding causation or disability. An employer may request both treatment and a fitness-for-duty evaluation for an employee in crisis. The employee's most pressing need may be emergency evaluation and treatment, not a fitness-for-duty evaluation, but the employer may assume that the mental health professional will provide both simultaneously.

A referral source may also assume that the evaluating psychiatrist or psychologist, even if not undertaking long-term treatment, will discuss the evaluee's condition with him or her, make referrals for treatment directly to the evaluee, or make treatment recommendations. The initial contact with the referral source should make clear that the mental health professional will be providing evaluation only. As reviewed in Chapter 2, evaluators should bear in mind that offering opinions directly to the evaluee may create a doctor–patient relationship along with the attendant duties associated with that relationship (Baum, 2005; Gold & Davidson, 2007). The only circumstances that justify a different stance involve an immediate threat to the life or limb of the evaluee or others (see Chapters 1 and 2).

Review Records and Collateral Information

The goal of the psychiatric disability evaluation is to correlate symptoms of mental disorders with occupational impairments. As discussed in Chapter 5, the development of disability and the evaluation of changes in an individual's work capacity and level of functioning require evidence of work capacity and level of functioning over a sufficiently long period of time before the date of examination. The case formulation analysis discussed in Chapter 5 is based on a longitudinal assessment of data collected from a variety of sources of information in conjunction with examination findings.

Collateral information and extensive record review is therefore a critical element of disability evaluations (American Medical Association, 2008; Krajeski & Lipsett, 1987; Melton et al., 2007; Drukteinis, 2004). Collateral information is often necessary to demonstrate the presence of a psychiatric disorder and associated impairment. No one source of information is sufficient in a disability evaluation. Collateral information may include formal written records obtained in the course of usual professional and business operations and third-party information obtained through personal interviews, witness statements, and depositions.

Typically, the referral source gathers and provides records to the evaluating mental health professional. Requests for documented information should be directed to the referral source to ensure that the referral source is aware of all the records that are being reviewed. The records reviewed and the source of these records may become significant issues should litigation arise. Nevertheless, with approval of the referring sources, evaluators can request a record release or permission to speak to a third party directly from the individual being evaluated. In collecting collateral information, evaluators must comply with requirements of the Health Insurance Portability and Accountability Act and other medical privacy laws (see Chapter 2).

The amount of documented information available and access to this information vary depending on the circumstances of the claim. For example, if a disability evaluation is conducted in the context of personal injury litigation, the legal discovery process may result in access to all recent treatment records, witness statements, depositions, and other background materials. In contrast, in cases such as an ordinary claim for Social Security disability benefits, collateral information may be limited, nonexistent, or difficult to obtain. Referral sources may not have access to all relevant information, such as job descriptions, performance reviews, and medical or pharmacy records, or may be unaware of their availability and relevance to the evaluation. If evaluators identify additional information that may be relevant, they should request that referral sources try to obtain or provide this information.

Occasionally, referral sources will send summaries of collateral information rather than the original documents. Evaluators should ask to review original documents and not rely solely on summaries of the referral source. Summaries can be of value, but they can omit important information or create distortions that reflect the summarizer's biases. In addition, the person preparing the summary may not recognize the psychological or medical importance of some original sources of information and thus may not include it.

Specific types of collateral information useful or necessary in workplace or disability evaluations include:

Written Records

Job Description

Evaluators should obtain and review a written job description, as discussed in Chapter 5. Assessment of impairment requires that evaluators understand the work skills required for a particular job. Without this understanding, correlating the potential impact of a symptom of a psychiatric disorder on specific job requirements is difficult.

The various physical and mental requirements of a job are frequently described in formal organizational job descriptions, but sometimes are not. Many job descriptions can be obtained from published information about the job, such as in the *Dictionary of Occupational Titles* (United States Department of Labor, 1991), which gives job descriptions for thousands of jobs, along with summaries of educational, strength, and cognitive requirements. Although somewhat obsolete and outdated, the *Dictionary of Occupational Titles* may contain relevant information and is utilized extensively at the Social Security Administration in litigation related to applications for Social Security disability benefits.

Psychiatric, Substance Use, Medical and Pharmacy Records

Mental health records are the most obvious source of longitudinal information regarding current and past disorders, impairments, treatment, and prognosis. The timeframe of such records should be taken into consideration. Individuals seeking treatment after filing a disability or legal claim may be attempting to establish a record supporting the claim rather than genuinely seeking treatment. Mental health records that predate the claim are more likely to indicate a process in which impairment is causing distress even before a disability claim has been made. However, many people will not seek treatment for psychiatric problems until their symptoms cause a significant problem, such as an adverse work event. So each case should be carefully considered on its own merits. Treatment records also frequently contain useful background information about an individual, sources of conflict or stress, previous job problems, evidence of personality trait disturbance, and motivational factors that can affect occupational functioning.

Other medical records may also contain useful information. Pharmacy records are often very helpful in corroborating claims regarding doctors seen for treatment, medications and dosages prescribed, and possible substance misuse or abuse. Medical treatment records may reveal psychiatric complaints made to a medical doctor rather than to a mental health professional (or absence thereof). Medical records may also demonstrate the presence of a physical disorder with psychiatric symptomatology or help rule out such disorders if diagnostic laboratory or imaging tests, such as electroencephalograms (EEGs), computed tomography (CT) scans, or magnetic resonance imaging (MRI) scans, have been performed.

Employment Records

Employment or personnel records are an important source of collateral information, especially when impairment in functioning arises in the context of an individual's current or recent employment. Employment records may provide evidence of difficulties in work performance, but they may also provide evidence of workplace factors that may influence or precipitate a claim of disability.

For example, good evaluations and the absence of performance problems can reduce concern about workplace factors influencing a claim. In contrast, employment records that contain documentation of personnel issues that precede a claim of disability might raise concerns that the claim represents an attempt to address workplace conflict or justify poor performance rather than reflect actual work impairment based on psychiatric symptoms. Records may include disciplinary or personnel actions that have threatened the claimant's job stability and perhaps led to disability claims. Personnel records from prior employers may also be a valuable collateral source of similar information.

Academic Records

Although these may also be difficult to obtain, academic records can shed light on an individual's intellectual abilities, earlier achievements or failures, limitations in functioning, or need for accommodations. They can also indicate whether an individual has a history of behavioral problems, an important historical aspect of certain disorders including personality disorders.

Other Experts' Evaluations

Evaluations performed by physicians or by other mental health experts can help determine the consistency of an evaluee's reports and allow comparison of diagnostic formulations. Evaluations that include psychological and neuropsychological testing can be helpful in establishing the validity of self-reports, clinical symptom patterns, and personality features of the individual.

Personal Records

A variety of other personal records may be helpful, depending on the circumstances, as sources of collateral information. Prior disability claims, criminal records, military records, and financial records, including tax returns, can provide relevant information to the evaluation of a claim of current disability. An individual's diaries or journals may also be useful if contemporaneous and not kept for self-serving purposes to validate a claim of disability.

Third-Party Information

Information from third parties can be useful in corroborating evaluees' accounts of their history, symptoms, and functioning. The reliability of all sources of collateral information should be carefully considered. The inherent bias of all informants as well as the consistency of reported information should be evaluated.

Family Members and Friends

These individuals often have first-hand knowledge of an evaluee's symptoms, the evolution of a disorder, and functional abilities. However, family members may be as invested in a disability or legal claim as claimants themselves and may distort or exaggerate reports of the individual's mental symptoms in support of the claim.

Treatment Providers

Conversations with treatment providers, with evaluee consent and when legally permissible, can be helpful. Physicians and therapists, particularly those who are aware that a legal or administrative disability claim is being made, may be circumspect in their documentation. They may be more forthcoming about their opinions in the course of a personal conversation.

Written Statements

Written statements, depositions, or affidavits provided by third parties may be informative. However, evaluators should be aware that they might be incomplete or biased. An employer or other party may be biased against the evaluee, especially in adversarial situations, such as personal injury litigation or workers' compensation claims, and may minimize symptoms or provide misleading information to indicate that the claim is fabricated. Multiple witness statements or depositions that corroborate each other may be more reliable and credible.

Surveillance

Surveillance may be useful and is at times a powerful source of collateral information. Nevertheless, surveillance information may be of limited value. A camera cannot capture an internal emotional state. Even in cases of alleged physical injury, pictures or video capture only discrete periods of time and may not accurately reflect the individual's overall functional ability. With psychiatric disorders, a discrete period of surveillance is even less likely to be representative of total functioning ability. However, surveillance may be able to disprove assertions that certain activities are impossible or never performed. Information gleaned from surveillance can also point out areas that bear further exploration with the evaluee.

Conduct a Standard Examination

Obtain Informed Consent

As in all forensic evaluations, evaluators are required to inform the evaluee of the nature and purpose of the examination and to obtain consent to proceed with the evaluation (see Chapters 1 and 2). This should be done before the interview and examination begin. Evaluators should clearly inform evaluees of the core issues that comprise informed consent. These include that

1. the purpose of the evaluation is to provide an opinion about the evaluee's mental state and level of impairment or disability, if any;
2. the evaluation is not for treatment purposes and the evaluee is not and will not become the evaluating mental health professional's patient; and
3. the information and results obtained from the evaluation are not confidential, and they will be shared with the referral source, and may be disclosed to the evaluee's, insurer, employer, the court, administrative body, or agency that makes the final determination of disability.

Other items that clarify the purpose and nature of the relationship, if relevant, should be discussed. These may include

1. the source of payment for the evaluation, which is typically the referring agency;
2. that the evaluations are voluntary and that requests for breaks needed are allowed and encouraged;

3. that an evaluee may choose not to answer questions but that refusal will be noted and may have consequences for the evaluation and the underlying claim or defense;
4. that although the mental health professional renders an opinion, the regulatory agency, employer, or court will make the ultimate determination of disability or other work-related issue; and
5. that a written report may be produced and, if so, will be turned over to the retaining third party. Once released to the third party, the evaluator does not control the report and who has access to it (Workgroup on Psychiatric Evaluation, 2006).

If an evaluee does not agree to the conditions of the evaluation as outlined, the evaluation should not be undertaken. The evaluee should be advised that refusal to consent will be noted in the report or testimony and reported to the referring agency.

Perform a Standard Interview, Including a Mental Status Examination and Review of Information Relevant to the Disability Claim

The importance of the mental health interview in workplace evaluations cannot be overstated. Mental health professionals should conduct a standard examination, including a mental status examination, in all disability evaluations (with the exception of those involving record reviews only, as discussed above). The elements used to evaluate and diagnose the presence or absence of a mental disorder follow the general principles elucidated in the American Psychiatric Association's *Practice Guideline for Psychiatric Evaluation of Adults*, Section III (American Psychiatric Association, 2006). This standard evaluation will be modified to some degree by the need to focus on the evaluee's functioning in general and other specific work-related issues. If an interpreter is needed, evaluators may have to advise referral sources to arrange interpretation services.

The interview process is generally best begun with open-ended questions exploring symptoms, impairment, and their relationship to the workplace. Most evaluees are anxious about being evaluated by a mental health professional. Many have never spoken with a psychiatrist or psychologist before. Most mental health disability and disability-related evaluations take place in a perceived, if not actual, adversarial context. Allowing evaluees to present "their side" of the narrative often facilitates obtaining a comprehensive interview. Generally this approach eases evaluees' anxiety because they feel they have been heard out at the start of the evaluation rather than interrogated.

The initial open-ended question approach also facilitates later inquiries from checklists or criteria within categories of function. The more structured part of the interview should explore psychiatric problems with a genetic causative factor, disorders of development, evidence of ability to handle stresses, educational, legal, and military history. Previous problems such as substance abuse, difficulties with others, and ability to maintain healthy and meaningful relationships inside and outside the workplace should also be reviewed (Enelow, 1988).

Disability and disability-related evaluations require a greater emphasis on occupational and functional history than is often obtained in evaluations conducted for treatment purposes. Information obtained during the interview should include a detailed history of past functioning and occupational history, including any problems previously encountered in the workplace or in attempts to obtain employment. Although some of this information may be available through documentary evidence, evaluees' accounts of their occupational history can provide useful information, particularly in regard to claims of previous high functioning or when issues of interpersonal problems are involved. Such information is best obtained in a sequential description of the evaluee's job history along with an assessment of career mobility and a discussion of difficulties and/or accomplishments in each occupational setting (Enelow, 1988).

The interaction between the interviewer and the evaluee provides data as critical to the assessment as the facts conveyed. The manner and affect with which an evaluee describes symptoms and past history, the consistency of the evaluee's account of events, and interpersonal styles of relating to the examiner are all important sources of data. Although most evaluees have a certain degree of anxiety and even suspiciousness at first, as noted above, many are able to become more comfortable if the evaluator presents a neutral environment in which the evaluee can speak freely. Persistent stances of distrust and defensiveness and consistent minimization or exaggeration of symptoms or events are all factors that provide significant information regarding the evaluee's coping styles, interpersonal skills, and mental status.

Avoid the Presence of Third Parties During the Evaluation

The presence of third parties unnecessary to the conduct of the evaluation should be avoided. Standard psychiatric interviews are typically conducted solely with the patient. In forensic evaluations, evaluees sometimes request or demand that they be accompanied during the examination. The presence of third parties, such as family, friends, therapists, or attorneys, inevitably results in some distortion of the interview process (Simon, 1996b). Audio and videotape recording is also beyond the scope of normal procedures and should be discouraged. However, if issues such as the presence of third parties, or audiotaping or videotaping an interview arise, optimally they should be addressed well before the examination begins (Grant & Robbins, 2003; Simon, 1996b).

The presence of a third party may be necessary to facilitate conducting a reliable interview, as in cases where an interpreter is needed for a non-English-speaking or deaf litigant (Simon, 1996b). If an interpreter is required, a professional interpreter, rather than family or friends, should translate. Professional interpreters understand that their role is to be the voice of the communicating parties rather than an active third party (Brodsky, 1987b; Grant & Robbins, 2003).

At times, attorneys or others are legally allowed to be present during a forensic examination. Evaluators should advise the representative not to interfere in the interview, either by offering information or by advising the evaluee not to respond to certain areas of inquiry (Grant & Robbins, 2003; Simon, 1996b). In these cases, evaluators should note if and how the dynamics of the interview have been affected. Although the presence of a third party inevitably alters the interview, it may not always do so in a manner that affects the quality of the information obtained, particularly if the third party cooperates with the evaluator's instructions.

Correlate the Mental Disorder with Occupational Impairment

Assess Categories of Function

As discussed in Chapter 5, the assessment of work capacity requires that evaluators assess specific areas of functioning. The setting of the evaluation and the nature of the claimed impairment may determine which categories of function should be evaluated. In any individual, multiple functions may be affected by psychiatric symptoms (Drukteinis, 2004).

A number of different classification systems for impairment are used in the United States and in other countries. Using these categories and their components may help evaluators avoid making vague or overgeneralized conclusions about impairment and disability. For example, as reviewed in Chapter 5, the Social Security Administration (Social Security Administration Office of Disability Programs, 2004) defines four specific categories of function:

1. activities of daily living;
2. social functioning;
3. concentration, persistence, and pace; and
4. deterioration or decompensation in complex or work-like settings.

Other classification systems are provided in the American Medical Association's *Guides to the Evaluation of Permanent Impairment, 6th Edition* (American Medical Association, 2008); the World Health Organization's *International Classification of Functioning, Disability and Health* (World Health Organization, 2001); and Diagnostic and Statistical Manual of Mental Disorders (DSM-IV-TR) Global Assessment of Functioning (GAF) scale (American Psychiatric Association, 2000).

The Bazelon Center for Mental Health has compiled a list of potential work functions that may be impaired due to psychiatric illness (Bazelon Center for Mental Health, 2008) specifically in relation to addressing accommodations for these impairments under the ADA. These specific work functions are applicable in all types of disability evaluations. Circumstances of the individual evaluation will suggest which areas of function or specific functions are most significant for evaluators to assess. Table 6.1, adapted from Bazelon Center's list, provides guidance regarding specific and basic work functions in three domains, namely social/emotional, cognitive, and physical, that may be impaired by psychiatric symptoms and should be considered in disability and disability-related evaluations.

Seek Descriptions and Clear Examples of Impairment

Evaluators should explore all claimed work impairments in detail, seeking specific behavioral examples and/or clear descriptions of how the evaluee's

Table 6.1 Work functions to be assessed in disability and disability-related evaluations

1. Social/emotional
Giving directions
Requesting clarification
Initiating interpersonal contact
Asking for feedback on job performance
Responding appropriately to negative feedback
Initiating corrective action
Providing explanations
Describing events
Communicating intelligibly, fluently, and coherently
Responding appropriately to supervision
Maintaining relationships with supervisors
Responding appropriately to supervisors
Responding appropriately to coworkers
Adapting to a new supervisor or new coworkers

2. Cognitive
Understanding, remembering, carrying out directions
Assessing own performance
Making decisions
Seeking information when necessary
Exercising judgment
Problem-solving capacity:

- managing multiple pressures or stresses;
- balancing work and home life;
- solving routine problems that make it possible to work, such as getting up on time, taking public transportation.

Recognizing when to stop doing one task and move on to another
Learning new tasks
Transferring learning
Adapting to a change in work assignment (e.g., in corporate re-organization)
Focusing on multiple tasks simultaneously
Screening out environmental stimuli (e.g., noise, visual distractions)
Processing information (e.g., understanding, analyzing, or synthesizing)
Maintaining boundaries of responsibility

3. Physical
Maintaining fixed work schedule, including issues such as

- need for flexible schedule or breaks or modified hours due to the impairment;
- the effects of medication;
- the need for appointments to receive treatment; and
- need for leave to receive acute treatment.

Maintaining work pace
Maintaining stamina throughout the workday

Adapted from the Bazelon Center for Mental Health (2008).

claimed psychiatric problems have affected functioning. If work impairment is suspected or claimed, mental health professionals should inquire

- when the evaluee reported an inability to work because of the symptoms;
- whether changes in work performance were noted by supervisors or coworkers and whether evidence exists to confirm this;
- whether these changes were unusual for the individual or whether the individual has had problems with work performance in the past; and
- if there have been previous instances of work-performance issues, were they related to the types of symptoms the individual is currently experiencing (Leclair & Leclair, 2001).

Evaluators should determine whether work capacity and degree of impairment have changed over time and the reasons for these changes. If an impairment is not present all the time, evaluators should specify the conditions under which specified functioning is or becomes impaired. Examples of this type of situation include specific phobias, or when interpersonal relationships in the workplace are impaired with one individual but not others, or when an evaluee has demonstrated an inability to cope with specific workplace conditions or stresses but not others.

Examples of impaired functioning outside the workplace should also be explored. Psychiatric impairments that affect workplace functioning are likely to affect functioning in other spheres. Individuals whose concentration is so impaired that they cannot manage finances in the workplace should have difficulty in managing personal finances of similar complexity. Alternatively, an individual who reports depression, social avoidance, and decreased energy, to the point where work attendance is problematic, but also reports continuing to engage in a demanding and high-energy hobby, such as playing on a competitive sports team, presents information that indicates less likelihood of globally impaired energy and social avoidance.

Examples of other types of impairments in social, personal, and family activities should also be elicited. Routine activities such as driving, household activities such as cooking, cleaning, and shopping, TV and reading habits, exercise habits, hobbies, travel, school, and sports activities should all be explored. Inquiries about the extent of and satisfaction with routine social interactions with relatives and friends, participation in community, religious, or professional organizations can demonstrate degrees of unimpaired or impaired interpersonal functioning. Again, changes in functioning over time should also be explored.

Asking evaluees to give a detailed account of their daily activities on an average or typical day, a good day, and a bad day is a useful way to obtain information regarding impairments, especially those present in the evaluee's personal life. Asking for an hour-by-hour description of activities can counteract the tendency of some evaluees to answer questions with sweeping descriptions of global impairment, such as "I don't do anything all day." Exploring through the evaluee's daily routines in detail can also sometimes reveal areas of preserved functioning that demonstrate the potential for work or rehabilitation.

Correlate the Requirements of the Evaluee's Job to the Claimed Impairments

Evaluators should correlate claimed impairments with specific job skills or requirements. Employment documents, including job descriptions, performance reviews, and other work assessments, should provide the basis for the evaluator to review the nature of the job with the evaluee. Evaluees' descriptions of their jobs may not match written descriptions in every detail but should be consistent with written descriptions. In addition, detailed inquiry into the actual work duties, the organizational structure of the workplace and work area, and the type of specific demands provide a framework for assessing impairment. Evaluators may find speaking with the evaluee's supervisor when permitted to so helpful in making this correlation.

Just as in cases of physical disorders and disability, individuals with mild or moderate symptoms of mental disorder may have significant impairment if their jobs are particularly hazardous or demanding. For example, an individual with chronic back pain and a restriction of lifting no more than 20 pounds might experience only mild impairment if employed at a sedentary desk job that does not routinely require heavy lifting. In contrast, a dockworker might be totally disabled by such a limitation. Similarly, an inability to maintain persistence and pace due to severe depression might be less of an impairment in an individual with flexible work demands but might represent a disabling impairment for an individual who has to meet daily deadlines.

Compare and Correlate Functional History with Current Level of Impairment

Evaluators should compare the individual's functioning before and after the development of the claimed disability or injury to arrive at a reasonable determination of severity of impairment. Mental health professionals should never assume that the onset of an evaluee's functional impairment, its cause, or consistency began with the illness or problem that precipitated the current evaluation. A longitudinal review of the evaluee's academic, military, social, and occupational functioning, as discussed above and in Chapter 5, is important to reach conclusions regarding the relationship between the claimed disorder and workplace impairments.

For example, an individual may claim a sudden change in previously high functioning due to posttraumatic stress disorder. A detailed review of functional history may, however, reveal a lifetime of poor or marginal functioning. Conversely, an individual who has suffered a head injury and depression may be so profoundly impaired that an interview cannot yield adequate information regarding previous levels of functioning. Only a detailed review of longitudinal functional history will reveal how much this evaluee's functional capacities have changed.

A longitudinal assessment of functioning therefore requires evidence of functioning over a sufficiently long period of time before the date of examination. This evidence should include treatment notes, hospital discharge summaries, work evaluations, and rehabilitation progress notes if they are available. Even tax records can reveal information about previous levels of functioning. The evaluator should describe the length and history of the impairment, points of exacerbation and remission, any history of hospitalization and/or outpatient treatment, and modalities of treatment used in the past. Examiners should determine whether mental or behavioral disorders previously resulted in work disruption, and if so, how long did the evaluee experience the work disruption and the circumstances under which the evaluee was able to return to work.

Other causes of changes in function should be explored and differentiated from impairments due to psychiatric illness. For example, changes in functioning related to use of medications may be significant in some evaluees. "Deconditioning" and other effects of not working or unemployment should also be considered in assessing current impairment. As discussed in Chapter 3, being away from the workplace for extended periods of time due to leave or unemployment can precipitate profound functional impairment. For example, an individual who has been on prolonged medical leave who complains of insomnia and associated fatigue may in fact be suffering from an altered sleep cycle due to the loss of the structure conferred by a regular work schedule. The inability to sleep at night in such individuals is often the result of habitual daytime napping rather than the result of insomnia associated with anxiety or depression.

Use Rating Scales Whenever Appropriate or Requested

Rating scales may be helpful in quantifying impairment, although the use of one is usually not required. If referral sources want evaluators to utilize a rating scale, they generally will identify the one they wish utilized. No analysis has examined the ways in which impairment rating practice guidelines apply to the evaluation of mental impairments (Pryor, 1997). In addition, given the complexities of attempting to quantify the relationship between psychiatric disorders, related impairment, and disability, no professional organization has developed an effective or convenient rating system for determination of psychiatric impairment as it pertains specifically to the determination of various types of work disability.

Nevertheless, the use of a standardized rating scale can assist in minimizing the potential biases in the use of subjective and idiosyncratic standards in the assessment of function (Gold & Simon, 2001). Several rating scales are available for use in assessing psychiatric disability and for inclusion in disability reports.[3] The American Medical Association *Guides* (American Medical Association, 2008) is the most widely used and accepted reference for evaluating permanent impairment for purposes of disability determinations and have been commonly used in state and federal workers' compensation cases.[4]

---

[3] One general rating scale is the International Classification of Functioning, Disability and Health (ICF), developed by the World Health Organization (World Health Organization, 2001), as a logical extension of the International Classification of Diseases, 10th revision (World Health Organization, 2004).

[4] Federal workers' compensation laws cover all federal employees (including postal workers) and citizens of Washington DC (American Medical Association, 2008). Federal disability systems that use the *Guides* also include the Federal Employees Compensation Act and the Longshore and Harbor Workers' Compensation Act.

Generally, the *Guides*, which adopted the terminology and conceptual framework of disability proposed by the World Health Organization's *Classification of Functioning, Disability and Health* (World Health Organization, 2001), uses a percentage rating system from 0 to 100% to score impairment in physiological and anatomic functions. However, the *Guides* have never used this percentage system for psychiatric or behavioral disorders. The 5th edition of the *Guides* (American Medical Association, 2001) noted that the Committee on Disability and Rehabilitation of the American Psychiatric Association advised against the use of percentages in evaluating impairments due to mental and behavioral disorders, and the contributors to the *Guides* agreed. "Unlike cases with some organ systems, there are no precise measures of impairment in mental disorders. The use of percentages implies a certainty that does not exist. Percentages are likely to be used inflexibly by adjudicators, who then are less likely to take into account the many factors that influence mental and behavioral impairment" (American Medical Association, 2001, p. 361). The 5th edition of the *Guides* proposed a classification system for the impact of impairments due to mental injury intended to provide a general assessment of overall impairment. These categories were discussed in terms of the amount of "useful functioning" the impairment will allow and were rated on a scale of permanent impairment ranging from 1, "no impairment," to 5, "extreme impairment."

The sixth edition of the American Medical Association *Guides to the Evaluation of Permanent Impairment* (American Medical Association, 2008), recognizing the limitations of the previous rating system for psychiatric impairment, proposed a new impairment rating system (Chapter 14). This new system is based on a process of calculating scores in three preexisting scales, namely the Brief Psychiatric Rating Scale, the GAF scale, and the Psychiatric Impairment Rating Scale. Evaluators are then asked to use the middle or median value of the three scores as the actual impairment rating.

The validity, reliability, and utility of this proposed rating system have yet to be demonstrated. Limitations of this system include its cumbersome and unwieldy application. In addition, only impairments for selected, well-validated major mental illnesses are considered. The rating system is limited to mood disorders, anxiety disorders, and psychotic disorders, the first two of which are, as noted in Chapter 4, the most commonly encountered in disability and disability-related evaluations. However, the *Guides* do not provide a method for assessing other disorders that also affect employment, such as personality disorders, substance use disorders, attention deficit hyperactivity disorder, and dementia.

Also, as noted above, the *Guides* rating system is intended for use in the assessment of permanent impairment. Although some individuals may reach a point where the impairments associated with their baseline mental status results in permanent disability, other individuals show variable patterns of impairment that wax and wane with the severity of an exacerbation or the relative lack of impairment in remission.

The rating scale that is generally most familiar to mental health professionals is the DSM GAF scale (American Psychiatric Association, 2000). The GAF scale is a standard component in multiaxial diagnostic assessment and is commonly used both in treatment and in forensic evaluations, including disability evaluations. This scale considers psychological, social, and occupational functioning on a hypothetical continuum of mental health and illness and assigns a numerical value from 1 to 100 to rate degree of functioning. The GAF scale has demonstrated both validity and reliability (Hilsenroth et al., 2000; Jones et al., 1995), although reliability has been found to be associated primarily with the raters' experience, knowledge, and training in using the scale (Soderberg et al., 2005).

Although the GAF scale is a valid measure of adaptive functioning, it too has limitations. The assessment of functioning in the GAF scale is that attributed to mental impairment alone. Instructions for the use of the GAF scale specify that impairment in functioning due to nonpsychiatric limitations, such as physical illness or environmental problems, should not be considered in determining a GAF score. Practically speaking, it may be impossible to disentangle the combined reduction in function imposed by mental, physical, and even environmental impairments. Another limitation arises from the GAF scale's single score, which combines the evaluation of psychological symptoms with academic, social, interpersonal, and occupational functioning. Applying a single common numerical value as a global measure for these distinct domains of functioning may be misleading in cases where an evaluee's psychological, social, and occupational functioning do not correlate neatly (Goldman et al., 1992).

Consider the Effects of Medical Illnesses and Medications

Many factors besides psychological symptoms and their associated impairments can affect work function. For example, evaluees may have chronic or acute physical disorders that present with or are accompanied by psychiatric symptoms. Physical disorders may produce psychological symptoms such as loss of sleep, loss of libido, poor concentration, depressed mood or fatigue, as can their prescribed medications' side effects. Anemia can be associated with anxiety or depression and fatigue. Chronic obstructive pulmonary disease can also cause anxiety or depression as well as cognitive impairment. Congestive heart failure can cause anxiety and depression. Hypothyroidism and hyperthyroidism can have symptoms that mimic affective and anxiety disorders.

The therapeutic as well as the nontherapeutic side effects of medications for both physical and psychiatric disorders should also be considered in evaluating the overall severity of the individual's impairment and ability to function. Attention must be given to the effects of medication on the individual's signs, symptoms, and ability to function. Psychoactive medications may cause drowsiness, blunted affect, or unwanted effects on other body systems. Side effects should be considered in evaluating the overall severity of the individual impairment and ability to function (American Medical Association, 2008).

Utilize Psychological Testing When Indicated

Psychological and neuropsychological tests, although not necessary for all evaluees, can be valuable sources of information in disability evaluations when conducted in conjunction with the psychiatric interview, examination of records, and information from collateral sources. Certain questions may arise which require evaluation through testing. For example, an individual with a head injury may also develop major depression. An individual who claims impairment in comprehension or memory so severe that it results in complete work disability may have this function best evaluated by neuropsychological testing, a far more sensitive instrument than the mental status examination. Neuropsychological testing may help evaluators discriminate whether the individual is exhibiting irreversible cognitive impairments due to the head injury or cognitive impairments due to depression that may be reversible with successful treatment.

Different psychological and neuropsychological tests evaluate specific psychological functions and can supplement an evaluation when questions regarding such issues arise. For example, cognitive testing, such as the Wechsler Adult Intelligence Scale-III (WAIS-III), can provide quantifiable and reproducible evidence of impairment of memory or other cognitive functions due to psychiatric symptoms. The Minnesota Multiphasic Personality Inventory-2 (MMPI-2), which includes reliable validity scales, can provide corroborating data regarding psychiatric diagnoses, personality characteristics or traits, and response styles that can indicate exaggeration or minimization of complaints. Comprehensive neurological tests such as the Halstead–Reitan Battery or the Luria-Nebraska Battery can be useful in assessing cognitive functioning in disability cases involving dementia, stroke, head injury, and neurological disorders with additional psychiatric symptoms (Shuman, 2005).

Self-administered tests and inventories, such as the Beck Depression Inventory, may be of value in research and treatment settings, but they are of limited usefulness in a forensic mental health or disability evaluation. These questionnaires provide evaluees an opportunity to give information about their complaints and their perceptions of their problems, which is of course relevant information. Nevertheless, these self-report lists of symptoms are not reliable indicators or evidence that the individual's complaints and perceptions are valid. These instruments often do little more than to confirm high complaint levels, somatic preoccupations, or attempts to convince the evaluator that disability exists (Enelow, 1988). To avoid the problems posed by such self-report instruments, the American Medical Association *Guides*, 6th edition (American Medical Association, 2008), recommends that any testing performed contain two or more symptom validity tests.

When evaluators feel that psychological testing may be useful in clarifying referral questions, they should so advise the referral source. The referral source either will arrange for the testing or will work with the evaluator to arrange for testing. Mental health professionals should not conduct any psychological testing that has not been preapproved by the referral source.

Psychological testing, if indicated, should be administered by mental health professionals trained in their administration and scoring (American Psychological Association, 2002). The conduct and administration of testing also affect its validity. Even if initial scoring is done by computer, the test administrator should be able to evaluate the raw data, clinically correlate findings, and explain why computer findings may not match clinical data.

The inappropriate use of self-report inventories or psychological or neuropsychological testing can pose significant problems in employment evaluations. Often inappropriate use of these instruments reflects bias on the part of the evaluators. Consider a patient who presents to an emergency room with complaints of leg pain. X-rays taken of the arm reveal no injury. The conclusion that the patient is malingering based on a normal arm examination is not supportable and reflects the inappropriate use of medical testing.

Similarly, conducting psychological testing that is not relevant to the questions involved in the evaluation represents an inappropriate use of testing. Inappropriate testing and conclusions based on them may result from lack of familiarity with the limitations or appropriate target areas of the testing. The inappropriate use of self-report inventories may also demonstrate bias on the part of the examiner. Basing opinions on self-report testing and presenting this as scientific data may indicate bias sympathetic toward the claimant. The use of testing for which there is no reasonable consensus regarding validity in the particular application being considered, for which standards to assure reliability have not been developed, or for testing normed on populations not relevant to the issue in question may also indicate bias on the part of the examiner (Battista, 1988).

Finally, psychological and neuropsychological testing, although useful, should not be used as the sole basis for judgments about impairment. Psychological testing, such as DSM diagnoses, was not designed for use in disability or other work-related evaluations (Shuman, 2002). Psychological testing can identify personality characteristics or neurocognitive impairments but does not correlate these findings with work impairment. In addition, the populations for which testing was developed and upon which testing has been normed are not those involved in litigation or applying for disability benefits. Thus, test results should be interpreted cautiously, and again, by a mental health professional with expertise in their administration, scoring, and interpretation.

Advise the Referral Source to Obtain Additional Opinions if Indicated

Forensic psychiatrists and psychologists alike are advised for both ethical and legal reasons to practice only within their areas of expertise (see Chapters 1 and 2). Some mental health professionals, who routinely conduct forensic evaluations of all kinds, including disability and disability-related evaluations, work in a multidisciplinary team setting. In these institutions or group practices, referrals to colleagues with necessary subspecialty expertise may be routine.

However, many mental health practitioners with private or limited group practices may not have immediate access to interdisciplinary team resources. If an evaluation requires expertise in an area in which the evaluating psychiatrist or psychologist is not an expert, referral sources should be advised to either refer the case to such an expert or get an adjunctive opinion. For example, most psychiatrists do not have the expertise to administer and hand-score psychological testing. Thus, psychiatrists often work with or refer psychological testing to psychologists who do have the necessary experience. Conversely, most psychologists are not experts in the use of medication or its side effects. Thus, cases referred to psychologists that require expertise in the use of psychotropic medication are also often referred to a psychiatrist for these opinions. Other mental health professionals, such as vocational rehabilitation counselors, may be required for some opinions.

Consider Alternatives That Might Account for Claims of Impairment and Disability

Consider Alternative Explanations

Evaluators should always consider alternative explanations for an individual's claim of impairment, psychological injury, or disability (Drukteinis, 2004). An evaluee whose poorly supported claims have arisen during an employment conflict may be in considerable distress but may be withdrawing from the workplace in an attempt to resolve their employment conflict rather than suffering from a psychiatric impairment that results in work impairment or disability. Claimants themselves sometimes do not understand the difference between "being too upset to work" and having a psychiatric impairment that affects work. In some cases, both dynamics may be present, resulting in symptom exaggeration or poor motivation despite minor impairment.

Mental health professionals may be confronted with the difficult task of assessing whether psychiatric impairment or other work or social issues are the most relevant factor in the claimed impairment or disability. Evaluators should explore the evaluee's circumstances both inside and outside the workplace. In any evaluation, psychiatrist and psychologists should expect to find factors related to primary gain, that is, tangible gains in the form of money or benefits, and/or secondary gain, that is, unconscious psychological gain such as that associated with adopting a "sick role." The presence of such factors does not discount or invalidate the existence or effects of true psychiatric symptoms and impairments related to these symptoms. However, failure to consider such factors may result in an inaccurate or incomplete assessment of psychiatric disability.

Personal, work-related, and nonwork-related factors may interact in the development of disability from injury or impairment (Brodsky, 1987a). For example, workplace crises, including disability claims and claims of discrimination or harassment, not uncommonly arise when an employee faces negative personnel action due to work performance problems, personality disorders, employment instability, or employee misbehavior (Brodsky, 1987a; Drukteinis, 1997). The presence of these factors may signal the possibility that evaluees are using a disability claim to protect themselves from adverse consequences of their workplace performance or behavior or from personnel action.

The models of disability development discussed in Chapter 5, based on a detailed longitudinal history tracing the evolution of the claimed impairment in relationship to the individual's work history, should be of assistance in this essential element of a disability assessment. A history of excellent work history in an individual who developed symptoms of depression and then became impaired implies that depression was responsible for work impairment. Nevertheless, other concerns should be investigated, such as whether the evaluee had depression in the past, whether previous episodes of depression resulted in impairment or work withdrawal, or whether treatment improved symptoms but impairment was still claimed. Even if a straightforward connection exists between the depressive symptoms and work impairment, the evaluator should assess whether the evaluee has reasons to withdraw from work irrespective of depression, such as job dissatisfaction or pending retirement.

Many individuals also report that problems over and above their disabling condition keep them from working (Druss et al., 2000). Outside the work setting, individuals may face a variety of overwhelming family or social problems unrelated to the workplace or an underlying psychiatric disorder that may be resolved by withdrawing from the workplace and filing claims for disability benefits. The timing of a claimed disability or claimed symptoms disproportionate to the claimed impairment, along with evidence of exaggeration and malingering, may be clues to such problems.

As discussed in detail in Chapter 5, motivation to work should always be considered in the evaluation of disability or workplace conflict. For some people, poor motivation can be a major cause of poor functioning. The determination of motivation is often nonempirical, and evaluators should be wary of their own biases when coming to conclusions in this area (see Chapters 1 and 5). As noted, in many cases an individual's motivation is not well understood even after careful assessment (American Medical Association, 2008).

Consider the Possibility of Malingering

Mental health professionals are frequently asked either directly or by implication to determine whether evaluees claiming psychiatric disability are malingering. As in all forensic evaluations, psychiatrists and psychologists should always consider the possibility of malingering for overt financial or other primary gain in claims of work-related psychiatric impairment or disability. Unconscious distortions, such as unintentionally exaggerating or overdramatizing symptoms, are related to personality characteristics or coping styles. In contrast, any type of malingering requires a deceitful state of mind (Resnick, 2003).

As discussed in Chapter 1, treating medical or mental health clinicians are unlikely to state that their patients are exaggerating, malingering, or displaying factitious disorders unless the evidence is overwhelming. Instead, they usually diagnose a somatoform disorder, or a physical disorder such as chronic pain syndrome or fibromyalgia that cannot be demonstrated or excluded by objective testing (Brodsky, 1996a). In contrast, forensic mental health evaluators are obligated to consider the unpleasant reality that some people will lie to obtain personal gain at the expense of others.

The incentives for frankly malingering or exaggerating a psychiatric disability may range from trying to obtain several paid months off work to effecting permanent withdrawal from the workplace with monthly disability payments or a large settlement check. Evaluators should bear in mind that the implications of a diagnosis of malingering, that is, pretending to have symptoms of illness, or dissimulation, that is, minimizing symptoms of illness, can be serious. Therefore, the determination that an evaluee is malingering mental illness should be based on convincing evidence (Appelbaum & Gutheil, 2006). Unsupportable conclusions regarding malingering or dissimulation represent substandard practice (see Rogers, 2008a).

Malingering may present as feigned disability, fabricated claims of harassment or discrimination, exaggerated effects of a medical or psychological condition upon "major life activities," exaggerated symptoms, misattribution of causes, and reversal of cause and effect (Rosman, 2001). Malingering can present on a spectrum from mild exaggeration of existing symptoms to complete fabrication of symptoms (Tisza et al., 2003). In disability and disability-related evaluations, symptom exaggeration or magnification is often more common than "complete faking" of illness or injury and can make the assessment of true impairment and symptoms more challenging (Rosman, 2001).

No method of detecting malingering is completely accurate. The most common method used to assess malingering is the clinical interview performed in an informed context (Resnick, 2003). Comprehensive reviews have described the interview skills used in nonstructured interviews to detect behavioral and verbal clues suggestive of dissimulation (see Melton et al., 2007; Resnick, 2003; Rogers, 2008b). A final determination of malingering requires the integration of data from a variety of sources, including collateral interviews or documentation, clinical records, third parties, unstructured and structured interviews, and standardized psychological tests.

An evaluee's report of impairments should be internally consistent as well as consistent with that provided by third-party information and documentary evidence. An evaluee providing an accurate history should be able to provide a description of the development, course, areas, and severity of impairment that contains little self-contradictory material. Again, the pattern of disability development as discussed in Chapter 5 should be determined and be consistent with the evaluee's report. Characteristically deceptive response strategies include the endorsement of rare, indiscriminant, fantastic, or preposterous symptoms (Resnick, 2003; Rogers, 2008b). Complaints grossly in excess of clinical findings or a pattern of disability development that does not fit one of the work capacity models in Chapter 5 should trigger consideration of malingering.

Voluntary symptom production, such as atypical symptomatic fluctuation consistent with external incentives, also suggests malingering (Rogers, 2008b). Such inconsistency is especially meaningful where the disparity directly reflects the examinee's awareness of the functional capacity being tested. Thus, an examinee may be able to follow a prolonged and detailed conversation, showing concentration ability, but claim inability to perform tasks requiring minimal concentration or straightforward tests of concentration on the mental status examination (Appelbaum & Gutheil, 2006). Unusual symptomatic response to treatment that cannot otherwise be explained also suggests malingering (Rogers, 2008b).

Other clues that an impairment or disability may be malingered or exaggerated include observations that

a. the nature of the condition claimed is not normally disabling, such as migraine headaches or the chronic low-grade depression associated with dysthymic disorder;
b. an employee claims to be disabled despite little evidence of disabling symptoms;
c. the disability is attributed to a specific work circumstance, such as a personality conflict with a supervisor or certain work environment; and
d. an employee is capable of performing tasks outside work that require the same skills as do work-related tasks (Rosman, 2001).

Other evidence suggestive of malingering includes discrepancies in an individual's report of illness and the history of the injury or illness and its treatment. For example, a history of treatment noncompliance but repeated contact with medical providers at times that medical documentation is required to maintain the disability claim may indicate a malingered or exaggerated disorder. An evaluee's legal and work histories may also be revealing. Evaluees sometimes repeat behaviors by claiming disability in a succession of different job positions and with different employers. This history alerts the evaluator to the evaluee's familiarity with the disability system and possible history of malingering for financial gain. The evaluee's history of substance use may also be helpful and reveal inconsistencies between self-reports and collateral information.

The mental status examination is essential in the detection of malingered disability. An evaluator may compare mood, affect, speech, and thought process during the evaluation to the individual's reported symptoms. A malingerer may show marked discrepancies between mood, affect, and behavior. For example, evaluees claiming major depression may assert they cannot concentrate, are irritable, and are easily confused, yet may demonstrate a pleasant affect and no impairment of concentration over a prolonged interview.

Psychological testing, as discussed above, is often used to supplement the clinical interview in the detection of deception or malingering of clinical symptoms. Information from such testing can be helpful in establishing certain aspects of response styles associated with malingering and can support a suspicion of malingering. The MMPI-2 is the most commonly used psychological test in forensic evaluations (Greene, 2008; Pope et al., 2006); it includes measurements of the tendency to underreport, exaggerate, or deny symptoms, and the consistency of the individual's response to test questions. These and other validity scales assess deviant response tendencies that may indicate defensive or deceptive responding. Defensive responding, inconsistent responding, and atypical MMPI patterns can reflect a general pattern of malingering on the test (Pope et al., 2006). As discussed above, the interpretation of such patterns requires that the test be administered and scored by a qualified and experienced psychologist.

Psychological testing should not provide the sole basis for a determination of malingering. The reliability of such tests in assessing specific areas of an individual's functioning may not necessarily be better than a careful assessment by a clinician who is able to consider relevant factors outside the scope of the test (Parry, 1998). The decision that an individual is malingering is ultimately made by assembling all of the clues from a thorough evaluation of a subject's past and current functioning with corroboration from other sources (Resnick, 2003; Rogers, 2008b). Nevertheless, when properly used, psychological testing can provide information that can be used in conjunction with the clinical interview and third-party reports to confirm or rule out malingering or dissimulation.

Generally, evaluators will gain little by directly confronting evaluees with suspicions of malingering. If malingering is suspected, the most useful approach is to focus opinions and questions on discrepancies in the data rather than becoming argumentative (Anfang & Wall, 2006). Evaluees who are malingering or exaggerating when directly confronted with accusations of malingering often become angry, respond defensively, and may even terminate the interview. None of these responses will provide additional information and may only serve to make a conflicted and adversarial situation even more complicated. Evaluators who remain neutral and politely ask for clarification of conflicting information or discrepancies in reports, admitting they are confused or puzzled and would like to understand, are likelier to get answers that will help them come to well-reasoned conclusions.

Formulate Well-Reasoned Opinions Supported by Data

An opinion regarding the presence of work impairment due to psychiatric illness should be based on clearly identified changes or limitations in functioning. If evaluators are only capable of speculation, this and the reasons why should be clearly articulated, such as lack of access to a personal interview with the evaluee or lack of access to critical collateral information. If evaluators have identified information that is critical to the formulation of an opinion but which has not been provided, they should inform the referral source that this information would need to be reviewed for an opinion to be reached.

Evaluators should not assume or base opinions regarding impairment or disability solely on the presence of a psychiatric disorder. As discussed, the presence of a psychiatric disorder does not automatically indicate the presence of impairment, and even less so disability, since the latter determination in particular involves nonmedical and vocational considerations. Therefore, unless a psychiatric disorder is so severe that global impairment of functioning and work impairment is overwhelmingly obvious from the manifest symptoms alone, conclusions about impairment should include specific factual reference to limitations in areas of functioning. Opinions regarding impairment (and if requested regarding disability) should demonstrate that the evaluator appreciates the requirements of the particular job description and how the impairment may affect job responsibilities.

Although experts are often advised that opinions should be held to a "reasonable degree of medical certainty" or to a "reasonable degree of medical probability" (Levin, 1998; Rappeport, 1985), the meaning of these phrases has never been entirely clear. In some instances, reasonable medical certainty appears to mean that the evaluator's opinions are as probable as other medical experts in the field could hope to achieve and are of the degree of certainty they would rely upon in making treatment decisions. In other instances it appears to correlate with the various legal standards of persuasion: preponderance of evidence, clear and convincing evidence, or evidence beyond a reasonable doubt.

This ambiguity reflects the confounding of two related but not identical legal concepts: the standards for admissibility of evidence and sufficiency of the evidence to support a verdict (Shuman, 2005). In the event that an evaluation is required to conform to legal rules and those rules include this standard, evaluators need to conform to local requirements. However, many disability and disability-related evaluations occur outside a legal context, and thus the concept of reasonable medical certainty is not relevant. The standard of reasonable medical certainty may become relevant if the case becomes contested in the courts, as many disability cases do. Since the meaning of reasonable medical certainty is unclear and the evaluating professional is unlikely to know whether it will become relevant, evaluators should focus instead on being certain that their opinions are based on standard evaluation procedures and the available, relevant data.

Write a Comprehensive Report That Addresses Referral Questions

In certain situations, such as personal injury litigation, referral sources may instruct evaluating mental health professionals to submit only a brief written report or to submit no report at all. In these cases, the evaluators' findings and opinions are likely to be disclosed through abbreviated expert disclosure statements and oral testimony. In most other evaluation contexts, however, referral sources ask evaluating psychiatrists and psychologists to produce written reports that fully describe their finding and opinions on impairment and disability, and the basis for those opinions.

General Practice Guidelines for Psychiatric Disability Evaluations 153

Most referral sources will request a full report of the evaluation without limitations on the scope or depth of the assessment. In such cases, reports should conform to standard suggested forensic report formats unless otherwise indicated by the referral source. A number of possible formats have been suggested (Allnutt & Chaplow, 2000; Group for the Advancement of Psychiatry, 1994; Silva et al., 2003) but there is no single correct style or format for writing a work-related or disability evaluation report.

The elements that should be included in all types of disability reports (unless otherwise specified as noted above) are found in Appendix C. Regardless of the format chosen for preparing written reports, mental health professionals should remember that the final arbiters of disability decisions typically have not had medical or psychiatric training. Reports should therefore be easy to read and should avoid technical jargon because parties without medical training need to understand the evaluator's findings, logic, and conclusions (Grant & Robbins, 2003).

Opinions

Many referral sources will ask evaluators to answer a set of written questions. All reports should contain the evaluator's opinions framed as responses to these questions, organized by listing each question followed by the response. When specific questions are asked, evaluators should limit themselves to providing opinions and supporting data responsive only to these questions unless otherwise specified. As mentioned earlier, some referral sources will expressly direct the evaluating mental health professional not to give an opinion about disability. Evaluators may be instructed only to provide opinions on impairment and other relevant factors that may influence a disability determination. If a broader discussion of the claimant's impairments and their relationship to disability is warranted, this can be included in the discussion/case formulation section as suggested in Appendix C.

The most common questions mental health providers are asked to address are listed in Table 6.2.

Table 6.2 Typical disability referral evaluation questions

1. Multiaxial diagnosis, including GAF score
2. Impairments in work function and the relationship to psychiatric symptoms
3. Disability from one or own type of work
4. Disability from any type of work
5. Current and past treatment, its adequacy and claimants response to treatment
6. Treatment recommendations, including recommendations for medical consultations or psychological testing
7. Prognosis
8. Motivation
9. Maximum medical improvement
10. Restrictions and limitations
11. Malingering, primary and secondary gain

Not every type of disability or disability-related evaluation will ask for responses to all these questions. For example, in Social Security Disability Insurance (SSDI) evaluations, mental health professionals are directed not to offer opinions regarding disability. In addition, SSDI evaluations and private disability insurers are not interested in causation of illness or disability, whereas causation is a central issue in a worker's compensation evaluation (see Chapter 7). Even though referral sources will not pose all these questions in every evaluation, evaluators should understand and be prepared to address all these issues when relevant.

Multiaxial Diagnosis, Including GAF Score

Diagnoses should utilize DSM categories and criteria. They should, at a minimum, include Axes I, II, and III, and may include all five DSM axes where appropriate, indicated, and/or requested. Reasons for any differential diagnoses should be given. In cases where a diagnosis is contingent on a factual determination, evaluators should provide adequate explanation regarding how the disputed fact could change the diagnosis.

Impairments in Work Function and the Relationship to Psychiatric Symptoms

Impairments in work function and their relationship to psychiatric symptoms and disorders are the central opinions in any disability evaluation, and the importance of these opinions cannot be overemphasized. The impairments most often associated with the most common psychiatric disorders encountered in the workplace were reviewed in Chapter 4, and a list of generally relevant work functions was provided in Table 6.1 above. In any evaluation, mental health professionals should be as specific as possible in relating work functions to impairments. Examples indicating the claimant's impairments and how they affect specific areas of functioning should be provided. These examples should not be limited only to job functioning but should include examples of social, interpersonal, and leisure functioning as well.

Causation

Causation is a complicated concept, particularly in the evolution of psychiatric disorders. Opinions regarding causality are even more complex in forensic evaluations than in treatment evaluations because medical causality and legal causality are two distinctly different concepts (Danner & Sagall, 1977). Although the concept of causation remains enigmatic even within the law (Shuman & Greenberg, 2003), it generally refers to proximate cause, that is, the last factor in a series of events rather than first or primary causes of an event. Practically speaking, proximate or legal causation has come to mean "the straw that broke the camel's back" (Simon, 1992, p. 550), that is, the immediate or most recent cause (Garner, 2004).

Difficulties in applying scientific causal research to the legal determination of causation in specific cases can lead to confusion for mental health professionals and administrative and legal systems struggling with causation of disability. Psychiatrists and psychologists examine and weigh multiple causative elements, including primary causes, when considering the etiology of any disorder (Simon & Shuman, 2007). These can include constitutional or genetic factors, social stressors, comorbid disorders, personality structure, personal history, and the availability of support systems as well as external events. Although one particular factor may have been the most immediate precipitant of the disorder in question, the interaction between a number of factors is generally considered to play a role in the development of illness.

Mental health professionals providing opinions regarding causation should be aware of the differences in definition between medical and legal causation. Nevertheless, if providing opinions regarding causation of disability or injury, they should sequentially consider and explain whether

- A causal event took place;
- The evaluee that experienced the event has a condition that is causing an impairment;
- The event could cause the condition and related impairment; and
- The event did cause or materially contributed to the condition and related impairment.

As a corollary to the question of causation, mental health professionals may be asked to offer opinions regarding aggravation of preexisting disorders. Although a single event can be the sole or primary cause of a given effect, in many instances evaluees have preexisting pathology that may underlie their current clinical condition. Evaluators should be aware that the terms exacerbation and aggravation again are not synonymous relative to disability evaluations. Aggravation is a circumstance or event that permanently worsens a preexisting or underlying condition. The terms exacerbation, recurrence, or flare-up generally imply temporary worsening of a condition that subsequently returns to baseline (American Medical Association, 2008).

Apportionment, that is, allocation of causation among multiple factors that caused or significantly contributed to the injury or disease and resulting impairment, is another corollary issue to causation regarding which evaluators may be asked to give opinions. Apportionment requires a determination of impairment directly attributable to preexisting illness as compared with that of the condition under consideration. If apportionment is required, evaluators must consider the nature of the impairment and its relationship to each alleged causative factor, along with an explanation of the medical basis for all conclusions and opinions (American Medical Association, 2008).

Disability for One Type of Work, Evaluee's Type of Work, or Any Type of Work

As discussed in this and previous chapters, opinions regarding disability are more than medical opinions and must take into consideration factors beyond those of the presence of psychiatric illness and associated impairments. If opinions regarding disability are offered, they should be well formulated and based on evidence from the interview, documentary evidence, and other relevant collateral information. Evaluators should bear in mind that they may have to defend opinions regarding disability in administrative or legal proceedings. If evaluators are unable to make this determination based on the available information, they should so inform the referral source. Evaluators should also be certain not to offer opinions regarding disability if they have not been asked to do or if they have been expressly asked not to do so.

Current and Past Treatment, Its Adequacy, and Claimant's Response

In many cases, an individual's impairments have evolved into a work disability because of issues related to treatment or treatment response. Any individual who claims disability on the basis of a psychiatric disorder should be receiving aggressive treatment. Although the individual's disorder may not meet criteria for inpatient psychiatric treatment since these are generally limited to dangerousness to self or others, the development of work disability without doubt merits a full court press in terms of available outpatient treatment.

Unfortunately, many individuals do not receive aggressive outpatient treatment. Claimants, and sometimes their mental health providers, may not understand that appropriate and aggressive treatment might restore work functioning even if some symptoms or mild impairments remain. Alternatively, both claimants and providers may believe that claimants are receiving appropriate and adequate treatment, when in fact, they are not. For example, an individual who claims she is unable to work due to depression may consider engaging in weekly psychotherapy adequate treatment but refuse to take medication. Although this claimant is in treatment, the treatment is not adequate given the demonstrated efficacy of antidepressant medications and a claim of work disability. At times, treatment providers may unintentionally collude with a patient's avoidance of appropriate treatment due to the misunderstanding of the nature of a responsible treatment alliance, as discussed in Chapter 1.

Conversely, evaluators should be able to identify individuals who have a history of inadequate response to prior appropriate treatment and who are receiving appropriate treatment without significant effect. These individuals may indeed have reached a point in their natural evolution of their illness where impairment has resulted in permanent disability. Residual problems may also represent side effects of medication. Nevertheless, this is not a reason for treatment to be withdrawn or abandoned. Further treatment may result in stabilization, even at a permanently disabled level, and/or prevent further deterioration and loss of other important functional abilities.

The conclusion that the claimant is unlikely to improve cannot be made without evaluation of past and current treatment and without application and evaluation of effectiveness of appropriate and aggressive treatment. Evaluators assessing an individual who claims permanent and total disability prior to receiving an adequate course of treatment or who is refusing recommended treatment should consider the possibility of other issues relating to the workplace as potentially more significant than psychiatric illness. A thorough assessment includes a history of the response to treatment and a determination of whether adequate treatment has been given. Evaluators should consider whether

- treatment has been sufficiently aggressive and of adequate duration;
- treatment resulted in improvement in patient function;
- a reasonable number of treatment options have been applied;
- the evaluee has been cooperative and compliant with recommended treatment;
- psychiatric symptoms related to illness (e.g., cognitive deficits, lack of insight) are interfering with the evaluee's ability to comply with treatment; and
- comorbid substance abuse and physical disorders have been considered and, if so, are they present and have they been addressed (American Medical Association, 2008).

Adequate treatment also involves an active return to work plan, with possibly incremental but nevertheless clear goals of increasing functioning and returning to work. These goals should be regularly assessed and adjusted as circumstances dictate. A work-return plan for psychiatric disability includes the following elements:

a. the intended outcome of the plan, that is, return to full-time work, part-time work, same job, different job;
b. what type of graduated transition back to the workplace is reasonable;
c. specific accommodation requirements and how long they are likely to be needed;
d. critical timelines, such as crucial events and stages associated with the recuperation process that have implications for work capacity, accommodation requirements, and resumption of productivity;
e. frequent assessment of functioning by stage or event, including a plan of action in response to specified crucial elements, stages, and events; and
f. supportive mechanisms, including monitoring success of accommodations, movement toward full work return, and procedures to address possible problems or relapses (Leclair & Leclair, 2001).

Treatment Recommendations, Including Recommendations for Medical Consultations or Psychological Testing

If the evaluee is not receiving appropriate or adequate treatment or is not responding to appropriate and aggressive treatment, evaluators should make specific treatment recommendations to the referral source. These may include trials of medication or specific types of psychotherapy such as cognitive behavior therapy or exposure therapy. Optimal psychopharmacological management includes trials of medications at therapeutic doses to ascertain which may be most effective with the least side effects.

Treatment recommendations may also include consultations with mental health providers with specialized area of expertise, for example, those who specialize in mental disorders comorbid with head trauma. Consultations with other medical professionals may also be recommended if physical problems are suspected to be causing or contributing to mental health disorders and impairments. Individuals whose subjective complaints of cognitive impairment are not congruent with mental status examination findings and their continued areas of intact functioning may need to be referred for psychological or neuropsychological testing in order to evaluate diagnosis and appropriate treatment interventions.

Referral sources should be encouraged to share treatment recommendations with the claimants and their treatment providers (see Chapter 2 for discussion regarding claimants' access to reports). Treatment providers often view these suggestions as a second opinion that assists them in providing more effective treatment or suggest avenues of treatment they had not considered. Claimants who are motivated to return to work may benefit from the evaluator's specific and candid recommendations regarding treatment, even if this includes suggesting seeking alternate treatment providers.

Prognosis

This includes the expected course of the evaluee's disorder(s), likelihood of recovery or chronicity, and expected duration of the impairment. The longitudinal work capacity model of disability discussed in Chapter 5 can inform this opinion. Extrapolating from past and present circumstances to form opinions regarding prognosis should take into account the natural history of the claimant's disorder, the presence of comorbid mental or physical disorders, previous response to treatment, treatment compliance, current response to treatment, and motivation for recovery.

Motivation

As discussed in Chapter 5, assessment of motivation to seek and comply with treatment, and to attempt to overcome or adapt to impairments so as to avoid or minimize disability, is an essential aspect of a disability evaluation. As noted, lack of motivation can be a symptom of psychiatric illness or side effect of psychiatric medication. Nevertheless, motivation itself is not a medical concept. Its assessment represents a judgment based on nonmedical evidence and influenced by a multitude of factors. As a result, evaluators should be certain their assessments consider all relevant factors while attempting to neutralize their own biases regarding motivation to work, as discussed in Chapter 1.

Maximum Medical Improvement

Mental health professionals are often asked to provide an opinion as to whether the claimant's impairments are permanent or whether the claimant has reached maximum medical improvement (MMI). MMI is usually synonymous with the concept of permanency of impairment, that is, the state wherein impairment becomes static or well stabilized with or without medical treatment. The American Medical Association *Guides* (American Medical Association, 2008) define a permanent condition or impairment as one that is "not expected to change significantly over the next 12 months" (p. 353). A claimant who has reached MMI is a claimant whose current condition reflects the end result of available treatment and illness status where symptoms can be expected to remain stable for at least the next 12 months or can be managed with palliative measures that do not, within medical probability, alter the underlying impairment substantially (American Medical Association, 2008). Usually, MMI is considered to have been reached when all reasonable medical treatment expected to improve the condition has been offered or provided.

Defining MMI in an individual with a psychiatric disorder is a difficult task and may be impossible in some instances (Leclair & Leclair, 2001). Many mental disorders are dynamic rather than static in nature and are, to some extent, never at permanency (American Medical Association, 2008). Remission may be incomplete at certain points in time and much more robust, to the point of lack of impairment, at other times. Chronic disorders, such as depression or generalized anxiety disorder, have patterns of recurrence and chronicity that may respond well or only minimally to therapeutic interventions. These disorders have their own clinical courses and degrees of impairment, and evaluation of MMI has to take into account that both may vary considerably among individuals with the same diagnosis. In addition, MMI is not predicated on the elimination of symptoms and/or subjective complaints nor does it preclude the inherent deterioration of a condition over time or the effects of maintenance treatment on the condition, which can possibly result in decrease in impairments (American Medical Association, 2008).

Opinions regarding MMI can be even more complex in the evaluation of claimants who have received inadequate treatment or who have refused treatment. Many individuals will, for example, refuse to engage in psychotherapy or refuse to take psychiatric medications. Mental health evaluators may still be asked to make a determination regarding MMI, even though inadequate treatment or treatment noncompliance precludes optimal disease control and functioning. In these cases, opinions regarding MMI will have to take these factors into consideration.

The fact that a claimant has refused treatment does not preclude or change the assessment of current impairment. However, evaluators should offer an opinion regarding the appropriateness of the suggested treatment and document the basis for the claimant's treatment refusal. Evaluators may conclude that the claimant is at MMI due to treatment noncompliance or inadequate treatment. Evaluators should also comment on whether appropriate treatment or treatment compliance could result in decrease in impairments and improvement in function.

Opinions regarding MMI are not strictly medical opinions. Similar to disability, an opinion about MMI is based on a combination of medical evaluations such as adequacy of treatment, treatment response, course of illness, and prognosis, as well as nonmedical factors, such as motivation, issues regarding entitlement, or secondary gain. If the referral provides the policy's or program's definition of permanent or of MMI, evaluators should be certain their opinions utilize that definition. If no definition is provided, evaluators should provide specific timeframes, if possible, and consider providing opinions that utilize medical concepts such as partial or total remission as well as potential for relapse. These opinions should also reference restrictions and limitations in functioning as well as possible accommodations that may preserve functioning, if appropriate.

Restrictions and Limitations

As discussed above, restrictions address what a claimant "should not do" because of the risk of exacerbating or precipitating psychiatric symptoms. In contrast, limitations address what a claimant "cannot do" because of psychiatric symptoms, that is, a reflection of documented loss of function. Referral sources commonly request opinions on an evaluee's restrictions and limitations, including the projected length of time restrictions will be present and remaining abilities or residual functioning. Reasonable restrictions can constitute an important aspect of functional capacity. Many treating clinicians will restrict an individual with some impairments from work altogether, rather than consider alternate duties, reasonable accommodations, or work restrictions that might preserve functioning. Mental health evaluators should carefully consider job requirements, symptoms, and impairments and provide more guidance regarding preserved functional capacities. Again, referencing accommodations that will assist or preserve areas of functioning may also be appropriate in this opinion.

Malingering, Primary Gain, and Secondary Gain

As previously noted, referral sources often ask directly or indirectly whether an evaluee is malingering or demonstrates elements of secondary gain in a claim of disability. Elements of malingering, primary gain, and secondary gain should be assessed in every evaluee. The evaluation of malingering is discussed above. Evaluators should bear in mind that malingering, that is, the exaggeration or feigning of symptoms and associated impairments, requires a conscious attempt to deceive. Malingering often occurs in an attempt to obtain primary gain, that is, overt and tangible benefits.

In contrast, secondary gain reflects unconscious processes aimed at the gratification of intrapsychic rather than external needs and does not necessarily involve a conscious attempt at deception. Secondary gain is reflected, for example, in the gratification of excessive dependency needs or the adoption of a sick role and the care and consideration attendant upon being considered ill or disabled. The presence of secondary gains (or even primary gains) in the circumstances surrounding an evaluee's claim of disability does not necessarily negate the validity of claims of illness, impairment, and dysfunction. Nevertheless, secondary gains inherent in a claim, such as the promotion of regression, may make recovery and return to functional status more difficult and should therefore be addressed if identified and if requested.

Conclusion

All assessments of workplace functioning and disability involve some extrapolation from evidence-based conclusions such as diagnosis and levels of impaired functioning. Nevertheless, the process of coming to reasonable conclusions regarding impairment and disability can be made more reliable by following the practice guidelines proposed in this chapter, which are largely based on the guidelines adopted by AAPL (Gold et al., 2008). Adherence to these suggested practices assure that evaluators will examine evidence from multiple, independent sources, probe categories of function in detail, seek clear examples of impairment, obtain dependable corroboration, understand the nature of the evaluee's work, and consider alternative explanations for claims of impairment or disability.

The goal of providing these practice guidelines is to assist mental health professionals in formulating well-reasoned opinions that are fair, complete, and competent assessments of the information obtained in their disability and disability-related evaluations. However, practice guidelines will vary in both usefulness and applicability on a case-by-case basis. In addition, even with use of practice guidelines, experts can and will come to different conclusions based on an evaluation of the same data. Honest disagreement between experts should be expected and respected.

The practice guidelines offered here are not specific to any individual type of disability or disability-related evaluation. The definitions used in programs designed to provide disability benefits or protections have a technical meaning conferred by legislation, case law, and/or contract. Mental health professionals providing disability evaluations need to understand the technical legal definition relevant to each specific type of evaluation. Chapter 7 will discuss common types of disability evaluations, including those involved in the Social Security Disability Income program, workers' compensations programs, and private disability insurance benefits. Chapter 8 will explore evaluations associated with the ADA and Chapter 9 will discuss fitness-for-duty evaluations. These chapters will offer discussion of the standards and rules governing the conduct of these specific evaluations and offer additional guidelines that will allow evaluators to adapt the general practice guidelines offered here to each particular type of disability or disability-related evaluation.

Chapter 7
The Maze of Disability Benefit Programs: Social Security Disability, Workers' Compensation, and Private Disability Insurance

Introduction

Impaired persons in the United States who cannot work and seek benefits to which they are entitled by law or by contract quickly learn that a compassionate, comprehensive system of accessing such assistance does not exist. Although as a society we share a loose consensus that those who cannot work due to illness or impairment should receive disability compensation, no agreement on the definition and measurement of disability exists and we are reluctant to give people money for not working. When asked to support workers who claim to be disabled, rather than conjuring an image of Studs Terkel's gritty American worker, they may imagine Maynard G. Krebs, the able-bodied beatnik who was allergic to work. Neither public agencies nor private insurance companies make it easy to successfully file a disability claim, particularly for psychiatric illness.

Disability benefit programs are a patchwork of uncoordinated public and private systems. The three largest and best known types of disability benefit programs in the United States are Social Security Disability Insurance (SSDI), administered by the Social Security Administration (SSA), a federal agency; the Workers' Compensation system, administered on a state-by-state basis; and private disability insurance programs, administered by private insurance carriers.[1] These programs' benefits, coverage, and eligibility differ in multiple and significant ways.

Mental health professionals play a variety of roles in the process of accessing these disability benefits. These roles range from that of treatment providers documenting their own patients' impairments to consultants or independent examiners providing opinions about a claimant's impairments to an employer, insurer, or agency. Regardless of the role, the contribution of the mental health professional in disability claims can be critical to the outcome of the claim.

---

[1] A variety of other programs exist, such as the Black Lung Disability Benefits, the Railroad Retirement Act, Civil Service Disability Retirement Benefits, and Federal Employees Compensation Act. However, this discussion will focus on the three largest sources of disability benefits named above.

Psychiatrists and psychologists providing disability evaluations need to be able to apply the concepts discussed in previous chapters to each specific type of disability evaluation. The process of translating the medical concept of impairment into nonmedical administrative or legal determinations of disability is complicated. Some challenges in the translation process arise as the result of the lack of congruence between legal and medical basic concepts and terminology, a problem that often occurs at the interface of psychiatry and psychology and any judicial or administrative system.

Mental health professionals providing disability evaluations face an additional challenge: understanding and responding to the requirements of the varied and widely differing disability benefits programs. Regardless of the mental health professional's expertise, the failure to understand the context in which the evaluation takes place can have profound consequences. Mental health professionals need to be able to address the relevant issues in each particular program and to communicate their findings and opinions in a language clearly understood by those who adjudicate the disability claims.

Different disability benefit programs have different definitions of mental disability, different levels of benefits, and different criteria for eligibility for benefits. Each program or administrative system defines the relevant terms that mental health professionals are expected to use. For example, Social Security disability programs have a single, rigid, statutorily determined definition of disability. Workers' compensation disability definitions vary from state to state. Private disability insurers offer definitions of disability that vary from policy to policy. None of these programs use the same definitions, terms, or criteria for eligibility for benefits.

This chapter will focus on discussion of psychiatric disorders and SSDI claims, workers' compensation claims, and private disability insurance claims. These three categories represent the most common contexts for evaluations of disability due to mental disorder. This chapter will also offer mental health professionals suggestions for adapting the principles and guidelines discussed in previous chapters to these specific types of disability evaluations.

Public Disability Insurance: The SSDI Program

The SSA, established by the Social Security Act in 1935, administers two disability benefits programs: the SSDI Program (Title II of the Social Security Act) and the Supplemental Security Income (SSI) (Title XVI of the Act).[2] SSDI

---

[2] SSI, enacted into law in 1972, is a social welfare program that differs from SSDI in several ways. SSI is a means-tested social welfare program that provides for a minimum income level for the needy, aged, blind, and disabled. Financial need, which is statutorily defined, determines a person's eligibility for SSI benefits. SSI is not linked to payment into the Social Security trust fund. Eligibility does not require insured status or any previous attachment to the work force, and its benefits reflect a flat rate, subsistence payment that is lower than

is a federally funded public disability insurance program enacted into law in 1956. This program provides disability cash benefits to citizens and lawful aliens who have not reached 62 years of age (when other benefit programs such as Old Age Assistance apply). SSDI is intended to benefit workers who experience catastrophic injuries or illnesses and are permanently and completely disabled. Eligibility for SSDI benefits, which is not means tested, is only available to those disabled workers (and their dependents) who have contributed to the Social Security trust fund through the Federal Insurance Contributions Act (FICA) tax on their earnings for at least 5 years over the 10-year period preceding the disability.

Mental health professionals with active clinical practices usually have some familiarity with Social Security disability claims. When patients file claims for public disability insurance, thereby beginning the SSDI administrative process, treating clinicians are required to provide documentation of impairments. Most clinicians therefore have seen and filled out SSDI paperwork for their patients.

SSA's disability determination process, definition of disability, and criteria for determining disability are highly specific, statutorily defined, and unique to SSA. They generally differ from those of workers' compensation programs, private disability programs, and other government disability programs. A person considered disabled under another program, such as workers' compensation, will not necessarily be deemed disabled under the Social Security program. In addition, unlike many other public or private programs, there is no "partial disability" under SSDI. A person is either totally or permanently disabled or not (Social Security Administration Office of Disability Programs, 2004).

SSDI Definitions and Process

Medical evidence is the cornerstone of a determination of Social Security disability. Mental health providers and the information they provide are integral to the adjudication of an SSDI claim. However, mental health providers are not asked to determine whether an individual is disabled and, if so, whether that individual is eligible for SSDI benefits. The SSA alone makes those determinations. Nevertheless, psychiatrists and psychologists should be familiar with SSDI's definitions and the process of claims adjudication in order to better understand what information is needed for SSA to make reasonable decisions regarding claims.

---

average SSDI payments. Although SSI will not be discussed further, mental health professionals should be aware that despite differences between the programs, the definition of a disability under SSI and SSDI is the same, and an individual can be eligible for benefits under both programs.

The Process of Filing an SSDI Claim

Claimants typically begin the SSDI process by filing a written application in an SSA district office. The claim is then referred to the Disability Determination Services (DDS), a federally funded state agency responsible for gathering medical records, obtaining medical and vocational evaluations, and rendering the initial determination of disability. Claimants are responsible for providing medical evidence to support their disability claim including information from their health-care providers.[3] One consequence of filing a claim is the loss of privilege or privacy claims that might otherwise apply to relevant records of treatment. Claimants may not place their psychiatric or medical condition in issue and then refuse to release relevant medical evidence of that condition.

Disability and Substantial Gainful Activity

The SSA's definition of disability was developed in the mid-1950s, at a time when a greater proportion of jobs were in manufacturing and required more physical labor than do many jobs today. People with severe impairments were therefore expected to be unable to engage in substantial gainful activity (SGA). Over the past decades, the nature of work has shifted from manufacturing more toward service industries. Medical and technological advances have made it possible for more severely disabled persons to be employed (Wunderlich et al., 2002). Moreover, changes in public attitudes and policy toward accommodating individuals with disabilities have resulted in the passage of the Americans with Disabilities Act (see Chapter 8) and creating more employment options for those who in the past would have had no choice but to accept a disabled status.

Nevertheless, the statutory definition of disability in the SSDI program has remained unchanged. SSA defines disability as the inability "to engage in any substantial gainful activity by reason of any medically determinable physical or mental impairment which can be expected to result in death or which has lasted or can be expected to last for a continuous period of not less than 12 months" (42 USC §423(d)(1)(A)). SGA is considered to be any productive work of a nature generally performed for remuneration or profit, involving the performance of significant physical or mental duties, or a combination of physical and mental duties (Silva et al., 2003).

The definition of SGA is intended to be more than a benchmark set by the claimant's previous employment or by the level of remuneration. It is neither limited by geographic convenience to employment available in the same town or time zone nor limited to fortuitous economics that assure full employment at

---

[3] The SSA will help claimants get medical reports and medical records from their own medical sources when the claimants give SSA permission to do so. The State DDS requests copies of medical records from physicians, psychologists, other health-care professionals, and from hospitals, clinics, and other health facilities where claimants have received evaluation or treatment.

prime wages for all members of the trade or profession (42 USC, §423(d)(2)(A)). It includes any kind of work the claimant is physically or mentally capable of performing for profit. If jobs that the claimant could do exist in substantial quantity somewhere in the country, then the claimant is not eligible for disability benefits (Social Security Administration Office of Disability Programs, 2004).

A statutorily recognized or "listed" medically determinable psychiatric impairment that causes disability is a diagnosis that the SSA has determined may meet the severity requirement of its definition of disability. The SSA has nine listed categories of mental disorders, based on Diagnostic and Statistical Manual (DSM) diagnoses and their criteria (American Psychiatric Association, 2000) (see Table 7.1). Each category or diagnostic group, except mental retardation, autism, and substance addiction disorders, consists of a set of clinical findings (paragraph A criteria), one or more of which must be satisfied for a listed diagnosis to be considered valid. The listings for mental disorders are so constructed that an individual meeting or equaling the criteria of the listings for mental disorders could not reasonably be expected to engage in gainful work activity.

Table 7.1 SSA's paragraph A criteria: Categories of mental disorder or "listed impairments"

1. Organic mental disorders
2. Schizophrenic, paranoid and other psychotic disorders.
3. Affective disorders
4. Mental retardation and autism
5. Anxiety-related disorders
6. Somatoform disorders
7. Personality disorders
8. Substance addiction disorders
9. Autistic disorders

The SSA recognizes that these nine categories of mental disorders do not encompass all types of clinical findings that may result in psychiatric impairments severe enough to preclude an individual from working. To assess whether the claimant suffers from a disability that does not fit into one of the listed impairments yet produces a sufficiently severe impairment to preclude SGA, the regulations direct an assessment of the functional limitation imposed by the disability. These include

1. activities of daily living;
2. social functioning;
3. ability to remain focused; and
4. decompensation in work-like settings.

SSA also allows for consideration and evaluation of severity of the effects of a combination of impairments in determining disability for work. If a combination of impairments precludes work, then the person would be considered disabled even if no single impairment alone would be considered severe. Claimants may also be found to be disabled based on reports indicating that they are experiencing medically equivalent impairments comparable to the criteria of the listings for mental disorders (20 CFR §404.1023).

If paragraph A criteria are satisfied, that is, if a claimant meets criteria for a DSM diagnosis that is a "listed impairment" or its equivalent, SSA then considers criteria assessing functional restrictions (paragraphs B and C criteria). The restrictions listed in paragraphs B and C must be the result of the clinical findings related to the mental disorder outlined in paragraph A. The criteria in paragraphs B and C are based on functional areas thought to be relevant to work and which are believed to establish the severity of the disorder. At least two or three of the four paragraph B criteria (see Table 7.2) must be met for claimants to demonstrate functional restrictions.

Table 7.2 SSA's paragraph B criteria: Criteria assessing functional impairment

Category	Examples of related activities
1. Marked restriction of activities of daily living	• cleaning, shopping, cooking • taking public transportation • paying bills • maintaining a residence • caring appropriately for grooming and hygiene • using telephones and directories • using a post office
2. Marked difficulties in maintaining social functioning	• ability to interact independently, appropriately, effectively, and on a sustained basis with other individuals • ability to get along with other persons, including family members, friends, neighbors, grocery clerks, landlords, or bus drivers • a history of altercations, evictions, firings, fear of strangers, avoidance of interpersonal relationships, or social isolation • cooperative behaviors, consideration for others, awareness of others' feelings, and social maturity • in work situations: interactions with the public, coworkers, and persons in authority (e.g., supervisors)
3. Deficiencies of concentration, persistence, or pace	• frequent failure to complete tasks in a timely and appropriate fashion in work settings • ability to work at a consistent pace for acceptable periods of time and until a task is completed • ability to repeat sequences of action to achieve a goal or an objective • ability or inability to complete tasks under the stresses of employment during a normal

Table 7.2 (continued)

Category	Examples of related activities
	workday or workweek (i.e., 8-h day, 40-h week, or similar schedule) • ability to complete tasks without extra supervision or assistance and in accordance with quality and accuracy standards, at a consistent pace, without an unreasonable number and length of rest periods, and without undue interruptions or distractions.
4. Repeated episodes of deterioration or decompensation in work or work-like settings	• withdrawal from the work situation • exacerbations or temporary increases in symptoms or signs accompanied by a loss of adaptive functioning, as manifested by difficulties in performing activities of daily living, maintaining social relationships, or maintaining concentration, persistence, or pace • worsening symptoms or signs that would ordinarily require increased treatment, a less stressful situation, or a combination of the two interventions • documentation of the need for a more structured psychological support system, such as hospitalizations, placement in a halfway house, or a highly structured and directed household

Paragraph C criteria (not reviewed here) were added for further evaluation of schizophrenic, paranoid, other psychotic disorders, and anxiety-related disorders. The addition of these criteria recognized the significant impact of impairments related to certain chronic mental illnesses even when such impairments are decreased by the use of medication or psychosocial factors such as placement in a structured environment (Metzner & Buck, 2003). SSA generally presumes that a person who is seriously limited in the areas defined by paragraphs B and C because of a listed disorder identified in paragraph A is unable to work (Krajeski & Lipsett, 1987; Melton et al., 2007; Metzner & Buck, 2003).

SSA evaluates functional restrictions as per paragraphs B and C criteria. In doing so, SSA expects mental health professionals to assess the independence, appropriateness, effectiveness, and sustainability with which the claimant can successfully negotiate the activities of daily living. Marked difficulties in maintaining social functioning refer to the claimant's ability to interact independently, appropriately, effectively, and on a sustained basis with other individuals in social or work settings. Deficiencies of concentration, persistence, or pace refer to the ability to pay attention and concentrate well enough to complete the sorts of tasks commonly involved in work settings in a timely and appropriate manner. Limitations in concentration, persistence, or pace are best observed in work settings, but can also often be assessed through clinical examination, including mental status examination or psychological testing.

Repeated episodes of deterioration or decompensation in work or work-like settings refer to exacerbations or temporary increases in symptoms or signs accompanied by a loss of adaptive functioning, as manifested by difficulties in performing activities of daily living, maintaining social relationships, or maintaining concentration, persistence, or pace. Episodes of decompensation may be demonstrated by worsening symptoms or signs that would ordinarily require increased treatment, placement in a less stressful situation, or a combination of these two interventions. Episodes of decompensation may also be inferred from the history of present illness, past psychiatric history, medical records that show significant changes in medication, documentation of the need for a more structured psychological support system (e.g., hospitalizations, placement in a halfway house, or a highly structured and directed household), or other relevant information in the record about the existence, severity, and duration of the episode.

Residual Functional Capacity

When a claimant has an impairment that is not sufficiently severe to justify benefits on the basis of medical evidence alone, the reviewing medical consultant is asked to assess the claimant's residual functional capacity (RFC). SSA defines RFC as "a multidimensional description of work-related abilities which an individual retains in spite of medical impairments," (20 CFR §4041545). RFC is a description of what the claimant can still do in a work setting despite the limitations caused by the claimant's impairments.

The elements of an RFC assessment are derivatives of paragraphs B and C criteria of the listings for mental disorders and describe an expanded list of work-related capacities that may be impaired by mental disorder (see Table 7.3). SSA assesses these qualities in the context of the individual's capacity to sustain the listed activity over a normal workday and workweek on an ongoing basis (American Medical Association, 2008). When a claimant's RFC is not sufficient to do his or her previous job, SSA considers other factors in assessing whether the claimant can do other types of work. Individuals who have an impairment not meeting one listed by the SSA and not equivalent to any listed disorder may in some instances be found disabled by the SSA if the demands of jobs in which the person might be expected to engage, considering the claimant's age, education, and work experience, exceed the individual's remaining capacity to perform (Kennedy, 2002; Krajeski & Lipsett, 1987; Metzner & Buck, 2003).

Public Disability Insurance: The SSDI Program 171

Table 7.3 Criteria for assessment of residual functional capacity (RFC)

Criteria	Examples for assessment
1. Understanding and memory	Ability to remember • procedures related to work • short, simple instructions • detailed instructions
2. Sustained concentration and persistence	Ability to • carry out short, simple instructions • carry out detailed instructions • maintain attention and concentration for extended periods of time • perform activities within a given schedule • maintain regular attendance • be punctual within customary tolerances • sustain an ordinary routine without special supervision • work with or near others without being distracted • complete a normal workday and workweek without interruptions from psychologically based symptoms • make simple work-related decisions • perform at a consistent pace without an unreasonable number of and unreasonably long rest periods
3. Social interaction	Ability to • interact appropriately with the general public • get along with coworkers and peers without distracting them or exhibiting behavioral extremes • maintain socially appropriate behavior • ask simple questions or request assistance • accept instructions • respond appropriately to criticism from supervisors • adhere to basic standards of neatness and cleanliness
4. Adaptation	Ability to • respond appropriately to changes in the work setting • be aware of normal hazards and take appropriate precautions • use public transportation and travel to and within unfamiliar places • set realistic goals • make plans independently of others

SSA's Adjudication of SSDI Claims

An understanding of the SSA's adjudicative process can assist mental health providers in supplying the information necessary for the system to make a reasonable determination of a patient's claim. As noted above, those supplying the medical evidence do not make the determination of disability nor are they asked or expected to do so. The SSDI program is administered on a day-to-day basis by the SSA outside of the direct scrutiny of the judicial system. The medical evidence furnished by the claimant's providers is reviewed by an adjudicative team, which makes the disability determination.

The SSA's disability determination process consists of a five-step "sequential evaluation" (see Table 7.4) (20 CFR §404.1520(a)(4)).

Table 7.4 SSA's adjudication process for SSDI claims

1. Is the claimant currently engaging in SGA? If so, claim denied. If not,
2. Does the claimant have a severe impairment? If not, claim denied. If so,
3. Does the claimant's impairment meet or equal a "listed" impairment? If so, and if claimant not engaging in SGA, claimant is deemed disabled. If disabled,
4. Does the impairment prevent the claimant from doing past relevant work, i.e., what is the claimant's RFC? If the claimant can still perform past relevant work, the disability claim is denied. If not,
5. Does the impairment prevent the claimant from doing any other work, If not, claim allowed. If so, claim denied

The first step in the process is the determination of whether the claimant is currently engaging in SGA. If claimants are working and earning over the prescribed level, SSA considers them to be engaged in SGA, and therefore not disabled, and denies their claims no matter how serious their medical condition.

If the claimant is not engaged in SGA for a time period expected to last for at least 12 months, SSA next turns to the severity of the disability. A medically determinable "severe" impairment is one that has more than a minimal impact on the claimant's ability to do basic work activities, such as the abilities to understand, carry out, and remember instructions, and to respond appropriately to supervision, coworkers, and work pressure in a work setting. If a medical impairment or combination of impairments is not "severe," the disability claim is denied.

If the medical impairment is severe, SSA next considers whether the claimant's impairment meets or equals a "listed" impairment, that is, a recognized DSM diagnosis as described above (see Table 7.1). If a claimant's medical impairments meet one of the listings (or is medically equivalent to a listed impairment) and the claimant is not engaging in SGA, the claimant is deemed to be disabled and the claim is allowed. If the impairment does not meet or equal a listing, SSA next considers whether the impairment prevents the claimant from doing past relevant work. At this stage, SSA determines whether claimants have the RFC to do the type of work they have done in the past. If the claimant can still perform past relevant work, the disability claim is denied.

The claimant bears the burden of proof in the first four steps (*Plummer v. Apfel*, 1999). If the claimant satisfies that burden of proof, the burden shifts to SSA to prove there are existing jobs the claimant can perform given his or her medical impairments, age, education, and past work experience. At this last step of the sequential evaluation, SSA determines whether claimants have the RFC to do other work that is appropriate to their age, education, and work experience. Claimants will be found disabled if they do not have the ability to perform any other work. If the claimant has the ability to perform other work that exists to a significant degree in the national economy, the claim is denied.

Most claimants receive or are denied benefits based solely on a determination by the SSA without direct judicial oversight. The initial determination of eligibility is subject to review by another disability examiner at one of the SSA's 10 regional offices or at SSA headquarters. Both of these reviews are strictly paper reviews. The claimant is not examined or interviewed at either of these steps in the process.

However, a multilevel appeals process is built into the law. A claimant unsatisfied with the SSA's decision may file a request for reconsideration at any field office or by calling SSA. If benefits are again denied at the DDS level, claimants may request a hearing before an administrative law judge (ALJ) at the SSA. Further appeals options include a request for review of the denial decision by SSA's Appeals Council, and, only when these avenues are exhausted, a review in the federal courts (Wunderlich et al., 2002).

The rules of evidence that apply in court (e.g., hearsay, judicial notice, Daubert) do not apply to the conduct or the presentation of the findings of an evaluation for Social Security disability benefits. In *Richardson v. Perales* (1971), the Supreme Court held that hearsay evidence relied on by a Social Security hearing examiner may support a decision to deny benefits. Unlike lay jurors who are thought to require protection in the form of evidentiary exclusionary rules like hearsay, it is assumed that experienced ALJs and agency decision makers can tell good hearsay from bad and therefore do not need to be protected from it. This permits evaluators to rely on hearsay in reaching an opinion and SSA to consider written reports by health-care professionals in their decisions.

Although hearsay may be relied on by an expert or by the SSA, vehicles to challenge such sources are available. A subpoena may be issued for the attendance of any witness the claimant wishes to cross-examine before an ALJ (*Barnhart v. Thomas*, 2003). In addition, although the hearsay rule does not result in per se exclusion of witnesses or evidence, it may or may not be given much weight. The weight given to a medical or psychological evaluation should be a function of its basis, all the relevant data, as well as the assessment of its impact on the claimant's ability to engage in gainful activity.

The Role of Mental Health Professionals in SSDI Disability Claims

The most common role for mental health professionals in SSDI claims is that of treatment providers supplying primary sources of information for Social Security disability claims. The SSA's process of determining psychiatric disability emphasizes medical evidence provided by the claimant's treating psychiatrist or psychologist. If additional information is needed, the SSA may ask psychiatrists or psychologists to provide consultative examinations as independent clinical examiners (see discussion below). Even as consultative examiners, however, the mental health professional's primary role is to supply enough information for SSA to adjudicate the SSDI claim.

As noted above, treatment providers (and consultative examiners) supplying the medical evidence for the initial review of an SSDI disability do not make the determination of disability. Notably, and in contrast to certain other types of disability evaluations, treatment providers are discouraged from discussing the claimant's ability to work or evaluating the claimant's work capacity. This determination is considered the sole purview of the state DDS or higher level review board (Pransky et al., 2001).

Nevertheless, psychiatrists and psychologists providing treatment play a critical role in the ultimate adjudication of their patients' claims and should understand how best to provide the information SSA needs to make a determination regarding a disability claim. Many disability claims are decided solely by reviewing the medical evidence from treating sources or consultative examiners. Thus, psychiatrists and psychologists must provide enough information in an SSDI report to allow lay administrators to determine whether the claimant meets SSDI criteria.

Treatment Providers and SSDI Claims

The Social Security Act requires that an impairment for purposes of SSDI benefits must result from an abnormality identified by medically or psychologically acceptable clinical and laboratory techniques. Lay testimony, while relevant, is not by itself sufficient to satisfy the disability determination required by the Act. Objective medical evidence is required. The SSA regards a mental status examination as objective medical evidence needed by disability adjudicators to establish the existence of a mental impairment and to determine the severity of the impairment (20 CFR 404 Appendix 1, §12.00(D)(4)).

This has led to the SSA practice of preferring the opinion of the claimant's treating clinician or consultative examiner over that of an independent examiner (*McGoffin v. Barnhart*, 2002) despite concerns regarding occupying dual roles (Shuman & Greenberg, 1998; also see Chapters 1 and 2 and discussion below). The SSA considers treating clinicians to be the medical professionals best able to provide a detailed, longitudinal picture of the claimant's impairments. They are also considered to bring a unique perspective to the medical evidence that is not obtainable from either medical findings alone, reports of an individual examination, or a brief hospitalization (Social Security Administration Office of Disability Programs, 2004).

As discussed, at the initiation of a claim, SSA requires that the treating mental health professional provide documentation of the existence of a mental disorder, which SSA refers to as "an impairment," and how it interferes with an individual's functioning. SSA facilitates the provision of the information they need to make a determination by providing treating mental health professionals with a standardized form focusing on clinical observations and evaluation. The SSA may also approve additional diagnostic testing to conclusively establish the extent and severity of an illness.

The request for medical information from the state DDS also usually specifies the level of detail required. This required information is based on explicit SSA medical eligibility criteria. Clinicians should therefore closely adhere to the format and provide the level of detail requested. This form also facilitates a relatively straightforward application of the relevant legal SSA criteria to the clinical data (Krajeski & Lipsett, 1987).

Requests from a DSS to fill out the disability paperwork should be accompanied by a signed release from the patient. Even though a release may be received with the request for information, prudent treatment providers should contact their patients and advise them they have received requests for information. They should at that time ensure that patients understand this means the mental health professional will be providing confidential information to the DSS.

SSA's administrative definitions and criteria for the determination of psychiatric disability translate in a relatively straightforward manner into three key mental health concepts. Treatment providers should understand that all three must be demonstrated to be present for an award of benefits:

1. whether the claimant has a medically determinable impairment, referred to as a "listed" mental disorder;
2. whether the mental disorder has resulted in an inability to work; and
3. whether the inability to work resulting from the mental disorder will last or is expected to last for at least 12 months.

Treating mental health professionals should therefore be certain that their SSDI report indicates whether an officially SSA-"listed" mental disorder or its equivalent is present. Only DSM diagnoses should be used. If clinical circumstances dictate, clinicians should point out that comorbidity or combinations of psychiatric disorders or psychiatric and physical disorders may be equivalent to a "listed" mental disorder.

In all cases, clinicians should be certain to document whether the disorder interferes with the individual's ability to function in a work setting. They should also indicate whether any limitations have lasted or are expected to last at least 12 months, even if there may be some periods of time during the 12 months when the claimant may function well (Metzner & Buck, 2003). Clinicians should provide specific details of the claimant's condition over time, including the length and frequency of exacerbations and remissions of the claimant's mental disorder, accompanied by descriptions of the claimant's exacerbations and remissions (Krajeski & Lipsett, 1987).

Clinicians should also make a connection between the functional restrictions and the existence of a mental disorder. In SSDI claims, functional restrictions must be related to the listed impairment (DSM diagnosis). Since functional restrictions may result from circumstances other than a mental disorder, reports should address whether restrictions in functioning arise from a mental disorder or other factors (Pransky et al., 2001).

Problems in adjudicating claims arise when treatment providers' reports fail to provide the supporting data necessary to establish a mental disorder, offer a non-DSM or idiosyncratic diagnosis, do not correlate impairments in function with the mental disorder, do not indicate severity of functional impairments, or do not indicate that impairments are expected to last for at least 12 months. Generalizations or overly broad conclusions rather than specific examples may reduce the credibility of a report and compromise the success of the claim.

Conflicts inherent in the relatively common circumstance of mental health professionals documenting impairments for their own patients for SSDI have been noted and discussed (Candilis et al., 2007). Mental health professionals should be mindful of both the needs of their patients and the needs of the SSA system. Even though this puts psychiatrists and psychologists in the position of "wearing two hats" (Strasburger et al., 1997), as discussed in Chapter 1, the structure of the SSA's public disability insurance program makes occupying a dual role difficult to avoid. Nevertheless, psychiatrists and psychologists providing information to SSDI should be aware of these potential ethical pitfalls and endeavor to be as objective as possible.

Consultative Examinations

Another common role for mental health professionals in SSDI claims is that of the consultative examiner. If the adjudicative team needs additional information beyond that provided by the treating clinician, a consultative examiner (CE) may be obtained on a fee-for-service basis. These examinations require specialized expertise and qualifications. All CE providers must have active licenses in the state in which they are performing their evaluations and they must have the training and experience to perform the type of examination or test SSA requests. Fees for CEs are set by each state and may vary from state to state. Each state agency is responsible for overseeing and managing its CE program.

Consistent with SSA's preference for information from the treating mental health profession, the claimant's treatment provider is still the preferred source for a CE if that physician is qualified, equipped, and willing to perform the examination for the authorized fee. However, this is not always possible. Therefore, SSA's rules provide for using an independent examiner for a CE or diagnostic study if

a. the treating source prefers not to perform the examination;
b. the treating source does not have the equipment to provide the specific data needed;
c. there are conflicts or inconsistencies in the file that cannot be resolved by going back to the treating source;
d. the claimant prefers another source and has good reason for doing so; or
e. prior experience indicates that the treating psychiatrist or psychologist may not be an adequate source of additional information.

Even so, the SSA generally gives more weight to the opinion of a treating physician than that of a non-treating physician, if the former opinion is well supported by medically acceptable clinical and laboratory diagnostic techniques and is not inconsistent with other substantial evidence in the record. As a general rule, the report of a consulting physician is not considered to be substantial evidence, especially when contradicted by a treating physician's opinion, unless it is supported by better or more thorough medical evidence or if the treating physician provides inconsistent opinions (Parry & Drogin, 2007).

The consultative examiner's primary role is to make a judgment as to the severity of the impairment, based on review, analysis, and interpretation of the clinical findings, test results, and other evidence in the case record. Therefore, consultants should request medical records from the DDS to determine their availability prior to the examination. The consultative examiner should obtain information concerning a claimant's functioning from both the evaluee and other sources including community mental health centers, family members, and friends.

The independent examiner also may be asked to provide additional detailed medical findings about the claimant's impairment or to provide technical or specialized medical evidence not available in the claimant's current medical file. Depending on the nature and scope of the CE, a general or focused physical examination may be indicated to determine whether the claimant's signs and symptoms are due to a mental or physical impairment or due to the adverse effects of psychotropic medications. Blood and urine testing, imaging studies, and psychological testing may also be requested. Psychological test results are considered in the context of all the evidence in file, and decisions regarding disability are not based on test results alone.

A CE report has many elements in common with a treatment provider's disability report but consultative examiners are usually expected to provide more information than treatment providers. CE reports should specifically include detailed information concerning mental restrictions, RFC, and functional limitations relative to activities of daily living; social functioning; concentration, persistence, or pace; and episodes of decompensation. Opinions about the claimants' residual capabilities despite their impairment(s) should describe the individual's ability to understand, to carry out and remember instructions, and to respond appropriately to supervision, coworkers, and work pressures in a work setting. Assessment of capability should also include whether the individual can manage awarded benefits responsibly.

Other Roles for Mental Health Professionals in SSDI Claims

Mental health professionals may also participate in the SSDI process as direct employees or consultants to the SSA and state Departments of Social Services, assisting in the evaluation of claims. In addition, as noted above, mental health professionals may serve as expert witnesses at appeals-level hearings. These roles do not require direct assessment of a disability but rather a review of the evidence and assessments of disability provided by others. These jobs or roles require additional forensic or administrative experience (Social Security Administration Office of Disability Programs, 2004), the discussion of which is beyond the scope of this chapter.

Additional Guidelines for Conducting SSA Disability Evaluations

1. Understand and utilize the relevant definitions and criteria used by the SSA.
2. Rely on and follow the format of the forms and referral questions supplied by the SSA.
3. Provide specific information as requested by the SSA regarding whether
   a. the claimant has a medically determinable impairment, referred to as a "listed" mental disorder;
   b. the mental disorder has resulted in an inability to work; and
   c. the inability to work resulting from the mental disorder has lasted or is expected to last for at least 12 months.
4. Use only DSM diagnoses.
5. Provide specific descriptions and examples of symptoms that support a diagnosis of a mental disorder.
6. Indicate how long impairments have lasted or are expected to last, bearing in mind that SSA requires that severe impairments that preclude substantial gainful employment last for at least 12 months.
7. Provide support for and specific examples of the severity of functional impairments.
8. Correlate functional impairments with the mental disorder if they are related to the mental disorder.
9. Do not offer opinions on disability.

Workers' Compensation Programs

Workers' compensation legislation, whose origins lie in nineteenth century Prussia, was created with the intent to provide timely and efficient compensation to injured workers for work-related injuries while controlling employer's costs. Workers' compensation laws impose liability on employers without regard to their fault in hiring, training, or supplying the injured employee, and reject fault defenses such as contributory negligence or assumption of the risk. Liability turns not on who was at fault but on the nexus between the injury and the employment.

The first American venture into workers' compensation laws occurred in the early twentieth century (Larson & Larson, 2000). Workers' compensation statutes gave employees and employers no choice whether to participate in this system, even though they stripped claimants of the right to trial by jury generally enjoyed in common law tort claims and stripped employers of established defenses against liability. Depending on the state, employers are required to obtain private insurance, state-funded insurance, or to be self-insured.

Today, workers' compensation statutes are accepted as part of the fabric of the employment relationship. However, when first instituted, these laws gave rise to many controversial constitutional questions. New York's 1911 workers' compensation act was held unconstitutional by the New York Court of Appeals (*Ives v. South Buffalo Ry.*, 1911). New York's legislators responded by adopting a constitutional amendment permitting the adoption of a compulsory worker's compensation law.

Workers' compensation laws are now well established in every state. The debate regarding the constitutionality of workers' compensation laws was settled in 1917, when the United States Supreme Court upheld the constitutionality of the 1913 New York law (*New York Central R.R. v. White*, 1917). Subsequently, all but eight states adopted workers' compensation acts. The last state of the then 48 states, Mississippi, came under the workers' compensation system in 1949. In the 1980s, following a report submitted in 1972 by the Presidential National Commission on State Workmen's Compensation Law, state workers' compensation statutes universally expanded to increase the range of covered employees to include unlimited medical benefits and occupational disease coverage.

Most federal employees are covered under the Federal Employees' Compensation Act, administered generally through the United States Department of Labor, Office of Workers Compensation Programs. The Federal workers' compensation programs are analogous to state workers' compensation programs in regard to the requirements of general issues of impairment and disability.

The Basic Components of Workers' Compensation Legislation

Each state and the federal government is entitled to fashion its own workers' compensation system. As a result, workers' compensation acts vary from state to state. Nevertheless, they typically share certain features, including

1. Employees of an employer required to participate are entitled to benefits when they suffer a personal injury by accident arising out of and in the course of employment or occupational disease.
2. Negligence and fault are largely immaterial to the validity of a claim or its amount.
3. Benefits include cash-wage benefits, usually around one-half to one-third of the employee's average weekly wage, and hospital, medical, and rehabilitation expenses. In death cases, benefits for dependents are provided, with arbitrarily imposed maximum and minimum limits.

4. Employees and their dependents, in exchange for these modest but assured benefits, give up their common-law right to sue the employer for damages for any injury covered by the act.
5. Rules of procedure and evidence are relaxed in application (Larson & Larson, 2000).

Differences Between Workers' Compensation, Tort Law, and SSDI

Workers' compensation laws differ in many ways from both tort law and the statutory law governing SSDI. In contrast to SSDI, workers' compensation is essentially a private disability compensation system; SSDI is a public disability benefits program[4] (Larson & Larson, 2000). SSDI costs are borne directly by the taxpayer; workers' compensation involves a financial arrangement between employers, insurance carriers, and employees. Also, unlike SSDI, in which disability is either total or nonexistent, workers' compensation programs provide for a spectrum of disability and jurisdictions differ as to the levels of disability that may be compensable.

Workers' compensation is also fundamentally different from tort liability. In contrast with tort law, the basic test of liability in workers' compensation is connection with work rather than fault. Defenses to employer liability under tort law include contributory negligence or comparative causation, both of which raise issues related to fault. Fault is not relevant to questions of liability in workers' compensation cases.

Workers compensation and tort law also differ in the nature of the injuries compensated and in the amount of compensation. Compensation in tort law is intended to restore to the claimant that which the claimant has lost. In contrast, workers' compensation benefits provide a sum, which, added to the claimant's remaining earning ability (if any), will prevent the claimant from becoming a burden to others or to society. Workers compensation amounts tend to be fixed, modest, and time limited.

Workers' compensation is an exclusive remedy. Employees are not given the option of bringing a tort claim for the same injury against their employers. Under workers' compensation statutes, employees are required to seek redress through workers' compensation. Despite this requirement, certain types of injuries that might be compensable in tort law, such as pain and suffering, are not compensable under workers' compensation (see, e.g., *Blailock v. O'Bannon*, 2001; *Ford v. Revlon, Inc.*, 1987; *Spangler, Jennings, & Dougherty P.C. v. Indiana Ins. Co.*, 2000).

---

[4] Nevertheless, the two programs are linked, in that SSDI benefits are offset by workers' compensation benefits to the extent that the sum of the payments under both programs does not exceed a certain percentage of the individual's average earnings. Many workers' compensation statutes also contain offset provisions relating to the receipt of SSDI and SSI benefits.

Causation in Workers Compensation: No Fault Does Not Mean No Conflict

The "no fault" component of workers' compensation is potentially misleading. It does not mean that employers must pay dubious claims or that bona fide claimants must accept less than they are entitled to in the name of civility. It means only that a finding of fault or liability is not required to award benefits. In fact, the required causal nexus of injury to employment is often a vigorously contested issue in workers' compensation claims (*Malave-Felix v. Volvo Car Corp.*, 1991).

Most workers' compensation acts require benefits are contingent upon an injury by accident or by accidental injury arising *out of* and *in the course of* employment. Thus, preexisting injury or concurrent injury caused by events or forces unconnected to the employment relationship falls outside workers' compensation. In the case of mental or emotional harm, the workers' compensation commissions and the courts look to psychiatrists and psychologists to provide guidance in judging the nexus between past and present events and current mental harm.

In the case of psychiatric disorders, generally claimants must demonstrate that they were placed at increased risk for exacerbation or injury or that stress or trauma precipitated the effects of the condition (Larson & Larson, 2000). In addition, if the primary injury is shown to be work connected, subsequent injury that is connected to the original compensable injury is also compensable; however, subsequent injury that is the result of an intervening cause attributable to a claimant's own intentional conduct may disqualify him or her from receiving additional benefits (Larson & Larson, 2000).

The Decision-Making Process in Workers' Compensation Claims

Each jurisdiction has its own procedures for filing and processing workers' compensation claims, for hearing contested cases, and for judicial review. Certain procedural features are commonly found in state administrative systems. Proceedings are generally summary and informal, as contrasted with judicial proceedings in state or federal court. The initial handling of claims and the first review are administrative in all but a few states.

The great majority of compensation claims are disposed of without contest. When claims are contested, controversial issues of liability, degree of disability, etc., may be subject to mediation and may result in compromise and settlement like any other claim, usually subject to approval by the compensation commission. Some states forbid agreements by which the claimant gets less than the amount specified in the statute (Larson & Larson, 2000).

Judicial review of awards is usually confined to questions of law. The parties' evidence is not weighed on review. It is the commission's function to weigh the evidence and make findings on questions of fact, which includes such matters as credibility of witnesses, extent of disability, ability to return to work, suitability of offered work, and, most common of all, medical causation. If the decision of the commission is supported by substantial evidence, it is considered conclusive.

Ordinarily, an order is not reviewable by the courts until a workers' compensation commission renders a final decision that awards or denies compensation. Typically, a judicial review is preceded by the decision of an ALJ whose finding are adopted, modified, or rejected by the agency board. A claimant may then seek judicial review of that final decision. State courts have jurisdiction to review the agency's or commission's decision for errors of law but generally not to retry the case anew (Larson & Larson, 2000).

Evidentiary Issues in Worker's Compensation Claims

The rules of evidence, often described as a product of the jury system, do not apply in workers' compensation proceedings or most other administrative proceedings where lay jurors play no role in the process. The only evidence rules that apply in these proceedings are those addressing relevance and privilege. Neither of these barriers is problematic for mental health professionals in a workers' compensation claim. As long as psychiatrists and psychologists know and address the correct legal standard, their reports or testimony will be relevant.

Examinations made at the behest of the workers' compensation board are not confidential. Claimants waive any physician, psychiatrist, or psychologist–patient privilege when they offer the records or the testimony of that psychiatrist or psychologist. In the case of an independent medical examination (IME) conducted for forensic purposes, as discussed in Chapter 2, no privilege comes into existence in the first place. In any case, in most jurisdictions the psychiatrist, psychologist, or physician–patient privilege has an exception for workers' compensation proceedings.

The primary evidentiary issue raised in workers' compensation cases is whether the award is supported by competent evidence, that is, whether sufficient evidence admissible under the traditional common law rules of evidence exists to support the award. Even though the rules of evidence do not apply in workers' compensation cases, there is good reason to know and abide by them. *Daubert* challenges to an opinion about this linkage are rare, but inclusion of transparent reasoning explaining why the conclusion is not just the "ipse dixit" of the expert is persuasive.

In some circumstances, the causal relationship between a workplace injury and mental or emotional harm could be supported by lay testimony alone. There is no requirement that expert testimony be offered to support workers' compensation claims. Compensation boards may rely to a considerable extent on their own knowledge and experience and awards or denials may be upheld without medical testimony (*Ex parte Price*, 1989; *Faria v. Carol Cable Co.*, 1987). Awards may even be upheld when they find a higher degree of disability than that supported by medical testimony (*McGowan v. Orleans Furniture, Inc.*, 1991).

However, choosing to pursue an emotional or mental injury workers' compensation claim without expert testimony can be a risky strategy. The suspicion that often accompanies claims for mental and emotional loss may make it difficult to demonstrate this type of injury with lay testimony only. In addition, if the commission or the court's opinion that the causal linkage is not obvious becomes apparent at the time of the hearing, claimants cannot remedy the situation by attempting to offer expert testimony later.

When expert testimony by a psychiatrist or psychologist is to be presented through live testimony or a written report, any opinion offered must be based on a personal examination and evaluation of the claimant when possible. Medical records must also be reviewed but are not of themselves a substitute for a personal examination in workers' compensation cases.

Definition of Disability in Worker's Compensation Cases

Although definitions of disability in workers' compensation law vary from state to state, surprising similarity between statutes exists. Typically disability is defined as the inability to perform work suitable to the claimant's qualifications and training as the result of a work-connected injury (Fla. Stat. §440.02(13); Tex. Lab. Code §401.011(16)). The degree of disability depends on impairment of earning capacity, which is presumptively determined by comparing pre-injury earnings with post-injury earning ability.

The definition of disability in workers' compensation claims, which combines medical or psychiatric impairment and the inability to earn wages, is unique to workers' compensation statutes. It is based on the concept of "compensable disability," a concept whose meaning is the result of the accumulation of years of legislation, judicial decisions, and local custom.

Both disability and wage-earning capacity can be found in varying degrees, with and without each other. For example, a claimant may be extremely and obviously impaired but, as previously discussed, may continue to work if he or she has motivation, appropriate support, or appropriate treatment interventions. Conversely, total disability may be found, in spite of sporadic earnings, if the claimant's physical condition rules out regular employment in the labor market (Larson & Larson, 2000).

Unlike SSDI evaluations, psychiatrists and psychologists are often asked to provide opinions regarding disability in worker's compensation cases. However, mental health professionals should be aware that the opinions they are asked to provide address only the assessment of impairment and disability related to the ability to perform work functions. Workers' compensation boards, which make the ultimate determination regarding disability in workers' compensation cases, also factor wage loss into their determination of disability. Mental health professionals should appreciate that their expertise extends only to the assessment of impairment and disability; the ability to assess a claimant's former, current, or future earning capacity is outside the range of expertise of most mental health professionals.

Psychiatric Claims in Workers' Compensation

All states allow claims for physical injuries that cause mental disorders. However, concerns regarding the validity of such claims, especially claims of mental injury or trauma leading to a mental disorder, have led many states to approach claims of mental or emotional injury by categorizing them as either

1. physical–mental injury claims;
2. mental–physical injury claims; or
3. mental–mental injury claims.

Physical–Mental and Mental–Physical Injury Claims

In a mental–physical claim, stress or an emotional problem is claimed to have led to an objectively measured physical disorder, such as stress leading to heart attack (Larson & Larson, 2000). In a physical–mental claim, a physical injury is alleged to have led to an emotional injury. An example of such a claim would be that of a firefighter who is burned in the course of duty but whose impairments and subsequent disability result primarily from posttraumatic stress disorder rather than from any physical problems.

All states' workers' compensation programs allow for claims for physical injuries that cause mental disorders and claims for injuries due to mental disorders that cause physical disorders. With certain exceptions, there is no difference in the general applications of principles of cause or proximate cause among the jurisdictions dealing with psychiatric cases. These types of claims are allowed because of the common understanding that physical injury can cause pain and because the connection to the physical condition lends these claims credibility. Medical evidence of an injury's effect on electroencephalogram or in metabolic studies has been held sufficient for establishing the physical causation of the mental injury (Lasky, 1993).

Originally, even in these types of claims, the mental injury had to arise from a clearly identified "nervous shock" or identifiable traumatic exposure. The specific event provided a limitation on the number of claimants and a rough map to begin to trace causation. Over time, some jurisdictions have relaxed the realm of compensable emotional injury to include prolonged or cumulative work stress, and there has been a trend to compensate for many conditions (e.g., asthma and peptic ulcers) that are claimed to result from such stress (*McDonald v. International Paper Co.*, 1981; *Townsend v. Maine Bureau of Public Safety*, 1979). Nevertheless, a minority of states still compensate mental injury leading to physical injury only when it can be traced to a specific recent traumatic workplace event but not when it arises out of the cumulative effect of everyday job stress (*Dunlavey v. Economy Fire & Casualty Co.*, 1995; *Holliday v. Conrail*, 1990).

Mental–Mental Injury Claims

The third and most controversial category of stress claim is the mental–mental claim, that is, a claim that a mental trauma has caused a mental disorder. Historically, the fear of fraud and malingering in the absence of a verifiable physical injury has loomed large over this type of claim. In addition, establishing a causal relationship between two intangible events seems at times an impossible task. The most straightforward mental–mental claims are psychiatric disorders caused by an obvious traumatic event or limited sequence of events, such as a fire at a plant (see, e.g., *Hecules Inc. v. Gunther*, 1991). While the fire burned, coworkers, family, and friends described the magnitude of the threat, the proximity of the threat to the worker, and the likely alarm created. These circumstances lent themselves to an atypical ability to verify important aspects of the claim.

In contrast, attempts to evaluate the cumulative effects of exposure to work-related stress, which, as discussed in Chapter 3, is a growing problem in the workplace, present a more difficult challenge.[5] This challenge becomes even greater when the perspectives of the worker and the employer widely differ. Because these types of mental–mental claims are more difficult to demonstrate convincingly, recovery for them is limited in ways that claims for physical injuries are not (Lasky, 1993; Nackley, 1989).

In fact, this type of worker's compensation stress claim has engendered some of the most restrictive legislation limiting claims involving workplace stress (Larson & Larson, 2000; Lasky, 1993, Nackley, 1989). Some states, such as Maryland and North Carolina, award benefits for mental–mental claims without differentiating between mental and physical injuries. In contrast, other states, including Kentucky, Florida, Oklahoma, Wyoming, and West Virginia, have completely excluded stress cases from workers' compensation and allow

---

[5] One of the earliest cases addressing this type of "mental–mental" claim, *Carter v. General Motors* (1960), was at one time considered a landmark workers' compensation case because it established the legitimacy of an occupational stress claim under a workers' compensation statute. In this case, expert testimony indicated that a machine operator had a personality disorder and a predisposition to the development of a schizophrenic process and that he sustained a disabling psychosis caused by emotional pressures produced by production line employment. The Michigan Supreme Court held that the operator had sustained a disability compensable under Michigan's Workmen's Compensation Act.

no relief for "mental–mental" claims (Larson & Larson, 2000). Kentucky, for example, defines "injury" in its workers' compensation statute so as not to include "a psychological, psychiatric or stress-related change" unless it is a "direct result" of physical injury (Ky. Rev. Stat. §342.0011(1)). Montana denies coverage for mental injury even when accompanied by disabling physical injury (Mont. Code Ann. 39-71-119(3)) (see *Yarborough v. Montana Municipal Ins. Auth.*, 1997).

Different states have adopted different approaches to administering this type of workers' compensation claim to address concerns regarding their costs and credibility. Some states address causal issues in mental–mental claims by only recognizing mental injury claims caused by a sudden or unusual emotional stimulus subject to independent verification (Lasky, 1993). State legislatures have enacted a variety of limitations governing stress claims short of an absolute bar (Larson & Larson, 2000). Restrictions fall into four broad categories:

1. Requiring a set amount or type of stress, such as "unexpected, unusual, or extraordinary" (Ariz. Rev. Stat. §23-1043.01). In Pennsylvania, a claimant must show that job stress is something other than the ordinary stresses of employment that all workers experience (*Romanies v. Workmen's Comp. App. Bd.*, 1994).
2. Raising the standard for proof of causation. For example, in Colorado, stress claims are not compensable "unless shown by competent evidence that such mental or emotional stress is proximately caused solely by hazards to which the worker would not have been equally exposed outside the employment" (Col. Rev. Stat. Ann. §8-41-302); (see also Ariz. Rev. Stat. §23-1043.01: mental stress must be a "substantial contributing cause" of the injury).
3. Imposing specific diagnostic guidelines. Arkansas, for example, mandates the use of diagnoses in the most current edition of the DSM (Ark. Code Ann. §11-9-113(a)(2)).
4. Limiting benefits. Again, Arkansas limits benefits for mental injuries to 26 weeks (Ark. Code. Ann. §11-9-113(b)(1).

Mental Health Evaluations in Workers' Compensation Claims

Mental health professionals play a critical role in mental injury claims in workers' compensation cases. As discussed above, although mental health testimony is not always required for the adjudication of workers' compensation claims, the evidentiary standard usually requires documentation of the claimant's injury or illness and its effects. If any part of the worker's claim alleges emotional stress or the presence of a mental disorder, claimants who are not already in treatment are commonly referred to a mental health professional for evaluation.

Psychiatrists and psychologists are typically asked to provide opinions regarding one or more of the following questions (Lasky, 1993):

1. Does the claimant have a mental disorder?
2. Is the mental disorder disabling?
3. Is the condition work related, and if so, how?
4. Is there apportionment to preexisting disability or nonindustrial factors?
5. Has the claimant reached a permanent and stationary condition, and if so, when?
6. Is the claimant's disability temporary-partial, temporary-total, permanent-partial, or permanent-total?
7. Is treatment indicated, and if so, what type, duration, and frequency?
8. If treatment has been rendered, was it appropriate, considering type, duration, and frequency?

When mental health professionals perform an evaluation of disability in conjunction with a worker's compensation claim, they should, as with all disability evaluations, assess whether a psychiatric disorder is present. However, unlike SSDI evaluations, mental health professionals are also asked to address causation and disability. Psychiatrists and psychologists should be familiar with particular language in the state or federal statutes that apply and address their inquiry and opinions to the standards articulated by that language.

Causation, as noted, is often a critical issue in workers' compensation cases and, as discussed, requires a determination of whether the mental disorder *arose out of* and *in the course of employment*. The majority of states impose no special requirement for causation in the case of mental injury that they do not impose in the case of physical injury (*Zundell v. Dade County School Board*, 1994). However, in the absence of a salient traumatic event, the task of demonstrating a causal nexus to the workplace rather than to nonwork-related problems is more difficult.

Stress claims related to personality disorders can present particular difficulties in assessment. Individuals with personality disorders often have a combination of factors that can result in deterioration in mental status and associated impairments. These include tenuous stability and lack of resilience in the face of stressors, inability to adapt to new difficulties or disruptions, poor interpersonal coping skills, episodic bouts of depression or anxiety, and externalization of blame on others (Lasky, 1993). These in turn can result in increased stress, which is typically blamed on workplace conditions but which actually is a consequence of the personality disorder itself. The workplace cannot be said to be the cause of the impairments or the resulting disability in these cases.

Mental health professionals may also be asked for a variety of other opinions related to disability that can affect the success of a workers' compensation claim. Opinions may also be requested as to whether the worker is impaired or disabled from performing the duties of the job where the injury occurred, what restrictions may be necessary so that the worker can perform that job, whether the worker has the ability to perform some other job, or whether the worker is completely disabled and unable to perform any job. Opinions regarding the need for treatment because of the work-related mental disorder, before and even after settlement of a claim, may also be required.

Workers' compensation adjudication of impairment and disability in most cases involving physical illness or injury relies on percentage ratings of impairment and disability provided by the American Medical Association *Guides to the Evaluation of Impairment* (American Medical Association, 2008). However, as discussed in Chapter 6, the use of the *Guides'* new rating system for psychiatric illness is problematic. The utility of this new edition's complex and cumbersome combined rating scale scores remains to be demonstrated. Some states may rely on their own percentage rating system for mental disorders fashioned from the general categories of function adopted by the SSA. As discussed in Chapter 6, percentage ratings of mental impairments should be used with caution.

Subcategories of Disability in Workers' Compensation Claims

Four subcategories of disability are used in workers' compensation claims to project loss and financial remuneration. Mental health professionals may also be asked to provide opinions regarding which category of injury is present and the basis for these opinions. These categories are

1. temporary-partial;
2. temporary-total;
3. permanent-partial; and
4. permanent-total.

Assessment of which of these categories most accurately describes the claimant's status is similar to the concept of RFC or maximum medical improvement. However, unlike SSDI claims in which only permanent disability meets criteria for eligibility for benefits, in workers' compensation, this assessment explicitly combines both evaluation of impairment with a prognostic assessment. Disability does not have to be permanent to be compensable in workers' compensation claims.

In fact, depending on the type of mental disorder, a claim of temporary disability may be credible where a claim of permanent disability would not. Similarly, a given mental disorder may cause an individual to be disabled from one type of work but not another, or may prevent the individual from working full-time but not part-time. Clinicians commonly offer an opinion that an individual can only work part-time. Such opinions may be reasonable in workers' compensation claims but only if based on a thorough understanding of the specific nature of the individual's work requirements and impairments.

Aggravation or Apportionment of Preexisting Injury

Unlike the statutory laws governing SSDI claims in which disability is total and permanent or nonexistent, workers' compensation laws allow for shades of gray in the assessment of disability. One such area, as discussed above, is the four subcategories of disability: temporary-partial, temporary-total, permanent-partial, and permanent-total. Another area involves claims that raise issues of apportionment, that is, claims involving aggravation or exacerbation of preexisting disorders (Larson & Larson, 2000). Mental health professionals are often asked to address this issue in workers' compensation claims involving psychiatric illness or injury.

Mental health professionals offering opinions regarding apportionment should understand that the concept is applied only to a *preexisting disability* not to a preexisting condition. The concept of a preexisting permanent disability means a disability would have been ratable under the workers' compensation law even before the present work-related event occurred. The disability or impairment did not necessarily have to previously interfere with the employee's ability to perform his or her particular job. Rather, a disability means an impairment in the ability to compete in the labor market for workers' compensation determination purposes (Lasky, 1993).

For example, a review of an individual's occupational and psychiatric history may demonstrate that he had disabilities that prevented him from engaging in activities such as customer sales due to a personality disorder that resulted in a pattern of poor interpersonal skills and coping with minor conflict by getting into altercations. If subsequently the individual got a job in sales and then claimed that wrongful termination caused an impairment in an ability to deal with the public, the previous history would be a basis for apportionment (Lasky, 1993). Findings of preexisting psychiatric disability may also be made even if previous employment was unimpaired by the psychiatric disorder and, in these cases, apportionment to a previous psychiatric disability would also be valid (Lasky, 1993; see also *Callahan v. Workers' Compensation Appeals Board*, 1978).

Apportionment of permanent disability in workers' compensation claims falls into three categories:

1. Apportionment to preexisting disability: if the disability can be demonstrated to have existed in a previous work environment, then the entire disability is apportioned to the preexisting history.
2. Apportionment to off-the-job stressors, such as family problems or other personal, nonwork-related issues: that percent that is identifiable is apportioned to the off-the-job stressor.
3. Apportionment to the natural course of the disorder: certain disorders, for example, unremitting substance use disorders, often have a natural course of declining function and increasing disability to which disability is apportioned (Lasky, 1993).

Workers' compensation laws also recognize that aggravation of a preexisting injury can be causally related to the workplace. An individual with a preexisting psychiatric disorder can often legitimately say that work stress has, at the least, caused an exacerbation or aggravation of the disorder, even though the stress is not necessarily the cause of the disorder. However, stress-related claims that are based only an *aggravation* of a preexisting condition have added to the complexity of mental–mental claims. Addressing this problem, for example, a New Hampshire court ruled that where there is a preexisting weakness, the workplace conditions must have contributed something substantial for the claim to be compensable (*New Hampshire Supply Company v. Steinberg* (1979).

In some states, workers' compensation statutes require that an employer only pay for disability that would have resulted in the absence of the prior disability. Under such statutes, it is important to distinguish prior disability (as noted, defined by workers' compensation as loss or permanent impairment connected to work) from prior, predisposing disorder or disease, which, although not disabling at the time of the injury, is precipitated by the work-related injury and contributes to its effects. Nevertheless, apart from apportionment statutes, the employer is generally held liable for the entire disability resulting from the combination of the prior disability and the present injury.

When work stress is merely one of several contributing causes of disability, such as work stress with concurrent marital or financial stress, no basis for apportionment exists, reaffirming the old rule that apportionment cannot be attributed to different sources of stress unless a discrete and discernable portion of the disability can be imputed to each source. In the absence of this, the industrial cause is sufficient to make the employer 100% responsible, even if the injury would not have occurred without the other causes of stress being present (Lasky, 1993; see also *Bstandig v. Workers' Compensation Appeals Board*, 1978).

The third type of apportionment involves the natural progression of a preexisting nonindustrial disease process. The critical requirement in this type of apportionment is that the disability would have manifested itself even in the absence of injury by the time of the adjudication of the case. For example, a person might have had either a deteriorating organic brain syndrome or perhaps a history of cyclical manic-depressive symptoms with reason to believe that a depressive portion of psychosis would have manifested itself again around the time of adjudicating a psychiatric injury (Lasky, 1993). A mental health professional who offers this opinion must address both the evidence of progressive deterioration and the reasons for believing its pace was such that it would have manifested itself by the time in question. The lack of such explanations has frequently been the reason for reversal of an apportionment decision on appeal (see, e.g., *Market Basket v. Workers' Compensation Appeals Board*, 1978).

Dual Roles in Worker's Compensation Claims

Workers' compensation cases provide a salient example of the ethical dilemmas and potential bias caused by occupying the dual roles of treatment provider and expert evaluation. As discussed above, treatment providers are not asked to provide opinions regarding disability in SSDI claims. Even so, concerns regarding ethical conflicts in simply providing information regarding one's own patients for the purposes of SSDI have been raised. The common practice in workers' compensation cases of asking the treating mental health professional for opinions regarding disability issues directly relevant to continued provision of workers' compensation benefits raises even more complex ethical dilemmas.

As noted, when claims of a mental injury arises in a workers' compensation claim, claimants are referred to a mental health professional for treatment if they are not already receiving treatment. The treating psychiatrist or psychologist to whom the claimant is referred is usually asked to provide both initial and ongoing evaluation of the patient/claimant's disability to the workers' compensation board. Therefore, in workers' compensation claims, the same mental health professional generally provides initial evaluation, treatment, and reevaluation of a claimant, including providing wide-ranging opinions regarding disability that workers' compensation boards consider objective evidence and upon which their patients' compensation may depend.

Empathy with claimant/patients or a misguided sense of obligation can bias mental health professionals' opinions regarding disability issues. As discussed in Chapter 1, mental health treatment providers are ethically obligated to be their patients' allies and advocates in the pursuit of health. Both claimant/patients and their providers may understand the treatment provider's ethical obligation to mean that the providers should support the patient's pursuit or maintenance of disability benefits. The combination of sympathy toward the claimant/patient and a tendency to justify one's own treatment renders the clinician who provides both treatment and workers' compensation evaluations for the same claimant/patient especially vulnerable to bias (Brodsky, 1990).

In addition, mental health professionals treating claimant/patients are far more likely to be sympathetic toward them and to become their advocates if the workers' compensation claim evolves into litigation. Also as discussed in Chapter 1, certifying disability that leads to long-term work absence may not be in the best interest of claimants/patients' mental health, even in the presence of a chronic psychiatric disorder. In many cases, patient advocacy may be best served by supporting recovery to maximum functioning and return to work. Such a position is not likely to be congruent with the claimant/patient's goal of obtaining compensation for a disability.

SSA and workers' compensation programs compel or encourage the assumption of dual roles. Ordinarily, mental health professionals treating workers' compensation claimants/patients do not consider it a conflict to treat the claimants they evaluate if treatment is indicated. Nevertheless, it is recognized that treatment providers are not truly "independent" and therefore their opinions and evaluations may be subject to greater scrutiny (American Medical Association, 2008). As discussed at length earlier, clinicians should be aware of the potential ethical conflicts and the bias inherent in assuming the dual role of treatment provider and disability evaluator, and attempt to address and neutralize them.

Additional Guidelines for Conducting Workers' Compensation Evaluations

1. Determine whether a DSM-defined mental disorder is present.
2. Assess whether the mental disorder leads to impairment and, if requested, to disability.
3. If the referral source asks for an opinion regarding causation, be familiar with the applicable terminology regarding causation in the relevant state or federal workers' compensation statutes, and address inquiries and opinions to the standards articulated in the statutes.
4. Determine whether the following are required to be used in the assessment of impairment and disability by the relevant jurisdiction and utilize as indicated:
   a. rating or percentage scale, and if so, which one and
   b. use of disability categories of "temporary-partial," "temporary-total," "permanent-partial," and "permanent-total."
5. Address specific referral questions, which may include
   a. whether the worker is impaired or disabled from performing the duties of the job where the injury occurred;
   b. whether restrictions may be necessary to allow the worker to perform his or her own job, and if so, what restrictions are recommended;
   c. whether the worker is able to perform some other job;
   d. whether the worker is able to perform any job at all;
   e. whether an individual has reached maximum medical improvement; and
   f. whether a continuing need for treatment exists, both before and after settlement of a claim, and whether that treatment is needed to address the work-related mental disorder.

Private Disability Insurance Claims

Despite the availability of public programs providing disability benefits, a thriving private market in which willing buyers and sellers come together to agree to terms for private disability insurance coverage continues to be an attractive option for those who can afford it. Private disability insurance can provide benefits in the event individuals are unable for to pursue their livelihood as a result of accident or illness. Unlike SSDI and workers' compensation programs, private disability insurance is a commercial insurance product. The insurance industry and its products are regulated by state and federal governments.

Individuals obtain private disability insurance through various avenues. Some people are covered by private disability insurance policies as part of their employment benefits. People may also purchase private disability insurance individually or through access to a group plan, such as may be offered through a membership in a professional organization.

Mental health professionals can become involved in claims of persons who hold private disability insurance policies in two ways. As in SSDI claims, patients may, in the course of their treatment, file a claim for private disability benefits. The private insurance company (the carrier) or the patient claiming disability (the claimant) may ask the treating mental health professional to submit clinical information to the carrier for use in deciding the claimant's eligibility to receive benefits. Insurance law generally recognizes that the insured bears the burden of proof in demonstrating that the policy covered the damage suffered. The information provided by treating clinicians is often critical in establishing proof of disability or damage.

Although treatment providers are the primary source of information regarding an individual's psychiatric diagnosis and associated impairments, the carrier may be entitled to additional information to process the claim (Appleman, 2007). Additional information may and often does include expert opinions, particularly regarding work capacity, of an independent mental health professional. When the basis of the disability claim is a psychiatric disorder, carriers will often seek an IME from a psychiatrist or psychologist to evaluate the insured person's claims of disability and to evaluate other aspects of the claimant's circumstances, such as treatment needs and prognosis.[6] Thus, insurers typically include provisions in the policy that require the claimant to undergo an independent medical evaluation and to provide records of treatment.

Private disability claims referred for independent psychiatric or psychological evaluations often encompass some of the most difficult mental health issues related to disability. First, the scope of issues with which private insurers concern themselves is wide, since policies may contain any number of provisions that can lead to payment or denial of the insured's benefits. Many private disability insurance policies require that incapacity arise from a physical or mental condition rather than from accident or injury (Appleman, 2007). Mental health professionals therefore may be asked to address a number of issues related to diagnosis; present and future work capacity; restrictions, limitations, and accommodations; past,

---

[6] Disability evaluations related to private insurance may also be necessary in life insurance claims that include a waiver of premium in the event of disability, medical benefits claims, personal injury claims, and even requests for premature withdrawal of funds from certain investment vehicles (Battista, 1988).

current, and future treatment; prognosis; and the social, personal, and employment circumstances that may be relevant to the claim.

In addition, issues regarding psychological and medical comorbidity and their contribution to the claim of psychiatric disability are common. These referrals frequently involve the relationship of psychiatric illness to poorly understood problems that lack objective medical evidence, such as chronic pain syndromes or chronic fatigue syndrome. Referrals for IMEs may be made on the basis of these medical diagnoses alone, if insurance companies have reason to believe that psychiatric illness, rather than the medical illnesses claimed, is the primary cause of the claimant's disability.

Other difficult issues may involve the relationship between evaluees and their work. As discussed in Chapter 3, changes in employment circumstances can result in disability claims. Individuals who purchase private disability insurance have historically been associated with fewer disability claims, and when claims are made, the disability claimed tends to be of shorter duration. However, the 1980s and 1990s saw a trend toward increasing numbers of claims, especially, for example, among physicians, a group previously noted to have a relatively low incidence of disability claims. This was due, in part, to changes in the practice of medicine resulting from increasing pressures from medical insurance and health maintenance organizations (Wall & Appelbaum, 1998). Evaluations of physicians claiming disability benefits based on depression should therefore consider whether claimants are unable to work due to depression or whether chronic dissatisfaction due to the stresses of working in a managed care environment and not major depressive disorder is the primary issue. Such an individual might not be disabled, even if depressed, if working in a different environment.

Finally, it is not unusual for an IME in a private insurance disability claim to already have become quite adversarial by the time the independent mental health professional evaluates the claimant. Carriers handle most private disability insurance claims through internal review processes, that is, by having their own employees and consultants examine the materials submitted by claimants and their treating clinicians. If a carrier has additional questions about disability status, it may request an IME. A referral from a carrier going beyond its standard internal reviews implies potential, if not actual, conflict between the carrier and the claimant.

Requests for IMEs in private disability insurance cases also arise in a litigation context. If benefits end before claimants believe they can return to work, or when carriers deny claims outright, legal disputes may arise between the carriers and claimants. In these circumstances, the claimant's treating mental health provider often informs the carrier that denying or revoking benefits will cause a relapse or exacerbation of the claimant's psychiatric condition, generating additional issues of evaluation for the independent examiner. In such situations, claimants' attorneys may request IMEs from psychiatrists or psychologists.

Private Disability Insurance: Benefits by Contract and Differences from Other Disability Benefits Programs

Provisions, definitions, and eligibility for benefits differ markedly in private disability insurance from the programs previously reviewed. SSDI is a federal program defined and administered by statutory law; workers' compensation programs are legislated by and administered through state governments and their agencies. In contrast, private disability policies are contract agreements between the individual or groups who purchase the policies and the insurance companies who sell the policies. The provisions of a disability insurance policy, like other health insurance policies, rest on fundamental principles of contract law. The terms of the contract are dispositive in determining the insured's right to collect disability benefits (Appleman, 2007).

In contrast to the highly structured and statutory definitions of disability found in Social Security and Workers' Compensation programs, the parties in a private disability insurance contract breathe life into the meaning of the policy. In workers' compensation programs, disability is a combination of medical impairment and loss of income. In private disability insurance programs, disability provisions ordinarily require only loss of capacity to work. Ultimately, as construed by the courts, private disability benefits are available when the insured cannot perform his or her usual occupation or any other for which he or she is qualified (Appleman, 2007).

No single legal or administrative institution system oversees the policies and provisions of private disability insurance. The insurance industry, its regulators, and the courts combine to give meaning to policies terms and definitions and will determine whether the claimant's circumstances meet the requirements specified by the policy to access benefits (Appleman, 2007). Each state has its own insurance regulatory system and each claim may take on an administrative life of its own.

Even within states, no comprehensive or integrated system exists for filing or processing private disability claims. The courts take on the role of interpreter to resolve disputes when conflicts between the parties arise over the meaning or application of policy language. Notably, a relevant contract principle in disputes over health insurance policies is that in the face of substantial disparity in bargaining power, any ambiguity in the policy language is construed against the party with the disparate power, the insurer (Appleman, 2007).

In private disability cases, preexisting injuries are treated the way the parties choose to treat them. This too differs from civil cases or workers' compensation cases in which causation issues associated with preexisting injury reflected in the common law's "eggshell skull" rule are relevant. An eggshell plaintiff is a person who is vulnerable to injury due to a preexisting problem. In common law and workers' compensation, the actor who cracks a plaintiff's eggshell skull, even if the trauma was minimal and would not have harmed an otherwise non-vulnerable person, is legally responsible for the damages that ensue.

Thus, in private disability insurance, if the disability arises after the contract date, and the contract did not state otherwise, the claimant's preexisting vulnerability, or eggshell skull, is immaterial. If an individual becomes disabled, even if due to a condition that preexisted the purchase of disability insurance benefits, they may be awarded benefits unless the policy specifically stated that a preexisting condition would disqualify the claimant from eligibility for benefits. For example, in *Lewis v. Paul Revere Life Ins. Co.* (2000), a federal district court rejected an insurer's contention that the insured was not entitled to disability benefits because the disabling conditions, anxiety and depression, were preexisting conditions.

Similar to some workers' compensation programs however, private disability insurance carriers concerns about quantifying psychiatric claims have resulted in certain restricting provisions in policies that cover psychiatric or mental disability claims. For example, some carriers place time limits on the benefit amount or the duration for which a psychiatric claim will receive compensation. As noted above, this can give rise to disputes when claimants feel their benefits are prematurely terminated.

Another significant difference between public disability programs and private disability insurance is the size of and required conditions for monetary compensation. The public benefits available through SSDI are relatively modest, available only to people whose employers have paid into the Social Security trust fund on their behalf in 5 of the 10 years before the disability, and who can demonstrate total and permanent disability. Workers compensation for injury or impairment is typically less generous than private disability insurance, and benefits are available only to those whose injury or disability satisfies the required nexus to workplace injury. Private disability insurance benefits tend to be very generous, even though they are available only to those whose employment benefits contain such coverage or who had the foresight, as well as the financial resources, to purchase a policy covering a risk that would not be realized until sometime later.

Also unlike the public disability programs in which amount and duration of payments are highly structured, the amount of compensation and the duration of time over which benefits are provided are contractually determined and vary from policy to policy and state to state. SSDI benefits are predicated on total and permanent disability and provide a minimal "substitute" income; workers' compensation benefits are intended to compensate only for lost earning power and associated medical expenses. In contrast, private disability insurance, in addition to providing a sizable payment based on previous earning capacity in the event of disability, may also make payments for the business expenses of a professional person or independent businessperson while that person is disabled.

Legal Disability vs Factual Disability

Cases in which mental health professionals are asked to determine whether a claimant's disability results from psychiatric disorders or legal problems arise primarily in private disability insurance claims. As discussed in Chapter 6, factual disabilities are based on medical impairments involving illness or injury. Legal disabilities result from the inability to perform occupational tasks due to a legal barrier such as incarceration or the loss of professional license.

Private disability insurance policies provide benefits for factual disabilities, not legal disabilities. The distinction between legal and factual disability is often a difficult one to make, both for mental health professionals and for the courts, and legal decisions do not provide consistent direction in these determinations. Certainly, psychiatric illness can result in impaired judgment that can lead to legal consequences, but just as certainly, not every individual becomes unable to work or pursue a profession because of legal consequences related to impaired judgment as a result of psychiatric illness.

Solomon v. Royal Maccabees Life Ins. Co. (2000) is an example of what courts consider legal disability not covered by disability insurance. In this case, a doctor suffering from bipolar disorder admitted to improper sexual relations with patients, left his practice, surrendered his medical license, and then sought disability benefits from his policy. The insurer denied benefits and the court from which he sought review agreed. Affirming, the Michigan Court of Appeals reasoned that the bipolar disorder did not prevent him from performing his occupation, as he had practiced medicine for at least 20 years despite the disorder. Rather, the court reasoned, it was the voluntary surrender of his medical license that stopped him from practicing medicine. The court determined that this was a legal disability for which he was not entitled to disability benefits.

A Florida District Court of Appeal decision (*Stern v. Paul Revere Life Ins. Co.*, 1999) provides a colorful example of a factual disability that might be covered. The insurer contended that claimant doctor was not disabled as a result of a sickness but because he engaged in sexual misconduct with patients resulting in the revocation of his license to practice medicine, two felony convictions, and incarceration. Reversing a summary judgment for the insurer in the trial court, the court of appeals found that the insurer could have written its policy to exclude this as a "legal disability" but did not. Accordingly, the appellate court found that summary judgment was premature and remanded to the trial court to determine whether the disability was caused by physician's incarceration, a legal disability, or the psychosexual disorder and anxiety/depression syndrome, a factual disability.

Private Disability Insurance: Definitions and Terms

Disability: Total or Partial

In private disability insurance policies, provision of benefits as well as conflicts and litigation over entitlement to benefits turn on the definitions in the policy. Courts, like mental health professionals and many others, often encounter difficulties in construing the term "total disability." The judicial position on total vs. partial disability lies somewhere between that of SSDI, in which disability is either total or nonexistent, and workers' compensation programs, which ideally would like to put a percentage value on any type of disability, including psychiatric disability.

A number of courts have held that a person is totally disabled if unable to perform the substantial duties of his or her work activities in the same manner as before. However, legal decisions regarding the definition of total disability have clarified that total disability is a relative concept to be determined in light of the insured's occupation, education, training, and injury. As one court ruled, "what may totally disable [a] manual laborer may not totally disable [a] business executive, physician, or lawyer within the scope of the total disability clause of the policy" (*Harker v. Paul Revere Life Ins. Co.*, 1965).

Generally, judicial interpretations of disability take into account the claimant's occupation as a whole in order to determine whether recovery should be allowed on the grounds that the insured can no longer perform occupational duties. Although not necessarily adhered to by every rule in every jurisdiction, if the insured is unable to perform any of the material, important, or substantial duties pertaining to his or her usual and customary occupation in substantially the same manner as before, the insured is entitled to receive the disability benefits. If the insured is able to do substantially all the acts material to the occupation and there are only a few immaterial things that the insured cannot do, he or she is not likely to be entitled to recover disability benefits. Moreover, some courts have held that the definition of total disability must be construed in light of the insured's understanding of the term or that the words must be interpreted as a layperson would understand them (*Sosnowski v. Aetna Life Ins. Co.*, 1939).

However, total disability generally must consist of more than an inability to carry on previous work that was trivial in nature. For example, an attorney who is substantially impaired in his work may recover disability benefits, but the occasional loss of use of a single hand due to intermittent circulation problems in the hand and fingers as a result of Raynaud's syndrome was not found sufficient to be interpreted to meet the terms of substantial impairment and disability (*Siegel v. Mutual Life Ins. Co.*, 1980).

In contrast, a surgeon suffering from hand tremors so severe that he could no longer perform surgery and was forced to discontinue his practice would be considered totally disabled (*Dixon v. Pc. Mut. Life Ins. Co.*, 1960). However, a surgeon who underwent cataract surgery and claimed that he was unable to maintain a full-time practice afterward was held not totally disabled to perform his duties within the meaning of his policy because he was still able to perform the substantial tasks of his occupation (*Girardeau v. Guardian Life Ins. Co.*, 1981).

Nevertheless, disability provisions should not be construed to require that an individual be utterly helpless to be considered disabled. For example, the fact that a person is able to do some temporary work is not a sufficient basis to deny recovery. The insured must be able to do gainful work with reasonable regularity and continuity. Ordinarily, an individual who cannot perform gainful work, that is, work that is profitable and advantageous rather than some trivial work that would yield only inconsequential compensation, has generally established total disability (Appleman, 2007).

Permanent vs. Temporary Disability

Depending on the terms of the policy, benefits may only become available when the condition becomes permanent or presumably permanent. Courts have been reluctant to abide solely by dictionary or statutory definitions in interpreting the words "permanent" and "temporary" in conflicts over disability insurance. The common interpretation of the expression "permanent" in private disability insurance is that a disability will persist for a long or indefinite period of time as opposed to a condition that is transient or temporary (Appleman, 2007).

Rather than considering the expression "permanent" to refer to a state of indefinite continuance, some courts have applied a higher test for recovery, defining permanent as "something incapable of alteration, fixed or immutable" (Appleman, 2007, p. 202). Under this rule, the disability must appear to be likely to continue for the remainder of the insured's life. If recovery from the injury or illness seems certain to occur within a short period of time, the claim is considered to be one of temporary total disability and no recovery is available, regardless of the seriousness of the injuries. Many personal disability insurance policies include provisions that specify after a certain time period, total disability should be presumed to be permanent, because the length of time that a disability is present is considered significant evidence of its nature. Nevertheless, benefits may not be available, again depending on the terms of the policy, until the disability is deemed permanent (Appleman, 2007).

Disability: Own Occupation or Any Occupation

Private disability insurance policies include terms that may specify that the insured, in order to receive benefits, must be disabled from their own particular occupation ("own occ") or disabled from any occupation ("any occ"). This distinction is often the subject of significant conflict between carriers and policyholders. Claimants whose policies specify disability as the inability to perform their own occupation may be eligible for benefits even if they can still do substantial work and make a substantial income in another occupation. In these evaluations, claimants' remaining abilities and work skills (similar to the SSDI's "RFC" concept) are not particularly significant if they are impaired in an area that precludes functioning in their own occupation.

However, many private disability policies require that to obtain benefits, the insured must be disabled not only from their own occupation but also from performing "any occupation" to which the insured is reasonably suited to engage by education, training, or experience. In these policies, remaining abilities and work skills are a critical part of the assessment. If a claimant is incapable of performing the substantial tasks of their own occupation but capable of performing other work, the requirements for obtaining benefits are not met (Appleman, 2007).

The fact that claimants might be able to perform some of the tasks associated with their occupation does not alter the fact of practical incapacity in the entirety of the occupation. For example, the capacity to continue to do certain types of minor tasks, such as occasional housework or driving to a doctor's office, is not considered evidence of continuing overall occupational capacity. In addition, the fact that the insured is able to earn a living post-disability is irrelevant, even if claimants earn more in the new occupation, if the disability policy provides benefits if claimants are disabled from engaging in their chosen profession (Appleman, 2007). For example, one court found that an obstetrician/gynecologist, employed as a hospital consultant in sex education and family planning, was totally disabled within the terms of his policy because he was unable to continue his medical practice after suffering a heart attack (*Niccoli v. Monarch Life Ins. Co.*, 1972).

Most courts hold that policy provisions that deny benefits unless the insured is totally disabled from engaging in any occupation refer to any occupation from which the insured has been accustomed to gain a livelihood. These courts permit recovery just as if the clause referred to the insured's ordinary vocation. As a result, these provisions become more restrictive in regard to considering what other kinds of occupations a person may engage in as their level of education, training, or experience increases. So, for example, a physician with an "any occ" disability policy who sustained loss of hearing in both ears, could not practice medicine, and could not retrain himself in allied specialties, was found wholly disabled from engaging in any gainful occupation for which he was reasonably fitted or qualified (*Littman v. Nat'l Cas. Co.*, 1966).

Some courts take a stricter view and will deny recovery of benefits if the insured is able to engage in any business or vocation, whether his own or another (Appleman, 2007). When the contract prohibits recovery if the insured can follow other occupations for gain or profit, claimants, if idle, must show that they made an effort to adapt to other work and that their health will not permit other work. The insurer is not liable if the evidence demonstrates that the insured has made no effort to secure other employment. Thus, an osteopathic surgeon could not recover when he made no attempt to have a skin infection treated and made no effort to test his ability in some other employment (*Mut. Life Co. v. Ellison*, 1955). Moreover, when total disability is defined as being incapable of performing "any and every duty of any gainful occupation," even a limited capacity to work, such as the ability to perform some duties on a part-time basis, may be sufficient to terminate benefits (Appleman, 2007).

Individuals who are found not to be disabled because they are employed consistently or able to do the substantial tasks of the employment and because they are earning reasonable compensation may rebut the conclusion of lack of total disability. To do so, an individual must demonstrate that

1. The disabling condition may not be chronic, and may be cured or resolved, but only if the individual refrains from ordinary exertions of any fixed employment; or
2. The disabling condition is chronic and incurable, and the insured is able to engage in employment; however, as a result of persisting in the ordinary exertions of any fixed employment, the condition would probably, not possibly, seriously and dangerously progress or become far worse, as compared with what would happen whether employed or unemployed; or
3. The condition results in pain and suffering, which is or will become unbearable by a person of average or normal fortitude (Appleman, 2007).

Mental Health Professionals and Private Disability Insurance Claims

Mental health professionals conducting IMEs in private disability insurance claims, whether retained by parties representing the claimant or the insurance carrier, have a significant role to play in the adjudication of these claims. The information mental health professionals provide in an IME can be critical both in the initial determination of eligibility for benefits and in subsequent conflicts over the interpretation of the policy. Although the ultimate determination regarding disability and the payment of benefits is not up to the evaluating psychiatrist or psychologist, the information the mental health expert provides may be central to the ultimate decision maker's determination, whether insurance carrier or court.

Carriers seeking to determine eligibility for benefits or whether to continue paying benefits already awarded may seek a review of records only from an independent mental health evaluator, rather than arranging a personal examination of the claimant. In such cases, carriers ask specific questions that they want independent reviewers to answer in order to obtain opinions from an independent source as well as to establish a record to support a claim determination. Often, at least one question in such referrals is whether the records support the degree of disability claimed.

Mental health opinions reached through record review alone are limited by lack of a personal interview with a claimant. In addition, they may be limited by the lack of other relevant or necessary information. The reviewing mental health professional should be certain to specify that the opinion offered is based only the records provided and suggest that the carrier obtain an IME if the questions asked cannot be answered without an interview of the evaluee.

Frequently, however, an IME with a personal evaluation of the claimant is requested. These independent evaluations have much in common with the type of independent medical or psychiatric evaluation that might be mandated by a court in the course of employment litigation. The referral source should clearly understand that the expert is providing evaluation and not treatment. In addition, the referral source should provide collateral information, including medical records, a description of the evaluee's job duties and responsibilities, and other relevant information. Experts should review these prior to meeting with the claimant.

Referrals for IMEs in private psychiatric disability claims also generally include specific questions derived from the policy. The language used in these questions is shaped by the courts and local custom, and should shape the evaluation and the presentation of the evaluator's opinions. Evaluators should be careful to answer these questions specifically. Assessments or opinions that have not been requested should not be offered. Doing so may cause complications for the referral sources as well as problems for the evaluating mental health professional should disputes regarding the carrier's determinations arise or in the litigation of a contested case.

Referral questions are often written in a manner that does not allow complete discussion of the case formulation and pattern of disability (see Chapter 5), the understanding of which is essential in understanding the dynamics of claimants' relationships to their work. Thus evaluators should consider including a brief case formulation in the written report. This allows evaluators to go beyond some of the "yes" or "no" answers to referral questions. A case formulation can be used to describe the salient features of how claimants have come to present themselves or perceive themselves as disabled, without offering an opinion on the validity of the disability claim.

Requests for opinions and findings will vary from case to case. Referral sources typically require a comprehensive IME report, with a full DSM multi-axial diagnosis, plus detailed findings and treatment recommendations. These are generally requested in the referral questions. In specific and detailed response to questions asked, evaluators should state whether the evaluee suffers from a psychiatric illness, whether that illness (if present) impairs the evaluee's ability to work, and the specific reasons for and areas of impairment. Evaluators may be asked whether current treatment meets the standard of care or includes return to work as a goal of treatment. Evaluators should indicate whether current treatment is not adequate for the condition or might generally be adequate but not aggressive enough given the degree of occupational dysfunction. Evaluators may also comment on the limitations, if any, of evaluation and treatment, the reasons for those limitations, and the evaluee's attitude and compliance toward treatment recommendations. Supporting data referenced should include past history of illness and its relationship to impairment and ability to work, current symptoms, whether treatment is organized to facilitate a return to work, and the motivation of the evaluee to seek appropriate treatment and return to work.

Despite the fact that the determination of disability goes beyond a purely medical assessment, as discussed in Chapter 6, many carriers and attorneys request and seriously consider the evaluator's opinion regarding disability

(Battista, 1988). Evaluators may be asked whether evaluees could return to work at their own occupation or some other occupation or whether the evaluee is subject to limitations and/or restrictions but could work with modified workplace conditions. If these opinions are requested, evaluators should provide detailed responses supported by objective evidence and specific examples. However, if mental health evaluators don't have enough information or are unable to formulate opinions based on objective data to answer these questions, they should so state.

Some referral sources may not want the independent evaluator to offer an opinion on whether the claimant is disabled. Instead, a referral source may ask the evaluator to discuss the evaluee's overall functional capacities so as to allow the referral source to make its own determination of disability status. If not requested, opinions regarding claimants' limitations, restrictions, and ability to return to work at their own or any occupation should not be offered. Regardless of whether an opinion on disability status is requested, the IME report should address the specific functional tasks of the particular evaluee's duties.

In addition to the usual elements of a comprehensive psychiatric assessment, independent evaluating mental health professionals should give special attention to determining the evaluee's level of function before the claimed disability began and what has changed in the evaluee's ability to function. For example, an individual may have had prior episodes of depression but been able to continue working. If the claimant is now stating that depression has resulted in total disability, the evaluator should be able to identify what has changed in the claimant's symptoms or work situation such that the claimant can no longer work, even though able to do so in the past despite symptoms of depression. As discussed, modeling such a formulation on the analysis suggested in Chapter 5 of disability development can be helpful in this formulation.

The evaluator should obtain a complete work history, including the evaluee's account of the current claimed disability, any past episodes of disability and the reasons for these, and any work performance problems. The evaluator should review efforts and results of any attempts to return to work during or after treatment. Evaluee's descriptions of typical activities before and after the onset of disability, self-assessment, self-prognosis, and future plans can also provide significant insight into the nature of the disability and which factors are most prominent in the claim of inability to work.

Other factors that may influence the decision to withdraw from the workplace through a claim of disability should be assessed. Although evaluees may volunteer information about their work performance problems, they can also be asked about their relationships with peers and supervisors, reprimands, or concerns voiced by others in the work environment. Individuals who feel they have been treated unfairly or feel their impairments were caused by the workplace often provide information about workplace problems and conflicts. Written records should also be able to provide evidence of workplace conflict or performance problems.

Evaluators should also have a reasonable understanding of the evaluee's pre- and post-disability income, disability benefits, policy terms, and other sources of income, as these may indicate the significance of financial factors in the evaluee's motivation to return to work or to seek disability benefits. Exploring these may also help provide information as to whether filing a disability claim represents the claimant's conscious or unconscious efforts to resolve nonemployment issues, such as family or marital problems (Brodsky, 1996a; Wall & Appelbaum, 1998). Evaluators should be aware that such questions raise the ethical problems involved in essentially taking on the role of an investigator, a role for which most mental health professionals lack specific training or expertise. Thus, evaluators should be cautious in coming to conclusions based on this type of information alone.

Evaluating mental health professionals should consider obtaining information about the evaluee's functioning by speaking with a spouse or significant other, work colleagues, or supervisors when possible and feasible. It is prudent to have evaluees sign a consent form or to document their consent to make these contacts. In cases where evaluees refuse to allow the necessary collateral contacts, evaluators should note the refusal and evaluees' stated reason for refusal in the report. Evaluators should also indicate that the report's conclusions might be limited by the lack of potentially relevant information.

Evaluating experts should attempt to speak with the evaluee's treatment providers, with consent of the referral source and the evaluee, even if these providers have supplied their treatment records. Additional and important information may be obtained by speaking directly with treatment providers. As noted in Chapter 6, individuals may be circumspect in their written documentation if they are aware that an insurance or legal claim may be pending. In addition, a written record of a therapy session or medication evaluation cannot reflect an entire therapy hour or cover every facet of patient contact, even assuming diligent documentation.

Mental health evaluators are also often asked various questions regarding the claimant's treatment. Many referral sources ask the evaluator to assess current treatment and to make additional treatment recommendations. These may be easier to answer once treatment providers have been contacted and directly questioned.

Evaluators should not contact treatment providers without the referral source's or evaluee's consent. Referral sources may have their own reasons for refusing to permit this direct contact. Evaluees should sign a consent form or document their consent to make these contacts. In cases where an evaluee refuses to allow contact with treatment providers, evaluators should note the refusal and the evaluee's stated reason for refusal in the report. Whether consent to contact treatment providers is refused by either referral sources or evaluees, evaluators should also indicate that the report's conclusions might be limited by lack of contact with the treatment providers if this is the case.

The possibility of malingering or, more commonly, exaggeration of symptoms, as discussed in Chapter 6, should also be assessed. Evaluators should not make conclusions about malingering lightly due to its implications. Although a claimant's presentation might suggest malingering, mental health professionals should consider various interpretations of these behaviors and affects. As in IMEs that occur in any adversarial situation such as litigation, defensiveness may reflect an evaluee's anger or anxiety at having to undergo an expert evaluation of their disability claim rather than their knowing exaggeration or misrepresentation of symptoms or functioning (Lanyon & Almer, 2002). Similarly, although an evaluee's illegal behavior or maladaptive personality traits may result in a disability claim, these types of problems do not necessarily result from impairment caused by a psychiatric illness. If no psychiatric impairment or diagnosis is found, evaluators should articulate this opinion and provide the data supporting this conclusion.

Sometimes, evaluating mental health professionals cannot obtain enough information to answer the referral source's questions. In such cases, evaluating psychiatrists and psychologists should inform the referral source that they do not have enough data to formulate a reliable opinion. When the information that has been provided indicates the existence of additional records that may provide essential information, evaluators should advise referral sources of the existence of such records and recommend that these records be obtained. In addition, a review of the records or an interview of the claimant may indicate that additional testing might provide useful information. If so, the evaluating psychiatrist or psychologist should suggest to the referral source that the claimant be referred for psychological, neuropsychological, or medical testing, urine screening or other laboratory tests, or other examinations. These should not be undertaken without prior discussion and agreement with the referral source.

Communicating Findings in Private Disability Insurance Evaluations

The written report is often the only final work product of the private disability IME. It should follow the format suggested by the referral source or some other standard format, such as the one suggested in Appendix C. Evaluators should list and respond to each referral question as posed. Regardless of what opinions are provided, evaluators should be certain to link the observed symptoms to the functional impairments and should provide specific examples of these. A comprehensive and objective report should make it easy for a reader to comprehend the clinical connections between an illness, the illness's impairing symptoms, and how those symptoms affect the evaluee's ability to work (Anfang et al., 2005). In addition, as discussed, the intended audience of the report typically comprises administrators or others who are not mental health professionals. The less the jargon used, particularly in the responses to the specific referral questions, the better.

No matter how thorough the evaluation and reports, referral sources often ask for clarification, pose follow-up questions, or forward additional records and ask whether the new information changes any of the evaluator's opinions.

Nevertheless, and especially if litigation is taking place or should ensue, well-substantiated and clearly articulated opinions with many specific examples presented in the initial report may prevent the problems that may arise with adding opinions or facts at a later time, such as in deposition or trial testimony.

Dual Roles and Ethical Conflicts in Private Disability Insurance Evaluations

As in SSDI and workers' compensation claims, treating mental health professionals are obligated to provide a patient's medical records to support disability claims if a patient so requests and provides appropriate authorization for release of the information. However, these requests do not abrogate a clinician's responsibility to consider the patient's best interests. Patients have the right to waive the privilege of confidentiality but treatment providers should advise their patients of the potential risks and consequences of releasing their mental health records.

For example, some patients' interests regarding their disability claims are better served by sending a summary report or letter, rather than copies of the records in their entirety. A written summary of the patient's mental health history and problems may assist a patient's claim more than providing handwritten chart notes, especially if those notes are sparse and difficult to read. This serves the dual purpose of providing the necessary information in a cogent (and legible) document while preserving a certain amount of the patient's privacy by not revealing details not relevant to the disability claim. Although some carriers may not accept a summary in lieu of records, this option is often worth exploring when a patient's privacy is at risk of being compromised.

More problematically, patients also often ask their treating clinicians to assist them in their private disability claims by requesting that their treatment providers provide opinions that require evaluation beyond that which has been conducted for treatment purposes. As discussed in Chapter 1, many patients and their clinicians believe the proper role for the treatment provider is that of unquestioning advocate of patients' requests. However, gathering information in the course of clinical care differs from conducting an IME or serving as expert witness for one's own patient's private disability claims.

Should a disability claim issue arise, patients and their attorneys should be advised that the patient is best served by obtaining an independent mental health evaluation of his or her impairments and disability. Treating mental health clinicians are not "independent" evaluators and therefore cannot, by definition, provide "independent evaluations" of their patients. Clinicians and patients alike often are unaware that providing such opinions without adequate evaluation and collateral or employment information creates ethical as well as practical difficulties for both the clinician and the patient/claimant. Opinions regarding disability that are not supported by an adequate disability evaluation will be easy to discredit should an adversarial situation with the insurance carrier arise.

The potential for bias in occupying the dual role of clinician and disability evaluator has been discussed in regard to both SSDI and, more significantly, in workers' compensation cases where treatment providers provide ongoing evaluation of disability to workers' compensation boards. In contrast to these contexts, and particularly in regard to the relatively informal administrative context of most workers' compensation claims, evaluations in private disability claims often must meet strict policy definitions in the provision of information. Moreover, if these claims result in litigation, the formal standards of rules of evidence will apply. Treatment providers may find that in an attempt to assist their patients in obtaining private disability benefits, they actually create more obstacles in successfully filing such claims than they resolve by providing opinions that are not adequately supported by the available data.

Treating mental health professionals who offer disability opinions may adversely affect the therapeutic relationship as well as the patient's claim. For example, as discussed in Chapter 1 and also above in regard to workers' compensation cases, certifying disability that leads to long-term work absence may not be in the best interest of claimants/patients' mental health, even in the presence of a chronic psychiatric disorder. In many such cases, patient advocacy may be best served by supporting recovery to maximum functioning and return to work.

Additional Guidelines for Conducting Workers' Compensation Evaluations

1. Clarify in writing the referral source's specific questions.
2. Understand the evaluee's policy terms and the relevant definition of disability. Utilize these definitions in response to referral questions.
3. Provide specific, clear, and well-substantiated answers to the referral source's questions.
4. Do not offer opinions regarding any aspect of psychiatric or work function, including the presence or absence of disability, unless specifically requested to do so.
5. If the referral source's questions cannot be answered due to lack of information, inform the referral source of this and suggest what additional information could or should be provided.
6. Opinions based on record review only should clearly indicate that only a record review has been conducted.
7. If request for record review only indicates the need for an IME to answer the referral sources' questions, evaluators should suggest that an IME be conducted.

Conclusion

Navigating complicated disability programs systems in order to obtain benefits is difficult at best. Individuals often find that regardless of the merits of their claims, they have to vigorously advocate for themselves to overcome bureaucratic and legal hurdles if they hope to obtain benefits. Individuals whose disabilities include mental illness are often at a disadvantage when filing a disability claim. These disorders often result in impairments in cognitive or emotional functioning needed to persist in advocating for themselves within or against disability systems with virtually unlimited resources, such as government or state agencies or wealthy and well-lawyered private insurance companies.

Mental health professionals providing assessments of impairment in disability claims should therefore maintain an acute awareness of their ethical obligations and be familiar with the relevant agency's proof requirements. Even when asked to offer opinions regarding disability, mental health professionals should be aware that the final determination of a claimant's disability status lies with rules and law regulating disability programs, and should tailor their opinions toward providing information to help these agencies come to fair and reasonable conclusions of participants' claims.

Chapter 8
Working with Disabilities: The Americans with Disabilities Act

Introduction

Many persons with mental or physical disabilities find that they are not able to work and seek disability benefits from programs such as Social Security Disability Income, workers' compensation, and private disability insurance, as addressed in Chapter 7. For many other people, the meaning that they derive from work is the spiritual core that sparks their lives (see Chapter 3). These individuals want to maintain their employment despite their impairments and believe they could perform the essential functions of their jobs if given some accommodations. The law does not recognize an individual right to employment. Nevertheless, the law does provide that all people who want to work, including those with disabilities, are entitled to a fair opportunity to participate in the competitive labor market and it provides for special measures to facilitate access to competitive employment for people with disabilities (Bonnie, 1997d).

The law most commonly associated with the right of persons with disabilities to participate in the mainstream of American society, including the workforce, is the Americans with Disabilities Act (ADA). The ADA, enacted in 1990, is a descendant of the civil rights movement of the 1960s. It was designed to protect the civil rights of disabled individuals in nearly every domain of public life, including housing, education, communication, transportation, governmental and public services, and employment. The ADA arguably has had a greater impact on the workplace than any other legislation since the Civil Rights Act of 1964 (Eddy & Schouten, 2003; Waldner & Hornsby, 2005). The enactment in 2008 of the Americans with Disabilities Act Amendments Act (ADAAA) may widen that impact significantly.

The implications of the ADA on persons already in the labor force have called attention to the outer boundaries of the definition of disability (Bonnie, 1997d), particularly in the case of psychiatric disability. The ADA and its judicial interpretations provide a set of requirements that facilitate demonstration of physical disabilities rather than mental disabilities (Paetzold, 2005). The ADA's application to mental disabilities therefore has needed continuous definition, primarily through legal challenges and judicial decisions (Bell,

1997). Employment, the cornerstone of independence for many persons with disabilities, has become a major source of litigation under the ADA (Parry & Drogin, 2007). The trend of those employment decisions led to the passage of the ADAAA, additional legislation attempting to broaden the application of the ADA.

Mental health opinions provided by a psychiatrist or psychologist with clinical expertise and a thorough grasp of the relevant issues in ADA evaluations can provide valuable guidance to employees, employers, and the courts in making ADA decisions. Identifying, proving, and accommodating a disability are particularly difficult tasks for persons with psychiatric disorders and raise problematic issues for both employees and employers. The obligation to provide reasonable accommodation has created considerable confusion about how to balance the needs of employers with those of disabled employees. Employers not infrequently find themselves in a quandary about how to accommodate workers who have psychiatric disorders, resulting in disputes that can lead to litigation.

Mental health professionals are often consulted in employment cases related to the ADA long before dispute or litigation has occurred. The invocation of the ADA by individuals with psychiatric disorders may result in a referral for a mental health evaluation. Employers may seek an evaluation to help clarify their responsibilities to an employee. Employees may seek documentation of psychiatric disability to demonstrate eligibility for ADA coverage. In a best-case scenario, a comprehensive ADA mental health evaluation may allow an employee who might otherwise have to assume disability status to remain in the workforce and may assist employers by facilitating the continued employment of a valuable worker. At a minimum, an ADA evaluation may help avert a confrontation that could lead to a claim of discrimination and costly litigation.

Psychiatrists and psychologists asked to provide opinions regarding ADA issues should be aware that ADA mental health evaluations differ in important respects from the more common and familiar disability evaluations reviewed in Chapter 7. Evaluations for purposes of qualifying for disability benefits focus on what individuals can no longer do. ADA evaluations focus not only on an individual's impairments but also on remaining work skills and what an employer can do to support them. In addition, mental health professionals conducting ADA evaluations need to understand and respond to questions involving unfamiliar statutorily defined terms unique to ADA evaluations. This chapter will review the ADA's legal and statutory requirements and the issues mental health professionals should understand in providing ADA evaluations.

The ADA in Action: How Does it Work?

The ADA prohibits discrimination based on a disability, a history of a disability, or a perception that a person has a disability. If individuals meet the ADA's definition of a disability, they are entitled to protection against discrimination due to disability under all sections of the ADA, one of which is employment. Many of the ADA's provisions regarding physical and mental disabilities are based on and encompass the provisions of the Rehabilitation Act of 1973. Rights established by the Rehabilitation Act and other laws predating the ADA are still in effect, but the ADA substantially extended the reach of those laws (Parry & Drogin, 2007).

Title I of the ADA prohibits private employers except those with less than 15 employees and all federal employers regardless of size from discriminating against a qualified individual with a disability in any aspect of that person's employment, including applications and hiring processes, and advancement, benefits, and discharge policies.[1] Title I requires employers to make "reasonable accommodations" for "disabled" but qualified individuals, unless the accommodation would impose an "undue hardship" on the employer. An "undue hardship" exists when an accommodation is too expensive, difficult, disruptive, or would fundamentally alter the position (Parry & Drogin, 2007). Factors courts consider in determining whether an accommodation represents an undue hardship include the nature and cost of the accommodations, the overall financial resources of the covered employer, and the type of operations performed by the employer (Parry & Drogin, 2007).

Notably, having sought disability benefits prior to seeking protection under the ADA does not invalidate a person's claim that he or she could perform the essential functions of a job with accommodations. The Supreme Court has ruled that pursuit and receipt of SSDI benefits does not as a matter of law preclude an ADA claim. In such a case, the plaintiff must be given the opportunity to explain the discrepancy between the claim that the person is totally disabled, integral to an SSDI application (see Chapter 7), and the ADA claim that the individual can perform the essential functions of the job if given accommodations (*Cleveland v. Policy Management Systems Corp.*, 1999).

An employer is obligated to provide a reasonable accommodation only if it knows of the "physical or mental limitations" of an "otherwise qualified" individual (42 USC §12112(b)(5)(A)). An employer owes no duty to an employee under the ADA to seek an accommodation unless and until the employee notifies an employer of a disability or the employer becomes aware that the employee is disabled (*Morisky v. Broward County*, 1996). Because many psychiatric disorders are not obvious and employers are prohibited from asking about or testing for disabilities during the preemployment process, the ADA does not come into play until the otherwise qualified person with a disability requests an accommodation (Campbell & Kaufmann, 1997).

Therefore, in most employment situations, an individual who chooses not to disclose their disability or chooses not to request an accommodation is choosing not to come under the protection of the ADA (Ritchie & Zonana, 2003). For

---

[1] In contrast, for example, Title V of the Rehabilitation Act of 1973 prohibited only federal government agencies and organizations that receive federal funds from discriminating against qualified individuals with disabilities.

example, in *Landefeld v. Marion General Hospital* (1993), a court of appeals upheld the termination of staff privileges of an internist who tampered with fellow physicians' mailboxes. The court of appeals noted that the board of directors had no notice of the internist's bipolar disorder and was merely reacting to the misconduct. In the absence of knowledge of a disability or a request for accommodation supported by medical documentation, the employer had no obligation to provide an accommodation to the employee.

In addition, simply advising an employer that the employer has a diagnosis such as bipolar disorder or depression is not sufficient. Courts have held that the employee is responsible for advising the employer of the need for accommodation and for providing enough specific information regarding limitations so that the employer can make reasonable accommodations. For example, in *Hammon v. DHL Airways, Inc.* (1999), a pilot suffered emotional problems after a traumatic experience during a flight simulator drill and resigned because he had "lost all confidence." The court ruled that the pilot's resignation, which stated he was "going backwards" and "this is not working," did not put the employer on notice that the pilot had a disability.

If an employer does not know about the disability, it cannot have a duty to accommodate the plaintiff. Nevertheless, case law suggests that the duty of the employer to accommodate a disabled employee may be higher when the employee suffers from a mental disability (Eddy & Schouten, 2003). A federal court of appeals indicated that when dealing with individuals with psychiatric problems, employers must make an extra effort to communicate and assist the employee to identify necessary accommodations (*Criado v. IBM Corp.*, 1998). The obligation to accommodate a disabled employee generally is triggered when an employee or his or her representative (such as a physician or family member) advises the employer that the employee requires an adjustment or change at work because of a disability. In one case, an appeals court found that a custodial employee whose psychiatrist submitted a letter suggesting assignment to a less stressful position constituted a request for an accommodation (*Bultemeyer v. Fort Wayne Community Schools*, 1996).

An employer may also owe a duty to an employee in the difficult circumstances that arise when, in the absence of the employee's disclosure of a disability, the employer comes to suspect that an employee is having performance difficulties that seem related to a serious mental illness. Despite the general rule that the employee has the obligation to disclose a disability and request an accommodation, an employer is obligated to initiate discussions regarding possible accommodations if the employer

1) knows the employee has a disability;
2) knows or has reason to know that the employee's disability is causing the employee to have problems at work; and
3) knows or has reason to know that the employee's disability prevents the employee from asking for an accommodation (Creighton, 2001; Eddy & Schouten, 2003).

The ADA in Action: How Does it Work?

Once an employer knows that an employee is mentally or physically disabled and seeks an accommodation, the employer is legally required to engage in an informal "interactive process" in which the employer and employee

1. identify the essential functions of the specific job;
2. consult with the employee to determine specific physical or mental limitations;
3. consult with the employee and identify potential accommodations and assess each accommodation's effectiveness; and
4. select the accommodation that best serves the need of the employer and the employee (29 CFR §1630.9).

The ADA requires this discussion to occur as early as possible after a disability has been identified. Any unnecessary delay in addressing the request for accommodation may lead to employer sanctions. If neither party identifies an accommodation after reasonable effort, the employer has fulfilled its duty under the ADA and the employee has no basis for a claim of discrimination.

On September 25, 2008, The ADAAA was signed into law. Congress explicitly stated that the purpose of the Amendment Act is "to restore the intent and protections of the Americans with Disabilities Act of 1990." Congress took exception to the narrowing of protections of the ADA as a result of a number of Supreme Court decisions and Equal Employment Opportunity Commission (EEOC) interpretations of the ADA, some of which are discussed below. The ADAAA was intended to liberalize and broaden the protection of the ADA and to reverse the Supreme Court and EEOC decisions that have restricted its application. When relevant to this discussion, the changes effected by the ADAAA will be discussed.

Title I of the ADA does not preempt federal state or local laws that provide greater or equal protection for persons with disabilities but does preempt laws that provide less protection (Parry & Drogin, 2007). For example, California's Fair Employment and Housing Act provides greater protection than the ADA. California's law does not require complainants to prove that their impairments are substantially limiting in order to demonstrate that they have a covered disability. They need only demonstrate that they have an impairment that makes the achievement of a major life activity difficult (Parry & Drogin, 2007).

Enforcement of the ADA

The EEOC is empowered to enforce the ADA. The EEOC provided enforcement guidance with respect to individuals with psychiatric disabilities in its "Enforcement Guidance on the Americans with Disabilities Act and Psychiatric Disabilities" (commonly referred to as the "Guidance") in March 1997 (Equal Employment Opportunity Commission, 1997). Courts may or may not accept the guidelines set forth by the EEOC, but they serve to inform and direct courts and litigants (Eddy & Schouten, 2003).

The EEOC has exclusive authority for 180 days after the discriminatory act to investigate and seek reconciliation, using the same procedures that govern Title VII of the Civil Rights Act of 1964. Thereafter, upon exhaustion of administrative remedies, concurrent jurisdiction exists in both the state and federal courts to hear claims by the United States government or private parties seeking compensatory as well as punitive damages and injunctive relief, plus attorney's fees (*Board of Trustees of University of Alabama v. Garrett*, 2001).

Successfully bringing claims under the ADA, particularly for psychiatric disabilities, has been extremely difficult, although this may change under the ADAAA (2008). To prevail in an ADA employment discrimination case, the plaintiff must demonstrate that he or she has a disability as defined by the ADA, is qualified to perform the job, with or without reasonable accommodation, and has been subjected to discrimination resulting in adverse employment decisions (*Horth v. General Dynamics Land Systems, Inc.*, 1997). Between 1997 and 2007, the EEOC received a total of over 253,000 complaints of ADA violations (United States Equal Employment Opportunity Commission, 2007). Of these, 25.4% were closed administratively and 55.6% were found to have no reasonable cause. Of the 6.2% (16,591) found to have reasonable cause over this 10-year period, only about one-third (5,852) were successfully litigated by the EEOC.

Claimants in private litigation also generally do not fare well. In private litigation between 2002 and 2004, employees have prevailed in only 3% of cases brought under the ADA (Allbright, 2005). In 2005, employees prevailed in only 6.2% (Allbright, 2006), in 2006, in only 2.8% (Allbright, 2007), and in 2007, in only 4.5% (Allbright, 2008). Fortunately, most ADA disputes are resolved without going to court (Ritchie & Zonana, 2003). The ADA encourages the use of alternative means of dispute resolution, including settlement negotiations, conciliation, mediation, fact finding, and arbitration. Nevertheless, when these interventions do not result in a compromise or settlement, the EEOC may choose to litigate or allow the plaintiff to litigate in the appropriate federal or state jurisdiction.

The conduct of ADA employment discrimination cases resembles tort cases. Prior to trial, discovery including interrogatories and depositions is available to the parties. The trial is a formal judicial proceeding with a jury and governed by the rules of evidence. Witnesses, including expert mental health professionals, testify in person, under oath, and are subject to cross-examination. *Daubert* and other relevant local tests of reliability and relevance apply to the admissibility of expert testimony. The rules of evidence governing hearsay and privilege apply and limit the facts on which the expert may rely in reaching an opinion (*Zwygart v. Board of County Com'rs of Jefferson County*, 2007).

Any recognized doctor–patient or psychotherapist–patient privileges are usually regarded as waived in ADA cases involving claims of mental disability. Courts have found that reliance on the records of the diagnosis or treatment of a mental disability to support a claim under the ADA is not consistent with the maintenance of confidentiality surrounding the disability. An ADA claimant therefore waives any psychotherapist–patient privilege (see, e.g., *Sarko v. Penn-Del Directory Co.*, 1997).

Although expert psychiatric or psychological testimony may be admissible in claims of mental impairment, the ADA does not require that a disability be proved with expert medical testimony (*Colwell v. Suffolk County Police Dept.*, 1997). In some cases, a finding that a disability exists relying on a claimant's testimony alone is not an abuse of judicial discretion. Whether it is tactically wise for a claimant to rely exclusively on lay testimony can only be evaluated on a case-by-case basis. The analysis is much like that made by an advocate in assessing whether to present or rebut an insanity defense in a criminal case without expert testimony. In most cases, presenting an ADA case without an expert witness is not considered good strategy, but if the right facts and witnesses are present, this strategy can be very powerful.

Mental Disabilities: The ADA and Employment

Passage of the ADA was accompanied by much optimism for doing away with discrimination against the disabled. A leading disability scholar observed with disappointment 5 years after the passage of the ADA, "Despite encouraging advances in job placement, education, and training since the ADA's enactment, the unemployment of many qualified persons with disabilities is a problem that remains unresolved" (Blanck, 1995, p. 390). In a study of disability status and functional impairment of over 100,000 people in the year 1994–1995, of individuals who reported disability but were working, 19.4% of individuals with mental disabilities reported job discrimination on the basis of their disability within the previous 5 years. The most common forms of discrimination cited were difficulty advancing in work (15.8%), being fired or laid off (10.8%), or being refused employment on the basis of disability (7.9%) (Druss et al., 2000).

Unfortunately, the number of EEOC complaints of discrimination based on psychiatric disability in the past decade also indicates that the high hopes associated with the ADA's effect on discrimination in employment have not been borne out. EEOC complaints of discrimination based on psychiatric disorders consistently represent the first or second single largest category of complaints since 1997 (the other leading category being orthopedic problems). In 2007, depression was the second most common basis for a complaint of discrimination, representing 6.8% of total claims, after claims based on orthopedic problems or injuries (15.9% of total ADA discrimination claims). The total number of ADA claims based on depression as a disability were more than those related to hearing and vision impairments combined (5.8%), diabetes (5.1%), and cancer (3.3%). Bipolar disorder (3.6%) and anxiety disorder (2.8%) were among the 10 most common impairments claimed as bases for complaints of discrimination. These statistics imply, as one group of authors has observed, "effective inclusion of individuals with psychiatric disabilities in the workforce has not yet been achieved fully" (Goldberg, Killeen, & O'Day, 2005).

The ADAAA is clearly intended to broaden the definition of disability and thus extend the protection of the ADA to more individuals. For example, the ADAAA retains the term "disability" but broadens terms used to define disability such as "substantial limitations" and "major life activities." Perhaps most significantly for psychiatric disorders, the amendment clarifies that an impairment that is episodic or in remission is a disability if it would substantially limit a major life activity when active. Whether this amendment to the ADA reverses the increasingly narrow judicial and administrative interpretations of the ADA over the past years remains to be seen.

Referrals for ADA Mental Health Evaluations

Employers may and usually do rely on health-care providers to supply information critical to their decision-making process in ADA claims (Waldner & Hornsby, 2005). Mental health professionals may be asked to provide evaluations and address ADA issues related to psychiatric disorders when an employee with a psychiatric disorder seeks an accommodation or claims to have been unfairly treated on the basis of the psychiatric disorder. Such evaluations may occur in the early, informal stages of discussions between employees and employers or in the context of litigation. Reaching reasoned opinions in these evaluations requires an approach that balances the needs of employees and employers with careful attention to potential legal concerns (Eddy & Schouten, 2003).

When a request for accommodations has been made, especially where the need for a requested accommodation is not obvious, the ADA permits employers to ask for information supporting the request. Employers are allowed to seek medical assessment to ascertain whether an employee is able to perform the essential functions of the job or to determine what interventions might constitute reasonable accommodation. Employers cannot request an employee's entire medical file but can request documentation regarding the impairment and its nature, its severity and duration, and the activities the impairment limits and the extent of the limitation of those activities.

Employers can also seek an independent medical evaluation if the information provided by the employee is insufficient. The need for additional information in requests for accommodations based on psychiatric disorders can result in referrals for psychiatric or psychological evaluation. When employees raise issues of psychiatric impairment, obtaining an evaluation from a mental health professional is a sensible response, particularly since employers have been trained to not ask questions about disabilities. In most cases, employee participation in such an evaluation is a condition of continued employment.

Implementation of certain provisions of the ADA's mandate to end employment discrimination has been straightforward in some instances, even for psychiatric disabilities. For example, preemployment physical examinations and employment entrance examinations to screen out persons with disabilities are prohibited. Although personality tests designed to predict job-related functions are permitted (42 USCA §12112), in general, psychological tests that support a diagnostic determination are regarded as medical tests and are prohibited under the ADA in preemployment evaluations (Blanck & Marti, 1997).

In contrast, providing reasonable accommodations for already employed individuals with psychiatric disorders can involve more complicated decisions and circumstances. Providing an access ramp or adequate restroom facilities for wheelchair-bound employees, although perhaps expensive, is a relatively straightforward accommodation. Providing accommodation becomes difficult when an employee, because of a psychiatric disorder, becomes unable to cope with workplace stress or supervisory criticism. In addition, individuals with a mental disorder often deny psychiatric illness or delay seeking help until some painful incident occurs, such as an adverse employment action or loss of a job, further complicating any request for accommodations for disability. Such circumstances often precipitate requests for mental health consultation and evaluation.

Further complicating ADA claims, some employees experiencing work difficulties for reasons other than mental disorders may attempt to characterize poor job performance or workplace misconduct as a product of a mental disorder in attempts to avoid disciplinary action (Creighton, 2001). Employers may be hard pressed to distinguish whether an individual's behavior is due to a psychiatric illness, which must be accommodated, or to poor work and interpersonal skills, which require disciplinary action. Similarly, determining whether an employee's requests represent a genuine appeal for consideration of accommodations or simply a request for special treatment may also be problematic. Mental health evaluations can often clarify these issues.

Not all problematic workplace behaviors or performance problems in individuals with psychiatric disorders are based on psychiatric disorders. Employees with mental disabilities may also demonstrate problems in work performance not related to their psychiatric diagnoses. For example, an individual with a history of attention deficit hyperactivity disorder (ADHD), inattentive type, may no longer be performing satisfactorily because of problems outside the workplace that cause him to be chronically late or absent. However, when confronted with problematic work performance, the employee may complain that the disabilities related to attention deficit disorder are the sole cause of poor performance and that he is entitled to a variety of accommodations and protection from discipline or discharge. At this point, the employer has to determine whether there is a relationship between performance problems and the claimed disability, and may turn to a mental health professional to help untangle these complicated situations.

The person claiming a disability needs to produce some evidence of a reasonable accommodation that would enable him or her to perform the essential functions of the job satisfactorily. The need for documentation supporting requested accommodations might also result in a referral for a mental health evaluation. Employees cannot simply ask for accommodations without providing some evidence of the accommodation's effectiveness. For example, one court found that an abusive, belligerent employee with bipolar disorder could not assert that accommodation was possible simply by pointing to the statutory list of examples of accommodation without explaining how a specific accommodation would enable him to meet the employers' legitimate expectations for performance and conduct (*Carrozza v. Howard County*, Maryland, 1995).

Another common situation that may lead to referral for an ADA mental health evaluation occurs when an employee presents an employer with information about a psychiatric disorder without a request for an accommodation. For example, an employee who justifies utilizing sick days with a note from a psychiatrist citing his depression has in effect put the employer on notice of a disability, triggering the employer's duty to consider whether the employee is entitled to reasonable accommodations for that disability (*Vinson v. Thomas*, 2002). The employer may then refer the employee for mental health evaluation. Requests for evaluations may also occur before an employee's return to the workplace following a psychiatric hospitalization.

The occurrence of a troubling event or employee problems in the workplace may also prompt a request for a disability evaluation under the ADA. The event may be as simple as an employee with known depression missing a week of work or as complex as an employee displaying bizarre behavior that is frightening coworkers but is not overtly threatening. Individuals who experience conflict with coworkers or supervisors may be referred for evaluation if they invoke the ADA to avoid disciplinary action.

An employer may also refer employees for mental health evaluation to clarify the employer's legal obligations under the ADA. As noted above, if a conflict between an employee and employer goes to litigation, courts make the final determination of any disputed aspect of the ADA. Although employers will often ask psychiatrists and psychologists to evaluate whether a limitation is substantial or whether a requested accommodation is reasonable, disagreements on these issues may not be settled by the mental health professional's opinions. Indeed, these questions form the basis of much ADA-related litigation, which must be settled by the courts.

Nevertheless, the mental health professional's opinion may help the parties reach a mutually beneficial agreement. Consider a work situation involving a valued employee who has posttraumatic stress disorder (PTSD) as a result of a sexual assault. Courts have differed on whether a diagnosis of PTSD establishes a mental impairment under the ADA.[2] A mental health evaluation might suggest a clinically and economically reasonable accommodation that allows the employee to take some leave yearly on the anniversary of the attack. This compromise would meet the needs of the employee, would allow the employer

---

[2] PTSD may qualify as an ADA disability (see *Farley v. Nationwide Mutual Ins. Co.*, 1999 and *Johnston v. Henderson*, 2001; but PTSD may also not qualify: see *Marschand v. Norfolk and Western Ry. Co.*, 1995). The impact of the 2008 amendment on this issue is as yet unclear.

Mental Health Professionals: Understanding the ADA

to maintain a valued worker, and would allow both sides to avoid the cost of litigating to determine whether PTSD is a disability as defined under the ADA and whether the worker is entitled to ADA coverage.

Mental Health Professionals: Understanding the ADA

Mental health professionals undertaking ADA evaluations should have a working knowledge of the ADA. Referral questions often use language taken directly from the ADA and include both medical and legal issues, such as

1) whether the individual in question meets diagnostic criteria for a particular disorder;
2) whether the disorder results in functional impairments of sufficient intensity and duration (relative to the ability of the average person in the general population to perform one or more major life activities) to qualify as having a "disability" as defined by the ADA;
3) whether the person can perform the essential functions of the job or related functions of the job with or without accommodation;
4) the specific ways that the impairments affect the individual's ability to function within a specific environment;
5) the types of accommodations that would allow the person to perform their job functions; and
6) the reasoning and basis of opinion for each recommended accommodation.

Mental health opinions in ADA evaluations will be relevant and useful only insofar as the mental health professional understands the definitions, regulations, and case law related to under the ADA. As noted above, ultimately, a court may have to determine whether an individual has a mental disability, whether a major life activity is substantially limited by a psychiatric disorder, or whether an accommodation is reasonable or presents an undue hardship for an employer. The recent implementation of the ADAAA, which changes the interpretations of these terms, makes predictions of future court decisions in ADA cases unclear. Nevertheless, the mental health expert's informed opinions can facilitate discussion, negotiation, and resolution when ADA issues arise in the workplace, potentially allowing parties to avoid costly and painful litigation. They may also provide guidance to the courts, as they reexamine the application of the ADA's protections in light of the ADAAA attempts to broaden the ADA's application and its requirements that courts interpret the ADA's provisions more liberally.

The ADA's Statutory Definitions and Relevant Terms

Disability

When an employer referral source asks whether the evaluee has a mental disability, they typically want to know whether the individual meets the definition of disability under the ADA. As in SSDI evaluations, where the definition of disability is statutorily defined, the ADA's definition of disability is also defined statutorily but differently from the definition of the Social Security Administration. The ADA defines disability as "a physical or mental impairment that substantially limits one or more of the major life activities of such individual; a record of such an impairment; or being regarded as having such an impairment" (42 USC §12102(2)). The ADAAA confirmed this definition.

As applied to psychiatric disorders, this definition includes individuals who are mentally ill, who have a history of mental illness, as well as those whom others regard as having a mental illness. These individuals are considered disabled if they have a mental impairment that substantially limits one or more major life activities compared to the average person in the general population for a significant duration of time.

As in other types of disability assessments, a diagnosis is necessary but not sufficient to cross the impairment threshold in the first part of the ADA's definition of disability (Hall, 1997). As discussed in previous chapters, the presence of a psychiatric disorder does not necessarily imply an impairment and the presence of an impairment does not necessarily imply disability. And, as in other types of disability evaluations, disability under the ADA is the interaction of a mental impairment (i.e., disorder or illness) with the environment in such a way that it that creates substantial limitations, that is, functional impairments, in a major life activity. The EEOC guidelines (1997) clearly state that the determination of whether an individual has a disability is not necessarily based on the person's diagnosis but rather on the effect of that disorder on the life of the individual. Some conditions may be disabling for particular individuals but not for others, depending on a variety of factors (56 FR 35741).

Mental Disorder

The ADA's definition of disability raises two major issues in regard to psychiatric disability. The first involves the requirement of a diagnosable mental illness for an individual to qualify for the ADA's protection. The ADA defines a mental impairment as "any mental or psychological disorder, such as mental retardation, organic brain syndrome, emotional or mental illness, and specific learning disabilities" (29 CFR §1630.2(h)(2)). Most major mental illnesses as defined by the Diagnostic and Statistical Manual of Mental Disorders (DSM) (American Psychiatric Association, 2000) meet this definition.[3]

Some employers may require specific psychological and neuropsychological testing as supportive documentation for psychiatric disorders, and evaluations of mental impairment in ADA assessments can include traditional diagnostic techniques regarding the existence of impairment and its functional limitations.

---

[3] According to the EEOC, the current edition of the American Psychiatric Association's *Diagnostic and Statistical Manual* is "relevant" for identifying mental disorders (Equal Employment Opportunity Commission, 1997).

For example, certain mental disorders such as ADHD or specific learning disorders typically require psychological and/or neuropsychological testing in addition to clinical interviews and thorough histories to support a finding that an individual is substantially impaired relative to the general population.

Certain DSM psychiatric disorders are excluded from ADA coverage, as are certain defined behaviors, such as homosexuality and bisexuality (42 USC §12211) (see Table 8.1).

Table 8.1 DSM disorders excluded from ADA coverage

1. Compulsive gambling
2. Kleptomania
3. Pyromania
4. Transvestitism
5. Transsexualism
6. Pedophilia
7. Exhibitionism
8. Voyeurism
9. Gender identity disorders not resulting from physical impairments
10. V Codes (which describe stressful personal events and issues)

When alcohol or drug use is at issue, ADA coverage turns on how recently the substance use stopped (Parry & Drogin, 2007). Current alcohol use involving on-the-job drinking, working while alcohol-impaired, and current use of illegal drugs are not covered (42 USC §12210). Employers may prohibit the use of alcohol in the workplace, require that employees not be under the influence of alcohol in the workplace, and hold an alcoholic employee to the same job performance and behavioral standards to which it holds other employees even if unsatisfactory performance or inappropriate behavior is related to the employee's alcoholism (Creighton, 2001).

Alcoholics and drug addicts who have used in the past but are not current users are not, on those grounds alone, covered under the ADA (Parry & Drogin, 2007). Similar to those with any other diagnosis, individuals with substance use disorders must demonstrate substantial limitation in a major life activity to meet the ADA's definition of disability. Alcohol dependence may be a disability under the ADA if it substantially limits an individual's major life activities.

Personality disorders are protected by the ADA (29 CFR §1630.2(h)(2)) if they result in substantial limitation of one or more major life activities. For example, a person might be able to demonstrate a pattern of severe self-injurious behaviors associated with borderline personality disorder that substantially impairs that person's ability to work or care for self. On the other hand, a person with a severe personality disorder would still need to meet the other requirements for ADA coverage such as being able to perform essential job functions with or without accommodations and overcome one or more of the exclusionary criteria (Ritchie & Zonana, 2003).

In contrast, personality traits or characteristics that are not symptoms of an Axis I or II mental disorder do not qualify as mental impairments or disabilities under the ADA. Requests to include these traits were rejected because the EEOC commissioners were concerned that it would facilitate claims of disability discrimination by employees challenging discipline for poor judgment or inappropriate behavior, a phenomenon observed under the Rehabilitation Act of 1973. The commissioners believed that persons with genuine psychiatric illnesses would be able to demonstrate disability status without providing other employees who had performance or behavior problems a basis for claiming discrimination (Bell, 1997). Although a variety of personality traits or characteristics may be associated with certain psychiatric disorders, they are not of themselves considered covered conditions (see Table 8.2) (Equal Employment Opportunity Commission, 1997; *Daley v. Koch*, 1989; *Fenton v. Pritchard Corp.*, 1996, *Greenberg v. New York State*, 1996; *Hindmann v. GTE Data Services*, 1994; *Weiler v. Household Finance Corp.*, 1994).

Table 8.2 Examples of personality traits, characteristics, or behaviors not considered mental impairments for purposes of the ADA[1]

- arrogance
- violent temper
- poor judgment
- irresponsible behavior
- irritability
- chronic lateness
- low stress tolerance
- poor social skills resulting in interpersonal conflict
- poor impulse control

[1] This table is not exclusive.

Individuals may become dissatisfied with aspects of their work responsibilities or environment and may attempt to use the ADA to address their job dissatisfaction. Such cases are difficult to evaluate, particularly when some history or evidence of psychiatric disorder is present. For example, individuals may claim that they cannot tolerate the stress of travel or deadlines due to a diagnosis of ADHD or depression. Travel and deadlines are stressful for most people. Under stress many people's performance deteriorates, resulting in anxiety, depression, and job dissatisfaction.

Evaluating mental health professionals should bear in mind that "The ADA does not protect people from the general stress of the workplace" (*Martin v. General Mills, Inc.*, 1996). The cost of covering such a common occurrence would be prohibitive. Beyond costs, the problems of allocating responsibility, determining limitations and what claims are barred are made easier for the courts when general stress levels do not trigger ADA coverage. Although some may disagree with this stance, the requirement of a distinct event, job responsibility, or employment requirement makes judicial oversight practicable.

A mental impairment does not have to be permanent to rise to the level of a disability for purposes of the ADA (Parry & Drogin, 2007). Chronic, episodic mental conditions may be covered if they are substantially limiting when acute or are highly likely to recur in a way that causes substantial limitations. The ADAAA has clarified and reinforced this by emphasizing that in assessing disability and substantial limitations, the illness or disorder should be considered in its active state.

To ease the claimant's evidentiary burden, disability advocates sought and believed that disability would be evaluated without consideration of the impact of corrective measures (Petrila & Brink, 2001). The Supreme Court surprised many disability advocates in their 1999 decision in *Sutton v. United Air Lines* (see also *Murphy v. UPS*, 1999 and *Albertson's, Inc. v. Kirkingburg*, 1999). In *Sutton*, the Court determined that the plaintiffs, unsuccessful applicants for employment as commercial airline pilots with uncorrected 20/200 vision, corrected to 20/20, but beyond the airlines requirement of uncorrected 20/100, were not disabled under the ADA.

The Supreme Court's interpretation of the ADA in *Sutton* required that the impact of corrective measures to mitigate the impairment play a central role in determining whether a condition constituted a disability under the ADA. Notably, the ADAAA states that mitigating measures other than "ordinary eyeglasses or contact lenses" shall not be considered in assessing whether an individual has a disability. Thus, the ADAAA has done away with the Court's finding that required mitigating effects of medication and other measures to be considered in the determination of disability.

Substantial Limitation of a Major Life Activity

The second requirement for psychiatric disability under the ADA is that the identified mental illness must "substantially limit one or more of the major life activities" (42 USC §12102(2)). Generally, these terms are not part of mental health professionals' clinical language. Yet they are crucial to a competent ADA evaluation. Similar to employers and employees seeking guidance, mental health professionals should be guided by the definitions and case law embodied in the ADA, EEOC clarifications, and judicial decisions.

The Supreme Court interpreted this language in the ADA to require a broad impact across multiple major life activities and to require that the major life activity must be significantly impaired compared to the average person. The landmark decisions in this regard were *Sutton* (1999) (discussed above) and *Toyota Motor Manufacturing, Kentucky, Inc. v. Williams* (2002). In regard to *Toyota*, the ADAAA stated that the Supreme Court "interpreted the term 'substantially limits' to require a greater degree of limitation than was intended by Congress" (§2(a)(7)).

The ADAAA, in seeking to restore some of the intended protections of the ADA, explicitly rejected the Supreme Courts reasoning and findings in *Sutton* and *Toyota*. The ADAAA expanded the definitions of "major life activities" by including two non-exhaustive lists. The first list includes many activities that the EEOC has recognized as a major life activity, such as walking, as well as activities that the EEOC has not specifically recognized, such as reading, bending, and communicating. The second list represents a new category of major life activity, that of "operation of major bodily function," and includes "functions of the immune system, normal cell growth, digestive, bowel, bladder, neurological, brain, respiratory, circulatory, endocrine, and reproductive functions" (§3(2)(B)). Again, the effect of the ADAAA on mental health evaluations and decisions remains to be seen, but presumably this definition also includes cognitive and emotional functions associated with the brain that are affected in psychiatric or neurological illness.

The significance for mental health professionals, however, is that momentum in regard to interpretation of the ADA is swinging in a less, rather than more, restrictive direction. It is therefore critically important that mental health professionals conducting ADA evaluations explore in detail the nature and extent of an evaluee's impairments and their effect on functioning in the workplace. Impairments that may not have resulted in qualifying as a disability and therefore for ADA protection may now be more likely to provide protection to individuals with mental disorders.

Essential Job Functions

The ADA does not guarantee disabled workers the right to continue working at their jobs or to be promoted or transferred because they are disabled. Persons with disabilities are entitled to employment only if they have the required training to perform the essential functions of their jobs. Essential job functions mean fundamental, as opposed to marginal, job duties (Parry & Drogin, 2007).

Determinations of what is "essential" to a specific job are made on a case-by-case basis. For instance, an essential job function for a letter handler at the post office might be to sort letters and put them in the appropriate bin. A nonessential function might be to work an occasional overtime shift until 3 a.m. In addition, employers are allowed to use their judgment in regard to defining what they consider essential to a job. Like the determination of the presence of mental disability, or the definition of substantial limitation, or major life activity, conflicts regarding what constitutes essential job functions issue ultimately have to be decided by a court. Legally, the employee bears the burden of proving he can perform the essential functions of the job; the employer bears the burden of production as to which functions are essential (*Benson v. Northwest Airlines*, 1996).

Psychiatric and psychological evaluators are often asked whether the disabled individual can perform essential job functions. Mental health experts who contemplate offering a response to this question should have a basic understanding of the job requirements and obtain a written job description from the employer as well as any relevant supplementary information from the evaluee. Review of a job description is essential, as is the evaluee's report of essential duties and his or her problems with performing these duties. If this is not sufficient to determine the essential duties of a job and distinguish essential from marginal duties, evaluators should obtain additional clarification from the employer.

The psychiatric or psychological evaluator should also determine whether the evaluee can carry out the essential functions of the job with or without accommodation. If individuals cannot perform essential job functions even with accommodation, they may not be covered by the ADA. For example, the ADA's protection has been found not to extend to an employee with depression whose workplace stress could not be controlled sufficiently by reducing overtime and avoiding deadline-intensive work (*Miller v. Honeywell, Inc.*, 1996). Similarly a customer service representative whose panic attacks prevented her from using the telephone (*Larkins v. CIBA Vision Corp.*, 1994) and a law enforcement officer who could no longer carry a gun because he had a paranoid delusional disorder (*Lassiter v. Reno*, 1997) were deemed not able to perform essential functions of their jobs even with accommodations and thus were not otherwise qualified, and therefore not protected by the ADA.

Courts determine on a case-by-case basis whether certain job functions are considered essential. Courts have held that interacting with customers or the general public, the ability to work independently, concentration, and licensure are essential functions with respect to certain jobs (Creighton, 2001). Some functions that may be considerably impaired by psychiatric disorders are at times the crux of an employment conflict regarding whether to discipline an employee or not. For example, an individual with severe irritability due to a mood disorder might have difficulty taking direction. In one case, a court found that "the ability to follow the orders of superiors is an essential function of any position. In other words, employees who are insubordinate are not otherwise qualified for the position" (*Mancini v. General Electric Co.*, 1993).

If the individuals do not have the necessary education or training for the position, even if they are disabled under the ADA, the ADA does not entitle them to the job. This issue is most relevant in a case where employees have misrepresented their training or have been promoted to a position that is beyond their level of training. Generally, in these cases the employees have demonstrated poor work performance that predates a claim of psychiatric disability, although they assert that their poor performance was due to the psychiatric disability.

Reasonable Accommodation

An essential difference between the ADA and other civil rights statutes lies in the ADA's requirement that "reasonable" accommodation be provided to a covered individual that will allow qualified persons with disabilities the opportunity to work. The ADA regulations define reasonable accommodations as "modifications or adjustments" to the work environment, to the way a position is performed, or those that allow disabled employees "to enjoy equal benefits and privileges of employment" as other employees (29 CFR §1630.2). Employers are required to provide such accommodations unless the accommodation would impose an "undue hardship" on the employer. Although the duty to create such accommodations is limited, failure to provide a reasonable accommodation to a disabled individual is a form of discrimination under the ADA (Parry & Drogin, 2007).

Mental health professionals conducting ADA evaluations are often asked to suggest accommodations for evaluees with psychiatric disabilities. Psychiatrists and psychologists may lack the information or expertise, and certainly lack the authority to determine whether accommodations would be reasonable or unreasonable. This authority is the province of the legal system. However, when asked to make suggestions for reasonable accommodations, mental health professionals should provide suggestions for possible accommodations based on clinical judgment and existing evidence regarding effective interventions, informed by the symptoms and severity of the evaluee's disorder and familiarity with the individual's work situation.

An understanding of what the EEOC and the courts have considered reasonable accommodations can guide these recommendations and help avoid unnecessary conflict. For example, flexible scheduling and use of intermittent leave on a regularly scheduled basis that allow an individual time to see a therapist are clinically reasonable interventions, and in fact are generally considered a reasonable accommodation. In contrast, several months' leave to address a mild episode of depression is not consistent with severity of the typical functional impairments associated with this condition, and so would not typically be a clinically indicated intervention. Similarly, it would be unlikely to be found a reasonable accommodation, although the mental health professional would not make that determination.

Mental health professionals should therefore suggest whatever clinical interventions seem reasonable to them, while bearing in mind their suggestions will be most useful if they fall within the general categories of accommodations already deemed reasonable. The employer and employee will have to work out whether a specific clinical intervention is or is not a reasonable accommodation. There are no standard or guaranteed accommodations for everyone with a particular disability or diagnosis. Rather, the ADA provides that an accommodation should match the needs of the disabled individual with the job's essential functions (29 CFR §1630.16). As with all other interpretations of the application of the ADA, case-by-case evaluations determine what accommodations will allow an otherwise qualified employee with a disability to perform the essential functions of the job and whether those accommodations are reasonable.

As noted, the ADA states that employers do not have to provide accommodations that constitute undue hardship, which is defined as an accommodation that is "excessively costly, extensive, substantial, or disruptive," or would "fundamentally alter the nature or operation of the business" (29 CFR §1630.2). Although the financial conditions of the employer may be taken into account in determining whether a proposed accommodation is reasonable, the costs involved in a particular accommodation will alone not be determinative of whether the accommodation represents an undue hardship. An accommodation may be so disruptive to the employer's business operation that it is unreasonable. If restructuring a job to accommodate a disabled individual creates a heavier workload for other employees, an undue hardship may result. However, an undue hardship would not exist merely because other employees complain about granting a disabled worker unpaid leave or a more flexible work schedule if the accommodation has no direct impact upon them (Creighton, 2001).

A requested accommodation that requires extensive job restructuring on the part of the employer might also be considered an undue hardship. In *EEOC v. Amego* (1997), the plaintiff was a behavior therapist who had attempted to overdose twice and whose job included dispensing medications to individuals. To reconfigure the job so that this employee had no access to medication would require the employer to hire an additional therapist or supervisor or restructure the position so that the employee worked only with clients not requiring medicine. The court determined that to do so would require the employer to exceed reasonable accommodation.

In addition, the accommodation has to be provided to an individual who would be "otherwise qualified" to perform essential job functions. In the case noted above, *Lassiter v. Reno* (1997), a deputy marshal with a paranoid personality disorder was not otherwise qualified because his condition prevented him from carrying a firearm. This was an essential function of his position, and there was no reasonable accommodation that would allow the employee to return to his former position or to carry a firearm despite the plaintiff's physician's statement that the plaintiff could return to general employment with follow-up treatment.

Mental health experts do not ordinarily have the authority or the expertise to determine whether an accommodation is reasonable or whether it creates an undue hardship for an employer. They may, however, be able to contribute to informed decision-making by recommending accommodations that have demonstrated benefit for individuals with psychiatric disorders and that the EEOC or the courts have deemed reasonable in other cases. This requires clinical familiarity of the employee as well as knowledge of the essential functions of the job. These include workplace surroundings, structure, and scheduling, a working knowledge of the types of accommodations typically provided, and familiarty with interpretation of reasonable accommodations as per the EEOC and case law (see Table 8.3 for some examples of possible job accommodations for individual with psychiatric disabilities).

Fortunately, many of the accommodations needed by psychiatrically disabled employees can be arranged through simple, inexpensive, commonsense interventions or changes that involve increased communication, schedule changes, or changes in surroundings or the physical environment (Blanck & Marti, 1997). Common forms of accommodation requested by psychiatrically disabled individual include unpaid leave, a flexible or modified work schedule, working at home, shift changes, and job transfers (Creighton, 2001). Relatively straightforward job restructuring, such as reassignment of nonessential job

Table 8.3 Examples of possible job accommodations for individuals with psychiatric disabilities

Changes in physical environment	Minimize noise distractions by moving equipment to a different location
	Move employee to enclosed work space to reduced distractions and increase privacy
	Install full-spectrum lighting to help improve mood and energy
Flexible scheduling	Allow longer or more frequent breaks
	Allow leave for regular counseling or medical appointments
	Develop flexible work schedules
Job restructuring/training	Restructure job to include only the primary or essential functions of the position
	Reassignment or transfer to another available position
	Telecommuting
	Provide additional time for training or learning new jobs or new responsibilities
Improved communication and support	Provide written instructions for job tasks
	Break duties into smaller steps
	Provide easy access to a supervisor to discuss work-related difficulties
	Utilize computer technology to assist with scheduling or work product

Parry (1998).

functions, is generally considered a reasonable accommodation. Reasonable accommodations for psychiatric disabilities might also include flexible scheduling, restructuring job duties or work environment, educating other employees, and job assistance (Mancuso, 1990; Parry, 1995).

Leave and flexibility in scheduling are the most frequently cited forms of reasonable accommodation for a person with a psychiatric disability (Bell, 1997). This includes adjusting arrival or departure times, providing periodic breaks, altering times when certain functions are performed, or allowing an employee to use accrued paid leave for time missed (Equal Employment Opportunity Commission, 1997). Additional unpaid leave may also be a form of reasonable accommodation.[4] The availability of paid and unpaid medical leave, voluntary time off, personal days, and vacation days are considered to be reasonable accommodations to allow employees to seek treatment or address symptoms of psychiatric disabilities (*Nunes v. Wal-Mart Stores*, 1999; *Rascon v.*

---

[4] The Family and Medical Leave Act (FMLA) of 1993 may also provide entitlement to leave. For example, although the ADA allows disabled employees to be terminated due to excessive absenteeism, if the FMLA applies to the employer and the employee's condition qualifies as a "serious health condition," as defined under the FMLA, the employee has 12 weeks of job-protected (but unpaid) leave whether used all at one time or intermittently. This could be used to protect an employee with a psychiatric disability prone to sporadic unpredictable absences.

US West Communications, 1998). In *Criado v. IBM* (1998), the court sustained a jury verdict for an employee who was terminated after she had asked for and been denied an extension of a leave for treatment for depression. The Court noted that there was evidence that an extended leave would have been both temporary and effective in producing a recovery.

Nevertheless, an employer's obligation to accommodate employees with psychiatric disabilities is not unlimited, even in regard to what are often considered reasonable accommodations. Accommodations relating to attendance or punctuality involve an analysis of "essential job functions" in conjunction with "reasonable accommodation." Case law is the main source for the continuing interpretation of the nature of "reasonable accommodation."

For example, in situations where an employer can show attendance or attendance during particular hours as an essential function, courts most likely will conclude that the modified schedule is not reasonable (Creighton, 2001). In *Tyndall v. National Education Centers* (1994), in response to a leave request as a form of reasonable accommodation, an appeals court ruled that presence at school is an essential function of a teacher position. In *Earl v. Mervyns, Inc.* (2000), the defendant fired an employee with obsessive compulsive disorder after she was late for work 33 times in a 365-day period because of her disability. The court held that the employer was not required to allow the plaintiff to start work once she arrived without reprimanding her or allowing her to make up time at the end of her shift.

Courts have almost uniformly held that although some leave is considered reasonable, unduly prolonged medical leave of absence or indefinite leave is not a reasonable accommodation (*Parker v. Columbia Pictures Indus*, 2000). Generally, when employees have requested medical leaves of absence for less than 1 year, courts have found that the employee is entitled to the accommodation. In contrast, courts have generally been reluctant to find that an employer has an obligation to provide unstructured leave to an employee to be determined by the employee (*Amadio v. Ford*, 2001; *Jovanic v. In-Sink-Erator*, 2000). Requests for leave where the employee would not be qualified to perform the essential functions of the job upon returning from leave have also been judged unreasonable accommodation (Creighton, 2001).

Drug- and alcohol-related disorders present additional challenges in regard to reasonable accommodations. For example, a leave of absence to obtain medical treatment for alcohol dependence is generally considered a reasonable accommodation. However, an employer is not required to provide repeated leaves of absence (or perhaps even a single leave of absence) for an alcoholic with a poor prognosis for recovery (see, e.g., *Evans v. Federal Express Corp.*, 1998). Courts have ruled that an employer is not required to give a leave of absence for an alcoholic employee to get treatment if such treatment would be futile (*Schmidt v. Safeway, Inc.*, 1994).

Employers may also have an obligation to allow employees to telecommute as a reasonable accommodation if the employee suffers from a substantially limiting impairment beyond the inability to drive and unless the employer can show that telecommuting would eliminate an essential job function or impose an undue burden. For example, in *Humphrey v. Memorial Hospital Association* (2001), a medical transcriptionist with obsessive compulsive disorder who was constantly late for work, if she arrived at all, requested to work at home when her prior accommodation of a flexible work schedule was not effective. The Ninth Circuit Court, in overturning summary judgment for the defendant, found that the case should be heard. The court reasoned that since the plaintiff's mental impairment did not interfere with her ability to type and transcribe, but only with her ability to leave her home, and the plaintiff's physician testified that working at home might accommodate the plaintiff's disability, she had a right to a determination as to whether her request constituted a reasonable accommodation.

As with leaves of absence, limits on telecommuting as a reasonable accommodation have also been recognized. For example, if attendance is an essential function of the job (*Kvorjak v. Maine*, 2001) or if the employee's productivity would be significantly reduced (*Smith v. Ameritech*, 1997), telecommuting is not a reasonable accommodation.

In certain circumstances, job transfers and reassignments have been determined to be a reasonable accommodation for a mental disability (*EEOC v United Parcel Serv.*, 2001; *Smith v. Midland Brake*, 1999). Nevertheless, job transfers or reassignments are generally considered accommodations of a last resort and are subject to a variety of limitations. Reassignment to a vacant position generally must be considered only when accommodation within the individual's current position would pose an undue hardship or when no accommodation that would enable the employee to perform his or her current job is available.

Job transfers or reassignments are also not required if the proposed position is not vacant or a new position has to be created (*Bristol v. Board of County Commissioners*, 2002), nor is an employer required to transfer an employee merely because of a conflict with a supervisor (Creighton, 2001). Other limitations on the obligation to reassign as an accommodation include bumping other employees to accommodate a disabled employee (*Cravens v. Blue Cross and Blue Shield*, 2000) and promoting a disabled employee in order to transfer him (*Lucas v. W. W. Granger, Inc.*, 2001). In addition, job transfers and reassignments that are not likely to effectively address the disabled employee's limitations and improve performance are not reasonable accommodations (*Hankins v. The Gap*, 1996). Case law also provides direction regarding the types of accommodations that have not been deemed reasonable for persons with mental disabilities (see Table 8.4).

Individuals with psychiatric disorders may request changes in work assignments or job restructuring to reduce stress. The ADA does not require an employer to eliminate stress from the work environment or to alter a particular position as an accommodation in order to eliminate stress. Courts have rejected such claims and have held that employers are not under an obligation to provide a stress-free environment (*Gaul v. AT&T, Inc.*, 1997). Courts have also determined

Table 8.4 Accommodations not considered "reasonable"
- Creating a new position
- Eliminating essential job functions
- Reducing performance standards
- Eliminating performance evaluations
- Providing a "stress-free" work environment
- Altering a position to reduce stress
- Excusing an employee from uniformly applied disciplinary policies
- Reassigning or transferring another employee, including supervisors
- Promoting an employee in order for the employee to be transferred
- Arranging a transfer if no vacant positions are available
- Providing erratic or indefinite leave
- Providing treatment for or monitoring of an employee's condition

that the elimination of performance evaluations as a means of reducing stress (*Carrozza v. Howard County, Maryland*, 1995) is not a reasonable accommodation. Similarly, the ADA does not require a change in supervisor whenever a dispute develops with an employee. The potential for abuse of such an accommodation by employees with poor performance or conduct problems when the causal link to a disability is unclear is evident (Bell, 1997).

The EEOC has also taken the position that an employer is not required to modify uniformly applied discipline policies as a reasonable accommodation (Equal Employment Opportunity Commission, 1997). Employees with disabilities are to be held to the same standard of conduct as other employees. Even when the misconduct is related to a disability, courts have found in favor of employers who terminated employees who engaged in serious misconduct. In *Garrity v. United Air Lines* (1995), for example, the court granted summary judgment to an employer who terminated a flight attendant who claimed to be an alcoholic, stole free-drink coupons, and became intoxicated on a flight on her employers' airline where she was a passenger. In *Bunevitch v. CVS Pharmacy* (1996), the court upheld the right of an employer to terminate an employee for repeatedly violating the employers' sexual harassment policies.

Similarly, in *Adams v. Alderson* (1989), a computer programmer with a personality disorder attacked a supervisor and destroyed office equipment. The employee requested reassignment to a different supervisor as a reasonable accommodation. The court held that the employer was not obligated to tolerate a propensity for violence and that reassignment away from a supervisor was not a reasonable accommodation. Similarly, in *Palmer v. Circuit Court of Cook County* (1997), an employee diagnosed with depression and a paranoid delusional disorder who threatened to kill her supervisor did not have to be accommodated.

Disabled employees are subject to the same disciplinary actions, including termination, to which nondisabled employees are subject. An employer is not required to forego discipline or termination of an employee who violates a workplace conduct standard that is job related and consistent with business necessity simply because the individual is disabled. Misconduct, absenteeism, and poor performance are all grounds for termination. Employers may terminate disabled employees for these as well as other legitimate nondiscriminatory reasons. An employer never has to tolerate or excuse violence, threats of violence, stealing, or destruction of property (Equal Employment Opportunity Commission, 1997). What the ADA prohibits is disciplinary action against an employee with a disability when no such action would be taken against a nondisabled employee who engaged in similar behavior (Eddy & Schouten, 2003).

Direct Threat or Risk of Danger

Concerns regarding the possibility of an individual presenting a risk of danger to self or others are a common reason for an ADA referral to a mental health professional (as well as a fitness-for-duty evaluation, discussed in Chapter 9). Individuals who meet the ADA's definition of disability may be discharged if they present a "direct threat" to themselves or others, despite job qualifications. An employer may terminate an employee who poses a direct threat, which is defined as "a significant risk to the health and safety of others that cannot be eliminated by reasonable accommodation" (42 USC §12111(3)). In fact, the ADA allows that an employer may require that an individual "not pose a direct threat to the health or safety of other individuals in the workplace" as a qualification standard (42 USC §12113(b)).

For example, in *Palmer v. Circuit Court of Cook County* (1997), an employee who had been diagnosed as paranoid and delusional had made various threats of physical violence against a coworker as well as her boss. After being fired she sued, claiming she was fired due to her mental disability. The Seventh Circuit Court found otherwise, stating, "She was fired because she threatened to kill another employee... [I]f an employer fires an employee because of the employee's unacceptable behavior, the fact that the behavior was precipitated by a mental illness does not present an issue under the Americans with Disabilities Act" (p. 352). The court stated that the ADA only protects qualified employees; threatening other employees disqualifies an individual for the job for which they were hired.

The ADA's provisions regarding a direct threat to others were derived from the Supreme Court's landmark decision in *School Board of Nassau County v. Arline* (1987). This case was brought by an elementary school teacher who was fired for having tuberculosis that could pose a threat to others because of the contagious nature of the disease. In determining whether the individual poses a "direct threat," the Court held that the determination must be based on reasonable medical judgments that assess the nature, duration, and severity of the risk to the individual and other parties, the probabilities that the disease will be transmitted and will cause harm, and whether any reasonable accommodation can be made by the employer to ameliorate the risk.

In *Arline*, the Supreme Court also held that the determination of "direct threat" must be based on an individual inquiry. The Court stated such an inquiry was essential if the legislation "is to achieve its goal of protecting handicapped individuals from deprivations based on prejudice, stereotypes, or unfounded fear, while giving appropriate weight to such legitimate concerns of grantees as avoiding exposing others to significant health and safety risks" (480 US at 288). An employer therefore cannot assume an employee with a mental disability poses a direct threat in the absence of objective evidence based on the employee's behavior such as recent acts or threats that caused or threatened harm.

However, the ADA does not allow an employee to deny employment to an individual with a disability because of a slightly increased risk of harm. The risk may be considered only when it is significant and poses a high probability of substantial harm (29 CFR §1630.2(r)). The relevant factors in determining whether an individual poses such a threat include

1. the duration of the risk;
2. the nature and severity of the potential harm;
3. the likelihood the potential harm will occur; and
4. the imminence of the potential harm (29 CFR §1630.2(r) app.).

Some courts have used a balancing test: the decision to consider that a direct threat is present may be made if a risk is small but the consequences of the risk are catastrophic (Creighton, 2001).

Thus, a person with a history of repeated assaultive behavior as a result of mental illness may be excluded from ADA coverage if it can be shown that the threat is significant and cannot be eliminated or reduced through reasonable accommodations. In contrast, a person with a mental illness including a prior history of assaultive behaviors only when psychotic would not be excluded if he is no longer psychotic and he is not likely to become psychotic in the near future, as indicated, for example, by a history of good medication compliance and lack of recurrence of psychosis when medication compliant (Ritchie & Zonana, 2003).

Risks to the public as evaluees perform the essential tasks of their jobs must therefore also be considered and evaluated as part of an ADA risk assessment. Unintended risk due to psychiatric illness, effects of medication, or even treatment noncompliance may also meet the definition of "direct threat" and should be considered. Law enforcement officers, fire fighters, and transportation workers such as pilots or bus drivers may require greater safety margins than some other jobs and therefore may have a lower threshold for what constitutes a "direct threat" to others in terms of mental or physical performance in order to meet the essential functions of the job (Ritchie & Zonana, 2003). These issues are addressed in Chapter 9, in the discussion of fitness-for-duty evaluations.

Risk Assessment: Treatment Providers vs. Forensic Examiners

If issues of threat of harm to others or self arise, employees already in mental health treatment often ask their treatment providers for documentation regarding the treatment provider's assessment of potential dangerousness. It is not unusual for treatment providers' opinions regarding their patients' dangerousness (as well as other aspects in ADA and disability evaluations) to differ from those of independent mental health examiners, as previously discussed in Chapters 1, 6, and 7.

Employers are allowed a certain amount of discretion in deciding whose opinions they will accept, as long as they have obtained and considered a thorough and objective analysis by a qualified examiner (Creighton, 2001). Nevertheless, the EEOC expressly warns employers to be cautious about relying solely on its own health-care professional's opinion that an employee poses a direct threat where that opinion is contradicted by documentation from the employee's own treating physician. The opinion of the treating physician is given weight by his or her presumed greater knowledge about and familiarity with the employee's medical condition and job functions and/or other objective evidence (Equal Employment Opportunity Commission, 1997).

An employer's decision to request or arrange an ADA evaluation often depends to a large degree on the extent to which the employer is satisfied that the treating clinician has conducted an objective, complete clinical assessment. As discussed in Chapter 1, employers should bear in mind that the treating clinicians often act as an advocate for the employee-patient in the event of an employment or legal conflict. If the disability is limited, the facts are well known, and the employer is familiar with the employee and the disability, an independent ADA evaluation may not be necessary. Nevertheless, if the employer has reason to doubt the adequacy or objectivity of the treating clinician's report, suspects that the treating clinician did not have all the relevant information, or believes the treatment that the employee is receiving is unsatisfactory, an independent evaluation may be necessary to address relevant forensic and treatment issues (Eddy & Schouten, 2003).

In the event of conflicting opinions, the EEOC has directed employers to consider

1. The area of expertise of each of the medical professionals;
2. Whether opinions are based on speculation or on current, objectively verifiable information about the risks associated with a particular condition;
3. The kind of information each person providing documented opinions has about essential job functions; and
4. whether the medical opinion is contradicted by information known to or observed by the employer, such as the employer's actual experience or information about the employee from previous jobs (Equal Employment Opportunity Commission, 1997, p. 7714).

These directions to employers for assessment of the validity of conflicting opinions underscore the need for mental health evaluators who conduct ADA evaluations to be certain they have the appropriate expertise and information upon which to base their opinions, particularly in regard to risk assessments.

Conclusion

In other types of disability evaluations, individuals are seeking compensation because they cannot work due to disability. In contrast, individuals invoking the protection of ADA are generally attempting to remain in the workforce despite impairments that might be disabling. Court decisions and legislation will continue to refine the interpretation and define the protections the ADA offers. The ADAAA is intended to reverse the judicial narrowing of the interpretation of the ADA's protection in the past decade. This new legislation is likely to result in new challenges regarding the boundaries of disability and accommodation in the workplace.

The interpretation of the ADA and determination of disputed issues of disability, substantial limitation, major life activities, and reasonable accommodations involve complex legal processes. Nevertheless, psychiatrists and psychologists can provide ADA assessments including a diagnostic evaluation, assessment of functional impairment, and recommendations for accommodations that may be used in assisting both employers and employees decide what is in the best interest of both parties as they negotiate to fulfill the ADA's requirements and protections. Each ADA evaluation requires an individualized approach, informed by clinical expertise as well as familiarity with the ADA, its statutory definitions and legal interpretations, as they apply to psychiatric impairments and disabilities.

Additional Guidelines for Conducting ADA Evaluations

1. Utilize the definitions and terms relevant to the ADA's statutory regulations.
2. Assess whether the evaluee meets criteria for a recognized psychiatric disorder.
3. Report all major life activities that are impaired by the disorder and the duration of the impairment of each activity.
4. Identify which of these impairments are substantial.
5. Be familiar with the essential functions of an evaluee's job.
6. Assess functional capacity related to essential and nonessential job functions.
7. Assess whether an evaluee can perform these functions with or without accommodations.
8. Provide specific examples for all opinions regarding impairments, functional capacity, and substantial limitations of major life activities.
9. If functional impairments are present but not related to a psychiatric disorder, identify other causes of impairment.
10. Suggest clinically reasonable accommodations that may enable individuals to perform essential job functions for which they are qualified based on clinical expertise and knowledge regarding effective interventions for the evaluee's disability.
11. Assess whether evaluees pose a direct threat of danger to themselves or others. If so, suggest clinical interventions, if any that may reduce the risk of threat or harm to others.
12. Remain mindful that despite the mental health professional's opinion, all of the above issues may become the subject of dispute that will be settled by a court, and advise referral sources to consult attorneys when appropriate.

Chapter 9
Fitness-for-Duty Evaluations

Introduction

The purpose of a fitness-for-duty (FFD) evaluation is to determine whether an employee[1] is able to safely perform a defined job. The FFD evaluation is an attempt by an employer or a regulatory agency to assess an employee whose psychological status is perceived as potentially unstable or threatening in some way that affects job performance or safety. FFD evaluations occur in the preemployment context as well as post-employment context. This discussion will address only post-employment FFD evaluations, which arise in less-structured circumstances than preemployment FFD evaluations and are less well addressed in the literature.[2] In direct contrast with preemployment FFD evaluations, referrals for post-employment FFD evaluations commonly arise in a context of acute crisis for both employer and employee.

Referrals for post-employment FFD evaluations are often generated by a sudden change in behavior that raises concern in the workplace. Coworkers may complain that the worker is not doing his or her job, or seems to be having memory problems, and is therefore burdening them with extra work. An employee may become uncooperative, suspicious, and irritable when he or she has not been so previously. Coworkers and supervisors may complain that a coworker is noticeably neglecting personal hygiene. A coworker may become

---

[1] In this discussion, the word employee is used to refer to the evaluee, although the evaluee may not be a direct employee of the referral source. Evaluees may also be individuals under the supervision or regulation of the referral source. Similarly, although the word employer is used to describe the referral source, referral sources can also include attorneys, independent evaluation companies, regulatory agencies, or licensing boards.

[2] Preemployment examinations are required in many professions involving public safety, but are not referred on a case-by-case basis to mental health professionals. Typically, the employment process in these professions includes standard provisions for obtaining these evaluations or retains employees whose jobs include conducting these routine evaluations. All additional references to FFD evaluations in this discussion will assume they are occurring in a post-employment context unless otherwise stated. In addition, this discussion addresses issues specific to independent FFD evaluations, not those performed by occupational mental health professionals directly employed by the agency or by a company for which the employee works.

contentious and confrontational, to the point where others are anxious or fear of assault. A supervisor may voice verbal threats against someone in a position of greater authority. FFD evaluations may even be initiated by a worker's request for leave because he or she feels unable to manage the responsibilities of his or her current position, where previously doing so was not problematic.

Mental health professionals should understand that post-employment FFD examinations typically arise in the context of a substantial disagreement between the employee and the employer regarding the employee's abilities to perform his or her job adequately or safely. These may involve public safety, such as in the case of medical care providers, airline pilots, air traffic controllers, commercial drivers, or law enforcement personnel. Other types of FFD evaluations may be related less to safety issues and more to performance issues, such as an individual who starts having problems with absenteeism that the employer suspects may be due to psychiatric illness. Regardless of whether a safety or performance issue is in question, typically the employee believes he or she is able to work, whereas the employer believes that the employee is not able to work or not able to work safely.

The stakes involved in an FFD evaluation for both employees and employers cannot be overstated. Even when motivated by genuine concern for the employee, misjudgment about FFD can cause job or career loss, with its attendant economic and emotional suffering. As discussed in Chapter 3, the loss of a job, particularly under adverse circumstances such as being told one is not psychiatrically fit to function, can be devastating to the individual employee. Just being referred for an FFD often stigmatizes an individual in the same way that being accused of a crime leaves a mark even if the accused person is eventually proved innocent (Brodsky, 1996a). Misjudgments can also cause an employer to lose a valuable worker or to maintain an employee in the workplace who may be disruptive, unproductive, or unsafe, with the attendant consequences on other coworkers and the organization.

Thus, of all the disability-related evaluations, FFD evaluations are often the most complex as well as the most adversarial, short of those conducted in the course of litigation. By the time mental health professionals are contacted to perform an FFD evaluation, generally the employer has already placed the employee on administrative or medical leave. Employees understand that they may lose their jobs and employers are acutely aware that continued employment might create risks of danger to others with public safety consequences. As a result, both sides are likely to have already contacted or retained attorneys, anticipating negative outcomes of the conflict and the possibility of litigation.

Maintaining an awareness of the sense of crisis and the actual or potential adversarial context is essential in conducting FFD examinations, especially as litigation may come to involve the mental health evaluator. Mental health professionals should therefore have a clear understanding of what event or events precipitated the post-employment FFD evaluation, the employee's job requirements, and the employer's concerns. In addition, they should understand the constraints under which they may have to function in providing FFD evaluations.

The Public's Stake in FFD Decisions

An FFD evaluation arises from an organization's obligations to society to assess their personnel, who are subject to human vulnerabilities and to committing human errors, and who have control over technology that can create profound consequences if mishandled (Stone, 2000). However much care we take in minimizing the risks inherent in daily life, we must often, of necessity, entrust our safety to FFD decisions made by others. These decision makers include licensing agencies, employers of law enforcement officers, emergency medical technicians, and firefighters, drivers, and pilots of common carriers (buses, planes, trains, etc.), as well as boards and agencies that regulate health-care professionals (physicians, nurses, psychologists, dentists, etc.).

The risk to the general public inherent in the FFD of certain professions mandates that mental health professionals also be acutely aware of the heightened standards for FFD in these occupations. Levels of tolerance for different types of behavior vary by occupation. Eccentricities or errors that may be accepted in one workplace, if displayed in another, may raise profound concerns regarding an employee's psychiatric stability. Certain jobs, by their nature, have low tolerance for error, particularly when the consequences of an error are substantial. Transportation workers, law enforcement agents, medical care providers, and nuclear power plant workers are some examples of these. Safety concerns are the most common reason for referral for an FFD evaluation.

FFD decisions, made on the public's behalf, can have life-changing consequences. The 1989 Exxon-Valdez disaster, in which the captain had a known history of alcohol abuse, is one widely known case involving the life-changing consequences of one employee's FFD. Another example is that of a Japan Airlines (JAL) DC-8 jet, which crashed into Tokyo Bay in 1982, killing 24 and injuring 141 (Aviation Safety Network, 1982). The captain who had been on leave for a "psychosomatic illness" allegedly pushed the nose down prematurely and pulled the inboard engines into reverse while on approach to the airport.

Given the risk posed by a mentally unstable commercial pilot, it is reasonable to expect an airline to protect the public. When an unstable employee acts in a manner that results in death and injury, the FFD evaluation may be at the center of civil litigation seeking to compensate those injured by a wrong decision and criminal litigation seeking to punish particularly bad decisions (*Lightenburger v. United States*, 1969; *Watson v. City of Miami Beach*, 1999). The merits of both types of litigation may turn on the competency with which the FFD evaluation was conducted.

A variety of systems are in place to ensure continuing competence in safety-related occupations. A common element of these systems is an oversight body, such as the Federal Aviation Administration, the Nuclear Regulatory Commission, and various state regulatory agencies such as state medical review boards. These administrative bodies generally have a system of rules, including standards relating to illegal drugs and job-related impairments (Stone, 2000). Many organizations and professions with less formalized methods for identifying emerging risk-related mental impairments, nevertheless, have organizational structures to identify problems that may threaten public safety. These include hospital oversight boards for physicians, plant safety officers in manufacturing plants, and informal internal systems based on the United States Department of Transportation policies for interstate truck drivers (Stone, 2000).

For example, a formal, independent psychiatric examination may be requested when aberrant behavior raises questions about a physician's fitness to practice. Usually, the observations and concerns about the physician's conduct will have been reported to an agency responsible for oversight of physicians such as a hospital administrative board, a hospital physician health committee, a state physician health committee, or a state licensing board. Any of these agencies may intervene and order a physician to undergo an assessment. Thus, requests for mental health evaluations of a physician's FFD may originate from state medical boards, hospital medical staffs, human resource departments of hospitals, impaired-physician or other diversion programs, or individual physicians and their attorneys. Some evaluations are voluntary; others are mandatory if the physician wants to maintain licensure or hospital privileges (Wettstein, 2005a).

Similarly, a law enforcement agency may order an FFD evaluation if it is job-related and consistent with business necessity. Post-employment FFD evaluations of law enforcement officers typically are requested when officers have exhibited behavior that has called into question their ability to perform the essential duties of their jobs safely and effectively. These questions generally center on the officer's ability to safely handle firearms. Despite the law enforcement employer's right to obtain an FFD evaluation, the referral process for FFD evaluations is frequently subject to agency guidelines and the provisions of union contracts (Pinals & Price, 2004; Rostow & Davis, 2004).

The Legal Basis for FFD Examinations

Disability evaluations arise from an employee's entitlements (see Chapter 7). Americans with Disabilities Act (ADA) evaluations are founded in an employee's civil rights (see Chapter 8). In contrast, FFD evaluations are based on an employer's or agencies' obligations. Employees are vicarious liabilities for their employers. Traditional common-law negligence claims, such as negligent hiring, negligent retention, negligent supervision, or vicarious liability, create multiple sources of potential liability for negligent employers (Schouten, 2008).

Employers are expected to monitor their employees' behavior and mental status. They are required to intervene appropriately when that employee's capacity has reached a threshold of serious threat (Stone, 2000). For example, the airlines owe a duty to the traveling public to regularly assess their employees. In addition, when specific information that raises concerns regarding a pilot's FFD comes to light, the carrier is obligated to act like a reasonable carrier would under the circumstances, determined ordinarily by normative considerations (*Terry v. Am. Airlines, Inc.*, 2004).

For example, in *Bonsignore v. New York* (1982), a New York City Police officer was widely known to have a serious psychological problem, yet the department failed to intervene and, in fact, required him to carry his department-issued weapon in the course of his employment. Officer Bonsignore shot his wife and then himself; he died, but his wife survived and brought suit against New York City for its negligence in failing to evaluate the officer's mental problem. In part of its ruling, the court held that the agency did have responsibility to monitor the mental state of its officers (see also *Sangirardi v. Village of Stickney*, 2003).

As noted above, an agency responsible for oversight of physicians such as a hospital administrative board or a state licensing board may also order a physician to undergo an FFD assessment (Anfang et al., 2005; Brent, 2002; Meyer & Price, 2006; Zuckerman et al., 1993). A formal, independent psychiatric examination may be requested when problematic behavior raises questions about a physician's fitness to practice (*Judice v. Hospital Service District No. 1*, 1996).

Employers are required by various obligations to take steps to increase the probability that a workplace is protected from the danger presented by employees who have become unstable. For example, the Occupational Safety and Health Act (OSHA) requires that employers maintain a safe workplace (29 USC 654 (5)(a)), implying a duty to protect employees from negligence acts committed by coworkers (Stone, 2000).

Nevertheless, organizations also have obligations to their employees that must be taken into consideration when the question of FFD arises. Individuals are protected by various laws in the workplace. In addition, a vast body of law protecting the rights of employees with health-related impairments against unfair discrimination is relevant to FFD evaluations, including the ADA, collective bargaining agreements, the Family and Medical Leave Act (FMLA), OSHA, and state occupational health regulations. Individuals wrongly suspected or accused of threats or violent acts may bring suit against their employers for violations of these rights, including defamation, violation of privacy, disability discrimination, and other types of civil rights violations (Schouten, 2008), as well as employment-based complaints such as wrongful termination.

Thus, employers or agencies requiring FFD evaluations must weigh and balance all these obligations against their duty to other workers, the organization's productivity, and the public. "This is a classic double bind, and regardless of which course of action is taken the organization could be violating its duty to the employee or others in one or a number of ways" (Stone, 2000, p. 3). This, of course, is one reason why litigation so commonly results from an employer's requirement that an employee undergo a psychiatric FFD evaluation.

Despite the potential conflict between employees' rights and employers' obligations to maintain safety in the workplace and to protect public safety, the ADA permits an employer to require employees to undergo FFD examinations when such examinations job related and consistent with business necessity (42 USC §12112(d)). The Equal Employment Opportunity Commission has stated that this requirement may "sometimes" be met when the employer has a reasonable belief, based on "objective evidence" that

1. an employee will pose a direct threat as a result of a medical condition or
2. an employee's ability to perform essential job functions will be impaired by a medical condition (which may also result in safety concerns).

This evidence may come from the employer's observation or from a third party (Equal Employment Opportunity Commission, 1997). If the information comes from a third party, an employer is supposed to consider the following factors in determining how much weight to give the information:

a. the relationship of the third party to employee;
b. the seriousness of the medical condition at issue;
c. the possible motivation of the third party in providing information;
d. how the third party has learned the information; and
e. other evidence concerning reliability (Equal Employment Opportunity Commission, 1997).

The quantum of proof necessary to support an FFD examination may vary depending on the functions of the job. Jobs involving public safety, for example, police officers, firefighters, physicians, and other health-care providers, often require less evidence than other types of jobs (Creighton, 2001). Individuals in these occupations are subject to special scrutiny if they display poor judgment, signs of cognitive impairment, or disruptive behavior.

An FFD evaluation addresses the ability to perform essential functions including a mental examination, which may be conducted by a psychiatrist or psychologist when, as a result of a mental disability (or the treatment for such disability):

1. the employee appears no longer able to perform the essential functions of the job (see, e.g., *Miranda v. Wisconsin Power and Light Co.*, 1996; *Sullivan v. River Valley School Dist.*, 1999) and
2. the employee behaves in an aberrant fashion or makes threats, suggesting that he or she may pose a danger to himself or others (Equal Employment Opportunity Commission, 1997).

Thus, FFD examinations should be based on job-related performance or threat issues and on an employee's known or suspected mental impairment. The absence of either job-related performance issues or suspected mental impairment does not raise sufficient legal basis for an FFD. That is, an individual with a mental impairment but no job-related performance or risk issues is not appropriate for an FFD evaluation. Conversely, an individual with job-related performance or safety issues but without a known or suspected mental impairment is also not an appropriate FFD referral (Stone, 2000).

An employee who may pose a direct threat may be terminated for refusing to submit to an FFD examination. However, an employer may not terminate an employee who refuses to submit to an examination or inquiry on the basis of refusal of the FFD examination if the FFD examination is motivated only by performance issues in the absence of a question of a mental health issue. Similarly, an employer may not require and an employee may not be terminated for refusing an FFD evaluation ordered in response to a request for reasonable accommodation (Creighton, 2001).

However, as noted in Chapter 8, an employee's request for accommodations can trigger an ADA-based inquiry that may include an independent psychiatric examination. The Equal Employment Opportunity Commission (EEOC) Enforcement Guidelines (1997) provide that a mandatory referral for evaluation is permitted if the employee fails to provide sufficient information to substantiate a mental impairment and/or to give guidance in developing an accommodation.

Many law enforcement agencies' departmental policies list behaviors that would suggest that an officer's ability to perform the essential functions of an armed peace officer may be compromised and may adversely impact job performance. Policies may reference the use of unnecessary or excessive force, inappropriate verbal or behavioral conduct indicating problems with impulse control, abrupt and negative changes in conduct, and a variety of psychiatric symptoms such as irrational speech or conduct, delusions, hallucinations, and suicidal statements or behaviors (Rostow & Davis, 2004). Courts have held that a required FFD evaluation in a police officer is justified even if based on evidence that he or she is only mildly paranoid or hostile, because of the high risk of direct threat or harm to others (*Watson v. City of Miami Beach*, 1999).

Employers may also require an employee to undergo an FFD examination where performance has declined or where an employee, previously without a disability, develops a mental disability during the course of employment that affects the employee's ability to perform the essential functions of the job (*Yin v. State of California*, 1996). An FFD mental examination may be required, for example, when an employee is disciplined for erratic attendance or for engaging in emotional outbursts with customers or coworkers. Such an examination can be used to determine what caused the performance problems.

For example, *Sullivan v. River Valley School District* (1999) involved a tenured teacher whose behavior had been satisfactory for nearly 20 years. He was asked to undergo a mental FFD examination after several instances of erratic behavior. When he refused to comply with the school board's request, which he challenged in court, he was suspended. The court found that the school board's request was job-related and consistent with business necessity.

In addition, an FFD mental examination may be used to determine whether an employee is able to return to work following a disability-related leave of absence (*Porter v. U.S. Alumoweld Co.*, 1997). Any such requirements must be specific to the employee's condition and job requirements (see *Norris v. Sysco Corp.*, 1994).

Forced FFD Evaluations

FFD evaluations lend themselves to potential misuse by employers. As noted above, employers have no legal basis to order FFD evaluations simply because of behavior issues or because an employee has filed a complaint or grievance. One of the two requirements that legally justify requiring an FFD evaluation is job-related performance or threat issues and an employee's known or suspected mental impairment. One of these in the absence of the other represents an insufficient basis for an FFD.

In the context of a workplace conflict, employees who have become problematic for reasons other than those involving their mental health may be referred for forced FFD evaluations. The requirement that an employee undergo an FFD may create the appearance of mental instability affecting workplace performance, which some employers may use to try to discredit or even terminate an employee. For example, an FFD referral may be made in an attempt to discharge a chronically underperforming employee or as a substitute for discipline, or as a way to gather information to harm the reputation of the evaluee who has brought a complaint against the employer.

Evaluators should therefore be alert for possible misuse of the FFD evaluation process. Participation in such an evaluation represents a misuse of mental health expertise. Psychiatrists and psychologists who identify a forced FFD evaluation should consider what type of response is appropriate on a case-by-case basis (Pinals & Price, 2004; Rostow & Davis, 2004). Options include participating and documenting lack of mental health issues or refusal to participate.

FFD Evaluations and the ADA

ADA and FFD evaluations are related, although they differ in significant respects. A person who meets the ADA's definition of disability (see Chapter 8) may be fit for duty and a person who is unfit for duty may not meet the ADA's definition of disability. The same may be said for any of the disability benefit entitlement programs. The applicable definition of disability may overlap with being fit for duty but is not synonymous with the definition of disability utilized by entitlement programs. However, because of the intertwining of the ADA with the FFD evaluation process, a discussion of the relationship between these two is in order.

The ADA requires that reasonable accommodations be provided to qualified but disabled individuals who can perform the essential functions of their jobs. Nevertheless, the question of FFD necessitates a determination of ability to perform essential job functions or potential for danger that may trump even antidiscrimination laws (*Metro. Gov't of Nashville and Davidson Co.*, 2008).

"[T]he ADA does not shelter disabled individuals from adverse employment actions if the individual, for reasons unrelated to his disability ... is not qualified for the job or is unable to perform the job's essential functions" (*Garg v. Potter*, 2008, p. 736). More to the point, "the ADA does not, indeed cannot, require a police department to forgo a fitness-for-duty examination to wait until a perceived threat becomes real or questionable behavior results in injuries" (*DePaoli v. Abbott Lab.*, 1998, p. 674).

Severe conduct problems, even if related to a disability, do not require accommodations under the ADA: "An employer may discipline an employee for engaging in misconduct if it would impose the same discipline on an employee without a disability.... [N]othing in the ADA prevents an employer from maintaining a workplace free of violence or threats of violence, or from disciplining an employee who steals or destroys property" (Equal Employment Opportunity Commission, 1997, p. 21). If a nondisabled employee would be disciplined or terminated for certain behavior, the disabled employee may also be disciplined or terminated for the same behavior.

The ADA specifically permits an employer to undertake mandatory evaluation of an employee's FFD, as the EEOC has confirmed, when there is a reasonable belief that an employee's ability to perform essential elements of the job will be compromised by a medical or psychological condition or that an employee will pose a direct threat due to the condition (CFR §1630; Equal Employment Opportunity Commission, 1997). An FFD evaluation may be requested when the question of whether mental impairments interfere with an employee's ability to perform the essential functions of his or her job. It may also be called for when the employee represents a direct threat, "a significant risk of substantial harm to the health or safety of the individual or others that cannot be eliminated or reduced by reasonable accommodations" (56 CFR 35736).

The role of the FFD in these circumstances is to investigate and document whether an employee has an impairment that affects performance of an essential job function or poses a threat based on mental impairment or psychiatric disorder. Assessments must be based on individual evaluation and not on stereotypes. The conclusion that an individual cannot perform job responsibilities or presents a direct threat "must be based on an individualized assessment of the individual's present ability to safely perform the functions of the job, considering reasonable medical judgment relying on the most current medical knowledge and/or the best available objective evidence" (Equal Employment Opportunity Commission, 1997, p. 16).

Nevertheless, the ADA does place some limitations on an employer's right to request an FFD evaluation. An examination for either inability to perform essential functions of the job or possible dangerousness must be tailored to seek only that information necessary to determine whether the employee can perform his or her job or whether he or she is a direct threat (*Riechman v. Cutler-Hammer, Inc.*, 2000; Equal Employment Opportunity Commission, 1997).

Referral Issues

FFD examinations occur typically after an employee has displayed behaviors that raise the possibility of psychiatric impairment adversely impacting job performance. They may also arise when employee behavior has raised concerns regarding risk of danger to self or others in the workplace, including those related to public safety issues or workplace violence. A teacher may be referred because of angry and inappropriate outbursts in the classroom. A police officer may be referred after demonstrating excessive irritability while on duty. Law enforcement agencies may also request an FFD evaluation of an officer after a critical incident exposure, or before an officer returns from sick or disability leave, particularly if there are indications of ongoing psychological or behavioral disturbance.

Triaging the FFD Referral

In many cases, the need for an FFD, particularly if a threat of violence is involved, is acute. When an FFD issue arises, the employer's first response is usually to place the employee on administrative or medical leave pending obtaining an FFD evaluation, creating problems for both the employee and the employer. Employees fear they may lose their jobs or be subjected to some other adverse employment action. For employers, employee absences create a need to have other workers fulfill the employee's responsibilities and may cause other disruptions of normal workplace activity or productivity.

Decisions made in the heat of the moment by employers lacking a standing FFD procedure with identified providers can compound the crisis. Not infrequently, the employer or agency, in the face of crisis, may seek to obtain sensitive information from the employee, select an inappropriate FFD provider (such as an established or new treatment provider), or implement a personnel action. Poor decision-making in any of these areas can lead to negative consequences, including harm to the employee, harm to other employees, or costly litigation (Stone, 2000).

Both employees and employers are anxious to obtain a speedy resolution to such crises. Consequently, referral sources often ask evaluators to complete FFD assessments quickly, on an urgent or even emergent basis. Mental health professionals should approach requests for expedited FFD evaluations cautiously. These complex assessments generally cannot be completed quickly for a variety of reasons, including the time required to obtain and review relevant documentation. In addition, because of the high level of anxiety, distress, and anger associated with these job crises, FFD examinations may involve safety issues for the evaluator. Conducting these examinations under a pressured timeframe and volatile circumstances is not advisable.

Moreover, the timing of a referral for FFD can substantially affect its findings and should also be considered upon request for provision of an FFD examination. Requiring an employee in the midst of an acute psychotic or manic episode to appear for an FFD evaluation is neither appropriate nor particularly useful. Evaluating an employee in the acute phase of an illness that may remit either partially or totally with treatment creates an incomplete picture of FFD. In these cases, the employee should be stabilized before undertaking the FFD. This course of action is not only humane but also reduces the potential iatrogenic harm that might be caused to the employee by requiring the FFD evaluation (Stone, 2000).

Mental health professionals should therefore approach FFD evaluation referrals as if they were performing triage. They should carefully assess the appropriateness of the referral and be prepared to make a recommendation regarding the most appropriate course of action. The employee may require an emergency clinical assessment (often in a psychiatric emergency room setting for safety purposes). Interventions designed to stabilize the potential evaluee should take place before beginning the FFD evaluation. FFD questions can be revisited and rescheduled if still indicated following completion of an urgent clinical assessment for treatment purposes. If there is no emergency or significant immediate danger, the mental health professional might suggest that the evaluation be postponed until the employee's own treatment provider indicates that the employee has stabilized and can undergo assessment (Stone, 2000).

Qualifications for Conducting FFD Evaluations

Another key FFD referral issue involves the ethical and legal issues discussed in Chapters 1 and 2, specifically, whether the mental health professional has the appropriate qualifications to conduct the evaluation. Some issues require no particular expertise beyond that of standard clinical training. For example, the assessment of the capability of a clerical worker with untreated and acute hypomania secondary to bipolar disorder does not require competence or expertise in the training or job functions of clerical workers. In contrast, questions involving highly specialized functions, such as certain types of medical jobs or law enforcement, might require a working knowledge of both the requirements of the evaluee's profession and alternatives for modified employment.

Constraints on FFD Evaluations

Because we are often dependent on the decisions of others for our safety, the processes we have set in place to assess FFD issues need to be given a full and fair opportunity to work. If we cannot act for ourselves in maximizing our safety, those who are charged with the obligation to do so must not be constrained. Nevertheless, as discussed above, the evaluee maintains certain protected rights. Therefore, prior to the evaluation, an agreement should be reached regarding the nature of the report that will be generated and who will have access to the report. Statute, policy, or procedure may restrict the scope of a report. Policy, law, or provisions of a union or employment contract may also limit the inquiry. The evaluating psychiatrist or psychologist, the referral source, and the evaluee should understand this agreement and the limitations of confidentiality. Review of these issues constitutes a significant part of the process of obtaining consent to conduct the evaluation.

Confidentiality

Issues of confidentiality are particularly complex in FFD evaluations due to the relationship between FFD evaluations and the workplace. Despite the inherent nonconfidential nature of the evaluation, as discussed in Chapters 1 and 2, maintaining confidentiality as far as possible is both an ethical and legal imperative. An FFD evaluation, as noted above, should be limited to relevant job-related issues. However, mental health professionals will inevitably uncover personal information through interview or record review. Sensitive personal data that are irrelevant to the purpose of an evaluation should be withheld in the interests of privacy.

Mental health professionals conducting FFD evaluations must comply with relevant state or federal confidentiality laws. These generally include obtaining consent to disclosure from the evaluee. Even with such consent, mental health professionals should be acutely aware that disclosure is permitted only for the purpose for which consent was provided. The report of the FFD examination should not be used for any other purpose without the evaluee's explicit supplemental consent. Similarly, obtaining records for use in an FFD assessment is not carte blanche for the use or dissemination of these records for any purpose. Mental health records obtained for one purpose may not be released or used for another purpose (*Moulton v. Vaughn*, 1998).

For example, in *McGreal v. Ostrow* (2004), an appeals court ruled that despite the signed waiver of confidentiality, the final document describing a police officer's FFD examination including diagnostic conclusions constituted a protected health record and had to be accorded confidentiality under the relevant jurisdictional statute. On appeal, the Illinois Supreme Court held that a police chief had the authority to order FFD evaluations of officers in the interest of public safety and that logically the police chief was entitled to the results of the examination. However, disclosure of the information was restricted to information necessary to accomplish a particular purpose (*Sangirardi v. Village of Stickney*, 2003). The court held that Mr. McGreal's psychological evaluation included sensitive personal information not relevant to his FFD and had been disseminated far beyond the superiors responsible for the determination of his fitness.

State and federal statutes, agency procedures, and employment contracts may dictate the extent of information and opinions that can be contained in the FFD report. For example, the International Association of Police Chiefs Police Psychological Services Section recommends that unless otherwise prohibited, the evaluator should provide a description of the officer's functional impairments or job-related limitations, an estimate of the likelihood of and timeframe for a return to unrestricted duty, and the evaluator's basis for that estimate (Police Psychological Services Section of the International Association of Chiefs of Police, 2004).

Mental health professionals have no control over who will see their reports and to what degree confidentiality will be maintained after the reports are forwarded to the referral source. Unlike a state or federal court judge in a person injury lawsuit, for example, participants in most FFD evaluations do not have the responsibility or authority to enforce privacy laws. Therefore, before beginning the assessment, evaluators should clarify the nature of the information and opinions that the report will disclose and know who will receive the report. This clarification should be part of the referral process and assists in preserving confidentiality. These matters vary from referral to referral and may change depending on referral questions, agency policies and procedures, and provision of the union/employment contract.

FFD reports often do not need to contain certain information that might normally be included in a standard clinical or disability evaluation. For example, FFD reports typically do not need to describe an evaluee's background (e.g., family history, social history) except to the extent that such information is directly related to the specific referral questions. Therefore, it may be appropriate to limit the detail of the report to specific referral questions, with less emphasis on sensitive personal information, especially if individuals or groups who know the evaluee will be able to review the report. Sensitive personal information can be omitted or summarized in a report if it does not bear directly on the referral concern (Anfang et al., 2005).

Withholding information in a report, especially in an adversarial situation, can raise concerns that the examiner is attempting to bias the report in favor of one side or the other. To avoid problems that may be caused by withholding information, mental health professionals should also consider clarifying with the referral source before conducting their evaluations the degree of personal information to be disclosed. If information is withheld, the report should document that the sensitive information (personal, medical, or social) was obtained and a more detailed report can be provided if necessary (Anfang et al., 2005). Should issues regarding the confidentiality of nonrelevant and sensitive personal information arise during the course of the evaluation, further discussion with the referral source is warranted.

Consent

As discussed in Chapters 1, 2, and 6, the mental health professional's role should be made as clear as possible to both the employer and the employee (Foote & Shuman, 2006). Whether referred to as assent, consent, or informed consent, to enhance admissibility and avoid tort lawsuits or ethical complaints, the role of the mental health professional, the purpose of the examination, and its potential consequences should be made clear to the evaluee. The sources of information on which the examiner may rely, and the potential and often inevitable disclosure of this information, must also be made clear before the examination begins.

Also as discussed in Chapter 6, consent should be reduced to writing and signed by the evaluee before starting the evaluation. If the evaluee is unwilling to give consent to go forward with the evaluation, mental health professionals should not proceed. In situations the employer and the employee clearly are not in agreement about how to move forward to resolve their conflicts, mental health professionals should step back. Evaluators are not in a position to resolve conflicts between referral sources and evaluees and should not advise or insist that the evaluee undergo or not undergo the evaluation. If the conflict has reached this impasse, the employee and the employer, often through their attorneys, have to work out issues involved in the conflict of the employee's rights and best interests and those of the employer (Stone, 2000).

Role Clarification and Dual-Agency Issues

The risk of the examinee's misunderstanding the examiner's role is greater and the corresponding obligation to clarify that role in the process of obtaining consent is more critical if evaluating mental health professionals occupy dual roles. If FFD issues arise and an evaluation is requested, employees already in treatment often ask their treatment providers for documentation regarding the treatment provider's assessment of potential dangerousness or ability to perform essential job functions. Dual-agency issues may also arise when an employer asks an employee to have his or her treatment provider to supply a letter attesting to the clinician's opinion that the employee/patient is fit for duty.

There may be circumstances where providing such information does not represent a conflict of interest, compromise patient confidentiality, or compromise the employer's obligation to assess the ability to safely and adequately perform job functions. However, as is often the case when mental health professionals occupy dual roles, the treatment provider's opinions may be reflective of the role of patient advocate rather than of an objective evaluator. It is not unusual for treatment providers' opinions regarding their patients' dangerousness and general fitness to perform their jobs to differ from those of independent mental health examiners. Such differences of opinion often result from the problems inherent in occupying the dual role of treatment provider and expert (see Chapters 2, 3, and 6).

Employers who ask employees to supply FFD documentation from treatment providers also put themselves into binds that may have legal consequences. An employer's refusal to accept a favorable opinion that the employer has solicited and the employee has supplied adds to an employee's anger and distress and may fuel litigation. Nevertheless, employers are often hesitant to accept these opinions and return the employee to work due to the nature of the behavior that led to the FFD request. Upon reviewing opinions provided by treating clinicians, employers may justifiably suspect they are based on the evaluee's self-reports, or suspect the report is inadequate or lacks objectivity, or suspect that the treating clinician did not have all the relevant information.

For example, in *Tokar v. City of Chicago* (2000), the plaintiff, a city truck driver, was removed from paid leave and placed on unpaid leave after two psychiatrists diagnosed her with various psychological disorders and stated that a risk to the public existed if she continued driving. The city asked her to submit any medical evidence she had that contradicted the psychiatrists' conclusions. She initiated treatment with a psychiatrist, who shortly thereafter requested that the plaintiff be reinstated with accommodations. The city responded that the plaintiff's psychiatrist's letter did not help it determine the plaintiff's FFD because it did not address which duties she could perform and what accommodations she would need. Four months later, the city had a different psychiatrist examine the plaintiff, who determined that she remained unfit to return to her job. The plaintiff's psychiatrist wrote several letters over the next months asking that the city reinstate the plaintiff, but it declined to do so.

The court found that the question of whether the decision to remove the plaintiff from paid leave was justified turned on whether the city honestly believed that she posed a danger. The difference of opinions between the city's doctors and the plaintiff's doctor did not mean that the city did not believe the opinion of the doctor who suggested that the plaintiff did not pose a risk to herself and others. The plaintiff's physician, the court noted, failed to provide support for his stance advocating her return, as is often the case when treatment providers adopt opinions that reflect patient advocacy rather than objective evaluation.

Dual-agency issues may also arise when mental health professionals have an ongoing relationship with a referral source. Such a relationship, whether as a direct employee or as a consultant, can potentially create or create the appearance of a bias toward taking positions that will benefit the referral source. An employer may lack sufficient documentation or may be constrained by collective bargaining agreements from pursuing disciplinary action, but a finding of psychologically unfit for duty would allow the employer to overcome these obstacles to terminating the employee (Stone, 2000). An evaluator who relies on the employer for income may feel pressured to provide the employer with a mental health report that finds the employee unfit for duty based on the employer's needs rather than on an objective evaluation.

An independent evaluation is almost always necessary to address relevant forensic and treatment issues in FFD evaluations. Dual relationships generally create insurmountable problems in almost every FFD case, and opinions generated by a mental health professional occupying both roles are not likely to bear up under legal scrutiny (Stone, 2000). Neither referral source nor employee is obtaining a fair, independent evaluation when the evaluating clinician has significant past or current obligations to either party.

Conducting a Mental Health FFD Evaluation

A mental health FFD examination is intended to answer very specific questions. Is the employee able to perform all or some of the duties of the job, and perform them safely, without danger to self or others, including the general public? Does psychiatric illness impair job performance or increase risk of danger in the performance of the job? As discussed, an examination for either inability to perform essential functions of the job or possible dangerousness must be tailored to seek only that information necessary to determine whether the employee can perform his or her job or whether he or she is a direct threat. Most FFD evaluations should be limited to the specific work-related function and impairment, unless otherwise indicated. Providing the answers to these questions requires both careful review of records and an interview with the evaluee.

Documentation

Mental health professionals should request a written document from the referral source specifically describing the work problems and stating the questions that the referral source wants answered. As noted above, FFD evaluations arise due to changes in an employee's behavior relative to job performance. Therefore, an FFD evaluation requires documentation of events and issues that have given rise to the referral and which may be relevant to job performance and mental health. Referral questions and related records should be reviewed carefully before conducting the evaluee's mental health FFD interview.

Mental health professionals may also need to request other specific types of documentation, as discussed in Chapter 6. The quality and quantity of the information upon which an FFD examination should be based is a function of the risk to which third persons may be exposed, the opportunity of those exposed to the risk to affect it by their own actions, and the examinee's interests. For example, when serious bodily harm is a potential risk, collateral data to verify possibly partisan information is a necessary component of competent decision-making.

Mental health professionals should therefore request that they be provided with specific categories of documentation (see Table 9.1) and should make considerable effort to obtain and review all relevant documents and records (Anfang et al., 2005).

Table 9.1 Documentation that should be requested to perform a FFD evaluation
1. Reason for referral
2. Collateral information from workplace
3. Job description
4. Past and current performance evaluations
5. Relevant medical/psychiatric records
6. Current job status
7. Description of any potentially relevant job related incident or stressor

Availability of information and documentation will vary on a case-by-case basis. In many cases existing documentation is minimal. When documentation does exist, its availability may also vary depending on legal issues. Both the ADA and the FMLA, for example, place restrictions on an employer's ability to access medical records.

Nevertheless, mental health professionals should request this information and make every effort to obtain and review these documents if they exist. The evaluator should record in the report the nature of any information that has been requested but withheld. If reliable or relevant opinions can't be offered in the absence of this information, they should state that the opinions offered are limited by lack of access to these records and that a final determination cannot be made without their review.

Review of documentation begins with written referral requests. Evaluators should review detailed information concerning the reason for the referral, including the nature of the behavior(s) that led to the referral and documentation from supervisors, coworkers, and/or customers concerning the behavior(s), and specific referral questions. Written referral requests will help minimize miscommunications between the referral source and the evaluating psychiatrist or psychologist. In addition, FFD evaluations differ depending on the referral source. For example, in the case of physicians, an evaluation for diversion to an impaired physician's program differs from an evaluation for discipline of a physician by a state medical board (Wettstein, 2005a).

Evaluators should also review documentation, even if limited to a few lines within the referral document, relating to the evaluee's current job status, that is, whether the evaluee is on medical or administrative leave, suspended, working, or in danger of being terminated. This should include relevant dates, such as when the suspension or leave began. Finally, evaluators should request any documentation regarding exposure to a specific stressor that may have precipitated unusual behavior or the FFD request, including exposure to a work-related critical incident or traumatic experience. Often these have had to be written up or documented as part of organizational policy, separate from FFD concerns about any individual employee, and may provide insight into the employee's current problems.

Evaluators also benefit from reviewing collateral information obtained from individuals with direct knowledge of the employee's behavior and its effect on coworkers and in the workplace. Written statements from coworkers and supervisors often help clarify whether the alleged incident is an isolated event and represents a response to a specific stressor, reflects an established pattern of misconduct, or is a recent change in behavior or functioning. This information can also clarify what events led to the referral and can help the evaluator formulate areas of inquiry during interviews with the evaluee.

At times, if written statements from coworkers or supervisors are not available or appear incomplete, interviewing the employee's supervisor or coworkers before interviewing the evaluee may be necessary. Such interviews must be arranged and conducted with full knowledge and consent of the employer. Finally, while the information provided by collateral sources should be considered, evaluators should bear in mind that such records or statements can be flawed, incomplete, or biased.

Evaluators should also carefully review the evaluee's job description. Different work skills and impairments will be significant in each type of profession or job. Each type of workplace also has different tolerance limits within which its employees must operate (Brodsky, 1996a). As reviewed in Chapter 6, the various physical and mental requirements of a job are frequently described in formal organizational job descriptions, but sometimes are not. Many job descriptions can be obtained from published information about the job, such as in the *Dictionary of Occupational Titles* (United States Department of Labor, 1991), which gives job descriptions for thousands of jobs, along with summaries of educational, strength, and cognitive requirements. Although somewhat obsolete and outdated, the *Dictionary of Occupational Titles* may provide relevant and useful information regarding job requirements.

Copies of past job performance evaluations can be invaluable in FFD evaluations. These provide data documenting changes in behavior and functioning. In addition, as noted above, an FFD referral may be generated in an attempt to resolve organizational issues regarding a chronically underperforming or otherwise problematic employee. Copies of past and present performance evaluations may clarify whether this is the case.

Medical and/or psychiatric records can provide information about problems that may be underlying causes of changes in behavior and functioning, past response to treatment, treatment compliance, and the role, if any, of substance use. For example, psychiatric or medical records may reveal a history of an episodic disorder that has previously been in remission, but which, due to treatment noncompliance, has again become acute. Alternatively, they may indicate that performance or behavior problems may be related to side effects of prescribed medications. Due to confidentiality concerns and limitations on employer's access to employees' medical records, evaluees are often responsible for supplying these nonemployment-related records, but requests for these records should be communicated to the evaluee through the referral source.

Previous medical and psychiatric records should include, again when available, previous post-employment FFD evaluations, preemployment FFD evaluations, or psychological testing associated with either. Police officers and some commercial transportation workers, for example, often receive psychological preemployment screenings before being offered a position, although the depth and quality of such screenings are variable. These prior evaluations may provide useful information and a comparative baseline when conducting an FFD examination (Anfang & Wall, 2006).

The FFD Interview

Regardless of the type of job involved, psychiatrists and psychologists will be asked to perform a thorough mental health evaluation, provide an opinion about FFD relative to the specific job duties, and risks associated with that job to the employee and to the safety and welfare of the general public. In addition to the standard elements of a comprehensive psychiatric evaluation, the examination should also include questions about any recent or past stressors such as exposure to critical incidents. In some cases, a formal violence risk assessment may be required.

Evaluators should consider and explore with the evaluee how a psychiatric condition, a medical condition, or a medication side effect might affect the evaluee's ability to perform specific and unique features of the job. For example, when assessing the FFD of an armed officer, evaluators usually will need to say whether contraindications to the officer's continuing to carry a weapon are evident. An officer who carries a firearm must be able to make on-the-spot, life-and-death decisions. With regard to the safe and appropriate use of firearms, evaluators need to consider whether psychiatric illness, medical illness, or the effects of medication may have effects on the officer's judgment, reaction time, memory, and fine motor skills (Pinals & Price, 2004; Rostow & Davis, 2004).

At the initial meeting, examinees should be encouraged to review the events leading to the FFD evaluation from their perspective and to include opposing points of view, even if they believe those opposing points of view are invalid. Allowing the evaluee to freely explain the events in question facilitates both the process and content of the examination. Evaluees may be reassured by having an opportunity to air their version of the events leading to the workplace problems. As discussed in Chapter 6, the opportunity to do so also may mitigate some of the anxiety and adversarial feeling that often precedes the examination (Meyer & Price, 2006).

After reviewing the employee's version of events, evaluators should be prepared to ask specific questions relevant to the referral issues. Ideally, as reviewed above, the referral source has provided the mental health evaluator with documents regarding the evaluee's work history, performance evaluations, and statements from those with whom the evaluee works. When this background is available, evaluators are able to frame specific and relevant questions. The evaluator should explore in detail any discrepancies between the evaluee's description of events and the versions of collateral sources. Evaluators should bear in mind that every conflict has at least two sides and should maintain their neutrality throughout the interview process. The fact that the explanations of either the employer or the employee are credible does not mean they are valid (Brodsky, 1996a).

The evaluee's responses to specific questions can also provide useful information. Evaluees' answers to questions based on information provided by the employer frequently add data that do not contradict the employer's report of events but which alter the meaning of the reported facts in a convincing and relevant way. Sometimes the response to such questions is an angry or a threatening explosion directed toward the examiner or others. Some evaluees threaten to leave or do leave the examination. More often, evaluees discuss with varying levels of emotional response the employer's concerns, explain why they may be valid or invalid, and explain what may have led to misinterpretation or distortions in the reports of their behavior or functioning. These responses provide needed information regarding the evaluee's impulse control, cognitive functioning, insight, and judgment.

Review of documentation may reveal performance or behavior changes, but evidence of associated cognitive impairment may not become apparent until an interview and mental status examination are conducted. Some evaluators use a mini-mental status examination or a screening neuropsychological examination, which includes tests of executive functioning, to detect more subtle impairment. If evaluators suspect cognitive impairment, the administration of a full neuropsychological battery should be considered. Similarly, the evaluee should be referred for a medical evaluation and for laboratory and imaging tests if evaluators suspect these may be appropriate. When documentation and/or an interview raises suspicion of a substance use disorder, appropriate testing can be obtained, if allowed by contract or law. All psychological testing, imaging, or medical evaluation should be organized through the referral source (Anfang et al., 2005).

As discussed, information from collateral sources should be obtained and reviewed prior to the evaluation. In addition, evaluators should encourage evaluees to identify any additional individuals who would have knowledge about the events that precipitated the evaluation. This is especially important in cases where the evaluee denies misconduct and maintains that the evaluation is retaliatory in nature or has arisen because of conflicts with supervisors. Information may be obtained from supervisors who can provide further context for understanding the problematic conduct. If at the end of the interview process evaluators feel they need more information, either because information that should have been provided was not adequate or because issues have been raised during the interview that need further clarification, they should request that the information be provided.

Finally, acute and long-term risk assessment and risk mitigation are an important part of all examinations of FFD evaluees referred for disruptive, threatening, or dangerous behavior, or for concerns regarding public safety. Evaluators should be certain they understand any safety or danger concerns relevant to the specific FFD evaluation and address them directly with the evaluee. Static and dynamic factors that indicate heightened risk of violence, if present, should be reviewed and discussed. As above, any discrepancies between the evaluee's report regarding safety concerns or risk of danger and that of collateral sources should be discussed with the evaluee in detail.

Dissimulation

In formulating opinions, evaluators should always consider whether the evaluee may be dissimulating. Dissimulation, that is, minimizing problems or feigning health, is a prominent concern in FFD evaluations. Unconscious minimization may arise from denial, lack of insight, or may represent a manifestation of illness (Rosman, 2001). For example, depressed individuals may not realize how depressed they are and may minimize their symptoms and impairments. Individuals with bipolar disorder rarely understand why others consider their manic symptoms a problem. Individuals with paranoid ideation often lack insight into the delusional nature of their beliefs and insist nothing is wrong with them.

Conscious dissimulation is a form of intentional deception. Evaluees may conceal problems to avoid negative consequences or sanctions for their behavior (Reynolds, 2002). More commonly in FFD evaluations, evaluees who intentionally minimize their problems are motivated by the desire to return to work, whether they are impaired or not, in order to maintain income or avoid the loss of a valued job. If the satisfaction or rewards of working are high, people are often willing to pay a high personal cost in emotional discomfort or take unreasonable risks with their mental or physical health to maintain a job or career.

Opinions

The utility of a mental health FFD evaluation turns on whether it accurately assesses mental health and possible impairments relative to the performance of essential job requirements and/or risk of danger at present and in the future. Referral sources will expect to see one of the following responses to these questions (although these responses may of course be worded differently depending on the referral questions):

1. The employee is fit for duty and able to return to work without restriction, with or without treatment.
2. The employee is fit for duty but with certain restrictions, with or without treatment.
3. The employee is temporarily unfit for duty but the likelihood that impairments may resolve with treatment is high. Return to work should be based on the condition that the evaluee receives treatment.
4. The employee is unfit for duty and likely to remain so permanently.
5. The employee is unfit for duty and it is too early or there is not enough information to determine whether the employee may be able to return to work in the future.

Mental health evaluators should offer opinions about the presence of a psychiatric illness and the extent, if any, to which the illness has interfered with the evaluee's ability to function effectively and safely in the specific work setting. The evaluator should provide a description of how the mental illness affects job-related capacities and thus FFD. These opinions should be accompanied by descriptions of specific areas of impairments, including insight and judgment, and should be well supported by data. The foundation for opinions should be discussed in detail in the report.

Unfortunately, circumstances sometimes dictate that FFD assessments, and the projections they entail, must be made even if the data upon which they are based are incomplete. Nevertheless, if evaluators feel they do not have enough information to come to an opinion because of lack of necessary documentary evidence or lack of cooperation with the interview on the part of the evaluee, they should so state and explain what they would need to reach an opinion.

Mental health professionals' opinions may be facilitated by understanding the process by which an employee progressed from being a satisfactory or even highly satisfactory worker to being a worker whose FFD is questioned (Brodsky, 1996a). This requires the exploration of internal factors, such as previous and current psychiatric illness, and external factors, such as changes in the evaluee's personal life or changes in the workplace. The models of development of disability discussed in Chapter 5 should be considered and utilized for this formulation when appropriate. Such a description is useful in providing a guide to suggesting treatment, accommodations, restrictions, alternate or modified duty, or workplace monitoring issues that may result in returning a valuable employee to the workplace and maintaining him or her in the workplace.

Evaluators may conclude that evaluees have no impairment and may return to the workplace. If so, the data supporting this conclusion need to be articulated with a logical explanation that clearly substantiates the conclusion and demonstrates evaluators' understanding of the reasons that prompted the referral. For example, illegal behavior or maladaptive personality traits that may prompt an FFD request do not necessarily result from disability or impairment due to psychiatric illness (Anfang & Wall, 2006). Reports should not simply conclude that there is no problem and therefore the examinee is fit for duty (Anfang et al., 2005; Anfang & Wall, 2006).

Evaluators might also reach the conclusion that the evaluee does not have a significant Axis I or Axis II psychiatric disorder, but has become impaired and unable to work safely in response to a serious personal stressor or work-related event. Such a finding should also be reported, along with potential treatment recommendations or oversight. Alternatively, evaluators may conclude that a psychiatric disorder has caused an evaluee to become unfit for duty. Such conclusions should be accompanied by opinions regarding whether such impairment is temporary or permanent, whether treatment might render the employee fit for duty, and what kind of treatment is indicated.

Most employers specifically request that mental health evaluators provide information regarding at least some of the following issues:

1. the likelihood of improvement;
2. the steps (such as treatment, accommodations) that might lead to improvement;
3. the length of time treatment might take for the employee to reach a level commensurate with safe return to work;
4. the viability of alternative job assignments while treatment is being undertaken;
5. how to know when (and if) improvement has occurred to the point that the employee could resume regular duties;
6. whether and how to structure return to regular duties so as to minimize risk; and
7. appropriate ongoing monitoring and how to recognize relapse or deterioration after improvement is shown (Stone, 2000).

An FFD evaluation often requires prospective opinions about the examinee's present and future capacity to function safely and effectively in the workplace, and the examinee's prospective needs for psychiatric treatment and workplace supervision. If psychiatric illness is present and evaluators believe that the evaluee's return to work should be conditioned on receiving treatment, they should suggest specific treatment modalities and provide indicators of improvement and treatment compliance. Treatment recommendations should be as specific as possible and should comment on the type and frequency of needed treatment. It may be important to comment on the limitations of prior evaluation and treatment, the reasons for those limitations, potential barriers to appropriate care as a consequence of the evaluee's health insurance benefits, and the examinee's attitude and resistance, if any, toward treatment and recovery (Anfang & Wall, 2006).

Where misconduct or poor performance is involved, employers may require that an employee undergo treatment to return to the workplace or face termination. However, the question of whether an employer may offer an employee the option of treatment or termination without violating the ADA is still undecided. Courts have almost uniformly permitted employers to put employees with alcohol-related problems whose work performance is deteriorating to a "treatment or termination" ultimatum. The courts have not decided whether an employer can put an employee who has a mental disability not involving drugs or alcohol to a choice between termination and treatment (Creighton, 2001). Nevertheless, if treatment is required to return an evaluee to a fit state for his or her employment, evaluators should make this clear and leave considerations regarding enforcing this recommendation to the employer and the employee.

In some cases, an employee who has undergone evaluation can return to work with accommodations or with modification of duties. Evaluators' recommendations may include reassigning the employee to light duty, part-time employment, mentoring, and training. The employer will make the decision as to whether to implement suggestions for job modification or accommodation. For example, some employers may have part-time or light-duty positions. However, employers are not required to create such positions if none have previously existed. As discussed in Chapter 8, reasonable accommodations for those protected by the ADA take into consideration the needs of the employer and whether the accommodation creates an undue burden on the employer. Nevertheless, evaluators should make recommendations regarding psychiatrically reasonable accommodations and restrictions based on the needs of the evaluee should such issues arise in an FFD evaluation.

FFD evaluations where dangerousness in the workplace or concerns of public safety have arisen also usually require an assessment of short- and long-term risk and suggestions for risk management and mitigation. Specific positive or negative findings about risk should be thoroughly explained and substantiated. An examiner's report of pertinent negative findings of risk factors may help reassure employers. However, the predictive power of an individual's current state of risk decreases over time. Evaluators' recommendations to the employer regarding future indicators and prospective monitoring of risk for the evaluee are as important as assessments of current risk.

Evaluators are often asked to move beyond a mental health treatment setting and consider how to implement monitoring and supervision of an evaluee, often in the evaluee's workplace. Referral sources may specifically ask evaluators to provide concrete suggestions for monitoring, oversight, and supervision of the evaluee in the workplace and how to educate workplace supervisors regarding relevant indicators of recurrence of diagnosed disorders (Meyer & Price, 2006). Oversight or monitoring suggestions may include periodic mental examinations, regular reports from treatment providers, or random urine screens for substance users. These suggestions may be incorporated into the provisions of a consent decree or a monitoring contract depending on the availability of such options in the specific workplace. Clinicians treating the examinee should on no account assume workplace supervision (Meyer & Price, 2006) and employers should not assume or expect that they will do so.

Recommendations for the monitoring and supervision of an examinee should include detailed guidance regarding signs of relapse that may precede or accompany psychiatric deterioration. Comments about an examinee's customary interpersonal style and conscious awareness of psychological and behavioral difficulties may also be essential in assisting an employer to develop effective oversight of the evaluee. An employer's understanding of the evaluee's long-term vulnerabilities and indicators of increasing risk can enhance the ability of supervisors to intervene promptly should symptoms recur and the efficacy of the workplace monitoring and supervision. Evaluators can also outline specific administrative and therapeutic steps that workplace monitors can take to respond in the event of the examinee's relapse (Anfang & Wall, 2006; Meyer & Price, 2006).

Under specific circumstances, workplace monitoring has been found to be job-related and consistent with business necessity (Equal Employment Opportunity Commission, 1997). For example, when an employee returns after rehabilitation, an employer can subject the employee to periodic alcohol testing if the employer has a reasonable belief based on objective evidence that the employee will pose a direct threat in the absence of such testing. Again, consistent with the ADA, a "reasonable belief" requires an individualized assessment of the employee and his or her position and cannot be based on generalized assumptions (Creighton, 2001). Therefore, if indicated by the FFD examination, evaluators should specifically indicate why such monitoring is recommended.

Other legal considerations in implementing ongoing monitoring include safety risks associated with the employee's position, the consequences of the employee's inability to perform his or her job functions, and how recently the events that caused the employer to believe the employee will pose a direct threat occurred. In addition, the duration and frequency of testing must be designed to address specific safety concerns and not used to harass the employee (see *Hinnershitz v. Ortep of Pennsylvania, Inc.*, 1998; Equal Employment Opportunity Commission, 1997).

Finally, evaluators should be certain to limit opinions to questions of psychiatric impairment. FFD examinations are not assessments of competence, unsafe general practices, or level of knowledge, skill, or training. If evaluators suspect that any of these are a basis of concern and may underlie performance or safety issues, they should report this and recommend to the referral source that appropriate evaluation of these problems be undertaken (Anfang et al., 2005).

Degree of Certainty of Opinions

Experts who conduct FFD evaluations may experience a range of certitude that includes a high degree of confidence that an individual is or is not fit to work in the foreseeable future to relative uncertainty that questions of safety or FFD can be answered beyond the very near future. Competent, ethical psychiatrists and psychologists should be aware of the concerns of risks posed by the employees they evaluate and clearly state the degree of certainty with which they hold their opinions. Uncertainties that surround predictions of the course of illness or injury, let alone progress in treatment and rehabilitation, may preclude projections beyond a brief period of time into the future.

Nevertheless, when issues of safety or danger to others are involved, even opinions that indicate only uncertainty on the part of the examiner may lead to serious consequences. In addition, since litigation commonly results from the type of workplace conflicts that give rise to FFD evaluations, mental health professionals should be prepared to defend their opinions in a legal arena. Therefore, when offering opinions, evaluators should be aware of the degree of certainty with which they hold their opinions regarding an evaluee's FFD and be prepared to demonstrate in specific detail the foundations for these opinions.

Return-to-Work Evaluations

Return-to-work (RTW) evaluations are similar to FFD evaluations, except that an RTW evaluation usually follows completion of an employment-related process. This process often involves a mental health FFD or disability examination that led to the decision for the employee not to return to work or for the employee to work at a modified job. During the time period that the employee was not working or was working at a modified job, the employee may have undertaken or completed some form of treatment that provided enough stabilization or symptom resolution to allow resumption of workplace responsibilities. Presumably, an employee undergoing an RTW evaluation desires to return to the workplace and the workplace is willing to restore the employee to his or her position.

The primary issue in an RTW evaluation is "What has changed?" RTW evaluations center on the issue of whether the impairment that led to leaving work or changing job responsibilities has resolved. The models of disability development reviewed in Chapter 5 should provide a framework for explaining the evaluee's changed situation. Some of these models indicate that even when work capacity falls below minimum required levels, it can, for reasons including effective treatment, result in sufficient recovery to allow return to work.

If the work-related impairments that led to withdrawal from the workplace are unchanged, it is unlikely that a transition back to the workplace will be successful. However, if the impairment is no longer present, the evaluator should recommend that the employee return to work, with or without restrictions as indicated. Opinions regarding oversight, supervision, continued treatment, assessment of future risk, and need for workplace monitoring, similar to those requested in an FFD evaluation, may also be required.

Opinions regarding the ability to return to work should reflect an understanding of the original issues leading to work withdrawal or modification and a detailed description of which internal or external circumstances have changed. Mental health evaluators should review documents relevant to the administrative decision to grant disability or leave or the evaluee's reasons for leaving the workplace, the length of time the evaluee has not worked, and what the evaluee has been doing to occupy his or her time. The referral source should provide written documentation concerning these issues. Evaluators should also review medical and mental health records, especially those generated during the period when the evaluee was unable to work. This includes current treatment (medication and/or therapy), response to treatment, and current mental and functional status.

If an evaluee is determined to be able to return to work, evaluators must delineate what has changed in the interim period and link the analysis to specific job functional capacities. Specific recommendations for further treatment, monitoring, or accommodations should be carefully described. If impairments have not resolved to the extent that full return to work is possible, evaluators should provide recommendations regarding restrictions, treatment, or accommodations that may facilitate this process. In either case, detailed consultation with the employer is typically necessary, both for understanding the circumstances that prompted the evaluation request and for explaining findings and recommendations (Anfang & Wall, 2006).

Conclusion

Ideally, an employer's dual set of obligations, namely, protecting the employment interests of its employees, especially those who might be disabled, and running a safe and productive workplace, are entirely compatible. However, when questions regarding job performance and safety in the workplace related to mental illness arise, FFD evaluations may be requested. Some are motivated by genuine concern for the well-being of the evaluee and his or her coworkers. Others arise as a result of liability issues. Regardless, the context of most FFD evaluations is one of workplace conflict regarding the employee's ability to continue working.

Mental health professionals have an obligation to undertake thorough and comprehensive FFD evaluations. A determination that an individual is fit or unfit for duty cannot be made lightly. The consequences of an FTD evaluation can be staggering. Individuals can lose the income and other tangible and intangible benefits associated with employment if found unfit for duty due to psychiatric illness without reasonable basis. Employers stand to bear moral, legal, and financial responsibility in millions if an individual deemed fit due to a less than thorough evaluation subsequently engages in negligent or violent behavior. When psychiatrists and psychologists conduct FTD evaluations, they should address themselves to mental health issues, examine all the data available, and provide thorough and well-reasoned opinions regarding job-related safety and performance issues.

Additional Guidelines for Conducting FFD Evaluations

1. Assess the appropriateness of the evaluation at the time of the referral. If it appears that a clinical evaluation for treatment should precede an FFD evaluation, the mental health professional should so advise the referral source.
2. Have the referral source provide specific, written questions for the evaluation.

3. Before interviewing the employee, obtain information about relevant behaviors and conflicts in the workplace.
4. Advise evaluees of the evaluation and limits of confidentiality before conducting the interview.
5. Perform a standard psychiatric examination with a focus on the evaluee's ability to perform relevant work functions as explained in the job description and other relevant referral questions.
6. Obtain psychological testing if clinical information indicates a need for such data to reach or support a conclusion. Carefully evaluate any differences or omissions between the evaluee's report of events and reports from the referral source.
7. Perform a thorough short- and long-term risk assessment relative to safety issues in the workplace and issues related to public safety.
8. Limit reports to information relevant to the referral.
9. Make a determination of FFD, with or without treatment and with or without accommodations and modification. Provide the basis for these opinions, correlating psychiatric illness and symptoms with job-related functions and safety issues.
10. Answer all other referral questions, including prognosis, present and future treatment needs, present and future safety risks, and workplace monitoring and oversight.

Key Points in Conducting RTW Evaluations

1. Establish a clear understanding of the reasons for the initial workplace withdrawal or change in responsibilities.
2. Base opinions regarding ability to return to work on documented changes in psychiatric symptoms or levels of impairment.
3. Specifically address the issues that resulted in change in the workforce status with concrete data and examples, and describe how these have resolved or may be mitigated enough to allow return to work, with or without restrictions or accommodations.
4. If requested, provide suggestions for continued treatment and workplace monitoring to help ensure adequate functioning or prevention of relapse of illness.

Conclusion

Disability and disability-related evaluations can appear deceptively straightforward. However, mental health evaluations related to disability benefit programs or insurance, the Americans with Disabilities Act (ADA), and fitness-for-duty (FFD) involve complicated psychiatric, psychological, and legal issues, often not evident until problems arise. Forensically trained and non-forensically trained clinicians frequently find themselves faced with practical, ethical, or legal dilemmas when what appeared to be a relatively simple disability evaluation turns into a complex civil rights or employment conflict.

Disability and disability-related mental health evaluations require specialized expertise. In recent years, the concept of disability has shifted from a focus on diseases, conditions, and impairments to the functional limitations caused by these factors, a concept that goes beyond the assessment and impairment of mental illness and takes into account the interaction between impairments and the environment. Criteria for eligibility in disability programs designed to provide benefits for individuals unable to work give disability a specific technical meaning conferred by statutory law, legislation, case law, and/or contract. The assessment of impairment is only the first step in the final administrative or legal determination of disability.

The persistent dominance of the medical model of disability has assured physicians and mental health professionals a continuing role in the determination of disability and disability-related issues such as accommodations or FFD in the workplace. This central role requires an acute awareness that, in contrast to the assessment of impairment, the determination of disability is *not* a medical assessment. In addition, it requires an understanding of attendant ethical and legal obligations and the agency's proof requirements. All these factors demand that psychiatrists and psychologists be aware of the limits of their competence or expertise, and not operate beyond them.

In addition, disability and disability-related assessments require a clinical understanding of the dynamic issues involved. Psychiatric diagnosis does not automatically imply significant functional impairment. Disability is a dynamic process between a psychiatric disorder and the environment in which an individual works and which can and often does fluctuate over time. At times the balance between psychiatric illness, personal issues, and the work environment may result in impairment evolving into disability; at other times, an individual may be impaired but may not be and may never be limited in the ability to work. The expertise required in making these assessments includes an understanding of the psychological meaning of work to an individual, the factors that influence the individual's working life and abilities, and an understanding of how that individual may go from an "abled" to "disabled" state and, in a best case scenario, back again.

In addition to clinical expertise, evaluators should be familiar with the legal and professional standards governing mental health workplace evaluations. Although legal and professional standards for conducting work-related evaluations are still evolving, psychiatrists and psychologists should be aware that legal and professional guidelines and rules governing the conduct of disability, ADA, and FFD evaluations do exist. We have reviewed these in detail and provided guidelines and suggestions congruent with those published by the American Academy of Psychiatry and the Law (AAPL) (Gold et al., 2008). The AAPL guidelines and those suggested here reflect best practices and the current state of the law governing mental health disability, ADA, and FFD evaluations.

Mental health professionals should be familiar with these standards and best practices. Evaluators do not have to adhere to every guideline or suggested best practice. Clinical judgment regarding the utility of guidelines has to be assessed on case-by-case basis. Some will not be relevant to the case under consideration; others require modification for clinical, practical, or legal reasons. However, evaluators who deviate from these suggested guidelines should be aware of the extent of the deviation, should be able to discuss their reasons for doing so, and should be prepared to do so in an adversarial arena.

Finally, and perhaps most importantly, clinicians with the requisite expertise who adhere to suggested guidelines and best practices reviewed here are likely to achieve one of the most valuable qualities in any type of clinical forensic evaluation, namely transparency. Existing empirical literature on the quality of forensic evaluations generally indicates that the work of forensic and non-forensic specialists is deficient in the consideration and evaluation of data from collateral sources; the use of irrelevant, unsound, or outdated psychological tests; extrapolation of the data; and commonly fails to link data, reasoning, and conclusions, resulting in lack of detailed support for expert opinions in the evaluation report (Heilbrun et al., 2008; Wettstein, 2005a).

All mental health assessments of workplace functioning and disability involve some extrapolation from evidence-based conclusions such as diagnosis and associated levels of impairment to issues such as disability, permanency, dangerousness, prognosis, response to treatment, ability to function with restrictions, modifications, or accommodations. Predicting outcomes and how to influence them (with treatment, accommodations, etc.) raises various issues that have yet to be definitively resolved. Whether disability, ADA, or FFD evaluations are considered, no outcome studies or statistics upon which to base determinations of the accuracy of mental health assessment exist. Moreover, examiners are often asked to give opinions on these non-evidence-based issues without access to important data. Under these circumstances, the fact that forensic assessments are inconsistent and demonstrate varying levels of skill in utilizing collateral data and extrapolating data into reasonable conclusions is not surprising.

Transparency lends itself to the improvement of quality and consistency of all forensic evaluations. Mental health professionals are regularly called upon to make assessments that are not purely empirical or scientific. However, when these judgments are made, ethics require our reasoning to be transparent. Utilization of the best interviewing skills, psychological testing, and evidence-based data does not guarantee an accurate assessment of opinions that requires extrapolation from that data. Mental health professionals are not required to guarantee the accuracy of their opinions. Nevertheless, disability and disability-related mental health evaluations are best made utilizing a structured approach that lends itself to others being able to follow the data and reasoning behind evaluators' conclusions.

The field of forensic mental health assessment has advanced empirically, conceptually, and ethically over the past decades. Courts, employers, insurers, and administrative boards must come to judicial and administrative decisions regarding disability and disability-related issues. These agencies all continue to rely on psychiatrists and psychologists to provide the information that helps them come to fair and reasonable determinations in making these life-changing decisions. Mental health professionals well versed in the clinical, ethical, legal, and administrative issues involved in these complex evaluations have much to offer the systems who depend on them. The information, guidelines, and suggestions presented here can assist psychiatrists and psychologists in fulfilling their responsibilities to provide well-reasoned, transparent opinions that facilitate just resolutions of important social, judicial, and administrative issues and conflicts in which they have been asked to participate.

Appendix A

The American Academy of Psychiatry and the Law: Ethics Guidelines for the Practice of Forensic Psychiatry, 2005

I. Preamble

The American Academy of Psychiatry and the Law (AAPL) is dedicated to the highest standards of practice in forensic psychiatry. Recognizing the unique aspects of this practice, which is at the interface of the professions of psychiatry and the law, the Academy presents these guidelines for the ethical practice of forensic psychiatry.

Commentary

Forensic psychiatry is a subspecialty of psychiatry in which scientific and clinical expertise is applied in legal contexts involving civil, criminal, correctional, regulatory, or legislative matters, and in specialized clinical consultations in areas such as risk assessment or employment. These guidelines apply to psychiatrists practicing in a forensic role.

These guidelines supplement the Annotations Especially Applicable to Psychiatry of the American Psychiatric Association to the Principles of Medical Ethics of the American Medical Association.

Forensic psychiatrists practice at the interface of law and psychiatry, each of which has developed its own institutions, policies, procedures, values, and vocabulary. As a consequence, the practice of forensic psychiatry entails inherent potentials for complications, conflicts, misunderstandings, and abuses.

Psychiatrists in a forensic role are called upon to practice in a manner that balances competing duties to the individual and to society. In doing so, they should be bound by underlying ethical principles of respect for persons, honesty, justice, and social responsibility. However, when a treatment relationship exists, such as in correctional settings, the usual physician–patient duties apply.

American Academy of Psychiatry and The Law, Reprinted with permission.

II. Confidentiality

Respect for the individual's right of privacy and the maintenance of confidentiality should be major concerns when performing forensic evaluations. Psychiatrists should maintain confidentiality to the extent possible, given the legal context. Special attention should be paid to the evaluee's understanding of medical confidentiality. A forensic evaluation requires notice to the evaluee and to collateral sources of reasonably anticipated limitations on confidentiality. Information or reports derived from a forensic evaluation are subject to the rules of confidentiality that apply to the particular evaluation and any disclosure should be restricted accordingly.

Commentary

The practice of forensic psychiatry often presents significant problems regarding confidentiality. Psychiatrists should be aware of and alert to those issues of privacy and confidentiality presented by the particular forensic situation. Notice of reasonably anticipated limitations to confidentiality should be given to evaluees, third parties, and other appropriate individuals. Psychiatrists should indicate for whom they are conducting the examination and what they will do with the information obtained. At the beginning of a forensic evaluation, care should be taken to explicitly inform the evaluee that the psychiatrist is not the evaluee's "doctor." Psychiatrists have a continuing obligation to be sensitive to the fact that although a warning has been given, the evaluee may develop the belief that there is a treatment relationship. Psychiatrists should take precautions to ensure that they do not release confidential information to unauthorized persons.

When a patient is involved in parole, probation, conditional release, or in other custodial or mandatory settings, psychiatrists should be clear about limitations on confidentiality in the treatment relationship and ensure that these limitations are communicated to the patient. Psychiatrists should be familiar with the institutional policies regarding confidentiality. When no policy exists, psychiatrists should attempt to clarify these matters with the institutional authorities and develop working guidelines.

III. Consent

At the outset of a face-to-face evaluation, notice should be given to the evaluee of the nature and purpose of the evaluation and the limits of its confidentiality. The informed consent of the person undergoing the forensic evaluation should be obtained when necessary and feasible. If the evaluee is not competent to give consent, the evaluator should follow the appropriate laws of the jurisdiction.

Commentary

Informed consent is one of the core values of the ethical practice of medicine and psychiatry. It reflects respect for the person, a fundamental principle in the practices of psychiatry and forensic psychiatry.

It is important to appreciate that in particular situations, such as court-ordered evaluations for competency to stand trial or involuntary commitment, neither assent nor informed consent is required. In such cases, psychiatrists should inform the evaluee that if the evaluee refuses to participate in the evaluation, this fact may be included in any report or testimony. If the evaluee does not appear capable of understanding the information provided regarding the evaluation, this impression should also be included in any report and, when feasible, in testimony.

In the absence of a court order, psychiatrists should not perform forensic evaluations for the prosecution or the government on persons who have not consulted with legal counsel when such persons are known to be charged with criminal acts; under investigation for criminal or quasi-criminal conduct; held in government custody or detention; or being interrogated for criminal or quasi-criminal conduct, hostile acts against a government, or immigration violations. Examinations related to rendering medical care or treatment, such as evaluations for civil commitment or risk assessments for management or discharge planning, are not precluded by these restrictions. As is true for any physician, psychiatrists practicing in a forensic role should not participate in torture.

Consent to treatment in a jail or prison or in other criminal justice settings is different from consent for a forensic evaluation. Psychiatrists providing treatment in such settings should be familiar with the jurisdiction's regulations governing patients' rights regarding treatment.

IV. Honesty and Striving for Objectivity

When psychiatrists function as experts within the legal process, they should adhere to the principle of honesty and should strive for objectivity. Although they may be retained by one party to a civil or criminal matter, psychiatrists should adhere to these principles when conducting evaluations, applying clinical data to legal criteria, and expressing opinions.

Commentary

The adversarial nature of most legal processes presents special hazards for the practice of forensic psychiatry. Being retained by one side in a civil or criminal matter exposes psychiatrists to the potential for unintended bias and the danger of distortion of their opinion. It is the responsibility of psychiatrists to minimize such hazards by acting in an honest manner and striving to reach an objective opinion.

Psychiatrists practicing in a forensic role enhance the honesty and objectivity of their work by basing their forensic opinions, forensic reports, and forensic testimony on all available data. They communicate the honesty of their work, efforts to attain objectivity, and the soundness of their clinical opinion by distinguishing, to the extent possible, between verified and unverified information, as well as among clinical "facts," "inferences," and "impressions."

Psychiatrists should not distort their opinion in the service of the retaining party. Honesty, objectivity, and the adequacy of the clinical evaluation may be called into question when an expert opinion is offered without a personal examination. For certain evaluations (such as record reviews for malpractice cases), a personal examination is not required. In all other forensic evaluations, if, after appropriate effort, it is not feasible to conduct a personal examination, an opinion may nonetheless be rendered on the basis of other information. Under these circumstances, it is the responsibility of psychiatrists to make earnest efforts to ensure that their statements, opinions, and any reports or testimony based on those opinions clearly state that there was no personal examination and note any resulting limitations to their opinions.

In custody cases, honesty and objectivity require that all parties be interviewed, if possible, before an opinion is rendered. When this is not possible, or is not done for any reason, this should be clearly indicated in the forensic psychiatrist's report and testimony. If one parent has not been interviewed, even after deliberate effort, it may be inappropriate to comment on that parent's fitness as a parent. Any comments on the fitness of a parent who has not been interviewed should be qualified and the data for the opinion clearly indicated.

Contingency fees undermine honesty and efforts to attain objectivity and should not be accepted. Retainer fees, however, do not create the same problems in regard to honesty and efforts to attain objectivity and, therefore, may be accepted.

Psychiatrists who take on a forensic role for patients they are treating may adversely affect the therapeutic relationship with them. Forensic evaluations usually require interviewing corroborative sources, exposing information to public scrutiny, or subjecting evaluees and the treatment itself to potentially damaging cross-examination. The forensic evaluation and the credibility of the practitioner may also be undermined by conflicts inherent in the differing clinical and forensic roles. Treating psychiatrists should therefore generally avoid acting as an expert witness for their patients or performing evaluations of their patients for legal purposes.

Treating psychiatrists appearing as "fact" witnesses should be sensitive to the unnecessary disclosure of private information or the possible misinterpretation of testimony as "expert" opinion. In situations when the dual role is required or unavoidable (such as Workers' Compensation, disability evaluations, civil commitment, or guardianship hearings), sensitivity to differences between clinical and legal obligations remains important.

When requirements of geography or related constraints dictate the conduct of a forensic evaluation by the treating psychiatrist, the dual role may also be unavoidable; otherwise, referral to another evaluator is preferable.

V. Qualifications

Expertise in the practice of forensic psychiatry should be claimed only in areas of actual knowledge, skills, training, and experience.

Commentary

When providing expert opinion, reports, and testimony, psychiatrists should present their qualifications accurately and precisely. As a correlate of the principle that expertise may be appropriately claimed only in areas of actual knowledge, skill, training, and experience, there are areas of special expertise, such as the evaluation of children, persons of foreign cultures, or prisoners, that may require special training or expertise.

VI. Procedures for Handling Complaints of Unethical Conduct

The American Academy of Psychiatry and the Law does not adjudicate complaints that allege unethical conduct by its members or nonmembers. If received, such complaints will be returned to the complainant for referral to the local district branch of the American Psychiatric Association (APA), the state licensing board, and/or the appropriate national psychiatric organization of foreign members. If the APA or the psychiatric association of another country expels or suspends a member, AAPL will also expel or suspend that member upon notification of such action. AAPL will not necessarily follow the APA or other organizations in other sanctions.

Commentary

General questions regarding ethical practice in forensic psychiatry are welcomed by the Academy and should be submitted to the Ethics Committee.

The Committee may issue opinions on general or hypothetical questions but will not issue opinions on the ethical conduct of specific forensic psychiatrists or about actual cases.

The Academy, through its Ethics Committee, or in any other way suitable, is available to the local or national committees on ethics of the American Psychiatric Association, to state licensing boards, or to ethics committees of psychiatric organizations in other countries to aid them in their adjudication of complaints of unethical conduct or the development of guidelines of ethical conduct as they relate to forensic psychiatric issues.

Appendix B
The American Psychology-Law Society, Committee on Ethical Guidelines of Division 41 of the American Psychological Association and the American Academy of Forensic Psychology: Specialty Guidelines for Forensic Psychologists (1991)

The Specialty Guidelines for Forensic Psychologists, while informed by the *Ethical Principles of Psychologists* (APA, 1990) and meant to be consistent with them, are designed to provide more specific guidance to forensic psychologists in monitoring their professional conduct when acting in assistance to courts, parties to legal proceedings, correctional and forensic mental health facilities, and legislative agencies. The primary goal of the Guidelines is to improve the quality of forensic psychological services offered to individual clients and the legal system and thereby to enhance forensic psychology as a discipline and profession. The *Specialty Guidelines for Forensic Psychologists* represent a joint statement of the American Psychology-Law Society and Division 41 of the American Psychological Association and are endorsed by the American Academy of Forensic Psychology. The *Guidelines* do not represent an official statement of the American Psychological Association.

The Guidelines provide an aspirational model of desirable professional practice by psychologists, within any subdiscipline of psychology (e.g., clinical, developmental, social, experimental), when they are engaged regularly as experts and represent themselves as such, in an activity primarily intended to provide professional psychological expertise to the judicial system. This would include, for example, clinical forensic examiners; psychologists employed by correctional or forensic mental health systems; researchers who offer direct testimony about the relevance of scientific data to a psycholegal issue; trial behavior consultants, psychologists engaged in preparation of *amicus* briefs; or psychologists, appearing as forensic experts, who consult with, or testify before, judicial, legislative, or administrative agencies acting in an adjudicative capacity. Individuals who provide only occasional service to the legal system and

---

Reprinted with kind permission from Springer Science and Business Media, Springer, Steven L. Golding, Ph.D., and *Law and Human Behavior*, Vol. 15. 1991, pp. 655–665, Committee on Ethical Guidelines for Forensic Psychologists, "Specialty Guidelines for Forensic Psychologists." The Specialty Guidelines for Forensic Psychologists are currently being revised; however, the revised draft has not yet been formally adopted. The September 2008 Draft of the Revised Specialty Guidelines for Forensic Psychologists may be viewed at http://www.ap-ls.org/links/professionals gfp.html.

who do so without representing themselves as *forensic experts* may find these *Guidelines* helpful, particularly in conjunction with consultation with colleagues who are forensic experts.

While the *Guidelines* are concerned with a model of desirable professional practice, to the extent that they may be construed as being applicable to the advertisement of services or the solicitation of clients, they are intended to prevent false or deceptive advertisement or solicitation, and should be construed in a manner consistent with that intent.

I. Purpose and Scope

A. *Purpose*

1. While the professional standards for the ethical practice of psychology, as a general discipline, are addressed in the American Psychological Association's *Ethical Principles of Psychologists*, these ethical principles do not relate, in sufficient detail, to current aspirations of desirable professional conduct for forensic psychologists. By design, none of the *Guidelines* contradicts any of the *Ethical Principles of Psychologists*; rather, they amplify those *Principles* in the context of the practice of forensic psychology, as herein defined.
2. The *Guidelines* have been designed to be national in scope and are intended to conform with state and Federal law. In situations where the forensic psychologist believes that the requirements of law are in conflict with the *Guidelines*, attempts to resolve the conflict should be made in accordance with the procedures set forth in these *Guidelines* [IV(G)] and in the *Ethical Principles of Psychologists*.

B. *Scope*

1. The *Guidelines* specify the nature of desirable professional practice by forensic psychologists, within any subdiscipline of psychology (e.g., clinical, developmental, social, experimental), *when engaged regularly* as forensic psychologists.

   a. "Psychologist" means any individual whose professional activities are defined by the American Psychological Association or by regulation of title by state registration or licensure, as the practice of psychology.

   b. "Forensic psychology" means all forms of professional psychological conduct when acting, with definable foreknowledge, as a psychological expert on explicitly psycholegal issues, in direct assistance to courts, parties to legal proceedings, correctional and forensic mental health

I. Purpose and Scope

   facilities, and administrative, judicial, and legislative agencies acting in an adjudicative capacity.
   c. "Forensic psychologist" means psychologists who regularly engage in the practice of forensic psychology as defined in I(B)(l)(b).
2. The *Guidelines* do not apply to a psychologist who is asked to provide professional psychological services when the psychologist was not informed at the time of delivery of the services that they were to be used as forensic psychological services as defined above. The *Guidelines* may be helpful, however, in preparing the psychologist for the experience of communicating psychological data in a forensic context.
3. Psychologists who are not forensic psychologists as defined in I(B)(l)(c), but occasionally provide limited forensic psychological services, may find the *Guidelines* useful in the preparation and presentation of their professional services.

C. Related Standards

1. Forensic psychologists also conduct their professional activities in accord with the *Ethical Principles of Psychologists* and the various other statements of the American Psychological Association that may apply to particular subdisciplines or areas of practice that are relevant to their professional activities.
2. The standards of practice and ethical guidelines of other relevant "expert professional organizations" contain useful guidance and should be consulted even though the present *Guidelines* take precedence for forensic psychologists.

II. Responsibility

A. Forensic psychologists have an obligation to provide services in a manner consistent with the highest standards of their profession. They are responsible for their own conduct and the conduct of those individuals under their direct supervision.
B. Forensic psychologists make a reasonable effort to ensure that their services and the products of their services are used in a forthright and responsible manner.

III. Competence

A. Forensic psychologists provide services only in areas of psychology in which they have specialized knowledge, skill, experience, and education.

B. Forensic psychologists have an obligation to present to the court, regarding the specific matters to which they will testify, the boundaries of their competence, the factual bases (knowledge, skill, experience, training, and education) for their qualification as an expert, and the relevance of those factual bases to their qualification as an expert on the specific matters at issue.
C. Forensic psychologists are responsible for a fundamental and reasonable level of knowledge and understanding of the legal and professional standards that govern their participation as experts in legal proceedings.
D. Forensic psychologists have an obligation to understand the civil rights of parties in legal proceedings in which they participate, and manage their professional conduct in a manner that does not diminish or threaten those rights.
E. Forensic psychologists recognize that their own personal values, moral beliefs, or personal and professional relationships with parties to a legal proceeding may interfere with their ability to practice competently. Under such circumstances, forensic psychologists are obligated to decline participation or to limit their assistance in a manner consistent with professional obligations.

IV. Relationships

A. During initial consultation with the legal representative of the party seeking services, forensic psychologists have an obligation to inform the party of factors that might reasonably affect the decision to contract with the forensic psychologist. These factors include, but are not limited to

   1. the fee structure for anticipated professional services;
   2. prior and current personal or professional activities, obligations, and relationships that might produce a conflict of interests;
   3. their areas of competence and the limits of their competence; and
   4. the known scientific bases and limitations of the methods and procedures that they employ and their qualifications to employ such methods and procedures.

B. Forensic psychologists do not provide professional services to parties to a legal proceeding on the basis of "contingent fees," when those services involve the offering of expert testimony to a court or administrative body or when they call upon the psychologist to make affirmations or representations intended to be relied on by third parties.
C. Forensic psychologists who derive a substantial portion of their income from fee-for-service arrangements should offer some portion of their professional services on a *pro bono* or reduced fee basis where the public interest or the welfare of clients may be inhibited by insufficient financial resources.

IV. Relationships

D. Forensic psychologists recognize potential conflicts of interest in dual relationships with parties to a legal proceeding, and they seek to minimize their effects.

1. Forensic psychologists avoid providing professional services to parties in a legal proceeding with whom they have personal or professional relationships that are inconsistent with the anticipated relationship.
2. When it is necessary to provide both evaluation and treatment services to a party in a legal proceeding (as may be the case in small forensic hospital settings or small communities), the forensic psychologist takes reasonable steps to minimize the potential negative effects of these circumstances on the rights of the party, confidentiality, and the process of treatment and evaluation.

E. Forensic psychologists have an obligation to ensure that prospective clients are informed of their legal rights with respect to the anticipated forensic service, of the purposes of any evaluation, of the nature of procedures to be employed, of the intended uses of any product of their services, and of the party who has employed the forensic psychologist.

1. Unless court ordered, forensic psychologists obtain the informed consent of the client or party, or their legal representative, before proceeding with such evaluations and procedures. If the client appears unwilling to proceed after receiving a thorough notification of the purposes, methods, and intended uses of the forensic evaluation, the evaluation should be postponed and the psychologist should take steps to place the client in contact with his/her attorney for the purpose of legal advice on the issue of participation.
2. In situations where the client or party may not have the capacity to provide informed consent to services or the evaluation is pursuant to court order, the forensic psychologist provides reasonable notice to the client's legal representative of the nature of the anticipated forensic service before proceeding. If the client's legal representative objects to the evaluation, the forensic psychologist notifies the court issuing the order and responds as directed.
3. After a psychologist has advised the subject of a clinical forensic evaluation of the intended uses of the evaluation and its work product, the psychologist may not use the evaluation work product for other purposes without explicit waiver to do so by the client or by the client's legal representative.

F. When forensic psychologists engage in research or scholarly activities that are compensated financially by a client or party to a legal proceeding, or when the psychologist provides those services on a *pro bono* basis, the psychologist clarifies any anticipated further use of such research or scholarly product, discloses the psychologist's role in the resulting research or scholarly products, and obtains whatever consent or agreement is required by law or professional standards.

G. When conflicts arise between the forensic psychologist's professional standards and the requirements of legal standards, a particular court, or a directive by an officer of the court or legal authorities, the forensic psychologist has an obligation to make those legal authorities aware of the source of the conflict and to take reasonable steps to resolve it. Such steps may include, but are not limited to, obtaining the consultation of fellow forensic professionals, obtaining the advice of independent counsel, and conferring directly with the legal representatives involved.

V. Confidentiality and Privilege

A. Forensic psychologists have an obligation to be aware of the legal standards that may affect or limit the confidentiality or privilege that may attach to their services or their products, and they conduct their professional activities in a manner that respects those known rights and privileges.

   1. Forensic psychologists establish and maintain a system of record keeping and professional communication that safeguards a client's privilege.
   2. Forensic psychologists maintain active control over records and information. They only release information pursuant to statutory requirements, court order, or the consent of the client.

B. Forensic psychologists inform their clients of the limitations to the confidentiality of their services and their products (see also Guideline IV E) by providing them with an understandable statement of their rights, privileges, and the limitations of confidentiality.
C. In situations where the right of the client or party to confidentiality is limited, the forensic psychologist makes every effort to maintain confidentiality with regard to any information that does not bear directly upon the legal purpose of the evaluation.
D. Forensic psychologists provide clients or their authorized legal representatives with access to the information in their records and a meaningful explanation of that information, consistent with existing Federal and state statutes, the *Ethical Principles of Psychologists*, the *Standards for Educational and Psychological Testing*, and institutional rules and regulations.

VI. Methods and Procedures

A. Because of their special status as persons qualified as experts to the court, forensic psychologists have an obligation to maintain current knowledge of scientific, professional, and legal developments within their area of claimed competence. They are obligated also to use that knowledge, consistent with accepted clinical and scientific standards, in selecting data collection methods and procedures for an evaluation, treatment, consultation, or scholarly/empirical investigation.

VI. Methods and Procedures 281

B. Forensic psychologists have an obligation to document and be prepared to make available, subject to court order or the rules of evidence, all data that form the basis for their evidence or services. The standard to be applied to such documentation or recording *anticipates* that the detail and quality of such documentation will be subject to reasonable judicial scrutiny; this standard is higher than the normative standard for general clinical practice. When forensic psychologists conduct an examination or engage in the treatment of a party to a legal proceeding, with foreknowledge that their professional services will be used in an adjudicative forum, they incur a special responsibility to provide the best documentation possible under the circumstances.

1. Documentation of the data upon which one's evidence is based is subject to the normal rules of discovery, disclosure, confidentiality, and privilege that operate in the jurisdiction in which the data were obtained. Forensic psychologists have an obligation to be aware of those rules and to regulate their conduct in accordance with them.
2. The duties and obligations of forensic psychologists with respect to documentation of data that form the basis for their evidence apply from the moment they know or have a reasonable basis for knowing that their data and evidence derived from it are likely to enter into legally relevant decisions.

C. In providing forensic psychological services, forensic psychologists take special care to avoid undue influence upon their methods, procedures, and products, such as might emanate from the party to a legal proceeding by financial compensation or other gains. As an expert conducting an evaluation, treatment, consultation, or scholarly/empirical investigation, the forensic psychologist maintains professional integrity by examining the issue at hand from all reasonable perspectives, actively seeking information that will differentially test plausible rival hypotheses.

D. Forensic psychologists do not provide professional forensic services to a defendant or to any party in, or in contemplation of, a legal proceeding prior to that individual's representation by counsel, except for persons judicially determined, where appropriate, to be handling their representation pro se. When the forensic services are pursuant to court order and the client is not represented by counsel, the forensic psychologist makes reasonable efforts to inform the court prior to providing the services.

1. A forensic psychologist may provide emergency mental health services to a pretrial defendant prior to court order or the appointment of counsel where there are reasonable grounds to believe that such emergency services are needed for the protection and improvement of the defendant's mental health and where failure to provide such mental health services would constitute a substantial risk of imminent harm to the defendant or to others. In providing such services, the forensic

psychologist nevertheless seeks to inform the defendant's counsel in a manner consistent with the requirements of the emergency situation.
    2. Forensic psychologists who provide such emergency mental health services should attempt to avoid providing further professional forensic services to that defendant unless that relationship is reasonably unavoidable [see IV(D)(2)].
E. When forensic psychologists seek data from third parties, prior records, or other sources, they do so only with the prior approval of the relevant legal party or as a consequence of an order of a court to conduct the forensic evaluation.
F. Forensic psychologists are aware that hearsay exceptions and other rules governing expert testimony place a special ethical burden upon them. When hearsay or otherwise inadmissible evidence forms the basis of their opinion, evidence, or professional product, they seek to minimize sole reliance upon such evidence. Where circumstances reasonably permit, forensic psychologists seek to obtain independent and personal verification of data relied upon as part of their professional services to the court or to a party to a legal proceeding.
    1. While many forms of data used by forensic psychologists are hearsay, forensic psychologists attempt to corroborate critical data that form the basis for their professional product. When using hearsay data that have not been corroborated, but are nevertheless utilized, forensic psychologists have an affirmative responsibility to acknowledge the uncorroborated status of those data and the reasons for relying upon such data.
    2. With respect to evidence of any type, forensic psychologists avoid offering information from their investigations or evaluations that does not bear directly upon the legal purpose of their professional services and that is not critical as support for their product, evidence, or testimony, *except where such disclosure is required by law.*
    3. When a forensic psychologist relies upon data or information gathered by others, the origins of those data are clarified in any professional product. In addition, the forensic psychologist bears a special responsibility to ensure that such data, if relied upon, were gathered in a manner standard for the profession.
G. Unless otherwise stipulated by the parties, forensic psychologists are aware that no statements made by a defendant, in the course of any (forensic) examination, no testimony by the expert based on such statements, nor any other fruits of the statements can be admitted into evidence against the defendant in any criminal proceeding, except on an issue respecting mental condition on which the defendant has introduced testimony. Forensic psychologists have an affirmative duty to ensure that their written products and oral testimony conform to this Federal Rule of Procedure (12.2 [c]) or its state equivalent.
    1. Because forensic psychologists are often not in a position to know what evidence, documentation, or element of a written product may be or may

lend to a "fruit of the statement," they exercise extreme caution in preparing reports or offering testimony prior to the defendant's assertion of a mental state claim or the defendant's introduction of testimony regarding a mental condition. Consistent with the reporting requirements of state or federal law, forensic psychologists avoid including statements from the defendant relating to the time period of the alleged offense.
2. Once a defendant has proceeded to the trial stage and all pretrial mental health issues such as competency have been resolved, forensic psychologists may include in their reports or testimony any statements made by the defendant that are directly relevant to supporting their expert evidence, provided that the defendant has "introduced" mental state evidence or testimony within the meaning of Federal Rule of Procedure 12.2(c) or its state equivalent.

H. Forensic psychologists avoid giving written or oral evidence about the psychological characteristics of particular individuals when they have not had an opportunity to conduct an examination of the individual adequate to the scope of the statements, opinions, or conclusions to be issued. Forensic psychologists make every reasonable effort to conduct such examinations. When it is not possible or feasible to do so, they make clear the impact of such limitations on the reliability and validity of their professional products, evidence, or testimony.

VII. Public and Professional Communications

A. Forensic psychologists make reasonable efforts to ensure that the products of their services, as well as their own public statements and professional testimony, are communicated in ways that will promote understanding and avoid deception, given the particular characteristics, roles, and abilities of various recipients of the communications.
   1. Forensic psychologists take reasonable steps to correct misuse or misrepresentation of their professional products, evidence, and testimony.
   2. Forensic psychologists provide information about professional work to clients in a manner consistent with professional and legal standards for the disclosure of test results, interpretations of data, and the factual bases for conclusions. A full explanation of the results of tests and the bases for conclusions should be given in language that the client can understand.
      a. When disclosing information about a client to third parties who are not qualified to interpret test results and data, the forensic psychologist complies with Principle 16 of the *Standards for Educational and*

Psychological Testing. When required to disclose results to a nonpsychologist, every attempt is made to ensure that test security is maintained and access to information is restricted to individuals with a legitimate and professional interest in the data. Other qualified mental health professionals who make a request for information pursuant to a lawful order are, by definition, "individuals with a legitimate and professional interest."
   b. In providing records and raw data, the forensic psychologist takes reasonable steps to ensure that the receiving party is informed that raw scores must be interpreted by a qualified professional in order to provide reliable and valid information.

B. Forensic psychologists realize that their public role as "expert to the court" or as "expert representing the profession" confers upon them a special responsibility for fairness and accuracy in their public statements. When evaluating or commenting on the professional work product or qualifications of another expert or party to a legal proceeding, forensic psychologists represent their professional disagreements with reference to a fair and accurate evaluation of the data, theories, standards, and opinions of the other expert or party.

C. Ordinarily, forensic psychologists avoid making detailed public (out-of-court) statements about particular legal proceedings in which they have been involved. When there is a strong justification to do so, such public statements are designed to assure accurate representation of their role or their evidence, not to advocate the positions of parties in the legal proceeding. Forensic psychologists address particular legal proceedings in publications or communications only to the extent that the information relied upon is part of a public record, or consent for that use has been properly obtained from the party holding any privilege.

D. When testifying, forensic psychologists have an obligation to all parties to a legal proceeding to present their findings, conclusions, evidence, or other professional products in a fair manner. This principle does not preclude forceful representation of the data and reasoning upon which a conclusion or professional product is based. It does, however, preclude an attempt, whether active or passive, to engage in partisan distortion or misrepresentation. Forensic psychologists do not, by either commission or omission, participate in a misrepresentation of their evidence, nor do they participate in partisan attempts to avoid, deny, or subvert the presentation of evidence contrary to their own position.

E. Forensic psychologists, by virtue of their competence and rules of discovery, actively disclose all sources of information obtained in the course of their professional services; they actively disclose which information from which source was used in formulating a particular written product or oral testimony.

VII. Public and Professional Communications

F. Forensic psychologists are aware that their essential role as expert to the court is to assist the trier of fact to understand the evidence or to determine a fact in issue. In offering expert evidence, they are aware that their own professional observations, inferences, and conclusions must be distinguished from legal facts, opinions, and conclusions. Forensic psychologists are prepared to explain the relationship between their expert testimony and the legal issues and facts of an instant case.

Appendix C
The Disability Report

The following information should be included in all types of mental health disability reports, unless otherwise specified by the referral source.

1. *Identifying information*: This includes the evaluee's name, date of birth, and, if relevant, last day worked and date of claim.
2. *Referral source*: Should specify whether the referral for evaluation was made directly from an employer, insurance company, attorney, or was requested by the evaluee, or if the referral was made through a medical benefits or claims management company.
3. *Referral issues*: List the specific referral questions. If none have been provided, discuss evaluating clinician's understanding of the general issue under evaluation.
4. *Identify report limitations*: Provide any data that may limit the usefulness or validity of the reported findings. This might include factors such as the necessity of conducting the examination through an interpreter, the failure of the evaluee to cooperate with the examination, or the fact that the opinions are based on a record review alone, without the benefit of an examination of the evaluee.
5. *Informed consent*: Evaluators should document that the evaluee understood the reason for the evaluation, the absence of a treatment relationship, the nonconfidential nature of the evaluation, and the evaluee's agreement to proceed with the evaluation after being informed of these conditions.
6. *Sources of information*:
    a. all records and other materials reviewed;
    b. dates and duration of interviews of the evaluee;
    c. collateral interviews (may include dates, amount of time, type of interview [telephone, in person]);
    d. assessment of the reliability of sources of information if relevant or significant; and
    e. any psychological tests utilized.

7. *Review of records*: Evaluators should document all relevant findings, including the results of any psychological testing, indicating which records provided the information. This can be combined with listing the sources of information as per item six above.
8. *History of the events or psychiatric disorder that have precipitated the evaluation*:
    a. onset and course of current symptoms;
    b. review of systems;
    c. claimed or observed impairments;
    d. current occupational status and relationship to impairments, if any; and
    e. workplace dynamics, that is, workplace factors that may be increasing stress or causing dissatisfaction, such as conflicts with supervisors, layoffs, decreased remuneration or benefits, perception of unfair treatment.
9. *Employment history and history of workplace functioning*:
    a. job history including promotions, demotions, firings, layoffs, reasons for leaving a job;
    b. history of any previous episodes of decreased work capacity and relationship, if any, to psychiatric illness;
    c. description of any gaps in employment, periods of umemployment, their duration and reasons for these, such as medical illness, family-related leave, work incapacity;
    d. history of complaints or grievances filed by or against the evaluee, including workers' compensation claims for work-related illnesses and injuries, any previous public or private disability insurance claims, and/or employment-related litigation.
10. *Psychiatric and mental health treatment history*.
11. *Medical history and current medications* including relevant physical examination findings obtained from medical records, if any, and relevant imaging, diagnostic or other test findings.
12. *Other relevant history*
    a. social history, including history of family of origin, significant relationships, marital history, current social situation, living arrangements, financial status, and legal status;
    b. academic history, including highest level of education attained;
    c. military history;
    d. history of substance use;
    e. history of trauma;
    f. family history;
    g. legal history; and
    h. criminal history.
13. *Mental status examination*.

Appendix C The Disability Report

14. *Conclusion: discussion and case formulation*: Mental health professionals should consider beginning the conclusion section of the disability report by providing their case formulation based on the work capacity/work demand model of disability development discussed in Chapter 5. A short discussion of the case formulation offers the evaluator the opportunity to succinctly present the salient issues of impairment and disability, factors significant in the evaluee's claim and presentation, and describes the evaluator's findings regarding pattern of development of disability. A description of one of the models of disability described in Chapter 5 and how it is relevant to the circumstances of the specific case is often informative and, as discussed previously, should naturally suggest discussion of the questions most commonly referred for evaluation.
15. *Opinions*: see Chapter 6 – General Guidelines for discussion of provision of opinions.

References

Adler, D. A., McLaughlin, T. J., Rogers, W. H., Chong, H., Lerner, D., & Lapitsky, L. (2006). Job performance deficits due to depression. *American Journal of Psychiatry, 163*, 1569–1576.
Allbright, A. (2005). 2004 employment decisions under the ADA: Title I survey update. *Mental and Physical Disability Law Reporter, 29*, 503–656.
Allbright, A. (2006). Employment decisions under the ADA Title I – survey update. *Mental and Physical Disability Law Reporter, 30*, 492–494.
Allbright, A. (2007). 2006 employment decisions under the ADA: Title I survey update. *Mental and Physical Disability Law Reporter, 31*, 328–330.
Allbright, A. (2008). 2007 employment decisions under the ADA: Title I survey update. *Mental and Physical Disability Law Reporter, 32*, 335–338.
Allnutt, S. H., & Chaplow D. (2000). General principles of forensic report writing. *Australian and New Zealand Journal of Psychiatry, 34*, 980–987.
Altshuler, L., Tekell, J., Biswas, K., Kilbourne, A. M., Evans, D., Tang, D., et al. (2007). Executive function and employment status among veterans with Bipolar Disorder. *Psychiatric Services, 58*, 1441–1447.
American Academy of Psychiatry and the Law: Ethical Guidelines for the Practice of Forensic Psychiatry. (2005). Retrieved November 29, 2008, from American Association of Psychiatry and the Law Website: http://aapl.org/ethics.htm (see Appendix A).
American Bar Association, Labor and Employment Law Section. Retrieved from http://www.abanet.org/labor/home.html, accessed on December 11, 2008
American Medical Association. (2001). *Guides to the Evaluation of Permanent Impairment* (5th ed.). Chicago: AMA Press.
American Medical Association. (2006). Code of medical ethics and current opinions. Retrieved January 15, 2006, from http://www.ama-assn.org
American Medical Association. (2006). Opinions on ethics, E-10.03 Patient-physician relationship in the context of work-related and independent medical examinations. Retrieved January 15, 2006, from http://www.ama-assn.org
American Medical Association. (2006). Opinions on ethics, E-5.09 Confidentiality: Industry-employed physicians and independent medical examiners. Retrieved January 15, 2006, from http://www.ama-assn.org
American Medical Association. (2006). Opinions on ethics, E-9.07 Medical testimony. Retrieved January 15, 2006, from http://www.ama-assn.org
American Medical Association. (2006). Opinions on ethics, H-265.992 Expert witness testimony. Retrieved January 15, 2006, from http://www.ama-assn.org
American Medical Association. (2008). *Guides to the Evaluation of Permanent Impairment* (6th ed.). Chicago: AMA Press.
American Psychiatric Association. (2000). *The Diagnostic and Statistical Manual* (4th ed., Text Rev.). Washington, DC: American Psychiatric Association.

American Psychiatric Association. (2006). *Practice Guideline for the Psychiatric Evaluation of Adults* (2nd ed.). Arlington, VA: American Psychiatric Association.
American Psychiatric Association. (2008). *The principles of medical ethics with annotations especially applicable to psychiatry*. Arlington, VA: American Psychiatric Association.
American Psychological Association. (2002). *Ethical principles of psychologists and code of conduct*. Retrieved December 4, 2007, from American Psychological Association Website: http://www.apa.org/ethics/code2002.pdf
American Psychological Association. (2005). Determination and documentation of the need for practice guidelines. *American Psychologist, 60*, 976–978.
American Psychology-Law Society. (2008). *Specialty guidelines for forensic psychology* (fourth draft). Retrieved November 9, 2008, from Committee on the Revision of the Specialty Guidelines for Forensic Psychology Website: http://ap-ls.org/links/92908sgfp.pdf
Anderson, K. E., & Savage, C. R. (2004). Cognitive and neurobiological findings in obsessive-compulsive disorder. *Psychiatric Clinics of North America, 27*, 37–47.
Anfang, S. A., Faulkner, L. R., Fromson, J. A., & Gendel, M. H. (2005). American Psychiatric Association resource document on guidelines for psychiatric fitness-for-duty evaluations of physicians. *Journal of the American Academy of Psychiatry and the Law, 33*, 85–88.
Anfang, S. A., & Wall, B. W. (2006). Psychiatric fitness-for-duty evaluations. *Psychiatric Clinics of North America, 29*, 675–693.
Appleman, J. A. (2007). *Appleman on insurance*. San Francisco: LexisNexis Mattew Bender.
Appelbaum, P. S. (1990). The parable of the forensic psychiatrist: Ethics and the problem of doing harm. *International Journal of Law and Psychiatry,13*, 249–259.
Appelbaum, P. S. (1997). Ethics in evolution: The incompatibility of clinical and forensic functions. *American Journal of Psychiatry, 154*, 445–446.
Appelbaum, P. S., & Gutheil, T. G. (2006). *Clinical Handbook of Psychiatry and the Law* (4th ed.). Philadelphia: Lippincott Williams & Wilkins.
Axelrod, S. D. (1999). *Work and the Evolving Self: Theoretical and Clinical Considerations*. Hillsdale, NJ: The Analytic Press, Inc.
AviationSafetyNetwork. (1982). Accident description. Retrieved 11/18/08 from Aviation SafetyNetwork Website, http://aviation-safety.net/database/record.php?id = 19820209-0
Barling, J., & Griffiths, A. (2003). A history of occupational health psychology. In J. R. Quick & L. E. Tetrick (Eds.), *Handbook of Occupational Health Psychology* (pp. 19–33). Washington, DC: American Psychological Association.
Barnett, R. C., Marshall, N. L., & Singer, J. D. (1992). Job experiences over time, multiple roles, and women's mental health: A longitudinal study. *Journal of Personality and Social Psychology, 62*, 634–644.
Barnett, R. C., & Shen, Y. C. (1997). Gender, high- and low-schedule-control housework tasks, and psychological distress: A study of dual-earner couples. *Journal of Family Issues, 18*, 403–428.
Battista, M. E. (1988). Assessing work capacity. *Journal of Insurance Medicine, 20*(3), 16–22.
Baum, K. (2005). Independent medical examinations: An expanding source of physician liability. *Annals of Internal Medicine, 142*, 974–978.
Bazelon Center for Mental Health. *Limitations on work activities*. Retrieved August 19, 2008, from Bazelon Center for Mental Health Law Website: http://www.bazelon.org/issues/disabilityrights/resources/lmtslist.htm
Beiser, M., Bean, G., Erickson, D., Zhang, J., Iacono, W. G., & Rector, N. A. (1994). Biological and psychosocial predictors of job performance following a first episode of psychosis. *American Journal of Psychiatry, 151*, 857–863.
Bell, C. G. (1997). The Americans with Disabilities Act, mental disability, and work. In R. J. Bonnie & J. Monahan (Eds.), *Mental Disorder, Work Disability, and the Law* (pp. 203–219). Chicago: The University of Chicago Press.

References

Bennett, J. B., Cook, R. F., & Pelletier, K. R. (2003). Toward an integrated framework for comprehensive organizational wellness: Concepts, practices and research in workplace health promotion. In J. R. Quick & L. E. Tetrick (Eds.), *Handbook of Occupational Health Psychology* (pp. 69–95). Washington, DC: American Psychological Association.

Berndt, E. R., Finkelstein, S. N., Greenberg, P. E., Howland, R. H., Keith, R., Russell, A. J., et al. (1998). Workplace performance effects from chronic depression and its treatment. *Journal of Health Economics, 17*, 511–535.

Bersoff, D. N. (1995). *Ethical Conflicts in Psychology.* Washington, DC: American Psychological Association.

Biederman, J., Mich, E., Fried, R., Aleardi, M., Potter, A., & Herzig, K. (2005). A simulated workplace experience for nonmedicated adults with and without ADHD. *Psychiatric Services, 56*, 1617–1620.

Binder, R. (2002). Liability for the psychiatrist expert witness. *American Journal of Psychiatry, 159*, 1819–1825.

Blanck, P. D. (1995). Assessing five years of employment integration and economic opportunity under the Americans with Disabilities Act. *Mental and Physical Disability Law Reporter, 19*, 384–393.

Blanck, P. D., & Marti, M. W. (1997). Attitudes, behavior, and the employment provisions of the Americans with Disabilities Act. *Villanova Law Review, 42*, 345.

Boardman, J., Grove, B., Perkins, R., & Shepherd, G. (2003). Work and employment for people with psychiatric disabilities. *British Journal of Psychiatry, 182*, 467–468.

Bonnie, R. J. (1997a). Mental disorder and labor force participation: An epidemiological perspective. In R. J. Bonnie & J. Monahan (Eds.), *Mental Disorder, Work Disability, and the Law* (pp. 11–12). Chicago: The University of Chicago Press.

Bonnie, R. J. (1997b). Work disability and the fabric of mental health law: An introduction. In R. J. Bonnie & J. Monahan (Eds.), *Mental Disorder, Work Disability, and the Law* (pp. 1–10). Chicago: The University of Chicago Press.

Bonnie, R. J. (1997c). To work or not to work: The constrained choices of persons with serious mental disorders. In R. J. Bonnie & J. Monahan (Eds.), *Mental Disorder, Work Disability, and the Law* (pp. 53–54). Chicago: The University of Chicago Press.

Bonnie, R. J. (1997d). Mental disorder and employment under the Americans with Disability Act. In R. J. Bonnie & J. Monahan (Eds.), *Mental Disorder, Work Disability, and the Law* (pp. 199–202). Chicago: The University of Chicago Press.

Bono, J. E., & Judge, T. A. (2001). Relationship of core self-evaluations traits -self-esteem, generalized self-efficacy, locus of control and emotional stability – with job satisfaction and job performance: A meta-analysis. *Journal of Applied Psychology, 86*, 80–92.

Book, H. E. (2003). How leadership and organizational structure can create a winning corporate culture. In J. P. Kahn & A. M. Langlieb (Eds.), *Mental Health and Productivity in the Workplace: A Handbook for Organizations and Clinicians* (pp. 205–232). San Francisco: John Wiley & Sons.

Borum, R., Otto, R., & Golding, S. (1993). Improving clinical judgment and decision making in forensic evaluations. *Journal of Psychiatry and Law, 21*, 35–76.

Braden, J. B., Zhang, L., Zimmerman, F. J., & Sullivan, M. D. (2008). Employment outcomes of persons with a mental disorder and comorbid chronic pain. *Psychiatric Services, 59*, 878–885.

Brent, N. J. (2002). Protecting physicians' rights in disciplinary actions by a medical board: A brief primer. *Medical Practice Management, 18*, 97–100.

Broadhead, W. E., Blazer, D. G., George, K. L., & Tse, C. K. (1990). Depression, disability days, and days lost from work in a prospective epidemiologic survey. *Journal of the American Medical Association, 264*, 2524–2528.

Brod, M. B., Perwien, A., Adler, L., Spencer, T., & Johnston, J. (2005). Conceptualization and assessment of quality of life for adults with Attention Deficit/Disorder. *Primary Psychiatry, 12*, 58–64.

Brodsky, C. M. (1984). Long-term work stress. *Psychosomatics, 24*, 361–368.
Brodsky, C. M. (1987a). Factors influencing work-related disability. In A. T. Meyerson & T. Fine (Eds.), *Psychiatric Disability: Clinical, Legal, and Administrative Dimensions* (pp. 49–65). Washington, DC: American Psychiatric Press, Inc.
Brodsky, C. M. (1987b). The psychiatric evaluation in workers' compensation. In A. T. Meyerson & T. Fine (Eds.), *Psychiatric Disability: Clinical, Legal, and Administrative Dimensions* (pp. 313–332). Washington, DC: American Psychiatric Press, Inc.
Brodsky, C. M. (1990). A psychiatrist's reflections on the workers' compensation system. *Behavioral Sciences and the Law, 8*, 331–348.
Brodsky, C. (1996a). Psychiatric aspects of fitness for duty. *Occupational Medicine, 11*, 719–726.
Brodsky, C. M. (1996b). The psychiatry of work. *Occupational Medicine, 11*, 685–698.
Brown, A., Kitchell, M., O'Neill, T., Lockliear, J., Vosler, A., Kubek, D., et al. (2001). Identifying meaning and perceived level of satisfaction within the context of work. *Work, 16*, 219–226.
Burton, W. N., Pransky, G., Conti, D. J., Chen, C. Y., & Edington, D. (2004). The association of medical conditions and presenteeism. *Journal of Occupational and Environmental Medicine, 46*, S38–S45.
Bush, S. S., Connell, M. A., & Denney, R. L. (2006). *Ethical Practice in Forensic Psychology: A Systematic Model for Decision Making*. Washington, DC: American Psychological Association.
Campbell, J., & Kaufmann, C. L. (1997). Equality and difference in the ADA. In R. J. Bonnie & J. Monahan (Eds.), *Mental Disorder, Work Disability and the Law* (pp. 221–239). Chicago: The University of Chicago Press.
Candilis, P. J., Weinstock, R., & Martinez, R. (2007). *Forensic ethics and the expert witness*. New York: Springer.
Cather, C., Mueser, K. T., & Goff, D. C. (2003). Psychosis: peculiar behaviors and inflexible bizarre beliefs. In J. P. Kahn & A. M. Langlieb (Eds.), *Mental Health and Productivity in the Workplace: A Handbook for Organizations and Clinicians* (pp. 517–539). San Francisco: John Wiley & Sons.
Centers for Disease Control and Prevention. *National health interview survey on disability (NHIS-D)*. Retrieved May 27, 2007, from http://www.cdc.gov
Charney, D. A., & Russell, R.C. (1994). An overview of sexual harassment. *The American Journal of Psychiatry, 15*, 10–17.
Cheng, Y., Kawachi, I., Coakley, E. H., Schwartz, J., & Colditz, G. (2000). Association between psychosocial work characteristics and health functioning in American women. Prospective study. *British Medical Journal, 320*, 1432–1436.
Chestang, L. W. (1982). Work, personal change and human development. In S. H. Akabas & P. A. Kurzman (Eds.), *Work, Workers, and Work Organizations: A View from Social Work* (pp. 61–89). Englewood Cliffs, NJ: Prentice-Hall Inc.
Claxton, A. M., Chawla, A. J., & Kennedy, S. (1999). Absenteeism among employees treated for depression. *Journal of Occupational and Environmental Medicine, 41*, 605–611.
Clemens, N. A. (2001). Psychotherapy and the workplace. *Journal of Psychiatric Practice, 7*, 273–275.
Cohen, M. J., & Hanbury, R. F. (1987). Psychiatric disability and substance use disorders. In A. T. Meyerson & T. Fine (Eds.), *Psychiatric Disability: Clinical, Legal and Administrative Dimensions* (pp. 83–117). Washington, DC: American Psychiatric Press, Inc.
Cohen, S., Janicki-Deverts, D., & Miller, G. E. (2007). Psychological stress and disease. *Journal of the American Medical Association, 298*, 1685–1687.
Comino, E. J., Harris, E., Chey, T., Manicavasagar, V., Wall, J. P., Davies, G. P., et al. (2003). Relationship between mental health disorders and unemployment status in Australian adults. *Australian and New Zealand Journal of Psychiatry, 37*, 230–235.
Committee on Ethical Guidelines for Forensic Psychologists. (1991). Specialty guidelines for forensic psychologists. *Law and Human Behavior, 15*, 655–665 (See Appendix B).

References

Committee on Psychiatry in Industry, Group for the Advancement of Psychiatry. (1994). *Introduction to Occupational Psychiatry.* Washington, DC: American Psychiatric Press.

Compton, W. M., Thomas, Y. G., Stinson, F. S., & Grant, B. F. (2007). Prevalence, correlates, disability, and comorbidity of DSM-IV drug abuse and dependence in the United States: Results from the National Epidemiologic Survey on alcohol and related conditions. *Archives of General Psychiatry, 64*, 566–576.

Coovert, M. D., & Thompson, L. F. (2003). Technology and workplace health. In J. R. Quick & L. E. Tetrick (Eds.), *Handbook of Occupational Health Psychology* (pp. 221–241). Washington, DC: American Psychological Association.

Cornell University. Disability Statistics. Retrieved August 12, 2007, from Cornell University Disability Statistics Online Resource for U.S. Disability Statistics Website, http://www.ilr.cornell.edu/edi/DisabilityStatistics/

Corrigan, P. W., Meuser, K. T., Bond, G. R., Drake, R. E., & Solomon, P. (2007). *Principles and Practice of Psychiatric Rehabilitation: An Empirical Approach.* New York: Guilford Press.

Crawford, M. & Unger, R. (2004), *Women and Gender: A Feminist Psychology* (4th ed.). New York: McGraw Hill.

Creighton, M. K. (2001). Mental disabilities under the Americans with Disabilities Act. In *Mental and Emotional Injuries in Employment Litigation* (2nd ed., pp. 659–776). Washington, DC: The Bureau of National Affairs, Inc.

Danner, D., & Sagall, E. L. (1977). Medicolegal causation: A source of professional misunderstanding. *American Journal of Law and Medicine, 3*, 303–308.

Dew, M. A., Bromet, E. J., & Penkower, L. (1992). Mental health effects of job loss in women. *Psychological Medicine, 22*, 751–764.

Dewa, C. S., Goering, P., Lin, E., & Paterson, M. (2002). Depression-related short-term disability in unemployed population. *Journal of Occupational and Environmental Medicine, 44*, 628–633.

Dewa, C. S., Lin, E., Kooehoorn, M., & Goldner, E. (2007). Association of chronic work stress, psychiatric disorders, and chronic physical conditions with disability among workers. *Psychiatric Services, 58*, 652–658.

Diamond, B. L. (1959). The fallacy of the impartial expert. *Archives of Criminal Psychodynamics, 3*, 221–236.

Dickerson, F. B., Boronow, J. J., Stallings, C. R., Origoni, A. E., Cole, S., & Yoken, R. H. (2004). Association between cognitive functioning and employment status of persons with Bipolar Disorder. *Psychiatric Services, 55*, 54–58.

Dixon, T., Kravariti, E., Frith, C., Murray, R. M., & McGuire, P. K. (2004). Effect of symptoms on executive function in bipolar illness. *Psychological Medicine, 34*, 811–821.

Dooley, D. (2003). Unemployment, underemployment, and mental health: Conceptualizing employment status as a continuum. *American Journal of Community Psychology, 32*, 9–19.

Dooley, D., & Catalano, R. (2003). Introduction to underemployment and its social costs. *American Journal of Community Psychology, 32*, 1–7.

Drukteinis, A. M. (1997). Personnel issues in worker's compensation claims. *American Journal of Forensic Psychiatry, 18*, 3–23.

Drukteinis, A. M. (2004). Disability. In R. I. Simon & L. H. Gold (Eds.), *The American Psychiatric Publishing Textbook of Forensic Psychiatry* (pp. 287–302). Washington, DC: American Psychiatry Publishing, Inc.

Druss, B. G., Marcus, S. C., Rosenheck, R. A., Olfson, M., Tanielan, T., & Pincus, H. A. (2000). Understanding disability in mental and general medical conditions. *American Journal of Psychiatry, 157*, 1485–1491.

Druss, B. G., Schlesinger, M., & Allen, H. M., Jr. (2001). Depressive symptoms, satisfaction with healthcare, and 2-year work out-comes in an employed population. *American Journal of Psychiatry, 158*, 731–734.

Dubovsky, S. L., Davies, R., & Dubovsky, A. N. (2003). Mood disorders. In R. E. Hales & S. C. Yudofsky (Eds.), *The American Psychiatric Publishing Textbook of Clinical Psychiatry* (pp. 439–542). Washington, DC: American Psychiatric Publishing Inc.

Eddy, S., & Schouten, R. (2003). Workplace forensic psychiatry: The Americans with disabilities act and the family and medical leave act. In J. P. Kahn & A. M. Langlieb (Eds.), *Mental Health and Productivity in the Workplace: A Handbook for Organizations and Clinicians* (pp. 369–385). San Francisco: John Wiley & Sons.

EEOC. (1997). Enforcement guidance: The Americans with Disabilities Act and Psychiatric Disabilities. Retrieved December 9, 2008, from EEOC Website: http://www.eeoc.gov/policy/docs/psych.html

El-Guebaly, N., Currie, S., Williams, J., Wang, J., Beck, C. A., Maxwell, C., et al. (2007). Association of mood, anxiety, and substance use disorders with occupational status and disability in a community sample. *Psychiatric Services, 58,* 659–667.

Elinson, L., Houck, P., Marchus, S. C., & Pincus, H. A. (2004). Depression and the ability to work. *Psychiatric Services, 55,* 29–34.

Elovainio, M., Steen, N., Kivimaki, M., & Kalliomaki-Levanto, T. (2000). Organizational and individual factors affecting mental health and job satisfaction: A multilevel analysis of job control and personality. *Journal of Occupational Health Psychology, 5,* 269–277.

Enelow, A. J. (1987). *The evaluation of permanent psychiatric disability: A report to the medical advisory committee of the California division of industrial accidents.* San Francisco: California Department of Industrial Relations, Division of Industrial Accidents – Workers' Compensation Appeals Board.

Enelow, A. J. (1988). Assessing the effect of psychiatric disorders on work function. *Journal of Occupational Medicine, 3,* 621–627.

Estroff, S. E., Zimmer, C., Lachicotte, W. S., Benoit, J., & Patrick, D. L. (1997). "No other way to go": Pathways to disability income application among persons with severe persistent mental illness. In R. J. Bonnie & J. Monahan (Eds.), *Mental Disorder, Work Disability and the Law* (pp. 55–104). Chicago: The University of Chicago Press.

Farager, E. B., Cass, M., & Cooper, C. (2005). The relationship between job satisfaction and health: a meta-analysis. *Occupational Environmental Medicine, 62,* 105–112.

Federation of State Medical Boards. (1996). Report on sexual boundary issues by the ad hoc committee on physician impairment. Retrieved March 15, 2006, from the Federation of State Medical Boards Website, http://www.fsmb.org/pdf/1996_grpol_sexual_boundary_issues.pdf

Federation of State Medical Boards. *Expert witness qualifications.* Retrieved December 20, 2007, from the Federation of State Medical Boards Website, http://www.fsmb.org/pdf/grpol_expertwitness.pdf

Fielden, S. L., & Cooper, C. L. (2002). Managerial stress: Are women more at risk? In D. L. Nelson & R. J. Burke (Eds.), *Gender, Work Stress and Health* (pp. 19–34). Washington, DC: American Psychological Association.

Fitzgerald, L. F., Drasgow, F., & Hulin, D. L. (1997). Antecedents and consequences of sexual harassment in organizations: A test of an integrated model. *Journal of Applied Psychology, 82,* 578–89.

Foote, W., & Shuman, D. W. (2006). Consent, disclosure, and waiver for the forensic psychological evaluation: Rethinking the roles of psychologist and lawyer. *Professional Psychology: Research and Practice, 37,* 437–445.

Frone, M. S. (2003). Work-family balance. In J. R. Quick & L. E. Tetrick (Eds.), *Handbook of Occupational Health Psychology* (pp. 143–161). Washington, DC: American Psychological Association.

Furnham, A. (1990). *The Protestant Work Ethic: The Psychology of Work-Related Beliefs and Behaviours.* London: Routledge.

Garner, B. A. (Ed.). (2004). *Black's Law Dictionary* (8th ed.). St. Paul, MN: West Group.

References

Gilbert, L. A., & Rader, J. (2001). Current perspectives on women's adult roles: Work, Family and Life. In R. K. Unger (Ed.), *Handbook of the psychology of women and gender* (pp. 156–169). New York: John Wiley & Sons.

Giorgi-Guarnieri, D., Janofsky, J., Keram, E., Lawsky, S., Merideth, P., Mossman, D., et al. (2002). Practice guideline: Forensic psychiatric evaluation of defendants raising the insanity defense. *Journal of the American Academy of Psychiatry and the Law, 30*, S3–S40.

Gold, L. H. (1998). Addressing bias in the forensic assessment of sexual harassment claims. *Journal of the American Academy of Psychiatry and Law, 26*, 563–578.

Gold, L. H. (2002). Psychiatric diagnoses and the retrospective assessment of mental status. In R. I. Simon & D.W. Shuman (Eds.), *Retrospective Assessment of Mental States in Litigation: Predicting the Past*. Washington, DC: American Psychiatric Publishing, Inc.

Gold, L. H. (2004). *Sexual Harassment: Psychiatric Assessment in Employment Litigation*. Washington, DC: American Psychiatric Publishing, Inc.

Gold, L. H., & Davidson, J. E. (2007). Do you understand your risk? Liability and third party evaluations in civil litigation. *Journal of the American Academy of Psychiatry and the Law, 35*, 200–210.

Gold, L. H., & Metzner, J. L. (2006). Psychiatric employment evaluations and the Health Insurance Portability and Accountability Act. *American Journal of Psychiatry, 163*, 1878–1882.

Gold, L. H., & Simon, R. I. (2001). Posttraumatic stress disorder in employment cases. In J. J. McDonald & F. B. Kulick (Eds.), *Mental and Emotional Injuries in Employment Litigation* (2nd ed., pp. 502–573). Washington, DC: The Bureau of National Affairs, Inc.

Gold, L. H., Anfang, S. A., Drukteinis, A. M., Metzner, J. L., Price, M., Wall, B. W., et al. (2008). AAPL Practice guideline for the forensic evaluation of psychiatric disability. *Journal of the American Academy of Psychiatry and the Law*, 36, S3–S50.

Goldberg, S. G., Killeen, M. B., & O'Day, B. (2005). The disclosure conundrum: How people with psychiatric disabilities navigate employment. *Psychology, Public Policy, and the Law, 11*, 463–500.

Goldman, H. H., Skodol, A. E., & Lave, T. R. (1992). Revising Axis V for DSM-IV. *American Journal of Psychiatry, 149*, 1148–1156.

Grant, R. L., & Robbins, D. B. (2003). Disability and workers' compensation. In J. P. Kahn & A. M. Langlieb (Eds.), *Mental Health and Productivity in the Workplace: A Handbook for Organizations and Clinicians* (pp. 347–368). San Francisco: John Wiley & Sons.

Greenberg, P. E., Kessler, R. C., Birnbaum, H. G., Leong, S. A., Lowe, S. W., Berglund, P. A., et al. (2003). The economic burden of depression in the United States: How did it change between 1990 and 2000. *Journal of Clinical Psychiatry, 64*, 1465–1475.

Greenberg, S. A., Shuman, D. W., Feldman, S. R., Middleton, C., & Ewing, C. P. (2007). Lessons for forensic practice drawn from the law of malpractice. In A. M. Goldstein (Ed.), *Forensic Psychology: Emerging Topics and Expanding Roles* (pp. 446–461). Hoboken NJ: Wiley.

Greenberg, S. A., Shuman, D. W., & Meyer, R. G. (2004). Unmasking forensic diagnosis. *International Journal of Law and Psychiatry, 27*, 1–15.

Greene, R. L. (2008). Malingering and defensiveness in the MMPI-2. In R. Rogers (Ed.), *Clinical Assessment of Malingering and Deception* (3rd ed., pp. 159–181). New York: The Guilford Press.

Greenglass, E. (2002). Work stress, coping, and social support: Implications for women's occupational wellbeing. In D. L. Nelson & R. J. Burke (Eds.), *Gender, Work Stress and Health* (pp. 85–96). Washington, DC: American psychological Association.

Group for the Advancement of Psychiatry. (1991). *The Mental Health Professional and the Legal System*. New York: Brunner.

Gutheil, T. G. (1998). *The Psychiatrist as Expert Witness*. Washington, DC: American Psychiatric Press, Inc.

Gutheil, T. G., & Simon, R. I. (1999). Attorneys' pressures on the expert witness: Early warning signs of endangered honesty, objectivity, and fair compensation. *Journal of the American Academy of Psychiatry Law, 27,* 546–553.

Hall, I. I. (1997). Making the ADA work for people with psychiatric disabilities. In R. J. Bonnie & J. Monahan (Eds.), *Mental Disorder, Work Disability and the Law* (pp. 241–280). Chicago: The University of Chicago Press.

Halleck, S. L., Hoge, S. K., & Miller, R. D. (1992). The use of psychiatric diagnoses in the legal process: Task force report of the American Psychiatric Association. *Bulletin of the American Academy of Psychiatry and the Law, 20,* 481–499.

Hand, L. (1915). Historical and practical considerations regarding expert testimony. *Harvard Law Review, 15,* 40–58

Harwood, H., Ameen, A., Denmead, G., Englert, E., Fountain, D., & Livermore, G. (2000). *The Economic Cost of Mental Illness.* Rockville, MD: National Institute of Mental Health.

Hays, R. D., Wells, K. B., Sherbourne, C. D., Rogers, W., & Spritzer, K. (1995). Functioning and well-being outcomes of patients with depression compared with chronic general medical illnesses. *Archives of General Psychiatry, 52,* 11–19.

Heilbrun, K., DeMatteo, D., Marczyk, G., & Goldstein, A. M. (2008). Standards of practice and care in forensic mental health assessment: Legal, professional and principles-based considerations. *Psychology, Public Policy and Law, 14,* 1–26.

Hilsenroth, M. J., Ackerman, S. J., Blagys, M. D., Baumann, B. D., Baity, M. R., Smith, S. R., Price, J. L., Smith, C. L., Heindselman, T. L., Mount, M. K., & Holdwick, D. J. (2000). Reliability and validity of DSM-IV axis V. *American Journal of Psychiatry, 157,* 1858–1863.

Hirt, E., McDonald, H., & Markman, K. (1998). Expectancy effects in reconstructive memory: When the past is just what we expected. In S. J. Lynn & K. M. McConkey (Eds.), *Truth in Memory* (pp. 62–89). New York: Guilford.

Hodson, C. (2001). *Psychology and Work.* New York: Taylor & Francis, Inc.

Hollander, E., & Simeon, D. (2003). Anxiety disorder. In R. E. Hales & S. C. Yudofsky (Eds.), *The American Psychiatric Publishing Textbook of Clinical Psychiatry* (pp. 543–630). Washington, DC: American Psychiatric Publishing Inc.

Hulin, C. (2002). Lessons from industrial and organizational psychology. In J. M. Brett & F. Drasgow (Eds.), *The Psychology of Work: Theoretically Based Empirical Research* (pp. 3–22). Mahwah, NJ: Lawrence Erlbaum Associates.

Iezzoni, L. I., & Freedman, V. A. (2008). Turning the disability tide: The importance of definitions. *Journal of the American Medical Association, 299*(3), 332–334.

Ilies, R., & Judge, T. A. (2003). On the heritability of job satisfaction: The mediating role of personality. *Journal of Applied Psychology, 88,* 750–759.

International Center for Disability Information. Retrieved August 12, 2005, from International Center for Disability Information Website: http://www.icdi.wvu.edu/

Jamison, K. R. (1995). *An Unquiet Mind.* New York: Knopf.

Jans, L., Stoddard, S., & Kraus, L. (2004). *Chartbook on Mental Health and Disability in the United States: An Info Use Report.* Washington, DC: National Institute on Disability and Rehabilitation Research.

Jansonius, J. V., & Gould, A. M. (1998). Expert witnesses in employment litigation. *Baylor Law Review, 50,* 267–331.

JHA. (2006). *JHA Disability Fact Book* (4th ed.). http://www.jhaweb.com/jhapp/publications/main.aspx

Jones, S. H., Thornicroft, G., Coffey, M., & Dunn, G. (1995, May). A brief mental health outcome scale-reliability and validity of the Global Assessment of Functioning (GAF). *British Journal of Psychiatry, 166*(5), 654–659.

Judd, L. L., Akiskal, H. S., Schettler, P. J., Endicott, J., Leon, A. C., Solomon, D. A., et al. (2005). Psychosocial disability in the course of bipolar I and II disorders. *Archives of General Psychiatry, 62,* 1322–1330.

Judge, T. A., Bono, J. E., Erez, A., Locke, E. A., & Thoresen, C. J. (2002). The scientific merit of valid measures of general concepts: Personality research and core self-evaluations. In J. M. Brett & F. Drasgow (Eds.), *The Psychology of Work: Theoretically Based Empirical Research* (pp. 55–77). Mahwah, NJ: Lawrence Erlbaum Associates.

Kahn, J. P. (2003). Workplace mental health quality: Effective recognition, management, evaluation, treatment and benefits. In J. P. Kahn & A. M. Langlieb (Eds.), *Mental Health and Productivity in the Workplace: A Handbook for Organizations and Clinicians* (pp. 3–27). San Francisco: John Wiley & Sons.

Kahn, J. P., & Unterberg, M. P. (2003). Executive distress and organizational consequences. In J. P. Kahn & A. M. Langlieb (Eds.), *Mental Health and Productivity in the Workplace: A Handbook for Organizations and Clinicians* (pp. 113–134). San Francisco: John Wiley & Sons.

Kates, N., Grieff, B. S., & Hagen, D. Q. (1990). *The Psychosocial Impact of Job Loss.* Washington, DC: American Psychiatric Press, Inc.

Kates, N., Grieff, B. S., & Hagen, D. Q. (2003). Job loss and employment uncertainty. In J. P. Kahn & A. M. Langlieb (Eds.), *Mental Health and Productivity in the Workplace: A Handbook for Organizations and Clinicians* (pp. 135–154). San Francisco: John Wiley & Sons.

Keller, M. C., Neale, M. C., & Kendler, K. S. (2007). Association of different adverse life events with distinct patterns of depressive symptoms. *American Journal of Psychiatry, 164*, 1521–1529.

Kennedy, C. (2002). Disability determination of mental impairments: A review toward an agenda for research in the measurement of work disability. In G. S. Wunderlich, D. P. Rice, & N. L. Amado (Eds.), *The Dynamics of Disability: Measuring and Monitoring Disability for Social Security Programs* (pp. 241–280). Washington, DC: National Academy Press.

Kesselheim, A. S., & Studdert, D. M. (2007). Role of professional organizations in regulating physician expert witness testimony. *Journal of the American Medical Association, 298*, 2907–2909.

Kessler, R. C., Akiskal, H. S., Ames, M., Birnbaum, H., Greenberg, M. A., Hirschfeld, R. M., et al. (2006). Prevalence and effects of mood disorders on work performance in a nationally representative sample of U.S. workers. *American Journal of Psychiatry, 163*, 1561–1568.

Kessler, R. C., Berglund, P., Demler, O., Jin, R., & Walters, E. E. (2005). Lifetime prevalence and age-of-onset distributions of DSM-IV in the National Comorbidity Survey Replication. *Archives of General Psychiatry, 62*, 593–602.

Kessler, R. C., Chiu, W. T., Demler, O., & Walters, E. E. (2005). Prevalence, severity, and comorbidity of the 12-month DSM-IV disorders in the National Comorbidity Survey Replication. *Archives of General Psychiatry, 62*, 617–627.

Kessler, R. C., Dupont, R. L., Berglund, P., & Wittchen, H.-U. (1999). Impairment in pure and comorbid generalized anxiety disorder and major depression at 12 months in two national surveys. *American Journal of Psychiatry, 156*, 1643–1678.

Kessler, R. C., & Frank, R. G. (1997). The impact of psychiatric disorders on work loss days. *Psychological Medicine, 27*, 861–873.

Kessler, R. C., Heeringa, S., Lakoma, M. D., Petukhova, M., Rupp, A. E., Schoenbaum, M., et al. (2008). Individual and societal effects of mental disorders on earnings in the United States: Results from the National Comorbidity Survey Replication. *American Journal of Psychiatry, 165*, 703–711.

Kessler, R. C., House, J. S., & Turner, J. B. (1987). Unemployment and health in a community sample. *Journal of Health and Social Behavior, 28*, 51–59.

Kessler, R. C., Mickelson, P. E., Meneades, L. D., & Wang, P. S. (2001). The effects of chronic medical conditions on work loss and work cutback. *Journal of Occupational and Environmental Medicine, 43*, 218–225.

Kimble, M., & Kaufman, M. (2004). Clinical correlates of neurological change in posttraumatic stress disorder: An overview of critical systems. *Psychiatric Clinics of North America, 27*, 49–65.

Kirsh, B. (2000). Factors associated with employment for mental health consumers. *Psychiatric Rehabilitation Journal, 24*, 13–21.

Klitzman, S., House, J. S., Israel, B. A., & Mero, R. P. (1990). Work stress, nonwork stress, and health. *Journal of Behavioral Medicine, 13*, 221–243.

Kokko, K., & Pulkkinen, L. (1998). Unemployment and psychological distress: Mediator effects. *Journal of Adult Development, 5*, 205–217.

Krajeski, J., & Lipsett, M. (1987). The psychiatric consultation for Social Security Disability Insurance. In A. T. Meyerson & T. Fine (Eds.), *Psychiatric Disability: Clinical, Legal and Administrative Dimensions* (pp. 287–311). Washington, DC: American Psychiatric Press, Inc.

Krantz, G., & Ostergren, P. O. (2001). Double exposure: The combined impact of domestic responsibilities and job strain in employed Swedish women. *European Journal of Public Health, 11*, 413–419.

Lanyon, R., & Almer, E. (2002). Characteristics of compensable disability patients who choose to litigate. *Journal of the American Academy of Psychiatry and the Law, 20*, 400–404.

Larson, L. K., & Larson, A. (2000). *Workers' Compensation Law: Cases, Materials, and Text* (3rd ed.). Newark, NJ: Matthew Bender & Co.

Lasky, H. (1993). *Psychiatric Claims in Workers' Compensation and Civil Litigation* (Vol. 1). New York: John Wiley & Sons.

LeBourgeois, H. W., III, Pinals, D. A., Williams, V., & Appelbaum P. A. (2007). Hindsight bias among psychiatrists. *Journal of the American Academy of Psychiatry and the Law, 35*(1), 67–73.

Leclair, N. J., & Leclair, S. W. (2001). Impairment and disability: Mental and behavioral disorders. *Clinics in Occupational and Environmental Medicine, 1*, 729–748.

Lehman, W. E., & Bennett, J. B. (2002). Job risk and employee substance use: the influence of personal background and work environment factors. *American Journal of Drug and Alcohol Abuse, 28*, 263–286.

Lennon, M. C. (1999). Work and unemployment as stressors. In A. V. Horwitz & T. L. Scheid (Eds.), *A Handbook for the Study of Mental Health* (pp. 284–294). Cambridge, UK: Cambridge University Press.

Lerner, D., Adler, D. A., Chang, H., Lapitsky, L., Hood, M. Y., & Perissinotto, C., et al. (2004). Unemployment, job retention and productivity loss among employees with depression. *Psychiatric Services, 55*, 1371–1378.

Lerner, D. J., Allaire, S. H., & Reisine, S. T. (2004). Work disability resulting from chronic health conditions. *Journal of Occupational and Environmental Medicine, 47*, 253–264.

Levi, L. (2003). Foreword. In J. R. Quick & L. E. Tetrick (Eds.), *Handbook of Occupational Health Psychology* (pp. ix–xiii). Washington, DC: American Psychological Association.

Levin, J.L. (1998). The genesis and evolution of legal uncertainty about "reasonable medical certainty." *Maryland Law Review, 57*, 380–441.

Lindemann, B., & Kadue, D. D. (1992). *Sexual Harassment in Employment Law*. Washington, DC: The Bureau of National Affairs, Inc.

Liu, P. M., & Van Liew, D. A. (2003). Depression and burnout. In J. P. Kahn & A. M. Langlieb (Eds.), *Mental Health and Productivity in the Workplace: A Handbook for Organizations and Clinicians* (pp. 433–457). San Francisco: John Wiley & Sons.

Lubit, R. H., & Gordon, R. P. (2003). Office politics: The good, the bad, and the ugly. In J. P. Kahn & A. M. Langlieb (Eds.), *Mental Health and Productivity in the Workplace: A Handbook for Organizations and Clinicians* (pp. 171–201). San Francisco: John Wiley & Son.

Mancuso, L. (1990). Reasonable accommodation for persons with psychiatric disabilities. *Psychosocial Rehabilitation Journal, 14*, 3.

Marcotte, D. E., & Wilcox-Gok, V. (2001). Estimating the employment and earnings costs of mental illness: Recent developments in the United States. *Social Science & Medicine, 53*, 21–27.

References

Marlowe, J. F. (2002). Depression's surprising toll on worker productivity. *Employee Benefits Journal, 27*, 16–21.

Martin, J. K., Blum, T. C., Beach, S. R., & Roman, P. M. (1996). Subclinical depression and performance at work. *Social Psychiatry and Psychiatric Epidemiology, 31*, 3–9.

Marvel, C. L., & Paradiso, S. (2004). Cognitive and neurological impairment in mood disorders. *Psychiatric Clinics of North America, 27*, 19–36.

Maslach, C. (1982). *Burnout: The Cost of Caring*. Englewood Cliffs, NJ: Prentice-Hall Inc.

Maslach, C., & Leiter, M. P. (1997). *The Truth about Burnout: How Organizations Cause Personal Stress and What To Do About It*. San Francisco: Jossey-Bass Publishers.

McDonald, J. J., & Kulick, F. B. (2001). Preface. In J. J. McDonald & F. B. Kulick (Eds.), *Mental and Emotional Injuries in Employment Litigation* (2nd ed., pp. xxxvi–xlv). Washington, DC: The Bureau of National Affairs, Inc.

Melton, G. B., Petrila, J., Poythress, N. G., & Slobogin, C. (2007). *Psychological Evaluations for the Courts: A Handbook for Mental Health Professionals and Lawyers* (3rd ed.). New York: Guilford Press.

Merikangas, K. R., Akiskal, H. S., Angst, J., Greenberg, P. E., Hirschfeld, R. M., & Petukhova, M., et al. (2007b). Lifetime and 12-month prevalence of bipolar spectrum disorder in the national comorbidity survey replication. *Archives of General Psychiatry, 64*, 543–552.

Merikangas, K. R., Ames, M., Cui, L., Stang, P. E., Ustun, T. B., Von Korff, M., et al. (2007a). The impact of comorbidity of mental and physical conditions on role disability in the US adult household population. *Archives of General Psychiatry, 64*, 1180–1188.

Metzner, J. L., & Buck, J. B. (2003). Psychiatric disability determinations and personal injury litigation. In R. Rosner (Ed.), *Principles and Practice of Forensic Psychiatry* (2nd ed., pp. 260–272). London: Arnold.

Meyer, D. J., & Price, M. (2006). Forensic psychiatric assessments of behaviorally disruptive physicians. *Journal of the American Academy of Psychiatry and the Law, 34*, 72–81.

Mossman, D. (1994). Is expert psychiatric testimony fundamentally immoral? *International Journal of Law Psychiatry, 17*, 347–368.

Mossman, D., Noffinger, S. G., Ash, P., Frierson, R. L., Gerbasi, J., Hackett, M., et al. (2007). Practice guideline for the forensic psychiatric evaluation of competence to stand trial. *Journal of the American Academy of Psychiatry and the Law, 35*, S3–S72.

Murphy, G. C., & Athanasou, J. A. (1999). The effects of unemployment on mental health. *Journal of Occupational and Organizational Psychology, 72*, 83–99.

Murray, C., & Lopez, A. D. (Eds.). (1996). *The Global Burden of Disease: A Comprehensive Assessment of Mortality and Disability from Disease, Injuries and Risk Factors in 1990 and Projected to 2020*. Cambridge, MA: Harvard University Press.

Murray, C. L., Gien, L., & Solberg, S. M. (2003). A comparison of employed and unemployed women in the context of a massive layoff. *Women & Health, 37*, 55–72.

Nackley, J. V. (1989). *Primer on Workers' Compensation* (2nd ed.). Washington, DC: Bureau of National Affairs.

Nasar, S. (1998). *A Beautiful Mind: The Life of Mathematical Genius and Nobel Laureate John Nash*. New York: Simon & Schuster.

National Institutes of Mental Health. (2007). Statistics. Retrieved May 26, 2007, from National Institutes of Mental Health Website: http://www.nimh.nih.gov/health/topics/statistics/index.shtml

Nelson, D. L., Burke, R. J., & Michie, S. (2002). New directions for studying gender, work stress and health. In D. L. Nelson & R. J. Burke (Eds.), *Gender, Work Stress and Health* (pp. 229–242). Washington, DC: American Psychological Association.

Nelson, D. L., & Simmons, B. L. (2003). Health psychology and work stress: A more positive approach. In J. R. Quick & L. E. Tetrick (Eds.), *Handbook of Occupational Health Psychology* (pp. 97–119). Washington, DC: American Psychological Association.

Noor, N. M. (2002). Work-family conflict, locus of control and women's well-being: Tests of alternative pathways. *Journal of Social Psychology, 142*, 645–662.

O'Brien, G. E. (1986). *Psychology of Work and Unemployment*. Chichester, UK: John Wiley & Sons.

Ormel, J., Oldehinkel, A. J., Nolen, W. A., & Vollebergh, W. (2004). Psychosocial disability before, during, and after a major depressive episode. *Archives of General Psychiatry, 61*, 387–392.

Ormel, J., Von Korff, M., Ustun, B., Pini, S., Korten, A., & Oldehinkel, T. (1994). Common mental disorders and disability across cultures: Results from the WHO collaborative study on psychological problems in general health care. *Journal of the American Medical Association, 272*(22), 1741–1748.

O'Toole, J. (1982). Work and love (but mostly work). *Journal of Psychiatric Treatment and Evaluation, 4*, 227–237.

Ozawa, M. N. (1982). Work and social policy. In S. H. Akabas & P. A. Kurzman (Eds.), *Work, Workers, and Work Organizations: A View from Social Work* (pp. 32–60). Englewood Cliffs, NJ: Prentice-Hall Inc.

Paetzold, R. L. (2005). Mental illness and reasonable accommodations at work: Definition of a mental disability under the ADA. *Psychiatric Services, 56*, 1188–1190.

Panzarella, J. P. (1991). The nature of work, job loss, and the diagnostic complexities of the psychologically injured worker. *Psychiatric Annals, 21*, 10–15.

Parry, J. W. (1995). Mental disabilities under the ADA: A difficult path to follow. *Mental and Physical Disability Law Reporter, 17*, 100.

Parry, J. W. (1998). *National Benchbook on Psychiatric and Psychological Evidence and Testimony*. Chicago: American Bar Association.

Parry, J., & Drogin, E. Y. (2007). *Mental disability law evidence and testimony: A comprehensive reference manual for lawyers, judges and mental disability professionals*. Chicago: American Bar Association.

Perlman, H. H. (1982). The client as worker: A look at the overlooked role. In S. H. Akabas & P. A. Kurzman (Eds.), *Work, Workers, and Work Organizations: A View from Social Work* (pp. 90–116). Englewood Cliffs, NJ: Prentice-Hall Inc.

Pernice, R. (1997). Employment attitudes and mental health of long-term unemployed people with disabilities: Implications for rehabilitation counselors. *Journal of Applied Rehabilitation Counseling, 28*, 21–25.

Perrewé, P. L., & Carlson, D. S. (2002). Do men and women benefit from social support equally? Results from a field examination within the work and family context. In D. L. Nelson & R. J. Burke (Eds.), *Work Stress and Health* (pp. 101–114). Washington, DC: American Psychological Association.

Petrila, J., & Brink, T. (2001). Mental illness and changing definitions of disability under the Americans with Disabilities Act. *Psychiatric Services, 52*, 626.

Pflanz, S. E., & Heidel, S. H. (2003). Psychiatric causes of workplace problems: Accidents, absenteeism and more. In J. P. Kahn & A. M. Langlieb (Eds.), *Mental Health and Productivity in the Workplace: A Handbook for Organizations and Clinicians* (pp. 276–296). San Francisco: John Wiley & Sons.

Pierce, R. (1987). Use of the Federal Rules of Evidence in federal agency adjudications. *Administrative Law Review, 39*, 1.

Pinals, D. A., & Price, M. (2004). Forensic psychiatry and law enforcement. In R. I. Simon & L. H. Gold (Eds.), *American Psychiatric Publishing Textbook of Forensic Psychiatry* (pp. 393–423). Washington, DC: American Psychiatric Publishing, Inc.

Police Psychological Services Section of the International Association of Chiefs of Police. *Psychological Fitness-for-Duty Evaluation Guidelines*. Retrived December 1, 2008, from http://theiacp.org/psych%5Fsection/

Pope, K. S., Butcher, J. N., & Seelen, J. (2006). *The MMPI, MMPI-2 & MMPI-A in Court: A Practical Guide for Expert Witnesses and Attorneys* (3rd ed.). Washington, DC: American Psychological Association.

Postol, L. P. (2003). The Medical-legal interface. In S. L. Demeter & G. B. J. Anersson (Eds.), *Disability Evaluations* (2nd ed., pp. 62–72). Chicago: American Medical Association.

Pransky, G., Wasiak, R., & Himmelstein, K. (2001). Disability systems: The physician's role. *Clinics in Occupational and Environmental Medicine, 1*(4), 829–842.

Price, R. H., Choi, J. N., & Vinokur, A. D. (2002). Links in the chain of adversity following job loss: How financial strain and loss of personal control lead to depression, impaired functioning, and poor health. *Journal of Occupational Health Psychology, 7*, 302–312.

Pro, J. D. (2005). Working with common psychiatric problems. In J. B. Talmage & J. M. Melhorn (Eds.), *A Physician's Guide to Return to Work* (pp. 305–320). Chicago: American Medical Association.

Probst, T. (2002). The impact of job insecurity on employee work attitudes, job adaptation and organizational withdrawal behaviors. In J. M. Brett & F. Drasgow (Eds.), *The Psychology of Work: Theoretically Based Empirical Research* (pp. 141–168). Mahwah, NJ: Lawrence Erlbaum Associates.

Pryor, E. S. (1997). Mental disabilities and the disability fabric. In R. J. Bonnie & J. Monahan (Eds.), *Mental Disorder, Work Disability and the Law* (pp. 153–198). Chicago: The University of Chicago Press.

Quillian-Wolever, R. E., & Wolever, M. E. (2003). Stress management at work. In J. R. Quick & L. E. Tetrick (Eds.), *Handbook of Occupational Health Psychology* (pp. 355–375). Washington, DC: American Psychological Association.

Rappeport, J. R. (1985). Reasonable medical certainty. *Bulletin of the American Academy of Psychiatry and the Law, 13*, 5–15.

Recupero, P. (2008). Clinical practice guidelines as learned treatises: Understanding their use as evidence in the courtroom. *Journal of the American Academy of Psychiatry and the Law, 36*, 290–301.

Resnick, P. J. (2003). Malingering. In R. Rosner (Ed.), *Principles and Practice of Forensic Psychiatry* (2nd ed., pp. 37–44). London: Arnold.

Reynolds, N. T. (2002). A model comprehensive psychiatric fitness-for-duty evaluation. *Occupational Medicine, 17*, 105–118.

Rice, D. P., Kelman, S., Miller, L. S., & Dunmeyer, S. (1990). *The Economic Costs of Alcohol and Drug Abuse and Mental Illness: 1985*. Washington, DC: United States Department of Health and Human Services.

Rigaud, M. C. (2001). Behavioral Fitness for Duty (FFD). *Work, 16*, 3–6.

Ritchie, A. J., & Zonana, H. V. (2003). Americans with Disability Act evaluations. In R. Rosner (Ed.), *Principles and Practice of Forensic Psychiatry* (2nd ed., pp. 273–281). London: Arnold.

Rogers, R. (Ed.). (2008a). *Clinical Assessment of Malingering and Deception* (3rd ed.). New York: The Guilford Press.

Rogers, R. (2008b). Detection strategies for malingering and defensiveness. In Rogers, R. (Ed.), *Clinical Assessment of Malingering and Deception* (3rd ed., pp. 14–35). New York: The Guilford Press.

Rosenstock, L., & Lee, L. J. (2000). Caution: Women at work. *Journal of the American Medical Women's Association, 55*, 67–68.

Ross, M. (1989). Relation of implicit theories to the construction of personal histories. *Psychological Review, 96*, 341–3577.

Ross, M., & Wilson, A. E. (2000). Constructing and appraising past selves. In D. L. Schacter & E. Scarry (Eds.), *Memory, Brain and Belief* (pp. 231–258). Cambridge, MA: Harvard University Press.

Rosman, J. P. (2001). Malingering: distortion and deception in employment litigation. In J. J. McDonald & F. B. Kulick (Eds.), *Mental and Emotional Injuries in Employment Litigation* (2nd ed., pp. 409–453). Washington, DC: The Bureau of National Affairs, Inc.

Rostow, C. D. (2002). Psychological fitness-for-duty evaluations in law enforcement. *The Police Chief*, 58–66.

Rostow, C., & Davis, R. A. (2004). *Handbook for psychological fitness-for-duty evaluations in law enforcement*. New York: Routledge.

Roth, R. M., & Saykin, A. J. (2004). Executive dysfunction in attention-deficit/hyperactivity disorder: Cognitive and neuroimaging findings. *Psychiatric Clinics of North America, 27*, 83–96.

Rothman, I., & Cooper, C. (2008). *Organizational and Work Psychology.* London: Hodder Education.

Roy-Byrne, P. P., Stein, M. B., Russ, J., Mercier, E., Thomas, R., McQuaid, J., et al. (1999). Panic disorder in the primary care setting: Comorbidity, disability, service utilization and treatment. *Journal Clinical Psychiatry, 60*, 492–499.

Rytsala, J. H., Melartin, T. K., Leskela, U. S., Sokero, T. P., Lestela-Mielonen, P. S., & Isometsa, E. T. (2005). Functional and work disability in major depressive disorder in Major Depressive Disorder. *Journal of Nervous and Mental Disease, 193*, 189–195.

Sanderson, K., & Andrews, G. (2002). Prevalence and severity of mental health-related disability and relationship to diagnosis. *Psychiatric Services, 53*, 80–86.

Schouten, R. (2008). Workplace violence and the clinician. In R. I. Simon & K. Tardiff (Eds.), *Textbook of Violence Assessment and Management* (pp. 501–520). Washington, DC: American Psychiatric Press, Inc.

Semmer, N. K. (2003). Job stress interventions and organization of work. In J. R. Quick & L. E. Tetrick (Eds.), *Handbook of Occupational Health Psychology* (pp. 325–353). Washington, DC: American Psychological Association.

Sherer, A. (1996). Psychiatric assessment: A semi-structured interview. In D.K. Shrier (Ed.), *Sexual Harassment in the Workplace and Academia: Psychiatric Issues* (pp. 79–94). Washington, DC: American Psychiatric Press, Inc.

Shirom, A. (2003). Job-related burnout: A review. In *Handbook of Occupational Health Psychology* (pp. 245–264). Washington, DC: American Psychological Association.

Shrier, D. K., & Hamilton, J. A. (1996). Therapeutic interventions and resources. In D. K. Shrier (Ed.), *Sexual Harassment in the Workplace and Academia: Psychiatric Issues* (pp. 95–112). Washington, DC: American Psychiatric Press, Inc.

Shuman, D. W. (1993). The use of empathy in forensic examinations. *Ethics and Behavior, 3*(3&4), 289–302.

Shuman, D. W. (2002). The role of mental health experts in custody decisions: Science, psychological tests, and clinical judgment. *Family Law Quarterly, 36*, 135–162.

Shuman, D. W., & Greenberg, S. A. (1998). The role of ethical norms in the admissibility of expert testimony. *Judges Journal, 37*, 4–9.

Shuman, D. W., & Sales, B. (1998). The admissibility of expert testimony based on clinical judgment and scientific research. *Psychology, Public Policy, and Law, 1*, 1226–1252.

Shuman, D. W., & Greenberg, S. A. (2003). The expert witness, the adversary system, and the voice of reason: Reconciling impartiality and advocacy. *Professional Psychology: Research and Practice, 34*, 219–224.

Shuman, D. W., & Sales, B. D. (2001). Daubert's wager. *Journal of Forensic Psychology and Practice, 1*, 69–82.

Shuman, D. W. (2005). Disability claims in the administrative setting. *Psychiatric and Psychological Evidence, 9*, 14.17.–14.22.

Silva, J. A., Leong, G. B., & Weinstock, R. (2003). Forensic psychiatric report writing. In R. Rosner (Ed.), *Principles and Practice of Forensic Psychiatry* (2nd ed., pp. 31–36). New York: Oxford University Press.

Simon, G., Revicki, D., Heiligenstein, J., Grothaus, L., Von Korff, M., Katon, W., et al. (2000). Recovery from depression, work productivity and health care costs among primary care patients. *General Hospital Psychiatry, 22*, 153–162.

Simon, R. I. (1992). *Clinical Psychiatry and the Law* (2nd ed.). Washington, DC: American Psychiatric Press, Inc.

Simon, R. I. (1996a). The credible forensic psychiatric evaluation in sexual harassment litigation. *Psychiatric Annals, 26*, 139–148.

References

Simon, R. I. (2002). Forensic psychiatric assessment of PTSD claimants. In R. I. Simon (Ed.), *Posttraumatic Stress Disorder in Litigation: Guidelines for Forensic Assessment* (2nd ed., pp. 41–97). Washington, DC: American Psychiatric Press, Inc.

Simon, R. I. (1996b). "Three's a crowd:" The presence of third parties during the forensic psychiatric examination. *Journal of the American Academy of Psychiatry and Law, 24,* 3–25.

Simon, R. I., & Gold, L. H. (2004). Psychiatric diagnosis in litigation. In R. I. Simon & L. H. Gold (Eds.), *The American psychiatric publishing textbook of forensic psychiatry* (pp. 117–138). Washington DC: American Psychiatric Publishing, Inc.

Simon, R. I., & Shuman D. W. (2007). *Clinical Manual of Psychiatry and the Law.* Washington, DC: American Psychiatric Press, Inc.

Simon, R. I., & Shuman, D. W. (1999). Conducting forensic examinations on the road: Are you practicing your profession without a license? *Journal of the American Academy of Psychiatry, 27,* 75–82.

Simon, R. I., & Shuman, D. W. (Eds.). (2002). *Retrospective Assessment of Mental States in Litigation: Predicting the Past.* Washington, DC: American Psychiatric Publishing, Inc.

Simon, R. I., & Wettstein, R. M. (1997). Toward the development of guidelines for the conduct of forensic psychiatric examinations. *Journal of the American Academy of Psychiatry and the Law, 25,* 17–30.

Smith, C. S., Folkard, S., & Fuller, J. A. (2003). Shiftwork and working hours. In J. R. Quick & L. E. Tetrick (Eds.), *Handbook of Occupational Health Psychology* (pp. 163–183). Washington, DC: American Psychological Association.

Social Security Administration: *HIPAA and the Social Security Disability Programs.* Retrieved January 30, 2006, from Social Security Administration Website: http://www.ssa.gov///cefactsheet.htm

Social Security Administration: Disability Programs Medical/Professional Relations. Retrieved January 30, 2006, from Social Security Administration Website http://www.socialsecurity.gov/disability/professionals/hipaa-cefactsheet.htm

Social Security Administration Office of Disability Programs. (2004). *Understanding Social Security's Disability Programs Mental Impairments.* (ERIC Document Reproduction Service No. 64–086).

Social Security Administration Office of Policy. (2004). *Annual statistical supplement, 2004, to the Social Security Bulletin.* Retrieved May 27, 2007, from Social Security Administration Website: http://www.socialsecurity.gov/policy/docs/statcomps/supplement/

Social Security Administration Office of Policy. (2005). *Annual statistical supplement, 2005, to the Social Security Bulletin.* Retrieved May 27, 2007, from Social Security Administration Website: http://www.ssa.gov.disability//html

Social Security Administration Office of Policy. (2006). *Annual statistical supplement, 2006, to the Social Security Bulletin.* Retrieved January 16, 2007, from Social Security Administration Website: http://www.ssa.gov.disability//html

Soderberg, P., Tungstrom, S., & Armelius, B. A. (2005). Reliability of global assessment of functioning ratings made by clinical psychiatric staff. *Psychiatric Services, 56,* 434–438.

Spielberger, C. D., Vagg, P. R., & Wasala, C. F. (2003). Occupational stress: Job pressures and lack of support. In J. R. Quick & L. E. Tetrick (Eds.), *Handbook of Occupational Health Psychology* (pp. 185–200). Washington, DC: American Psychological Association.

Statt, D. A. (1994). *Psychology and the World of Work.* New York: New York University Press.

Stein, D. J., & Hollander, E. (2003). Anxiety and stress. In J. P. Kahn & A. M. Langlieb (Eds.), *Mental Health and Productivity in the Workplace: A Handbook for Organizations and Clinicians* (pp. 407–432). San Francisco: John Wiley & Sons.

Stellman, J. M. (2000). Perspectives on women's occupational health. *Journal of the American Medical Women's Association, 55,* 69–72.

Stewart, W. F., Ricci, J. A., Chee, E., Hahn, S. R., & Morganstein, D. (2003). Cost of lost productive work among US Workers with depression. *Journal of the American Medical Association, 289,* 3135–3144.

Stone, A. A. (1984). The ethical boundaries of forensic psychiatry: A view form the ivory tower. *Bulletin of the American Academy of Psychiatry and the Law, 12*, 209–219.

Stone, A. V. (2000). *Fitness-for-Duty: Principles, Methods and Legal Issues.* New York: CRC press.

Strasburger, L. H. (1987). "Crudely, without any finesse": The defendant hears his psychiatric evaluation. *Bulletin of the American Academy of Psychiatry and the Law, 15*, 229–233.

Strasburger, L. H. (1999). The litigant-patient: Mental health consequences of civil litigation. *Journal of the American Academy of Psychiatry and the Law, 27*, 203–211.

Strasburger, L. H., Gutheil, T. G., & Brodsky, A. (1997). On wearing two hats: Role conflict in serving as both psychotherapist and expert witness. *American Journal of Psychiatry, 154*, 448–456.

Straus, J. S., & Davidson, L. (1997). Mental disorders, work and choice. In R. J. Bonnie & J. Monahan (Eds.), *Mental Disorder, Work Disability and the Law* (pp. 105–130). Chicago: The University of Chicago Press.

Styron, W. (1990). *Darkness Visible: A Memoir of Madness.* New York: Random House.

Swanson, N. G. (2000). Working women and stress. *Journal of the American Medical Women's Association*, 76–79.

Talmage, J. B., & Melhorn, J. M. (2005a). Preface. In J. B. Talmage & J. M. Melhorn (Eds.), *A Physician's Guide to Return to Work* (pp. xi–xiv). Chicago: American Medical Association.

Talmage, J. B., & Melhorn, J. M. (2005b). Why staying at work or returning to work is in the patient's best interest. In J. B. Talmage & J. M. Melhorn (Eds.), *A Physician's Guide to Return to Work* (pp. 1–17). Chicago: American Medical Association.

Tausig, M. (1999). Work and mental health. In C. S. Aneshensel & J. C. Phelan (Eds.), *Handbook of the Sociology of Mental Health* (pp. 255–274). New York: Kluwer Academic Publishers.

Terkel, S. (1972). *Working: People Talk About What They Do All Day And How They Feel About What They Do.* New York: The New Press.

Tetrick, L. E., & Quick, J. C. (2003). Prevention at work: Public health in occupational settings. In J. R. Quick & L. E. Tetrick (Eds.), *Handbook of Occupational Health Psychology* (pp. 3–17). Washington, DC: American Psychological Association.

Thomas, N. K. (2004). Resident burnout. *Journal of the American Medical Association, 292*, 2880–2889.

Tisza, S. M., Mottl, J. R., III, & Matthews, D. B. (2003). Current trends in workers' compensation stress claims. *Current Opinion in Psychiatry, 16*, 571–574.

Tse, S., & Yeats, M. (2002). What helps people with bipolar affective disorder succeed in employment: A grounded theory approach. *Work, 19*, 47–62.

Tseng, W. S., Matthews, D., & Elwyn, T. S. (2004). *Cultural Competence in Forensic Mental Health: A Guide for Psychiatrists, Psychologists and Attorneys.* New York: Brunner-Routledge.

United States Equal Employment Opportunity Commission. (2008). *Enforcement Statistics and Litigation.* Retrieved May 21, 2009, from http://www.eeoc.gov/stats/enforcement.html

United States Department of Health and Human Services: Office of Civil Rights Summary of the HIPAA Privacy Rule. Retrieved January 30, 2006, from http://www.hhs.gov/ocr/privacy/hipaa/understanding/summary/

United States Department of Health and Human Services. *Health information privacy and civil rights questions and answers.* Retrieved December 1, 2008, from http://www.hhs.gov/ocr/privacy/hipaa/faq/about/index.html

United States Department of Health and Human Services. (1999). *Mental health: A report to the Surgeon General.* Retrieved May 27, 2007, from http://www.surgeongeneral.gov/library/mentalhealth/home.html

United States Department of Health and Human Resources, Office for Civil Rights-HIPAA. (2007). Compliance and Enforcement. Retrieved September 14, 2007, from http://www.hhs.gov/ocr/privacy/hipaa/enforcement/index.html

United States Department of Labor (Ed.). (1991). *Dictionary of occupational titles* (4th ed.). Retrieved from http://www.oalj.dol.gov/LIBDOT.HTM

United States Department of Labor, Bureau of Labor Statistics. (2005). *Women in the Labor Force: A Databook.* Retrieved July 7, 2007, from http://www.bls.gov/cps/databook2005.html

United States Department of Labor, Bureau of Labor Statistics. (2005a). *Employee benefits in private industry*. Retrieved May 27, 2007, from http://www.bls.gov/ncs/ebs/sp/ebsm0003.pdf

United States Department of Labor, Bureau of Labor Statistics. (2008). *Highlights of women's earnings in 2007*. Retrieved November 22, 2008, from United States Department of Labor Website: http://www.bls.gov/cps/cpswom2007.pdf

United Stated Department of Labor, Bureau of Labor Statistics. *Labor Force Statistics (CPS)*. Retrieved November 22, 2008, from United States Department of Labor Website: http://www.bls.gov

Vik, P. W., Cellucci, T., Jarchow, A., & Hedt, J. (2004). Cognitive impairment in substance abuse. *Psychiatric Clinics of North America, 27*, 97–109.

Von Korff, M., Crane, P., & Lane, M., et al. (2005). Chronic spinal pain and physical-mental comorbidity in the United States: Results from the National Comorbidity Survey Replication. *Pain, 113*, 331–339.

Waldner, P. F., & Hornsby, L. E. (2005). The medical and legal aspects of return-to-work decision making. In J. B. Talmage & J. M. Melhorn (Eds.), *A Physician's Guide to Return to Work* (pp. 95–111). Chicago: American Medical Association.

Wall, B. W., & Appelbaum, K. S. (1998). Disabled doctors: The insurance industry seeks a second opinion. *Journal of American Academy of Psychiatry and the Law, 26*, 7–19.

Wang, P. S., Beck, A. L., Berglund, P., McKenas, D. K., Pronk, N. P., Simon, G. E., et al. (2004). Effects of major depression on moment-in-time work performance. *American Journal of Psychiatry, 161*, 1885–1891.

Warr, P. B. (1987). *Work, Unemployment and Mental Health*. Oxford, UK: Oxford University Press.

Weinstock, R., & Garrick, T. (1995). Is liability possible for forensic psychiatrists? *Bulletin for the American Academy of Psychiatry and the Law, 23*, 183–193.

Weinstock, R., & Gold, L. H. (2004). Ethics in forensic psychiatry. In R. I. Simon & L. H. Gold (Eds.), *The American Psychiatric Publishing Textbook of Forensic Psychiatry* (pp. 91–115). Washington, DC: American Psychiatric Publishing, Inc.

Wells, K. B., Stewart, A., Hays, R. D., Burnam, M. A., Rogers, W., Daniels, M., et al. (1989). The functioning and well-being of depressed patients; results from the medical outcomes study. *Journal of the American Medical Association, 262*, 914–919.

Wettstein, R. M. (2005a). Commentary: Quality improvement and psychiatric fitness-for-duty evaluations of physicians. *Journal of the American Academy of Psychiatry and the Law, 33*, 92–94.

Wettstein, R. M. (2005b). Quality and quality improvement in forensic mental health evaluations. *Journal of the American Academy of Psychiatry and the Law, 33*, 158–175.

Williams, J. (2000). *Unbending gender: Why family and work conflict and what to do about it*. Oxford: Oxford University Press.

Williams, J. C. (1999). The sameness/difference (or equality/difference) debate. In B. Taylor, S. Rush, & R. J. Munro (Eds.), *Jurisprudence, women and the law: Critical essays, research agenda, and bibliography* (pp. 23–38). Littleton, CO: Fred B. Rothman & Co.

Willick, D., Weinstock, R., & Garrick, T. (2003). Liability of the forensic psychiatry. In R. Rosner (Ed.), *Principles and Practice of Forensic Psychiatry* (pp. 73–78). London: Arnold.

Winefield, A. H., Winefield, H. R., Tiggeman, M., & Goldney, R. D. (1991). A longitudinal study of the psychological effect of unemployment and unsatisfactory employment on young adults. *Journal of Applied Psychology, 76*, 424–431.

Wittchen, H. U., Carter, R. M., Pfister, H., Montgomery, S. A., & Kessler, R. A. (2000). Disabilities and quality of life in pure and comorbid generalized anxiety disorder and major depression in a national survey. *International Clinical Psychopharmacology, 15*, 319–328.

World Health Organization. (2001). International Classification of Functioning, Disability and Health. Geneva, Switzerland: World Health Organization.

World Health Organization. (2004). *International classification of diseases and related health problems* (2nd ed., 10th Rev.). Geneva, Switzerland: World Health Organization.

Wright, T. A., & Cropanzano, R. (1998). Emotional exhaustion as a predictor of job performance and voluntary turnover. *Journal of Applied Psychology, 83*, 486–493.

Wunderlich, G. S., Rice, D. P., & Amado, N. L. (Eds). (2002). *The Dynamics of Disability: Measuring and Monitoring Disability for Social Security Programs.* Washington, DC: National Academy Press.

Yelin, E. H., & Cisternas, M. G. (1997). Employment patterns among person with and without mental conditions. In R. J. Bonnie & J. Monahan (Eds.), *Mental Disorder, Work Disability and the Law* (pp. 25–51). Chicago: University of Chicago Press.

Zonana, H. (2008). Commentary: When is a practice guideline only a guideline. *Journal of the American Academy of Psychiatry and the Law, 36*, 302–305.

Zuckerman, D., Debenham, K., & Moore, K. (1993). *The ADA and People with Mental Illness: A Resource Manual for Employers.* Washington, DC: American Bar Association and National Mental Health Association.

Legal Citations

Cases

Adams v. Alderson, 723 F. Supp. 1531 (D. D.C. 1989)
Albertson's, Inc. v. Kirkingburg, 527 U.S. 555 (1999)
Amadio v. Ford Motor Co., 238 F.3d 919 (7th Cir. 2001)
Austin v. American Association of Neurological Surgeons, 253 F.3d 967 (7th Cir. 2001)
Bar-Av v. Psychology Examining Board, 728 N.W.2d 722 (Wis. App. 2007)
Barcai v. Betwee, 50 P.3d 946 (Ha. 2002)
Barnhart v. Thomas, 540 U.S. 20, 24 (2003)
Bayne v. Provost, 359 F. Supp. 2d 234 (N.D.N.Y. 2005)
Bd. Of Trustees of the Univ. of Alabama v. Garrett, 531 U.S. 356 (2001)
Benson v. Northwest Airlines, 62 F.3d 1108 (8th Cir. 1996)
Blailock v. O'Bannon, 795 So.2d 533 (Miss. 2001)
Bonsignore v. New York, 683 F.2d 635 (2d Cir. 1982)
Briscoe v. LaHue, 460 U.S. 325 (1983)
Bristol v. Bd. of County Comm'rs, 312 F.3d 1213 (10th Cir. 2002)
Bruce v. Byrne-Stevens, 776 P.2d 666 (Wash. 1989)
Bruni v. Tatsumi, 346 N.E.2d 673 (Ohio 1976)
Bstandig v. Workers' Comp. Appeals Bd., 137 Cal. Rptr. 713 (Cal. App. 1978)
Budwin v. Am. Psychological Ass'n, 24 Cal. App. 4th 875 (Cal. App. 1994)
Bultemeyer v. Fort Wayne Community Schools, 100 F.3d 1281 (7th Cir. 1996)
Bunevitch v. CVS Pharmacy, 925 F. Supp. 89 (D. Mass. 1996)
Calkins v. Sumner,13 Wis. 193 (Wis. 1860)
Callahan v. Workers' Comp. Appeals. Bd., 149 Cal. Rptr. 647 (Cal. App. 1978)
Canterbury v. Spence, 464 F.2d 772 (D.C. Cir. 1972)
Carrozza v. Howard County, Md., 847 F. Supp. 365 (D. Mich. 1994), aff'd 4 AD Cas. 512 (4th Cir. 1995)
Carter v. GM, 106 N.W.2d 105 (Mich. 1960)
Cleveland v. Policy Mgmt. Sys. Corp., 526 U.S. 795 (1999)
Colwell v. Suffolk County Police Dept., 967 F. Supp. 1419 (E.D.N.Y. 1997)
Cravens v. Blue Cross and Blue Shield, 214 F.3d 1011 (8th Cir. 2000)
Criado v. IBM Corp.,145 F.3d 437 (1st Cir. 1998)
Daley v. Koch, 892 F.2d 212 (2d Cir. 1989)
Dalton v. Miller, 984 P.2d 666 (Colo. App. 1999)
Daly v. United States, 946 F.2d 467 (9th Cir. 1991)
Daubert v. Merrell Dow Pharmaceuticals, 509 U.S. 579 (1993)
Debose v. USDA, 700 F.2d 1262 (9th Cir. 1983)
Dehn v. Edgecombe, 865 A.2d 603 (Md. 2005)
DePaoli v. Abbott Lab, 140 F.3d 668, 674 (7th Cir. 1998)

Dixon v. Pc. Mut. Life Ins. Co., 268 F.2d 812 (2d Cir. 1959), cert. denied, 361 U.S. 948 (1960)
Dunlavey v. Econ. Fire and Casualty Co., 526 N.W.2d 845 (Iowa 1995)
Dyer v. Trachtman, 679 N.W.2d 311 (Mich. 2004)
Earl v. Mervyns, Inc., 207 F.3d 1361 (11th Cir. 2000)
EEOC v. Amego, 110 F.3d 135 (1st Cir. 1997)
EEOC v. UPS, 249 F.3d 557 (6th Cir. 2001)
Ervin v. American Guardian Life Assur. Co., 545 A.2d 354 (Pa. Super. 1988)
Estelle v. Smith, 451 U.S. 454 (1981)
Evans v. Federal Express Corp., 133 F.3d 137 (1st Cir. 1998)
Ex parte Price, 555 So.2d 1060 (Ala. 1989)
Faria v. Carol Cable Co.,527 A.2d 641 (R.I. 1987)
Farley v. Nationwide Mut. Ins. Co.,197 F.3d 1322 (11th Cir. 1999)
Fenton v. Pritchard Corp., 926 F. Supp. 1437 (D. Kan. 1996)
Ford v. Revlon,734 P.2d 580 (Ariz. 1987)
Frye v. United States, 293 F.3d 1013 (D.C. Cir. 1923)
Garg v. Potter, 521 F.3d 731 (7th Cir. 2008)
Garrity v. United Air Lines, 653 N.E.2d 173 (Mass. 1995)
Gaul v. AT&T, 955 F. Supp. 346 (D. N.J. 1997)
General Electric v. Joiner, 522 U.S. 136 (1997)
Gilbert v. Daimler-Chrysler Corp.,685 N.W.2d 391 (Mich. 2004)
Girardeau v. Guardian Life Ins. Co.,287 S.E.2d 324 (Ga. App. Ct. 1981)
Greenberg v. New York,919 F. Supp. 637 (E.D.N.Y 1996)
Greenberg v. Perkins, 845 P.2d 530 (Colo. 1993)
Hafner v. Beck, 916 P.2d 1105 (Ariz. App. 1995)
Hammon v. DHL Airways, Inc., 980 F. Supp. 919 (S.D. Ohio 1997), aff'd, 165 F.3d 441 (6th Cir. 1999))
Hankins v. The Gap, 84 F.3d 797 (6th Cir. 1996)
Harker v. Paul Revere Life Ins. Co.,137 N.W.2d 395 (Wis. 1965)
Harris v. Kreutzer,624 S.E.2d 24 (Va. 2006)
Hecules v. Gunther, 412 S.E.2d 185 (Va. App. 1991)
Hindmann v. GTE Data Services, 3 AD Cas. 641 (M.D. Fla. 1994)
Hinnershitz v. Ortep of Pennsylvania Inc., 1998 WL 962096 (E.D. Pa. 1998)
Holliday v. Conrail, 914 F.2d 421 (3d Cir. 1990)
Horth v. General Dynamics Land Sys., 960 F. Supp. 873 (M.D. Pa. 1997)
Humphrey v. Memorial Hosp. Ass'n, 239 F.3d 1128 (9th Cir. 2001)
Ives v. S. Buffalo Ry., 94 N.E. 431 (N.Y. 1911)
Jaffee v. Redmond,518 U.S. 1 (1996)
Johnson v. Henderson, 144 F. Supp. 2d 1341 (S.D. Fla 2001)
Joseph v. McCann,147 P.3d 547 (Utah App. 2006)
Jovanic v. In-Sink-Erator, 201 F.3d 894 (7th Cir. 2000)
Judice v. Hosp. Serv. Dist. No. 1, 919 F. Supp. 978 (E.D. La. 1996)
Keshecki v. St. Vincent's Medical Center, 785 N.Y.S.2d 300 (N.Y. Sup. Ct. 2004)
Kumho Tire Co. v. Carmichael, 526 U.S. 137 (1999)
Kvorjak v. Maine, 259 F.3d 48 (1st Cir. 2001)
Lambley v. Kameny, 682 N.E.2d 907 (Mass. App. Ct. 1997)
Landefeld v. Marion General Hospital, 994 F.2d 1178 (6th Cir. 1993)
Larking v. CIBA Vision Corp., 86 F. Supp. 1572 (N.D. Ga. 1994)
Lassiter v. Reno, 885 F. Supp. 869 (E.D. Va. 1995)
Lassiter v. Reno, 86 F.3d 1151 (4th Cir. 1996), cert. denied, 519 U.S. 1091 (1997)
Levine v. Wiss, 478 A.2d 397 (N.J. 1984)
Lewis v. Paul Revere Life Ins. Co., 80 F. Supp. 2d 978 (E.D. Wis. 2000), vacated 2001 US Dist LEXIS 21709

Legal Citations

Lightenburger v. United States, 298 F. Supp. 813 (D. Cal. 1969), rev'd 460 F.2d 391 (9th Cir. 1972), cert denied, 409 U.S. 983 (1972)
Littman v. Nat'l Cas. Co., 266 N.Y.S.2d 183 (N.Y. Civ. Ct. 1966)
Lucas v. W.W. Granger, Inc., 257 F.3d 1249 (11th Cir. 2001)
Malave-Felix v. Volvo Car Corp., 946 F.2d 967 (1st Cir. 1991)
Mancini v. GE Co.,820 F. Supp. 141 (D. Vt. 1993)
Marine Transp. Corp. v. Methodist Hosp., 221 S.W.3d 138 (Tex. App.—Houston [1st Dist.] 2006, no pet.)
Market Basket v. Workers' Compensation. Appeals Board., 149 Cal. Rptr. 872 (Cal. App. 1978)
Marschand v. Norfolk and Western Ry. Co., 876 F. Supp. 1528 (N.D. Ind. 1995)
Martinez v. Lewis, 969 P.2d 13 (Colo. 1998)
Martin v. General Mills, Inc., 1996 WL 648721 (N.D. Ill. 1996)
Massachusetts Mutual v. Ouellette, 612 A.2d 132 (Vt. 1992)
McDonald v. International Paper Co., 406 S.2d 582 (La. 1981)
McGoffin v. Barnhart, 288 F.3d 1248 (10th Cir. 2002)
McGowan v. Orleans Furniture Inc., 586 S.2d 163 (Miss. 1991)
McGreal v. Ostrow, 368 F.3d 657 (7th Cir. 2004)
McKinnie v. Barnhart, 368 F.3d 907 (7th Cir. 2004)
Metro. Gov't of Nashville and Davidson Co., 2008 U.S. App. LEXIS 13909 (6th Cir. 2008)
Miller v. Honeywell, Inc., 1996 WL 481525 (Minn. App 1996)
Miranda v. Wisconsin Power and Light Co., 91 F.3d 1911 (7th Cir. 1996)
Morisky v. Broward County, 80 F.3d 445, 448 (11th Cir. 1996)
Moulton v. Vaughn, 982 S.W.2d 107 (Tex.App.—Houston [1st Dist.] 1998)
Murphy v. A.A. Matthews, 841 S.W.2d 671 (Mo. 1992)
Murphy v. UPS,527 U.S. 516 (1999)
Mut. Life Co. v. Ellison, 223 F.2d 686 (5th Cir.), cert. denied, 350 U.S. 845 (1955)
Nam v. Ashcroft, 354 F.3d 652 (7th Cir. 2004)
New Hampshire Supply Co. v. Steinberg,400 A.2d 116 (N.H. 1979)
New York Cent. R.R. v. White, 243 U.S. 188 (1917)
Niccoli v. Monarch Life Ins. Co.,332 N.Y.S.2d 803 (N.Y. Sup. Ct. 1972)
Nines v. Wal-Mart Stores, 164 F.3d 1243 (9th Cir. 1999)
Norris v. Sysco Corp.,191 F.3d 1043 (9th Cir. 1994)
Palmer v. Circuit Court of Cook County, 117 F.3d 351 (7th Cir. 1997)
Parker v. Columbia Pictures Indus., 204 F.3d 326 (2d Cir. 2000), rev'd on other grounds 260 F. 3d 100]
Pasha v. Gonzales, 433 F.3d 530 (7th Cir. 2005)
Pettus v. Cole, 57 Cal. Rptr. 2d 46 (Cal. App. 1996)
Plummer v. Apfel, 186 F.3d 422, (3d Cir. 1999)
Porter v. U.S. Alumoweld Co., Inc.,125 F.3d 243 (4th Cir. 1997)
Rascon v. US West Communication, 143 F.3d 1324 (10th Cir. 1998)
Reed v. Metro Gov't of Nashville and Davidson Co., 2008 LEXIS 13909 (6th Cir. 2008)
Richardson v. Perales, 402 U.S. 389 (1971)
Riechman v. Cutler-Hammer Inc.,95 F. Supp. 1171 (D. Kan. 2000)
Riffe v. Armstrong, 477 S.E.2d 535 (W. Va. 1996)
Rodriguez Galicia v. Gonzales, 422 F.3d 529 (7th Cir. 2005)
Rogers v. Horvath, 237 N.W.2d 595 (Mich. App. 1975)
Romanies v. Workmen's Compensation Appeals Board, 644 A.2d 1164 (Pa. 1994)
Ryans v. Lowell, 484 A.2d 1253 (N.J. Super. Ct. App. Div. 1984)
Sangirardi v. Village of Stickney, 32 Ill. App. 3d 1 (Ill. App. Ct. 2003)
Sarko v. Penn-Del Directory Co., 170 F.R.D. 127 (E.D. Pa. 1997)
Schloendorff v. Society of New York Hospital, 105 N.E. 92 (N.Y. 1914)
Schmidt v. Safeway, 129 F. Supp. 857 (D. Or. 1994)
School Board of Nassau County v. Arline, 480 U.S. 273 (1987)

Siegel v. Mutual Life Ins. Co., 490 F. Supp. 367 (D. Mass. 1980)
Smith v. Ameritech, 129 F.2d 857 (6th Cir. 1997)
Smith v. Midland Brake, 180 F.3d 1154 (10th Cir. 1999)
Smith v. Welch, 967 P.2d 727 (Kan. 1998)
Solomon v. Royal Maccabees Life Ins. Co., 622 N.W.2d 101 (Mich. App. 2000)
Sosnowski v. Aetna Life Ins. Co.,13 N.Y.S.2d 791 (N.Y. App. 1939)
Spangler, Jennings, and Dougherty, P.C. v. Indiana Ins. Co., 729 N.E.2d 117 (Ind. 2000)
Stern v. Paul Revere Life Ins. Co., 744 S.2d 1084 (Fla. Dist. Ct. App. 1999)
Sugarman v. Board of Registration in Medicine, 662 N.E.2d 1020 (Mass. 1996)
Sullivan v. River Valley School District, 197 F.3d 804 (6th Cir. 1999)
Sutton v. United Air Lines, 527 U.S. 471 (1999)
Terry v. American Airlines Inc., 2004 LEXIS 19712 (N.D. Ill. 2004)
Tokar v. Chicago, 2000 WL 1230489 (N.D. Ill. 2000)
Tomko v. Marks, 602 A.2d 890 (Pa. Super. 1992)
Townsend v. Maine Bureau of Public Safety, 404 A.2d 1014 (Me. 1979)
Toyota Motor Manufacturing, Kentucky, Inc. v. Williams, 534 U.S. 184 (2002)
Twelker v. Shannon and Wilson, 564 P.2d 1131 (Wash. 1977)
Tyndall v. National Education Centers, 31 F.3d 209 (4th Cir. 1994)
Vinson v. Thomas, 288 F.3d 1145 (9th Cir. 2002)
Waldron v. Secretary of Health, Education, and Welfare, 344 F. Supp. 1176 (D. Md. 1972)
Watson v. Miami Beach, 177 F.3d 932 (11th Cir. 1999)
Weiler v. Household Finance Corp., 3 AD Cas. 1337 (N.D. Ill. 1994)
Wilkinson v. Times Mirror Corp., 264 Cal. Rptr. 194 (Cal. App. 1989)
Yarborough v. Montana Municipal Ins. Auth., 938 P.2d 679 (Mont. 1997, reh'g denied, June 19, 1997)
Yin v. California, 95 F.3d 864 (9th Cir. 1996)
Zimmerman v. Burch, 494 U.S. 117 (1990)
Zundell v. Dade County School Board, 636 S.2d 8 (Fla. 1994)
Zwygart v. Board of County Commissioners of Jefferson County, 483 F.3d 1086 (10th Cir. 2007)

Statutes, Regulations, Model Acts

Administrative Procedure Act, 5 U.S.C. § 556(d) (2006)
Americans with Disabilities Act of 1990, Pub. L. No. 101-336, 104 Stat. 327 (1990) (current version at 42 U.S.C. § 12101 et seq. (2006))
The Americans with Disabilities Act Amendments Act, Pub. L. No. 110-325, 122 Stat. 3553 (2008)
Black Lung Disability Benefits: 30 USC Chapter 22, §§ 901–945
Cal. Gov. Code § 12940(f) (2004)
California's Fair Employment and Housing Act, Cal. Gov. Code § 12900 et seq. (2006)
Civil Rights Act of 1964, Title VII, 42 U.S.C. § 2000e et seq. (2006)
Civil Service Disability Retirement Benefits: 5 USC § 8451
Confidentiality of alcohol and drug abuse patient records, 42 C.F.R. § Part 2 (2008)
Emergency Medical Treatment and Active Labor Act (42 USC § 1395);
The Family and Medical Leave Act of 1993, 29 U.S.C. § 2206 et seq. (2006)
Federal Employees' Compensation Act, 5 U.S.C. § 8101 et seq. (2000)
Federal Insurance Contributions Act (FICA) 42 USC §423 (2004)
The Health Insurance Portability and Accountability Act, 5 U.S.C.A. § 601 (1996)
Health Insurance Portability and Accountability Act Privacy Rule, 67 Fed. Reg. 53182 (2006)
Longshore and Harbor Workers' Compensation Act
Medical Practice Act of Texas, 16 V.T.C.A § 159 (2007)

Legal Citations

Occupational Safety and Health Act (1970) US Code title 29,. Chapter 15, §651 et seq
Old Age Assistance (CITE) Act? Program?
The Public Health and Welfare Act, 42 U.S.C. § 423(d) (2006)
Railroad Retirement Act of 1974: 42 USC § 231
Rehabilitation Act of 1973, 29 U.S.C. § 701 et seq. (2006)
Restatement (Second) of Torts §588 (1981)
Social Security Act, 20 C.F.R. § 401 (2006)

Rules

Fed. R. Evid. 1101
Fed. R. Civ. P. 26 (b)
Tex. R. Evid. § 510(d)(4)

Index

A
Absenteeism, 53
Adams v. Alderson, 231
Administrative law judges (ALJs), 41, 173
Administrative Procedure Act, 41
Advocacy bias, 11–12
Agoraphobia, 87
Albertson's, Inc. v. Kirkingburg, 223
Alcohol abuse, effects, 91
Alzheimer's dementia, 111
Amadio v. Ford, 229
American Academy of Psychiatry and the Law (AAPL), xxvi, 2, 4, 5, 6, 7, 8, 10, 11, 19, 20, 23, 266
   guidelines, 269–274
American Bar Association, xix
American Law Institute, 35
American Medical Association (AMA), xxiii, 2, 4, 6, 7–10, 23, 70, 71, 99, 100, 118, 119, 124, 126, 127, 142–145, 148, 155, 157, 159, 170, 188, 191, 269
American Psychiatric Association (APA), 2–4, 3, 6, 8, 14, 16, 17, 22, 23, 71, 72, 79, 123–125, 127, 136, 138, 143, 144, 167, 220, 269, 273, 274
American Psychiatric Association clinical practice guidelines, 124
American Psychological Association, 2–4, 7, 9, 23, 123, 146, 275, 276, 277
American Psychology-Law Society (AP-LS), 2–4, 5, 6, 8, 9, 10, 11, 12, 19, 20, 275–284
Americans with Disabilities Act (ADA), xix–xx, 15, 58, 71, 129, 166, 209–235, 240, 265
   effect on employment, 215–216
   employment discrimination, 214
   enforcement, 213–215

Equal Employment Opportunity Commission (EEOC) interpretations, 212, 220, 226, 231, 234
   guidelines for evaluations, 235
   implications of, 209–210
   importance of mental health opinions, 210
   private litigation, 214
   problematic workplace behaviors, 217
   procedures, 210–213
   referrals for examination, 216–219
   role of mental health professionals, 219
   role of psychiatrists and psychologists, 210
   statutory definitions and relevant terms
      disability, 219–220
      essential job functions, 224–225
      mental disorders, 220–223
      reasonable accomodation, 225–232
      risk assessment, 233–234
      substantial limitations on life activities, 223–224
      threat or risk of danger, 232–233
   Title I of, 211, 213
   traits and behaviors not considered mental impairments, 222
Americans with Disabilities Act Amendments Act (ADAAA), 209, 213, 220, 224
Anticipatory anxiety, 88
Anxiety, 16
Anxiety disorders, 87–91
APA Principles of Medical Ethics, 4
Austin v. American Association of Neurological Surgeons, 23, 35

B
Bar-Av v. Psychology Examining Bd., 41
Barcai v. Betwee, 28
Barnhart v. Thomas, 173

Bayne v. Provost, 38
Bazelon Center for Mental Health, 138
Beck Depression Inventory, 145
Benson v. Northwest Airlines, 224
Bias, in employment evaluations
 advocacy bias, 11–12
 associated with diagnosis, 14–17
 associated with extrapsychic or external focus, 13–14
 associated with role conflict, 17–20
 associated with work ethics, 20–22
 intrapsychic, 12–13
 sources in disability and disability-related evaluations, 10–11
Biederman, J., 77, 81
Binder, R., 23, 25
Bipolar disorder, 83–87
 cognitive impairments, 84
 degree of workplace impairment, 85
 impairments related to manic and hypomanic symptoms, 86
 psychomotor speed deficits, 84–85
 psychosocial disabilities, 85
 psychosocial outcomes, 84
 subsyndromal depressive symptoms, 87
 treatment, 86
Blailock v. O'Bannon, 180
Board of Trustees of University of Alabama v. Garrett, 214
Brief PsychiatricRating Scale, GAF scale, 143
Bristol v. Board of County Commissioners, 230
Bruce v. Byrne-Stevens, 36
Bruni v. Tatsumi, 47
Bstandig v. Workers' Compensation Appeals Board, 190
Budwin v. American Psychological Assn., 23
Bultemeyer v. Fort Wayne Community Schools, 212
Bunevitch v. CVS Pharmacy, 231
Burnout, 60–62

C
Calkins v. Sumner, 35
Callahan v. Workers' Compensation Appeals Board, 189
Carrozza v. Howard County, 218
Carrozza v. Howard County, Maryland, 231
Centers for Disease Control and Prevention, xvii, xviii
Cleveland v. Policy Management Systems Corp., 211
Colwell v. Suffolk County Police Dept., 215

Committee on Ethical Guidelines for Forensic Psychologists, 2–4, 3, 8, 19, 20, 124
Committee on Psychiatry in Industry, Group for the Advancement of Psychiatry, xv
Comorbidity, 92–94
Confidentiality associated, with disability and disability-related evaluations, 7–8
Constant effect determinants, psychological effects of job, 51
Cravens v. Blue Cross and Blue Shield, 230
Criado v. IBM Corp., 212, 229

D
Daley v. Koch, 222
Dalton v. Miller, 36
Daubert standards, 40, 182, 214
Daubert v. Merrell Dow Pharmaceuticals, Inc., 40
Dehn v. Edgecombe, 31
Demoralization, 120
DePaoli v. Abbott Lab., 245
Depressive disorder, major
 and absenteeism, 80–81
 antidepressant medication, 82–83
 cognitive deficits, 81–82
 and dysthymic conditions, 80
 functional levels, 80
 judgment effects, 81
 level of disability, 79
 and lost productivity, 79–80
 motor impairments, 82
 number of episodes, 80
 and presenteeism, 80–81
 refractory, 83
 and social impairments, 81
Diagnostic and Statistical Manual (DSM), 14, 70, 138, 167, 220
 diagnoses, 16
Diagnostic and Statistical Manual of Mental Disorders (DSM-IV-TR), 14, 70, 138
Diagnostic judgments, role in employment evaluations, 13–14
Dictionary of Occupational Titles, 132, 254
Disability benefit programs
 and concentration deficiencies, 169–170
 criteria assessing functional impairment, 168–169
 and episodes of decompensation, 170
 private disability insurance
  avenues of coverage, 193

definitions and terms, 197–201
dual roles and ethical conflicts in, 206–207
eligibility for benefits, 195–196
issues in requests for IMEs, 194
issues regarding evaluee relation with work, 194
issues regarding psychological and medical comorbidity, 194
legal disability *vs.* factual disability, 196–197
and mental health personnels, 201–206
referrals, 194
source of information, 193–194
residual functional capacity (RFC) assessment, 170–171
role of mental health professionals, 163–164
SSDI Program
definitions and process, 165–173
guidelines, 178
role of mental health professionals, 173–178
Workers' compensation program
causation in, 181
components, 179–180
decision making process, 181–182
definition of disability, 183–184
dual roles, 190–192
evidentiary issues, 182–183
guidelines, 192
mental health evaluations for claims, 186–190
mental–mental injury claims, 185–186
vs. other programs, 180
physical–mental and mental–physical injury claims, 184–185
Disability, definition of, 71
Disability Determination Services (DDS), 37, 166, 177
Disability reports, 287–289
Disciplinary actions and mental health employment evaluations, 22–23
Disclosure issues, with employment evaluations, 5–7
Dixon v. Pc. Mut. Life Ins. Co., 198
Dunlavey v. Economy Fire & Casualty Co., 185
Dyer v. Trachtman, 32

E

Earl v. Mervyns, Inc., 229
EEOC v. Amego, 227
EEOC v. United Parcel Serv., 230

Emergency Medical Treatment and Active Labor Act, 30
Environmental clarity, 52
Equal Employment Opportunity Commission (EEOC), xix, xviii, 41, 213, 214, 222, 228, 231, 232, 234, 242, 243, 245, 261
Ervin v. American Guardian Life Assur., Co., 30
Estelle v. Smith, 28
Ethical obligation, for objectivity, 11
Ethics, associated with disability and disability-related evaluations
area of expertise, 2–3
confidentiality, 7–8
disciplinary actions, 22–23
disclosure and informed consent, 5–7
honesty, *see* bias, in employment evaluations
implications for impeachment, 23–24
objectivity, *see* bias, in employment evaluations
references for, 2
sources of bias, *see* bias, in employment evaluations
in third-party evaluations, 3–5
Evans v. Federal Express Corp., 229
Extrapsychic bias, in employment evaluations, 13–14
Expert testimony, 41

F

Falsifiability in science, 40
Faria v. Carol Cable Co., 183
Federal Employees' Compensation Act, 179
Federal Insurance Contributions Act (FICA), 165
Federal Rules of Civil Procedure 26(b), 8
Federal Rules of Evidence (FRE), 40–41
Federation of State Medical Boards, xxiii, 128
Fenton v. Pritchard Corp., 222
Fitness-for-duty (FFD) evaluations, 265
and ADA, 244–245
and adversarial contexts, 238
conducting mental health evaluation
degree of certainty of opinions, 261–262
dissimulation, 257
documentation, 252–255
interview, 255–257
opinions, 257–261
constraints
confidentiality, 248–249
consent, 250

Fitness-for-duty (FFD) evaluations (*cont.*)
    role clarification and dual-agency
        issues, 250–252
    EEOC guidelines, 242–243
    forced, 244
    legal examinations, 240–243
    objective evidence, 242
    public's stake, 239–240
    qualification requirements, 247
    referral issues, 246–247
    return-to-work (RTW) evaluations,
        262–263
Ford v. Revlon, Inc., 180
Forensic psychiatry, 3
Frye v. United States, 39

G
The GAF scale, 138, 143, 144
Garg v. Potter, 245
Garrity v. United Air Lines, 231
Gaul v. AT&T, Inc., 230
General Electric v. Joiner, 40
Generalized anxiety disorder (GAD), 75, 76,
    87, 89, 93, 159
Gilbert v. DaimlerChrysler Corp., 41
Girardeau v. Guardian Life Ins. Co., 198
Greenberg v. New York State, 222
Greenberg v. Perkins, 30, 32
Guidelines, for conducting
    ADA evaluations, 235
    FFD evaluations, 263
    SSA disability evaluations, 178
    workers' compensation evaluations, 192, 207

H
Halstead–Reitan Battery, neurological
    tests, 145
Hammon v. DHL Airways, Inc., 212
Hankins v. The Gap, 230
Harker v. Paul Revere Life Ins. Co., 198
Harris v. Kreutzer, 31, 32
Health Insurance Portability and
    Accountability Act, xxvii, 132
Health Insurance Portability and
    Accountability Act's (HIPAA)
    Privacy Rule, 37–38
Hecules Inc. v. Gunther, 185
Hindmann v. GTE Data Services, 222
Hinnershitz v. Ortep of Pennsylvania, Inc., 261
Holliday v. Conrail, 185
*Horth v. General Dynamics Land Systems,
    Inc.,* 214

*Humphrey v. Memorial Hospital
    Association,* 230
Hypochondriasis, 20

I
Identity and work, 46
Independent medical examination (IME),
    xxiii, 9, 10, 30, 182
Informed consent and employment
    evaluations, 5–7
Insomnia, 16, 70, 108
Intrapsychic bias, in employment
    evaluations, 12–13
Ives v. South Buffalo Ry., 179

J
Job dissatisfaction, 49
Job elimination, 52
Job loss, effects, 62–67
Job satisfaction, 48
Joseph v. McCann, 30
Jovanic v. In-Sink-Erator, 229

K
*Keshecki v. St. Vincent's Medical
    Center,* 38
Kumho Tire Co. v. Carmichael, 40
Kvorjak v. Maine, 230

L
Lambley v. Kameny, 27
Landefeld v. Marion General Hospital, 212
Lurkins v. CIBA Vision Corp., 223
Lassiter v. Reno, 225, 227
Legal obligations, for disability and
        disability-related evaluations
    for administrative purpose, 40–41
    breach of duty, 34
    communication of critical information,
        32–33
    confidentiality, 33
    of evaluee, 29–36
    explicit agreement, 27
    and immunity, 35–36
    for judicial purpose, 39–40
    for perspective of physician–patient
        relationship, 27–29
    privacy and confidentiality, 36–39
    qualitative standards, 39, 40–41
    of third party who enters into contract,
        27–29

Index   319

Levine v. Wiss, 36
Lewis v. Paul Revere Life Ins. Co., 196
Littman v. Nat'l Cas. Co., 200
Lucas v. W. W. Granger, Inc., 230
Luria-Nebraska Battery, neurological tests, 145

M
McDonald v. International Paper Co., 185
McGoffin v. Barnhart, 185
McGowan v. Orleans Furniture, Inc., 183
McGreal v. Ostrow, 33, 248
McKinnie v. Barnhart, 41
Malave-Felix v. Volvo Car Corp., 181
Malingering, 149, 150
Mancini v. General Electric Co., 225
Marine Transp. Corp. v. Methodist Hosp., 27
Martinez v. Lewis, 30, 32
Martin, J. K., 80, 81
Martin v. General Mills, Inc., 222
Maximum medical improvement (MMI), 116, 158–160, 188, 192
Medical eligibility, for social security disability benefits, 19
Mental disorders at workplace, cost and cost analysis, xvi–xix
  disability and disability-related mental health evaluation, xix–xxii
  disability-related assessment, xxv
  model, xxvi–xxvii
  role of forensic specialists, xxii
Mental health treatment, 18
Mental–mental injury claim, 185–186
Mental–physical injury claim, 184–185
Miller v. Honeywell, Inc., 225
Minnesota Multiphasic Personality Inventory-2 (MMPI-2), 145, 151
Miranda v. Wisconsin Power and Light Co., 242
Mood disorders, 16, 87
Morisky v. Broward County, 211
Motivation to work, 118–120
Moulton v. Vaughn, 248
Murphy v. A.A. Matthews, 36
Murphy v. UPS, 223
Mut. Life Co. v. Ellison, 200

N
National Council on Compensation Insurance, 53
National Health Survey Interview, xvii

National Institutes of Mental Health, xvi, xvii, 92
Negative psychological effects, of work, 48–49
Negligence, 28
New Hampshire Supply Company v. Steinberg, 190
New York Central R.R. v. White, 179
New York's 1911 Workers' Compensation Act, 179
Niccoli v. Monarch Life Ins. Co., 200
"No-duty-to-rescue" rule, 31
Nonfinancial benefits, of work, 46
Noor, N. M., 58, 59
Norris v. Sysco Corp., 243
Nunes v. Wal-Mart Stores, 228

O
Obsessive compulsive disorder (OCD), 76, 87–89, 230
Occupational disability, 97
Occupational Safety and Health Act, xix, 241
Occupational stress, 15, 53–59
  burnout and withdrawal, 60–62
Occupational stressors, for men, 58
Ordinary negligence, 30

P
Palmer v. Circuit Court of Cook County, 231, 232
Panic disorder, 87, 88
Parker v. Columbia Pictures Indus, 229
Pascal's Wager, 40
Pettus v. Cole, 33
Physician–evaluee relationship, in employment evaluations, 4–5
Plummer v. Apfel, 172
Polydrug-abusing individuals, 92
Porter v. U.S. Alumoweld Co., 243
Posttraumatic stress disorder (PTSD), 15, 76, 87, 90, 141, 184, 218
Practice guidelines, disability and related work capacity assessments benefits, 123–125
  categories of functions, assessment, 138–139
  claim accounts, 147–151
  for collateral information, 131–135
  correlation of claimed disorder and level of severity, 141–142
  correlation of claimed impairments with specific job skills or requirements, 141

Practice guidelines, disability (cont.)
 definitions and related issues
  disability and impairment, 125–127
  impairment vs. illegal behavior, 127–129
  restrictions and limitations, 127
 descriptions and examples of impairment, 138–140
 effects of medical illness and medications, 144
 insurance issues for forensic evaluators, 129
 malingering issues, 147–151
 mental health interview, 136–137
 mental status examination, 136–137
 nature and purpose of informed consent, 135–136
 opinions regarding presence of work impairment, 151–152
 presence of third parties during evaluation, 137–138
 rating scales, 142–144
 for record review, 131–135
 for referrals and referral sources, 130–131
 referral sources, 146–147
 report writing
  causation, 154–155
  disability for one type of work, evaluee's type of work, or any type of work, 155–156
  impairments in work function and their relationship to psychiatric symptoms, 154
  malingering, primary gain and secondary gain, 160–161
  maximum medical improvement (MMI), 158–160
  motivation, 158
  multiaxial diagnosis, 154
  prognosis, 158
  restrictions and limitations, 160
  treatment and treatment recommendations, 156–158
 safety issues for evaluators, 129–130
 use of psychological testing, 145–146
Private disability insurance
 avenues of coverage, 193
 definitions and terms, 197–201
 dual roles and ethical conflicts in, 206–207
 eligibility for benefits, 195–196
 issues in requests for IMEs, 194
 issues regarding evaluee relation with work, 194
 issues regarding psychological and medical comorbidity, 194
 legal disability vs. factual disability, 196–197
 and mental health personnels, 201–206
 referrals, 194
 source of information, 193–194
Probst, T., 48, 49, 56
Protected health information (PHI), 37
Protestant work ethics, 20
Psychiatric disabilities
 concept of work capacity and disability development
  and baseline rapid recovery, 109–110
  cumulative effects, 111–112
  due to changes in work supply, 113–114
  due to progressive illness, 110–111
  due to sudden illness and impairment, 108–109
  and episodes of impairment, 114–116
  prototypic models, 107–108
 and cultural and ethnic factors, 120–122
 episodic, 114
 and motivation to work, 118–120
 relationship between impairment and disability, 99–101
 relationship between job demands and work supply
  diagnosis and treatment, 106
  job description, 102–103
  performance and employment history, 104–106
  personal and social circumstances, 107
  significance of, 101–102
 retrospective assessment, 98–99
Psychiatric disorders
 assessment, 70
 disabilities, 71
 evidence-based assessment
  affective disorders, 78–87
  anxiety disorders, 87–91
  comorbidity, 92–94
  substance use and dependence, 91–92
 use of diagnoses, 71–74
 in workplace, 74–78
Psychiatric Impairment Rating Scale, 143
Psychodynamic theory, 11
Psychological stress, 49
Psychological testing, treatment recommendations, 157, 158
Psychosis, 83

Index

Q
Quasi-judicial immunity, 36

R
Rascon v. US West Communications, 228–229
Residual functional capacity (RFC), assessment, 170, 171
Richardson v. Perales, 173
Riechman v. Cutler-Hammer, Inc., 245
Riffe v. Armstrong, 35
Rogers v. Horvat, 30
Role conflict, in disability and disability-related evaluations, 17–20
Romanies v. Workmen's Comp. App. Bd., 186
Ryans v. Lowell, 27

S
Sangirardi v. Village of Stickney, 248
Sarko v. Penn-Del DirectoryCo., 215
Schizophrenic disorders, 87
Schloendorff v. Society of New York Hospital, 27
Schmidt v. Safeway, Inc., 229
School Board of Nassau County v. Arline, 232
Self-esteem, 63–64
Siegel v. Mutual Life Ins. Co., 198
Smith v. Ameritech, 230
Smith v. Midland Brake, 230
Smith v. Welch, 28–29
Social anxiety disorder, 87
Social isolation, 52
Social Security Act, 71, 128
Social Security Administration (SSA), xviii, 37, 105, 132, 138, 163, 220
    SSA's disability determination process, steps in, 172
Social Security Administration Office of Disability Programs, 138, 165, 167, 174, 178
Social Security Disability benefits, xxiii
Social Security Disability Income, 71
Social Security Disability Insurance (SSDI) evaluations, 154
Social Security Disability Insurance (SSDI) program
    adjudicative process, 171–173
    criteria for assessment of residual functional capacity (RFC), 170–171
    definitions and process, 165–173
    guidelines, 178
    restrictions as per paragraphs B and C criteria, 168–170
    role of consultative examinations (CEs), 173–174, 176–177
    role of mental health professionals, 173–178, 177–178
    treatment providers and, 174–176
Solomon v. Royal Maccabees Life Ins. Co., 197
Sosnowski v. Aetna Life Ins. Co., 198
Spangler, Jennings, & Dougherty P.C. v. Indiana Ins. Co., 180
SSA's disability determination process, 165
SSA's paragraph B and C criteria, 168–169
Stern v. Paul Revere Life Ins. Co., 197
Stress at work, 15
Stressful life events, 55
Substance use and dependence, 91–92
Substantial gainful activity (SGA), 128, 129, 166
Sullivan v. River Valley School District, 242, 243
Supplemental Security Income (SSI) (Title XVI of the Act), 164
Sutton v. United Air Lines, 223

T
Third-party evaluations, 1, 3–5, 7–8
Title II of the Social Security Act, 164
Tokar v. City of Chicago, 251
Tomko v. Marks, 30
Townsend v. Maine Bureau of Public Safety, 185
Toxic cultures, 53
Toxic workplaces, 53
Toyota Motor Manufacturing, Kentucky, Inc. v. Williams, 223
Transient symptoms, 16
Traumatic brain injury, 32
Twelker v. Shannon & Wilson, 35
Tyndall v. National Education Centers, 229

U
Unemployment, effects, 62–67
United States Bureau of Labor Statistics, 57, 58
United States Department of Health and Human Services, xvi, 37
United States Department of Health and Human Services:Office of Civil Rights-HIPAA, 37

United States Department of Labor, xviii, 58, 59, 132, 179, 254
United States Equal Employment Opportunity Commission, xviii, 214

V
Variable effect determinants, psychological effects of job, 51–53
Vinson v. Thomas, 218

W
Watson v. City of Miami Beach, 243
Wechsler Adult Intelligence Scale-III (WAIS-III), 145
Weiler v. Household Finance Corp., 222
Wellbeing and work, 44–45
Wilkinson v. Times Mirror Corp., 28
Witness immunity, 36
Women
  and family work relationship, 59
  occupational stressors for, 58
World Health Organization, 126
Work
  assessment of work functions, 105
  benefits, 45–48
  burnout and withdrawal, 60–62
  demand domains, 103
  effect on mental health, 44–45
  general abilities, 104–105
  "goodness of fit" between the individual and the job, 49–53
  job loss and unemployment, 62–67
  negative psychological effects, 48–49
  occupational stress, 53–59
  role in daily life, 43–44
Work capacity models and disability evaluations, 116–118
Workers' compensation, 19

Workers' compensation program, 178
  aggravation or apportionment of preexisting injury, 189–190
  causation in, 181
  components, 179–180
  decision making process, 181–182
  definition of disability, 183–184
  dual roles, 190–192
  evaluation, guidelines, 207
  evidentiary issues, 182–183
  guidelines, 192
  laws, 179
  mental health evaluations for claims, 186–190
  mental–mental injury claims, 185–186
  vs. other programs, 180
  physical–mental and mental–physical injury claims, 184–185
  psychiatric claims, 184
  subcategories of disability, 188
Work ethics, in disability and disability-related evaluations, 20
  and mental health professionals, 21
Workplace conflicts, xvi
Workplace relationships, complexity, xvi
Work-related impairments, xvi
Work-related stress, 15
Work relationships, importance, 47

Y
Yarborough v. Montana Municipal Ins. Auth., 186
Yin v. State of California, 243

Z
Zinermon v. Burch, 27
Zundell v. Dade County School Board, 187
Zwygart v. Board of County Com'rs of Jefferson County, 214